Jews and Protestants
From the Reformation to the Present
Originally edited by Irene Aue-Ben-David, Aya Elyada, Moshe Sluhovsky and Christian Wiese
This edition edited by Anthony Uyl _{MTS}

Devoted Publishing
Ingersoll, Ontario. Canada 2023

Jews and Protestants
From the Reformation to the Present
Originally edited by Irene Aue-Ben-David, Aya Elyada, Moshe Sluhovsky and Christian Wiese
This edition edited by Anthony Uyl ₘₜₛ

This book was originally published by Walter de Gruyter GmbH, Berlin/Boston.

The reformatted text of Jew and Protestants is all protected under Copyright ©2023 Devoted Publishing. The covers, background, layout and Devoted Publishing logo are Copyright ©2023 Devoted Publishing. This edition is published by Devoted Publishing a division of 2165467 Ontario Inc.

Note on Creative Commons 4.0 Attribution status: Although all the text in this document is from the CC-BY, the layout, formatting and note changes makes this book a copyrighted work. The original document remains in the CC-BY and can be found here:

https://doi.org/10.1515/9783110664713

Unless written permission is given for any material, all use of this material to be reproduced, stored in a retrieval system, or transmitted in any form by any means, electronic, mechanical, photocopying, recording or otherwise is forbidden. All rights reserved.

Drop Cap and Table of Contents fonts are AnglicanText by Typographer Mediengestaltung and used under a Free For Commercial Use License (FFC).

ISBN: 978-1-77356-448-7

Contact Us Online:
Email: office@devotedpub.com
Facebook: @devotedpublishing
Editors' Twitter: @AnthonyUyl
For more information on Biblical Demonology and issues with the occult in modern evangelicalism, check out the editors' Substack Blog Reformed Demonology: reformeddemonology.substack.com

Table of Contents

Acknowledgements - 5

Introduction - 7
    By Moshe Sluhovsky and Aya Elyada

The Impact of the Reformation on Early Modern German Jewry - 21
    By Dean Phillip Bell

Edom versus Edom - 39
    By Markéta Kabůrková

Eschatology and Conversion in the Sperling Letters - 57
    By Alexander van der Haven

The Legacy of Anti-Judaism in Bach's Sacred Cantatas - 79
    By Lars Fischer

A New Model of Christian Interaction with the Jews - 97
    By Yaakov Ariel

The Vernacular Bible between Jews and Protestants - 111
    By Aya Elyada

Christian Images of the Jewish State - 127
    By Ofri Ilany

Standard-bearers of Hussitism or Agents of Germanization? - 145
    By Johannes Gleixner

Luther's Shadow - 167
    By Christian Wiese

Exclusive Space as a Criterion for Salvation in German Protestantism during the Third Reich - 195
    By Dirk Schuster

Nazi Racism, American Anti-Semitism, and Christian Duty - 209
    By Kyle Jantzen

Lutheran Churches and Luther's Anti-Semitism - 235
    By Ursula Rudnick

German Guilt and Hebrew Redemption - 245
    By Johannes Becke

List of Contributors - 261

Acknowledgements

It is our great pleasure to thank all the institutions that contributed to the Reformation Conference at the Leo Baeck Institute Jerusalem in February 2017, including the Hebrew University of Jerusalem, the Martin Buber Chair in Jewish Thought and Philosophy at the Goethe University in Frankfurt, the Evangelical Church in Germany, the Center for the Study of Christianity at the Hebrew University, the Institute for the History of the German Jews in Hamburg, the Stephen Roth Institute for the Study of Contemporary Antisemitism and Racism in Tel Aviv University, and the Minerva Institute for German History, Tel Aviv University.

We are grateful to Sara Tropper for the professional copy-editing, to Joel Swanson for preparing the index and to Alice Meroz from De Gruyter Verlag for her help and cooperation in bringing the volume to publication. A special thanks is extended to Daat Hamakom – I-Core In The Study of Modern Jewish Culture at the Hebrew University of Jerusalem for generously supporting the publication of the book. We are also grateful to the Hessian Ministry for Science and Art funded research hub "Religious Positioning: Modalities and Constellations in Jewish, Christian, and Muslim Contexts" at the Goethe University Frankfurt and the Justus-Liebig University Gießen for their support.

INTRODUCTION
By Moshe Sluhovsky and Aya Elyada

The year 2017 marked the five-hundredth anniversary of the eruption of the Protestant Reformation. Among the thousands of events commemorating the occasion was a conference that took place in Jerusalem, dedicated to 500 years of interactions between Protestants and Jews. The conference was organized by the Leo Baeck Institute Jerusalem, together with the Hebrew University of Jerusalem, the Martin Buber Chair in Jewish Thought and Philosophy at the Goethe University in Frankfurt as well as the Frankfurt research hub "Religious Positioning: Modalities and Constellations in Jewish, Christian and Islamic Contexts," the Evangelical Church in Germany, the Center for the Study of Christianity at the Hebrew University, the Institute for the History of the German Jews in Hamburg, the Stephen Roth Institute for the Study of Contemporary Antisemitism and Racism, Tel Aviv University, and the Minerva Institute for German History, Tel Aviv University. Some of the papers that were first presented at the conference comprise the core of this volume.

Since 1996, discussions of Protestant-Jewish relations, the impact of the Reformation on the history of Germany, Jews, and German-Jews, and, in fact, European history tout court, have been shaped by Daniel Jonah Goldhagen's best-selling and controversial *Hitler's Willing Executioners: Ordinary Germans and the Holocaust*.[1] While many, if not most, historians reject the book's main thesis, that, in its own way, revived the Sonderweg explanation of German history, in public opinion and the media Goldhagen's book reaffirmed the alleged persistence, in German history, of an eliminationist German type of antisemitism. Martin Luther stands at the beginning of this uniquely German and German-Protestant trajectory, a straight historical path that led from Luther's call to destroy the material presence of Jews in the Holy Roman Empire to Hitler's actual destruction of the Jews

---

1. Daniel Jonah Goldhagen, Hitler's Willing Executioners: Ordinary Germans and the Holocaust (New York: Random House, 1996).

in modern Germany. In tracking the spread of modern antisemitism in nineteenth-and twentieth-century Germany, Goldhagen reminds his readers of the reluctance of some segments of the Catholic Church under Nazism to adopt racist theories while positioning Protestant churches, the Protestant media, and especially the Protestant *Sonntagsblätter*, the weekly Sunday newspapers, as active agents in shaping antisemitic public opinion.[2]

There is no denying Luther's own antisemitism, nor the immense influence of his antisemitic writings on Protestant theology and theologians in later periods. Lutheran theology concerning Jews and Judaism was, in its turn, molded by the Pauline theology of supersession, and by Luther's own trajectory from hoping to bring about a mass conversion of the Jews following his purported purification of Christianity of foreign pagan elements, to the vicious and even exterminatory theology of his later years. It is equally self-evident that Luther's personal struggle with the Jewish refusal to accept his purified theology had an inestimable impact on later generations of Lutheran theologians. This was true throughout the past half a millennium and even more so since 1945. In fact, as Thomas Kaufmann rightly observes, "[Luther's] attitude to the Jews has become a sort of pivotal issue in understanding his character and theology."[3]

Just as Luther's own virulent antisemitism should not be whitewashed, one ought never to dismiss or forgive the brutal, racist, and in many cases eliminationist antisemitism of large segments of the Protestant hierarchy in the modern period. Nonetheless, the articles in this volume posit that there was no direct line leading from Luther to Hitler. And while some papers in the collection address Luther's antisemitism as well as the *Glaubensbewegung Deutsche Christen*, we have sought to broaden the scope of the investigation. Protestant-Jewish theological encounters shaped not only antisemitism but also the Jewish Reform movement and Protestant philosemitic post-Holocaust theology; interactions between Jews and Protestants took place not only in the German-speaking sphere but also in the wider Protestant universe – in Poland, Bohemia, the Low Countries, England, and the United States; theology was crucial for the articulation of attitudes toward Jews, but music and philosophy were additional spheres of creativity that enabled the process of thinking through the relations between Judaism and Protestantism. Generally speaking, Luther and Lutheranism spelled trouble for the Jews, but there were times that they constituted an attractive model of 'purified'

---

2. Ibid., 106–10; 284–5, among other places.

3. Thomas Kaufmann, Luther's Jews: A Journey into Anti-Semitism (2014; Oxford: Oxford University Press, 2017), 5.

Christianity that could potentially lead to a rapprochement between the faith communities. For a few generations of secularized Jews in Germany, conversion to Protestantism was a means of acculturation into *Deutschtum*, Protestantism's essence as a belief system brushed aside. Thus, rather than a single history of Protestant-Jewish relations and a single history of the theological mis/understandings between the two religions, it is, in fact, multiple histories and engagements that have helped to fashion both the religions and their peoples over the past 500 years. The collection aims to disentangle some of the intricate perceptions, interpretations, and emotions that have characterized contacts between Protestantism and Judaism, and between Jews and Protestants. As the presence of Dr. Martin Hauger, the *Referent für Glaube und Dialog* of the Evangelical Church in Germany, at the conference in Jerusalem, and some of the articles below make clear, Jewish-Protestant relations are an on-going project, a project to which this collection hopes to contribute.

In 1523, Martin Luther published his first major tract on the 'Jewish Question' under the title *That Jesus Christ was Born A Jew*.[4] Considering the anti-Jewish stance advocated by Luther in earlier theological writings,[5] and particularly in light of the deeply rooted anti-Jewishness that characterized medieval society and culture, the new treatise of the young reformer was marked by a surprisingly tolerant tenor, and even evinced a certain congenial tone toward the Jews. To be sure, Luther did not promote any tolerance toward the Jewish religion itself, nor did he call to accept Jews as Jews. The explicit aim of this work was to encourage mission among the Jews, with the goal of bringing about their conversion to the new Protestant Church. Yet, some of the main notions Luther presented in the text clearly broke from the hitherto prevalent attitudes toward the Jewish minority. To begin with, Luther laid the blame for the Jews' persistent refusal to convert to Christianity squarely at the feet of the Catholic Church. It was the centuries old Catholic perversion of Christianity that had kept the Jews from joining this corrupt, half-pagan religion, he maintained. Moreover, the Catholic Church had treated the Jews so badly, persecuted and exploited them, "that anyone who wished to be a good Christian would almost have had to become a Jew. If I had been a Jew and had seen such dolts

---

4. Martin Luther, "Daß Jesus Christus ein geborner Jude sei" (1523), in D. Martin Luthers Werke: Kritische Gesamtausgabe. 120 vols. (Weimar: Böhlau, 1883–2009), vol. 11: 307–36 (henceforth: WA). English translation in Luther's Works. 55 vols. (Philadelphia: Fortress Press; and Saint Louis: Concordia Publishing House, 1955–1986), vol. 45: 199–229 (henceforth: LW).

5. See especially his first and second lectures on the Psalms (*Dictata super psalterium*, from 1513/14, and *Operationes* in psalmos, from 1518).

and blockheads govern and teach the Christian faith," Luther admonished, "I would sooner have become a hog than a Christian."[6]

Recommending the termination of the harsh and obviously futile traditional methods used by the Catholic Church to achieve Jewish conversion, Luther endorsed a fresh, twofold strategy. Christians would instruct the Jews kindly and carefully in Scripture, according to its 'true Christian' (namely, Lutheran) understanding, and allow the Jewish minority to integrate into Christian society, as a means of exposing them to Christian belief and way of life.[7] Luther was certain that, when offered the option of converting to a pure, correct, and unadulterated form of Christianity, and after existing barriers and obstacles had been removed, many Jews, if not all, would choose to convert to the new confession.

Yet Luther's hopes for Jewish conversion did not materialize, and from the late 1530s we witness the publication of several anti-Jewish tracts from the pen of the aging reformer, the most notorious of which was *On the Jews and Their Lies* from 1543, three years before Luther's death.[8] In this work, which became a hallmark of Luther's – and Lutheran – antisemitism, Luther warns his Christian readers of their most dangerous, indeed devilish, eternal enemy – the Jews residing among them. "Therefore, dear Christian," Luther writes, "be advised and do not doubt that next to the devil, you have no more bitter, venomous, and vehement foe than a real Jew who earnestly seeks to be a Jew."[9] And elsewhere he writes,

> They are real liars and bloodhounds who have […] continually perverted and falsified all of Scripture with their mendacious glosses […] The sun has never shone on a more bloodthirsty and vengeful people than they are who imagine that they are God's people who have been commissioned and commanded to murder and to slay the Gentiles.[10]

Fortunately, Luther states, they lack the power to do so. Yet the threat posed to Christian society by the Jewish minority is no less real: since the Jews habitually lie and blaspheme, they might implicate the entire society – both Jews and Christians – in their depravity. If we tolerate the Jews and their calumnies, Luther exhorts his readers, the wrath of

---

6. LW 45, 200.
7. Ibid., 200–201, 229.
8. Martin Luther, "Von den Juden und ihren Lügen" (1543), WA 53, 417–552. English translation from LW 47, 137–306. Two other important works in this respect are *Wider die Sabbather* (*Against the Sabbatarians*, 1538) and *Vom Schem Hamphoras* (*On the Ineffable Name*, 1543).
9. LW 47, 217.
10. Ibid., 156–57.

God shall be upon us all.[11]

What do we do then, asks Luther, with the Jews? We are unable to convert them, yet we cannot tolerate their presence among us. The solution he now suggests to the Christian authorities is the mirror opposite of the one he offered twenty years before. Instead of integrating the Jews into Christian society and approaching them with compassion, Luther advocates applying to them "sharp mercy": burning their synagogues and schools, destroying their homes, confiscating their books and forbidding their rabbis to teach, denying them safe conduct, prohibiting their dealing with finance and putting them to hard labor. But the best solution, Luther advises, would be to follow in the footsteps of other European countries and expel the Jews from the German lands altogether.[12]

Scholars have long attempted to account for what seems to be Luther's dramatic change of heart regarding the Jews and the 'Jewish Question.' First and foremost, Luther's disappointment concerning the continued refusal of the Jews to convert to his new confession clearly drove him to the conclusion that they were entirely under the wrath of God. Thus, as he makes explicit at the beginning of *On the Jews and Their Lies*, it is impossible – and therefore useless – to try and convert them. Indeed, considering the anti-Jewish stance he advocated already in his early writings, the 1523 text would seem to be the exception, as though Luther had 'suspended' his animosity toward the Jews in order to give their conversion a chance.[13] Once this opportunity was not partaken of, the old animus could make a horrifying comeback.

But the rancor of Luther's attacks from the 1540s, which were considered exceptionally severe even in the anti-Jewish atmosphere of the sixteenth century, also merits inquiry. Here scholars have proposed, alongside Luther's conversionary letdown, his increasing decrepitude; his bitterness in the face of Reformation setbacks; his apocalyptic set of mind; and the fact that during those years Luther spoke ruthlessly about all his enemies – the 'papists,' the Anabaptists, the Turks, and basically anyone who did not affirm his theology as the one and only true understanding of Christianity. Specifically, with regard to the Jews, it has been suggested that what Luther perceived as 'Judaizing' tendencies within the Protestant camp (Sabbath-observing sects,

---

11. Ibid., 268.
12. Ibid., 268–72.
13. It is important to note, in this respect, the last sentence of *That Jesus Christ was Born A Jew*, where Luther makes the following statement: "Here I will let the matter rest for the present, until I see what I have accomplished" (LW 45, 229). This concluding sentence should probably be taken as a kind of warning made by Luther, suggesting that the advocated tolerance toward the Jews was entirely conditional, and clearly had an expiry date.

certain circles within Protestant Hebraism, etc.) sharpened his view of the 'Jewish danger' that he perceived as placing his Reformation in peril. Finally, it is important to note the influence of the book *Der gantz Jüdisch glaub* (*The Entire Jewish Faith*, first published in Augsburg, 1530) on the stance taken by the older Luther toward the Jews. Written by Antonius Margaritha, the son of a rabbi and a convert from Judaism, the book claimed, among other things, to expose the Jewish blasphemies and anti-Christian sentiments allegedly contained in their religious books and daily prayers. Luther referred to Margaritha's influential and highly popular book on several occasions as a crucial source of knowledge for contemporary Judaism. It appears that the work contributed to the reformer's view of the hostility of the Jews toward the Christians and of their outrageous blasphemies against God and the Christian religion – two prominent motifs in his 1543 antisemitic tract.

While the aforementioned factors may well have contributed to Luther's antisemitic attacks, one thing is certain: his existential fear of the Jews, and his profound conviction that they must be converted or otherwise banished entirely from Christian Germany, persisted up to his very final days. On February 7, 1546, less than two weeks before his death, Luther added to one of his last sermons, preached at St. Andrew's Church in his hometown of Eisleben, *An Admonition against the Jews*.[14] As he noted in two letters to his wife from February 1 and 7,[15] Luther was quite upset by the presence of a small Jewish community in Eisleben and in a small town close by. He decided to encourage Count Albrecht in their expulsion – by advocating it from the pulpit. "More than others, you still have Jews in your land who do great harm," he warned his listeners, emphasizing again the great sin of tolerating Jewish slander and blasphemy, as well as the eternal enmity of the Jew toward the Christian religion and its adherents. In conclusion to his final will with regard to the Jews Luther wrote:

> This is the final warning I wanted to give you, as your countryman: [...]
> If the Jews will be converted to us [...] we will gladly forgive them. But if not, then neither should we tolerate or endure them among us.[16]

Luther died in 1546, leaving his newly founded Church with a Janus-faced legacy concerning the Jews and their prospective conver-

---

14. Martin Luther, "Warnung vor den Juden" (1546), in WA 51, 195–96; English translation in LW 58, 458–59. See also Brooks Schramm and Kirsi I. Stjerna (eds.), Martin Luther, the Bible, and the Jewish People: A Reader (Minneapolis: Fortress Press, 2012), 200–202.

15. For English translation of the letters see ibid., 198–99.

16. Ibid., 201, 202.

sion. The legacy of the younger Luther, advocated most clearly by the Pietist movement of the late seventeenth and eighteenth centuries, emphasized the responsibility of Christians to convert Jews via friendly engagement. The legacy of the older Luther, by contrast, which characterized Lutheran Orthodox circles from the mid-sixteenth until the early eighteenth century, denied the possibility of converting the Jews through human efforts and stressed the need for Christians to defend themselves in the face of the Jewish threat.

As the eighteenth century drew to a close and the nineteenth century opened, the anti-Jewish part of Luther's legacy seems to have fallen into oblivion. The Pietistic roots of German Enlightenment contributed considerably to the diffusion of a relatively pro-Jewish stance among German theologians of the time, and to the image of Luther as a proponent of tolerance toward the Jews. Anti-Jewish writings from this period and throughout the nineteenth century tended to cite the sinister work of the Calvinist scholar Johann Eisenmenger, *Entdecktes Judentum* (*Judaism Unmasked*, 1700) as their source of inspiration and authority, rather than Luther's later works. Only in the 1830s, following the first modern edition of Luther's writings,[17] did Luther's anti-Jewish writings gain renewed attention. While some Lutheran scholars condemned the reformer's hostility to the Jews, others utilized his work to propagate antisemitic notions. This was especially the case toward the end of the nineteenth century, when the formation of the Second Reich propagated a new image of Luther as a German national hero who mobilized his people against external enemies. Soon enough, and under the influence of racially based ideologies, Luther was also mobilized against internal enemies. His antisemitic writings enjoyed a growing popularity in the last quarter of the nineteenth century and, usually stripped of their theological message, were often integrated into a new *völkisch*-racist understanding of German-ness.

By the early twentieth century, the later Luther, the author of vitriolic antisemitic sermons and treatises, came to dominate scholarship on Luther. The impact of this antisemitic reading of Luther's theology was such that even the Munich edition of Luther's writings, which was closely linked to the Confessing Church (*Bekennende Kirche*), sang the praises of Luther's *On the Jews and their Lies*'s antisemitism.[18] By the 1930s, Luther's writings were used to justify the exclusion of Jews from public life, the burning of synagogues, and the promotion of ethnic and racist notions of German-ness. After Kristallnacht, the

---

17. Erlangen Edition, 1826–1886. The volume with the late writings on the Jews appeared in 1832. In the Weimar Edition (WA) this volume saw light only in 1919.

18. Kaufmann, Luther's Jews, 7.

publication and circulation of Luther's antisemitic writings increased dramatically, the most popular compendium of the genre being Martin Sasse's *Martin Luther über die Juden: Weg mit ihnen!* (*Martin Luther on the Jews: Away with Them!*). Sasse was a leading Lutheran theologian who merged world Jewry, Catholicism, liberal Protestants abroad, and western democracies into a vast conspiracy against the Führer's sacred struggle. He also did not fail to point out the expiatory symbolism of *Kristallnacht* taking place on Luther's birthday.[19]

This being said, one ought to bear in mind that Luther's antisemitism was rather akin to the antisemitism of his contemporaries, Catholics and Protestants alike. Luther did not call for an annihilation of the Jews, and while he talked about the degeneration of Jews since Jesus' time, he – unlike the Nazis – never denied Jesus' Jewish ethnicity. Nor should one forget that German Lutherans' engagement with Luther's antisemitic writings and with Jews did not end in 1945. In fact, Lutheran theology of the second half of the twentieth century became the core of a reckoning and a fundamental departure from a stained past. Already in 1950, the synod of the Protestant Church in Germany (EKD) in Berlin-Weissensee declared that God's selection of the Jews was not revoked with the crucifixion of Christ, a theological novelty without precedent that abrogated 1700 years of supersessionist theology. Since then, the covenant with Israel has become a crucial component of German and non-German Lutheran theology. In 1983, as is well known, on the 500th anniversary of Luther's birth, the council of the EKD pronounced Luther's late texts on the Jews "calamitous," and a few years later the EKD recognized the implication of the Protestant Church in the crimes of the Nazi state against the Jews. In 2017, in conjunction with the 500th anniversary of the Reformation, the synod published a new declaration concerning the EKD's relations to Jews. Recognizing the mistakes made by reformers and by the Reformation churches, the EKD expressed its regrets that the Reformation failed to put an end to medieval antisemitism, and that Luther's antisemitism, in fact, contributed to Nazi antisemitism. Furthermore, unlike previous discourse on Luther's theology, which emphasized the break between the early and the late Luther, the EKD stated that "Luther's early statements and his late writings from 1538, with their undisguised hatred of Jews, show continuity in his theological judgment." The declaration attributed to the founding father irrational fear of and stereotypical thinking about Jews and draws a direct line between his writings and the

---

19. Martin Sasse (ed.), Martin Luther über die Juden: Weg mit ihnen! (Freiburg/Br.: Sturmhut-Verlag, 1938), 2.

justification of hatred and persecution of Jews, in particular with the emergence of racist antisemitism and at the time of National Socialism. It is not possible to draw simple continuous lines. Nevertheless, in the 19th and 20th century, Luther was a source for theological and ecclesial anti-Judaism, as well as for political antisemitism.

Last, but not least, the EKD declared that "Luther's judgment upon Israel therefore does not correspond to the biblical statements on God's covenant faithfulness to his people and the lasting election of Israel."[20]

DEAN PHILLIP BELL's article looks at the impact of the Reformation on German Jewry and the development of Jewish historiography of the topic. Bell warns against a teleological perspective that ignores Lutheran-Jewish moments of interaction and collaboration. He recalls the role of Jews in the development of Lutheran Hebraism, the growing interest of theologians in Hebrew texts and traditions, and the Jewish support of the idea of a godly community. Using the concept of Confessionalization, which denotes the early modern processes that reshaped relations between state and church after the Reformation, Bell demonstrates how these processes also influenced Jewish communities in the Holy Roman Empire. Bell concludes that even if German Jews totally rejected the theological message of the Reformation, its organizational and political transformations of society still had a significant impact on Jewish communities. MARKÉTA KABŮRKOVÁ explores the large and diverse body of Jewish views on Luther, and on the Reformation as it unfolded. She shows that the Jewish reaction to the religious upheavals in Christianity was far from monochromatic: while some Jewish authors saw the Reformation as a purification of Christianity and its return to Jewish roots, others were more apprehensive, fearing the impact of Luther's Reformation on the fate of the Jews in the German lands. Still other Jewish authors, especially those of Sephardi origin, viewed Lutheranism as the Catholic Church's comeuppance for its mistreatment of the Jews. All agreed, however, that the reformers misunderstood Scripture.

Moving chronologically, the next papers examine various aspects of Protestant-Jewish relations during the seventeenth and the eighteenth centuries. ALEXANDER VAN DER HAVEN investigates the changing relations between notions of conversion and eschatological expectations in the aftermath of the Thirty Years' War. While eschatological thinking typically prompts exclusivist notions of conversion, insisting that there is only one true religion, Van der Haven suggests that early modern eschatology also had the potential to bring different religious groups together. To support this claim, he analyzes two letters written

---

20. https://www.ekd.de/en/Martin-Luther-and-the-Jews-272.htm

by a convert to Judaism in Amsterdam in 1682, in which the author presented a scenario of an imminent eschaton that assigned positive roles to more than one religious group. This was done, however, without relinquishing a clear line of demarcation between the forces of light and darkness. LARS FISCHER's discussion of the antisemitic nature of Bach's sacred cantatas brings us back to the theme of anti-Jewish inclinations within German Lutheranism. Arguing that this attitude was to be expected in light of Bach's adherence to Lutheran orthodoxy and his position as cantor in the Lutheran Church of the early eighteenth century, Fischer asks how, and to what extent, did the anti-Jewish sentiment of the time find expression in Bach's oeuvre. With Cantata 42 as a central case-study, he wishes to raise awareness of these troubling aspects in Bach's music, awareness that he finds to be lacking among Bach scholars and fans of our time.

Questions of mission and conversion, especially in the context of the Pietist and the Evangelical movements within Lutheranism, come to the fore in the next two papers. YAAKOV ARIEL discusses the rise of the Pietist mission to the Jews, its underlying assumptions, and the way it was carried out at the *Institutum Judaicum*, the great Pietist missionary center founded in 1728 in the Prussian city of Halle. Ariel highlights the use of Yiddish in the missionary endeavors of the Halle Pietists, first and foremost for the missionary publications produced in Halle. He also shows how eighteenth-century Pietism helped shape the agenda and methods of Evangelical missions to the Jews which emerged in English speaking countries at the beginning of the nineteenth century. AYA ELYADA tackles the project undertaken by the Halle Pietists during the first half of the eighteenth century, of publishing missionary works in Yiddish for distribution among the Jews. In particular, Elyada attempts to explain why the Pietists found it important to publish Yiddish versions of biblical books despite the centuries-long availability of such translations among Ashkenazi Jews. Elyada raises the possibility that the Pietist missionaries, like earlier Lutheran theologians from the sixteenth and seventeenth centuries, rejected the existing Jewish, Yiddish versions of the Bible on the basis of both style and content. These publications, she suggests, were then to be replaced by 'decent' – that is, Protestant and Germanized – versions of the holy text.

The vagaries of Protestant-Jewish relations in the modern period are the second focus of the collection. From the eighteenth century on, these relations were often also related to different configurations of the nation and the *Volk*. OFRI ILANY traces the trajectory of the notion of the 'Hebrew Republic' in legal theory and theology in the German-speaking lands. This concept was central to numerous authors, among them the most prominent theologian of the German Enlightenment, Johann David Michaelis. In Michaelis' writings, Moses the Lawgiver is portrayed as the man who, in his republican-theocratic innovations, overcame the division of the Hebrews into tribes, thus enabling the creation of a nation. The Hebrew Republic could thus serve as a model for a hopeful unification of the German people. JOHANNES GLEIXNER probes the position of Jews and Protestants in relation to the political changes in the Czech-speaking parts of the Habsburg Empire at the turn of the twentieth century. During that time, Gleixner argues, the two communities were pressured in a similar manner to assimilate into mainstream, Catholic society, and there are strong parallels in the ways in which both of these minorities responded to the challenge, while struggling to maintain their own religious and cultural identity. Gleixner also signals the political achievements of the Czech Jewish-Protestant alignment and its impact on the discourse surrounding the foundation of the new Czechoslovak republic in 1918. CHRISTIAN WIESE analyses the way Jewish historians and philosophers in Germany interpreted Luther's significance for contemporary debates on Jewish emancipation and integration, either praising him as a forerunner of freedom of thought and Enlightenment or criticizing his contribution to Protestantism's submissiveness towards the authoritarian state. Those who referred to the reformer's *Judenschriften* between 1917 and 1933, he argues, insisted on a strong discontinuity between the early and the later writings, in a desperate attempt to counter nationalist or *völkisch* readings and to convince non-Jewish Germans to embrace the attitude of the – idealized – young Luther and, as a consequence, reject antisemitism. Wiese demonstrates that, unfortunately, this narrative of a 'tolerant' creator of Germanness remained without an echo among the majority of Protestant theologians of the time.

Entering deeper into the twentieth century, DIRK SCHUSTER and KYLE JANTZEN both address Lutherans' responses to Aryan racism during the period of National Socialism. Schuster considers how ideas of racial purity influenced the theological as well as practical stance of certain movements in the German Protestant Church towards Jews, Judaism, and Jewish converts to Christianity. He shows how these movements perceived Protestantism as an exclusive Aryan religion, and how racial considerations became for their adherents a precondition to belonging to the Protestant Church. Thus, they not only aimed to 'de-Judaize' Christianity, but also denied the Jews the only possibility, in their eyes, to reach salvation. Turning our gaze to the other side of the Atlantic, Kyle Jantzen's paper examines how U.S. Protestants perceived Hitler, Nazism, and the persecution of Germany's Jews in the prewar era, and what kinds of responses they proposed. Analyzing a sample of Protestant publications and journals, he contends that prior to the Second World War, American Lutherans did not ignore the danger of Nazism, but were primarily concerned with the Nazi persecution of Christians. Above all, Jantzen claims, they identified Nazism as an enemy of religion. As far as the Jews were concerned, American Protestants both condemned and perpetuated forms of antisemitism in the United States. Over time, they developed an anti-antisemitic attitude, which did not prevent them from adhering to supersessionist and conversional attitudes toward Jews.

Post-Holocaust reckoning is crucial for Lutheran theology of the second half of the twentieth century, and it is the main concern of the last pair of articles. URSULA RUDNICK addresses the impact of the Holocaust in her discussion of the process undertaken by the Lutheran church in condemning the antisemitic writings of Martin Luther, while at the same time renewing theological dialogue between Jews and Lutherans after the Shoah. She offers a detailed chronology of the activities and pronouncements of the Lutheran Commission on Church and Judaism over the 40-year period which led to the Declaration of Driebergen in the year 1990. The article scrutinizes pan-European and pan-Lutheran developments and declarations, reminding us that the process of reckoning and rethinking Jewish-Lutheran relations after the Holocaust took place across the globe. Finally, JOHANNES BECKE analyzes contemporary attitudes of Lutherans toward Judaism and the reconfigurations of theology in the shadow of the Arab-Israeli conflict. Studying the history of *Aktion Sühnezeichen Friedensdienste* (ASF) in Israel from the 1960s onwards, Becke presents both theological and sociological evidence for shifting notions of guilt, responsibility, and atonement among different generations of German Lutheran youth. After situating the history of the organization within the conceptual frameworks of Philosemitism and Philozionism, Becke spotlights the rupture in the long history of Protestant-Jewish relations brought about by the foundation of a Jewish state.

As can be seen from this brief overview, the present volume aims to shed light on various chapters in the long history of Protestant-Jewish relations, from the Reformation to the present day. Spanning five centuries and a vast geographical area, it demonstrates the manifold manifestations of these complex relations in ever-shifting historical contexts. The volume brings together the work of scholars who differ not only with respect to religious, national, and institutional backgrounds, but also in their methodological approaches and fields of expertise. By this, we hope to showcase current trends in present-day scholarship on Protestant-Jewish relations, and to open up directions for future research on this intricate topic, which bears both historical significance and evident relevance to our own time.

The Impact of the Reformation on Early Modern German Jewry
Politics, Community, and Religion
By Dean Phillip Bell

Introduction

It seems somewhat unnecessary by now to state candidly that the Reformation, at least as traditionally understood, never occurred. While something most assuredly happened in Germany in the sixteenth century, it is impossible to conceive of what that something was absent a discussion of what came before and what came after. In other words, any inquiry into the 'Reformation' calls for coverage of a daunting range of topics, personalities, and localities.

We do know that anniversaries, such as the one commemorating the 500th anniversary of Luther's 95 Theses, are historical constructs. As Robert Scribner, the renowned historian of the German Reformation, has reminded us in a slender but provocative book on another anniversary – the occasion of the 500th anniversary of the birth of Martin Luther – for most of us, the Reformation began when Luther brazenly, if rather commonly, posted his 95 Theses on the door of the Castle Church in Wittenberg in 1517. But, Scribner cautions,

> Despite much scholarly debate, it remains uncertain whether the theses were ever posted; the real significance of the alleged incident resided in the fact that much later in the sixteenth century a myth was created that this was how 'the Reformation' began. This myth is typical of a number of myths about the Reformation. It involves a teleological view of history, an arrangement from hindsight of the course of events into an inevitable pattern in which no other outcome is envisaged than 'the Reformation' as later ages understood it.[1]

Ruing what he deems an excessive focus on Luther, Scribner points to the complexity of a protracted historical process that better reflects

---

1. Robert W. Scribner, The German Reformation (Atlantic Highlands, NJ: Humanities Press, 1986), 1.

the Reformation as a historical phenomenon.² For Scribner and for us, however, such myths and historical constructions provide a valuable opportunity to question handed-down assumptions and to seek a broader context for understanding both the past and present.

Like other scholars, Scribner observed that the term 'Reformation' was itself somewhat anachronistic in the sixteenth century. It was used in the modern sense to describe a period in Church history only beginning in the seventeenth century under particularly polemical circumstances, eventually becoming a self-legitimating mantra for confessional churches in the nineteenth and twentieth centuries.³ Still, while the Reformation in the modern sense was a construction, the term Reformation did have important currency in the late medieval period and the sixteenth century in three specific contexts: first, as a legal code; second, as a restructuring of a university curriculum; and finally, as internal reform of the church (coming closest here to later Reformation notions). The term also carried a popular sense, almost of apocalyptic dimensions, of ushering in a great change.⁴ In this regard, there is some overlap with more recent discussions of Confessionalization (see below).

Recognizing the complexity of something called the Reformation, as well as the need to take a long view of events and developments, including earlier trends (which some scholars suggest we seek already back in the twelfth century) and later developments, beginning with Confessionalization, we have a remarkable opportunity to (re)consider developments within German Jewry during the Reformation period.

Jewish historiography has balanced its treatment of the Reformation and the Jews between two poles, reflected in the varying interpretations of Luther as the embodiment of the German *lauter*, pure,⁵ or the Hebrew *lo-tahor*, impure.⁶ On the one hand, the Reformation is recognized as a decisive event that led to increasingly bitter and abusive theological and political, and in some cases even 'racial,' discrimination and concomitant expulsion from various cities and territories

---

2. Ibid., 2.
3. Ibid., 4.
4. Ibid.
5. "Light" in Hayyim Hillel Ben-Sasson's translation; see Haim Hillel Ben-Sasson, "The Reformation in Contemporary Jewish Eyes," The Israel Academy of Sciences and Humanities Proceedings 4:12 (1970): 239–326.
6. See ibid., 272 and n. 96, and 288; see also Joseph M. Davis on Eliezer Eilburg; as Davis points out, an anonymous polemical treatise played with Luther's first name as well, since 'martina' was the Aramaic word for clay, it could note that "In 1520 a priest named Martin arose [...] and his name proves that he is common clay [...]"; Joseph M. Davis, "The 'Ten Questions' of Eliezer Eilburg," Hebrew Union College Annual 80 (January, 2009): 173–244, here at 229.

throughout central Europe. Indeed, according to some scholars, the reformers' attitude towards the Jews paved the way for the centuries-later annihilation of European Jewry – the *Sonderweg* theory.[7]

On the other hand, in the view of other scholars, the Reformation ushered in a dissolution of the homogeneous and all-powerful church and led to the eventual removal of anti-Jewish motifs such as host desecration and ritual murder. Further, the Reformation, with its emphasis on the Hebrew Bible and the refashioning of Protestants as the ancient Israelites and Christian cities as new Zions, by the end of the sixteenth century led to an unprecedented degree of toleration of Jews through the reception of Roman Law and the interest in Hebrew language, the Hebrew Bible, and Jewish customs. Jews, too, felt the burning apocalyptic sense of the age, envisioning their own redemption and the beginning of a messianic era. Moreover, many scholars suggest that the Reformation, with its alleged Protestant Ethic, led to the economic reintegration of European Jewry by the end of the sixteenth century.[8]

Well representing an older stream of historical interpretation – one which noted the ill treatment of the Jews but also their essential Otherness – the towering nineteenth-century Jewish historian Heinrich Graetz (1817–1891) once wrote that,

> It is astonishing, yet not astonishing, that the surging movement, the convulsive heaving that shook the Christian world from pole to pole in the first quarter of the sixteenth century scarcely touched the inner life of the Jews [...] Having had no 'Middle Ages,' they needed no new epoch. They needed no regeneration, they had no immoral course of life to redress, no cankering corruption to cure, no dam to raise against the insolence and rapacity of their spiritual guides. They had not so much rubbish to clear away [...].[9]

---

7. See Salo Wittmayer Baron, A Social and Religious History of the Jews, vol. 13 (2nd ed.) (New York: Columbia University Press, 1969), 217: "Hence it was mainly in the territory of the Holy Roman Empire that the great drama of the Reformation immediately affected many Jewish communities and constituted a major factor in the subsequent destinies of the Jewish people, down to the Nazi era and beyond."

8. According to Baron, for example, "At the same time, the chronologically preceding influences of the Protestant Reformation upon Jewish history had to be treated in a subsequent chapter as an integral factor in the transformation of modern Europe and the ensuing emancipation of the Jews" ; Salo W. Baron, "Emphases in Jewish History," in History and Jewish Historians: Essays and Addresses (Philadelphia: Jewish Publication Society of America, 1964): 65–89, here at 69. Baron argues that, "[...] in the long run, the Reformation contributed to the religious diversification, and subsequently to the growing secularization, of Europe. In time, these forces were bound to affect deeply also the position of Jews in the modern world"; Baron, A Social and Religious History of the Jews, vol. 13, 206.

9. Heinrich Graetz, History of the Jews, vol. IV (Philadelphia: Jewish Publication Society of America, 1956 [orig. 1894]), 477.

One of the few, early scholars to examine the contemporary Jewish view of the Reformation was Haim Hillel Ben-Sasson (1914–1977). As Ben-Sasson noted at the beginning of one of his by now dated, but still important and landmark essays:

> Essentially this conflict within the Christian community no doubt left the Jew in the role of an outside observer. Nevertheless, there were some Jews who regarded themselves as involved in this struggle, whether through force of circumstances, or as a result of certain illusions that they chose to nurture. Whatever the cause, it can hardly be denied that many of the phenomena of the Christian controversy and attendant problems had a definite bearing upon Jewish life and thought.[10]

Ben-Sasson identified the fact, a bit begrudgingly perhaps, that the Reformation clearly had resonance in Jewish life and thought. In the years since his research, the regular rejection of traditional historiographical emphases on intellectual accomplishments and persecution, in favor of a more nuanced and frequently less pristine, harmonious, and isolated society than was once imagined has fruitfully complicated our image of early modern German Jewry.

Thus, an abundance of recent studies have added significant depth to our understanding of the position of Jews and the Jewish community in the larger non-Jewish world and have pointed to remarkably rich social interactions and intellectual engagements between Jews and Christians. Yet historians often remain reticent to explore the extent to which the broader changes associated with the Reformation affected the social and communal aspects of 'internal' Jewish life. This is true to such a degree that we may even allow for the standard bifurcation of 'internal' and 'external,' or even the segregation of what were once distinct fields of inquiry such as social, political, intellectual, economic, and cultural history.[11] The representation of Jews and Judaism, the accomplishments and activities of some Jewish scholars, and even the impact of Judaism and Jews on the Reformation have received much attention in scholarship and continue to garner interest

---

10. Ben-Sasson, "The Reformation in Contemporary Jewish Eyes," 239. In another article, Ben-Sasson reflected that, "On closer inspection Jewish culture in Germany turns out to be much more receptive to nonnative elements, more variegated, than current views about it would allow"; Hayyim Hillel Ben-Sasson, "Jewish-Christian Disputation in the Setting of Humanism and Reformation in the German Empire," Harvard Theological Review 59 (1966): 369–90, here at 369.

11. There are, however, a number of contributions to this discussion, including Dean Phillip Bell, Jewish Identity in Early Modern Germany: Memory, Power and Community (Aldershot: Ashgate Publishers, 2007); Debra Kaplan, Beyond Expulsion: Jews, Christians, and Reformation Strasbourg (Stanford, CA: Stanford University Press, 2011); and Rachel L. Greenblatt, To Tell Their Children: Jewish Communal Memory in Early Modern Prague (Stanford, CA: Stanford University Press, 2014).

from Jewish and Christian scholars alike. Less attention, however, has been paid to other aspects of the Reformation and the Jews. A recent exception is the book *Jews, Judaism, and the Reformation in Sixteenth-Century Germany*, which appeared in 2006. The volume attempts to place the issue of the Reformation into conversation with the topic of Judaism and the Jews through the exploration of a longer historical and intellectual context and the consideration of a broad range of reformers' (beyond Luther's) attitudes towards Judaism and the Jews. Particularly helpful for present purposes, it also probed the impact of the Reformation on Jewish intellectual, legal, religious, and communal developments.[12]

The short shrift paid until recently to the internal effects of the Reformation on the Jews is undoubtedly due, at least in part, to the dearth of sources available to scholars. Plausibly, too, the focus of Reformation studies and the assumption – among Christian and Jewish scholars alike – that Jewish and Christian interaction was quite limited, likely also contributed to this neglect. A range of diverse studies, however, has shown that the multi-faceted early modern German Jewish communities were closely linked to a longer and broader Jewish tradition, and that they variously engaged with, borrowed from, and at times rejected the momentous changes sparked by the Reformation.[13]

This topic calls for some caution. While we have certainly witnessed a broadening of perspective and historical recalibration (as demonstrated in some of the scholarship referenced in the notes), one might argue that in our recent rush to repudiate the older lachrymose view of Jewish history we may be going too far in the other direction, running the risk of over-emphasizing notions of convivencia and acculturation. The balance of this essay, therefore, will rehearse some of the valuable opportunities to contextualize early modern German Jewish developments in the era of Reformation, but also remind us that Jewish communal history and development were also marked by

---

12. Dean Phillip Bell and Stephen G. Burnett, eds., Jews, Judaism, and the Reformation in Sixteenth-Century Germany (Leiden and Boston: Brill, 2006).

13. Traditionally, the Reformation has been interpreted to have had little direct impact on the religion of sixteenth-century Jews. As one early twentieth-century scholar wrote, "Despite the spread of Luther's writings among the Jews, it left the spirit of the people untouched, and only in isolated instances did conversions to Lutheranism occur; Luther himself complained that Jews read his works only to refute them": Louis Israel Newman, Jewish Influences on Christian Reform Movements (New York: Columbia University Press, 1925), 629. The same author notes, however, that the Reformation did have a significant impact on later Jewish history, ushering in a new era for European Jewry and paving the way and serving as a model for the nineteenth-century Reform movement within Judaism (ibid.).

boundaries and unique concerns as well as a connection with longer-term internal trajectories and discourse.

The Politics of Jewish and Christian Relations

I begin with the question of whether the Reformation affected Jewish and Christian relations,[14] which I consider through policies on Jewish settlement and expulsion. There were numerous expulsions of Jews in German lands – in cities and territories – in the later Middle Ages and on the eve of the Reformation.[15] The late medieval expulsions reflected a number of important political, economic, and social changes in the German commune, including discussions about the nature of ministry and political power, for example. In addition, the religious

---

14. There is a large and ever growing literature on many aspects of Jewish and Christian relations in the Reformation period. Among the more recent works, consider the following: Miriam Bodian, "The Reformation and the Jews," in Rethinking European Jewish History, eds. Jeremy Cohen and Moshe Rosman (Oxford: Littman Library of Jewish Civilization, 2009): 112–32. Regarding the Reformation and the Jews in a more traditional religious and intellectual context, see, for example, Achim Detmers, Reformation und Judentum: Israel-Lehren und Einstellungen zum Judentum von Luther bis zum frühen Calvin (Stuttgart: Kohlhammer, 2001); Avner Shamir, Christian Conceptions of Jewish Books: The Pfefferkorn Affair (Copenhagen and Lancaster: Museum Tuscalanum Press and Gazelle, 2011); David H. Price, Johannes Reuchlin and the Campaign to Destroy Jewish Books (Oxford and New York: Oxford University Press, 2011); Debra Kaplan, "Sharing Conversations: A Jewish Polemic against Martin Luther," Archiv für Reformationsgeschichte 103 (2012): 41–63; Brooks Schramm and Kirsi I. Stjerna, Martin Luther, the Bible and the Jewish People: A Reader (Minneapolis: Fortress Press, 2012); Yaacov Deutsch, Judaism in Christian Eyes: Early Modern Descriptions of Jews and Judaism (Oxford and New York: Oxford University Press, 2012); Stephen G. Burnett, Christian Hebraism in the Reformation Era (1500–1660): Authors, Books, and the Transmission of Jewish Learning (Leiden and Boston: Brill, 2012); and, Jewish Books and their Readers: Aspects of the Intellectual Life of Christians and Jews in Early Modern Europe, eds. Scott Mandelbrote and Joanna Weinberg (Leiden and Boston: Brill, 2016). On Luther and the Jews there is a vast literature by now. See, for example, Thomas Kaufmann, Luther's Jews: A Journey into Anti-Semitism, trans. Lesley Sharpe and Jeremy Noakes (Oxford and New York: Oxford University Press, 2017).

15. Among the significant regional expulsions we can number: The Palatinate (1390/91); Thuringia (1401); Austria (1420/21); Breisgau (1421); Bavaria-Munich (1442); Bavaria-Landshut (1450); Mecklenburg/Pomerania (1492); Carniola (1496); and Styria (1496). In the first half of the sixteenth century, regional expulsions occurred in a number of areas, including Brandenburg (1510); Alsace (ca. 1520), and Saxony (1540). The regional expulsions might also include large archbishoprics, such as Cologne (1429), Mainz (1470), and Magdeburg (1493), or clusters of cities, as throughout Bohemia in 1454. During the fifteenth century, Jews were expelled from numerous German cities, such as Vienna (1421), Cologne (1424), Augsburg (1438/40), Mainz (1438 and 1470), Munich (1442), Würzburg (1450), Breslau (1453/54), Erfurt (1453/54), Hildesheim (1457), Bamberg (1478), Salzburg (1498), Nuremburg (1499), Ulm (1499), Nördlingen (1504), Regensburg (1519), and Rothenburg ob der Tauber (1520).

changes prior to the Reformation, which led to a sacralization of German communal life, help to explain the growing marginalization of the Jews in late medieval German society. The Reformation continued this marginalization, while also revamping the terrain in some crucial ways.

Jewish life in early modern Germany was subsumed under different layers of experience and authority. While Jews lived in specific cities, towns, or villages, they were also subject to territorial and imperial conditions. These territorial realities – which were themselves influenced by the Reformation – could affect Jewish settlement and Jewry law, at times creating opportunities and at times leading to restriction or expulsion. In such cases, Jewish relations with the emperor and the imperial court could be pivotal. Jewish delegates made their way to the emperor and to imperial diets to plead the case of their communities and to offer much-needed financial support. The famous *Shtadlan*, Josel of Rosheim (1476–1554), came, in time, to side with the Catholic emperor. Ben-Sasson attributes this to his "conservative turn of mind and social ideology,"[16] though it is also related to general political conditions.[17] According to Josel:

> At all times – as we have now seen with our own eyes in the case of a people *that has established a new faith, with all kinds of leniencies in order to cast off the yoke*. And their aim was to set upon us and annihilate the people of Israel by various and harsh legal measures and massacres. But God, seeing the affliction of His people, sent His angel, merciful kings, to give power and might to his majesty, the Emperor Charles – long may he live! – that he might prevail over them on many occasions, breaking their covenant and voiding their – conspiracy. […] And by a miracle he triumphed and saved the people of Israel from the hands of the new faith established by the priest called Martin Luther, an unclean man, who intended to destroy and slay all the Jews, both young and old. Blessed be the Lord, who foiled his counsel and frustrated his designs and allowed us to behold His vengeance and many salvations to this day.[18]

The status of the Jews in Hesse provides an intriguing prism through which to look at discussions of toleration and expulsion of the Jews in a Reformation context. In the 1530s, the Landgrave Philip sought to clarify the position of the Jews living in his territory. Eminently practical in his economics and often his politics as well, Philip granted the Jews limited protection while turning to reforming theologians, espe-

---

16. Ben-Sasson, "The Reformation in Contemporary Jewish Eyes," 293.
17. Sefer ha-Miknah, translated in Ben-Sasson, ibid., 291.
18. Joseph of Rosheim, Sefer ha-Miknah, ed. Hava Fraenkel-Goldschmidt (Jerusalem: Mekizei Nirdamim, 1970), 73–4; translated in Ben-Sasson, "The Reformation," 291. The italics belong to Ben-Sasson.

cially Martin Bucer (1491–1551), for advice on what position to adopt on the Jewish question.[19] Continuing a long line of Christian analysis, Bucer distinguished between the biblical Israel of the elect (or of the spirit) and empirical Judaism (or corporeal Israel), providing numerous historical examples of rulers expelling the Jews. Philip, however, cast the Jews as a noble race, who might reestablish their covenant with God. Along the way, they might also prove to be of financial benefit to the territory.

Underlying these various positions on the fate of the Jews of Hesse, one discerns several core 'Reformation' issues. First, the debate over true religious identity and the notion of *ad fontes*, in which different religious groups strove to claim historical, and thereby a certain spiritual, legitimacy and primacy. This battle would continue at the end of the sixteenth century, through Confessionalization, as Catholics and Protestants debated the calendar and Jews such as David Gans (1541–1613) attempted to make Jews into historical actors, with a role in shaping the past and present.[20] Second, we find a close relationship between matters of state and religious tolerance (not toleration in the modern sense), with an emphasis on moral behavior and a certain Godly law that even Josel referenced.[21] Third, we see the

---

19. On Bucer and the Jews, see Timothy J.Wengert, "Bucer, the Jews, and Judaism," in Bell and Burnett, eds., Jews, Judaism, and the Reformation, 137–69. See also Dean Phillip Bell, "Jewish Settlement, Politics, and the Reformation," in ibid., 421–50. See also Carl Cohen, "Martin Bucer and his Influence on the Jewish Situation," Leo Baeck Institute Year Book 13 (1968): 93–101; R. Gerald Hobbs, "Martin Bucer et les Juifs," in Martin Bucer and Sixteenth Century Europe: Actes du colloque de (28–31 août 1991), eds. Christian Krieger and Marc Lienhard (Leiden and New York: Brill, 1993): 681–89; Wilhelm Maurer, "Butzer und die Judenfrage in Hessen," in Kirche und Geschichte, vol. II, eds. Ernst Wilhelm Kohls and Gerhard Müller (Göttingen: Vandenhoeck & Ruprecht, 1970): 347–65; and Willem Nijenhuis, "A Remarkable Historical Argumentation in Bucer's 'Judenratschlag'," and "Bucer and the Jews," in idem, Ecclesia Reformata: Studies on the Reformation (Leiden and New York: Brill, 1972), 23–37, 38–72. More recently, see Christoph Strohm, "Martin Bucer und die Juden," in Protestantismus, Antijudaismus, Antisemitismus: Konvergenzen und Konfrontationen in ihren Kontexten, eds. Dorothea Wendebourg, Andreas Stegmann, and Martin Ohst (Tübingen: Mohr Siebeck, 2017): 79–96; and Görge K. Hasselhoff, "Ein ehemaliger Dominikaner als Reformator: Martin Bucer und die Juden," in Dominikaner und Juden: Personen, Konflikte und Perspektiven vom 13. bis zum 20. Jahrhundert, eds. Elias H. Füllenbach and Gianfranco Miletto (Berlin and Boston: de Gruyter, 2015): 349–73.

20. See Dean Phillip Bell, "Jewish and Christian Historiography in the Sixteenth Century: A Comparison of Sebastian Münster and David Gans," in God's Word for Our World: In Honor of Simon John DeVries, eds. J. Harold Ellens, Deborah L. Ellens, Rolf P. Knierim, and Isaac Kalimi, vol. 2 (London: Continuum International Publishing Group, 2004): 141–58.

21. In his "Article and Ordinance" of 1530, Josel refers to "godly law" when discussing what happens when a Christian has a complaint against a Jew; see Ludwig

reality, veiled in criticism, of religious change. While it is true that late medieval Jews grappled with informers and apostasy, Josel raised the discussion of these groups to an entirely new level, reflecting many of the debates current within the Christian world of conversion between Christian religions, particularly significant after the middle of the sixteenth century.[22] At the same time, Josel noted that Bucer's writings had the effect of stirring up the common people and inciting them against the Jews.[23] In their defense, Josel insisted that Jews were the true Chosen People of God and stressed the continuity of the Jewish

---

Feilchenfeld, Rabbi von Rosheim: Ein Beitrag zur Geschichte der Juden in Deutschland im Reformationszeitalter (Strasbourg: J.H.E. Heitz, 1898), 156. Later on he notes, "We are also men, created by God the almighty to live on the earth, to live and deal among them and with them" (ibid., 157).

22. Elisheva Carlebach has noted that in his depiction of the expulsion of the Jews from Regensburg Josel's emphasis on apostates as a primary hostile Other deflects responsibility for oppression of the Jews from territorial rulers to an internal malefactor; Elisheva Carlebach, "Between History and Myth: The Regensburg Expulsion in Josel of Rosheim's *Sefer Ha-Miknah*," in Jewish History and Jewish Memory: Essays in Honor of Yosef Hayim Yerushalmi, eds. Elisheva Carlebach, John M. Efron, and David N. Myers (Hanover, NH: Brandeis University Press, 1998): 40–53, here at 46. This is Yosef Hayim Yerushalmi's notion of the "profound internalization and concomitant glorification of the myth of the royal alliance" amongst Jews noted by David Myers; see David N. Myers, "Of Marranos and Memory: Yosef Hayim Yerushalmi and the Writing of Jewish History," in Jewish History and Jewish Memory, 1–21, here at 6. The work of Jacob Katz and other historians forced a re-evaluation of the once perceived monolithic nature of Jewish religious belief and community boundaries. Katz articulated concepts he labeled "halakhic flexibility" and the "semi-neutral society" that revealed a Jewish society able to encompass degrees of deviation from rabbinic or communal norms in pre-modern times. Evidence for such divergence can be found in a range of texts. Yom-Tov Lipmann Mühlhausen's polemical Sefer ha-Nizzahon, to give one example, served both to argue against Christian theology as well as Jews who deviated and apostatized from Judaism; see Israel Jacob Yuval, "Kabbalisten, Ketzer und Polemiker: Das kulturelle Umfeld des Sefer ha-Nizachon von Lipman Mühlhausen," in Mysticism, Magic and Kabbalah in Ashkenazic Judaism, eds. Karl Erich Grözinger and Joseph Dan (Berlin: de Gruyter, 1995): 155–71, here at 161, 170. Mühlhausen addresses his polemic to Christians, heretics, and various sectarians. See Yom-Tov Lipmann Mühlhausen, Sefer ha-Nitsahon, ed. Frank Talmage (Jerusalem: Merkaz Dinur, 1984) [Hebrew], especially 20–22 in the editor's introduction, as well as the first page of the author's introductory remarks (47). See also Joseph M. Davis, "Drawing the Line: Views of Jewish Heresy and Belief Among Medieval and Early Modern Ashkenazic Jews," in Rabbinic Culture and Its Critics: Jewish Authority, Dissent, and Heresy in Medieval and Early Modern Times, eds. Daniel Frank and Matt Goldish (Detroit: Wayne State University Press, 2008): 161–94.

23. Pointing to the events on the streets of Friedburg where "a poor Jew was struck and his life taken, while the perpetrators jeered: 'see, Jew, the writings of Bucer say that your goods should be taken and distributed among the poor.'" Joseph of Rosheim, Trostschrift, in Joseph of Rosheim: Historical Writings, ed. Hava Fraenkel-Goldschmidt (Jerusalem: Magnes Press, 1996), 328–49, here at 331 [German].

people.[24] Josel thus placed the Jews and Judaism squarely within the confines of Reformation debates, but he did so by maintaining their exceptionalism.

Confessionalization and the Jews: A Long View of the Reformation

Taking a long view of the Reformation, Confessionalization – namely, the social and theological process of denominational identity construction during and after the Reformation – is a highly charged concept that has been much discussed in recent historiography. It is worth considering in the context of German Jewry.[25] Four central, and over-

---

24. In his reading of many of the historical cases of expulsion of the Jews, Josel located the machinations of apostates and informers. See Dean Phillip Bell, Sacred Communities: Jewish and Christian Identities in Fifteenth-Century Germany (Boston and Leiden: Brill, 2001), chapter 8.

25. Wolfgang Reinhard, a central scholar of Confessionalization, has provided a rich overview in his assessment of Catholic Confessionalization. Reinhard argues that Confessionalization was caused by religious innovation and the origin of and competition between more churches with absolute claims. He divides the forms of Confessionalization between processes and institutions. See also Wolfgang Reinhard, "Zwang zur Konfessionalisierung? Prolegomena zu einer Theorie des konfessionellen Zeitalters," Zeitschrift für historische Forschung 10 (1983): 257–77, here at 258, 263; and idem, "Gegenreformation als Modernisierung? Prolegomena zu einer Theorie des konfessionelles Zeitalters," Archiv für Reformationsgeschichte 68 (1977): 226–52. See also the work of Heinz Schilling, including: "Die Konfessionalisierung im Reich," Historische Zeitschrift 246 (1988): 1–45; and, "Confessionalization: Historical and Scholarly Perspectives of a Comparative and Interdisciplinary Paradigm," in Confessionalization in Europe, 1555–1700: Essays in Honor and Memory of Bodo Nischan, eds. John M. Headley, Hans J. Hillerbrand, and Anthony J. Paplas (Aldershot: Ashgate, 2004), 21–35. On Confessionalization and the Jews, see Gerhard Lauer, "Die Konfessionalisierung des Judentums: Zum Prozess der religiösen Ausdifferenzierung im Judentum am Übergang zur Neuzeit," in Interkonfessionalität – Transkonfessionalität – binnenkonfessionelle Pluralität: Neue Forschungen zur Konfessionalisierungsthese, eds. Kaspar von Greyerz, Manfred Jakubowski-Tiessen, Thomas Kaufmann, and Hartmut Lehmann (Gütersloh: Gütersloher Verlaghaus, 2003): 250–83. See also Dean Phillip Bell, "Confessionalization and Social Discipline in Early Modern Germany: A Jewish Perspective," in Politics and Reformations: Studies in Honor of Thomas A. Brady, Jr., eds. Peter Wallace, Peter Starenko, Michael Printy, and Christopher Ocker (Leiden and Boston: Brill, 2007): 345–72, and idem, "Polemics of Confessionalization: Depictions of Jews and Jesuits in Early Modern Germany," in 'The Tragic Couple:' Encounters between Jews and Jesuits, eds. James Bernauer and Robert Maryks (Leiden and Boston: Brill, 2014): 65–86; Michael Driedger, "The Intensification of Religious Commitment: Jews, Anabaptists, Radical Reform, and Confessionalization," in Bell and Burnett, eds., Jews, Judaism, and the Reformation in Sixteenth-Century Germany, 269–99; and Yosef Kaplan, "Between Christianity and Judaism in Early Modern Europe: The Confessionalization Process of the Western Sephardi Diaspora," in Judaism, Christianity, and Islam in the Course of History: Exchange and Conflicts, eds. Lothar Gall and Dietmar Willoweit (Munich: R. Oldenbourg, 2011): 307–41.

lapping, topics raised by the Confessionalization paradigm resonate with what we now know about early modern German Jewry: questions of conformity (orthodoxy?) and the role of customs; the marginalization and eradication of dissident behavior; the formalization and monopolization of education; and, communal or institutional (re)organization.

Early modern German Jewish customs books sought to codify local and regional customs, especially as regional identities developed and as German Jews responded to a broader pull in early modern Judaism towards codification. The tension between more universal codes and particular local practices and scholars highlights nicely what appears to be a period of transition in which standards of belief and practice were coalescing. Early modern Ashkenazic authorities initially had distinctly mixed responses to the codification reflected in the *Shulhan Arukh*. Hayyim ben Bezalel (c. 1520 –1588) grumbled that such codification complicated the problem by which "there are many uneducated who are not worried about the ancient writings, do not even understand them, and in the meantime forget the Torah."[26] Initially hostile Ashkenazic reactions to codification[27] gave way, within a generation or so, to an engagement with, if not complete embrace, of Joseph Karo's (1488–1575) and Moses Isserles's (1530–1572) codes of Jewish law.[28] Joseph Davis has argued that, despite the ongoing production of collections of local customs, the synods of late sixteenth-century German Jewry "gave evidence of the new, clearer sense of forming a single community."[29] Ironically, however, both localized customs and broader codification could create greater uniformity, albeit at different levels and in different ways.

In early modern German Jewry, dissidence was not merely moralized against; it was also punished, specifically through fines and

---

26. Moritz Güdemann, Quellenschriften zur Geschichte des Unterrichts und der Erziehung bei den deutschen Juden: Von den ältesten Zeiten bis auf Mendelssohn (Amsterdam: Philo Press, 1968), 77. His brother, the Maharal of Prague (c 1512/25–1609), was an even more outspoken opponent. Maharal believed that such codes allowed, even forced, people to make decisions from ignorance and lowered the level of knowledge more generally. He wrote that it was better to decide from the Talmud itself (relying on a collection of decisions allows one to decide without knowing); see ibid., 69.

27. Joseph Davis, "The Reception of the Shulhan 'Arukh and the Formation of Ashkenazic Jewish Identity," AJS Review 26:2 (2000): 251–76.

28. Ibid., 273; see Isadore Twersky, "Law and Spirituality in the 17th Century: A Case Study in R. Yair Hayyim Bacharach," in Jewish Thought in the Seventeenth Century, eds. Isadore Twersky and Bernard Septimus (Cambridge, MA: Harvard University Center for Jewish Studies, 1987), 447–67, here at 449. Bacharach urged the study of codes (ibid., 452–53).

29. Davis, "The Reception of the Shulhan 'Arukh," 267.

excommunication (*herem*). Among the more common forms of dissidence, aside from informing[30] and apostasy, we find Sabbath desecration (as well as the transgression of other religious laws, such as shaving the beard),[31] the disruption of prayer or synagogue decorum,[32] disrespect for the authority of communal officials,[33] the violation of sumptuary laws, scandalous behavior (including participation in games of chance and violence),[34] problematic writings,[35] and inappropriate relations with Christians – either relations that were too intimate or actions that might provoke negative Christian reaction.[36]

The Reformation could provide a sounding-board against which to measure Jewish behavior and religious observance. Josel's famous twentieth-century biographer, Selma Stern, saw Josel as a social critic and social reformer of German Jews who, like the humanists, brought the Jews back to the wellsprings of their history and, like adherents of the *devotio moderna*, patterned his own conduct and lifestyle after the Pietists of Germany.[37] Stern attributed to Josel's petition to the Royal Commission the same spirit that animated broadsides and articles of the rebellious peasants of the 1520s.[38] Indeed, she saw his "Articles and Regulations" as the first large-scale attempt to purge the life of Jews, improve deteriorating social and economic conditions, and facilitate the adjustment to changing social and economic realities.[39]

Various *pinkasim* (communal ledgers) and communal legislation

30. Apparently considered the most dangerous infractions. See Yosef Kaplan, "The Place of the Herem in the Sefardic Community of Hamburg during the Seventeenth Century," in Die Sefarden in Hamburg: Zur Geschichte einer Minderheit, part 1, ed. Michael Studemund-Halevy (Hamburg: Buske Verlag 1994): 63–87, here at 72.

31. Including mention in Hamburg of people "careless" or "lacking conscience;" ibid., 77; 81 regarding transgressions against halakah.

32. See also Güdemann, Quellenschriften, 55ff. for the 1583 Jewish-German book *Buch des ewigen Lebens*. It is indicated that one should not speak or hear Neuigkeiten said during the Torah reading in the synagogue.

33. Kaplan, "The Place of the Herem," 81.

34. Ibid.

35. Ibid., 72.

36. See statutes from 1685 in: Die Statuten der drei Gemeinden Altona, Hamburg und Wandsbek: Quellen zur Jüdischen Gemeindeorganisation im 17. und 18. Jahrhundert, ed. Heinz Mosche Graupe (Hamburg: Christians Verlag, 1973), for example, "[for every] man or woman, young man or maiden, it is forbidden, on the Sabbath and on holidays to go to drink in a non-Jewish inn. Likewise it is forbidden to visit on Shabbat [a] skittle floor, a comedy, fencing school – with penalty of 4 Rt. Women and girls should generally not go to the opera, not even on weekdays – with the same punishment" (86).

37. Selma Stern, Josel of Rosheim: Commander of Jewry in the Holy Roman Empire of the German Nation, trans. Gertrude Hirschler (Philadelphia: Jewish Publication Society of America, 1965 (orig., 1959), xviii.

38. Ibid., 70–71.

39. Ibid., 119.

also addressed these issues. Famously, the important Frankfurt synod of 1603 attempted to formulate German-wide standards of behavior and governing mechanisms. It devised punishments for a variety of transgressors, including Jews who compelled opposing litigants to go to secular courts,[40] who informed on the community, or who used their wealth or power to press their own advantages;[41] created centralized courts and tax collection centers;[42] and attempted to regulate rabbinic jurisdiction[43] and rabbinic titles,[44] as well as the publication of books.[45] Of course, earlier, late medieval, German synods had also grappled with some of these and other challenges, and the ordinances of the early seventeenth century synod need to be read in the context of those discussions as well as the Confessional discussions of the later sixteenth century.

The defining and punishment of dissent was a recurrent topic in early modern German Jewish sources. On one hand, such discussions continued late medieval considerations;[46] on the other, they revealed increased concern with generating and regulating communal norms of behavior, for both internal organization and external accountability. In this sense, the Jewish communities were indeed a part of the early modern territorialization of the state, which itself took even greater interest in the internal boundaries and affairs of the Jewish communities than its late medieval predecessors.

Jewish education in the early modern period similarly maintained important links with previous traditions, all the while evidencing new emphases. In the early modern period, the educational institution of the *Talmud Torah* became better structured and more formally organized, serving a broader communal population.[47] The spread of printing made seminal works more standardized and accessible. Leading rabbinic authorities increasingly promoted a 'proper' order of study. This, along with the possession of certain standard works, such

---

40. Louis Finkelstein, Jewish Self Government in the Middle Ages (New York: The Jewish Theological Seminary of America, 1964), 257.

41. Ibid., 258.

42. Ibid., 259.

43. Ibid., 263. See also Eric Zimmer, Jewish Synods in Germany during the Late Middle Ages (1286–1603) (New York: Yeshiva University, 1978), 140 –47 for excerpts from the Frankfurt synod of 1542 that detailed the issue of jurisdiction.

44. Finkelstein, Jewish Self Government in the Middle Ages, 260–61.

45. Ibid., 263.

46. See, for example, the complex community dynamics related to violence within the community, as described in Dean Phillip Bell, "Early Modern Comparative Topics and Emerging Trends," in The Routledge Companion to Jewish History and Historiography, ed. Dean Philipp Bell (London: Routledge, 2019): 207–20, esp. 212–17.

47. Encyclopedia Judaica, "Jewish Education, Italy."

as popular grammars, opened the door to more consistency in Jewish education. Alongside a lament for the dismal Hebrew skills of many Jews, a call for a return to the text and a certain Reformation Biblicism could sometimes be detected among some Jewish writers.[48] Jews also similarly drew from and imbibed non-Jewish literature, thought, and practices. The work of the late sixteenth-century Prague astronomer and historian David Gans, for example, has been seen within the context of contemporary German and Czech chronicles as well as within the context of burgeoning burgher literature in early modern Germany.[49] According to Mordechai Breuer,

> In his low opinion of the rabbinical titularies and hierarchy Gans may have been influenced by the elevation of the lay element in the congregation effected by the Lutheran Reformation, and more particularly by the egalitarianism practiced by the Bohemian Brothers who required their priests to make their living through the work of their own hands.[50]

Early modern German Jewry evinced signs of growing communal organization, despite thinly spread settlement and often small community size. Increasingly, Jews – like their non-Jewish peers – turned to more bureaucratic tools and practices.[51] Not surprisingly, the early modern period witnessed a growing number of community *pinkasim*, memorybooks, formal constitutions, community offices, and institutions, such as those for the sick. In some cases, the impetus for communal institutional re-structuring came from the outside, as Christian civic, territorial, or even imperial agents required Jews to adhere to particular codes, policies, or practices.

Consider the protocol book of Friedberg for the year 1574. According to the document, the rabbi was closely supervised and his powers and duties clearly circumscribed.[52] In this case, the rabbi was

---

48. Though see the Maharal's opposition to Azariah de Rossi (1511–1587), more generally, in Lester A. Segal, Historical Consciousness and Religious Tradition in Azariah de' Rossi's Me'or 'Einayim (Philadelphia: Jewish Publication Society of America, 1989). See also Ben-Sasson, "The Reformation," 303, 307–8, 309.

49. See Bell, "Jewish and Christian Historiography in the Sixteenth Century," 157–58.

50. Mordechai Breuer, "Modernism and Traditionalism in Sixteenth-Century Jewish Historiography: A Study of David Gans' Tzemah David," in Jewish Thought in the Sixteenth Century, ed. Bernard Dov Cooperman (Cambridge, MA: Harvard University Center for Jewish Studies, 1983): 49–88, here at 70. Of course, the shifting of power from rabbinic to lay authorities was hardly new to the Jewish community after the Reformation, though there are some intriguing parallels.

51. See Bell, Jewish Identity in Early Modern Germany.

52. Stefan Litt, Protokollbuch und Statuten der Jüdischen Gemeinde Friedberg (16.–18. Jahrhundert) (Friedberg: Bindernagel, 2003), 274–76 (beginning at 74 in the Hebrew).

obligated to remain in his position for four years, without residing in another area; the council, for its part, was obligated to refrain from seeking another rabbi during this period. The rabbi in question was not to ostracize/excise or place under the ban any residents in the holy community, or from any of the surrounding area, without the agreement of the council. The council, however, retained the authority to ostracize/excise community members without the agreement of the rabbi. The council was to provide the rabbi twelve Gulden in salary every year, and he was freed from all customary taxes (though not every tax obligation). The rabbi was also to receive one Gulden from each betrothal and a Gulden for the lodging of each student in the yeshivah. Other regulations and agreements were also outlined. Importantly, the rabbi was restricted from making changes in the community's customs without the consent of the community board.[53]

Rabbinic contracts only emerged in the sixteenth century, as did formal processes for selecting a rabbi by a community.[54] The development, or professionalization, of the rabbinate that began in Germany in the fourteenth century has been placed within the context of social and religious (pastoral) changes that occurred among Jews and Christians after the Black Death.[55] It has also been seen as part of late medieval, especially fifteenth-century developments in law and university education (in which the rabbinic diploma is paralleled to that of the university doctor).[56] It has been further compared to the development of city councils, guild structures, and the professionalization of lawyers and physicians in the later Middle Ages.[57]

A comprehensive comparison of these documents and communal contracts made with Christian priests in the late medieval and Reformation period may shed light on early modern German Jewish communal developments and engagement with the non-Jewish world. Setting aside for the moment their important religious practices and orientations, sixteenth-century Church ordinances grappled with similar concerns to Jewish synods and rabbinic contracts. The 1582 Church ordinance from Nassau-Dillenburg, for example, noted the need for

---

53. See Simon Schwarzfuchs, A Concise History of the Rabbinate (Oxford: Blackwell, 1993), 19–21.

54. Ibid., 24.

55. See Simon Schwarzfuchs, "The Making of the Rabbi," in Das aschkenasische Rabbinat: Studien über Glaube und Schicksal, ed. Julius Carlebach (Berlin: Metropol, 1995): 133–40, here at 137; Israel Yuval, "Juristen, Ärzte und Rabbiner: Zum typologischen Vergleich intellektueller Berufsgruppen im Spätmittelalter," in Das aschkenasische Rabbinat, 119–31, here at 122–3.

56. Schwarzfuchs, "The Making of the Rabbi," 138; see Yuval, "Juristen," and his criticism of Robert Bonfil's model, 124.

57. Ibid., 126.

proper recognition and jurisdiction of clergy, and stipulated that the clergy should serve as moral role models. Other contracts specified the moral upbraiding of congregants and citizens.[58] Contracts for priests set out term limits and a range of salaries and benefits that paralleled those found in rabbinic contracts.[59] Christian clergy had particular financial responsibilities, ritual tasks (e. g., Mass and baptism),[60] teaching and supervision of scriptural and doctrinal interpretation, and pastoral duties (i. e., visiting the sick[61] and the delivery of sermons) that differentiated their contracts from those of appointed rabbis, however.[62] On the one hand, sixteenth-century German Jewish communal developments mirrored late medieval and Reformation changes in which the community arrogated important authority, and lay leaders could see themselves as encompassing some aspects of sacral power and exercising the ability to appoint and remove clergy.

On the other hand, Christian (even Protestant and Lutheran concerns, as reflected in Luther's own, often changing, notion of ministry)[63] discussions of sacral authority were, almost by definition, differently focused, drawing as they did from general contemporary concerns as well as specific Christian traditions and innovations. What is more, the context for discussions about the roles and authority of the rabbi and other related issues involved a range of Talmudic materials and prior, late medieval, German Jewish communal discussions and rabbinic responsa.

Conclusions

The Reformation – particularly in a broad sense that began in the fifteenth century and continued beyond the sixteenth – had a notable impact on Jews and Jewish life. Jews did not live in a vacuum, and their exposure to major issues in the non-Jewish world shaped how they perceived that world and themselves. One need not resort to formal Jewish and Christian dialogue to see that the religious, social, and political discussions of the Reformation era significantly impacted early modern German Jews. In its daily life, in its communal organization,

---

58. See Saulle Hippenmeyer, Nachbarschaft, Pfarrei und Gemeinde in Graubünden 1400–1600: Quellen (Chur: Kommissionsverlag Bündner Monatsblatt, 1997), no. 160.

59. See also Rosi Fuhrmann, Kirche und Dorf: Religiöse Bedürfnisse und kirchliche Stiftung auf dem Lande vor der Reformation (Stuttgart: G. Fischer, 1995), 162, 331–2.

60. Ibid., 179, 205.

61. Ibid., 191.

62. See the table in ibid., 200.

63. Martin Luther, Luther's Works, vol. 40, ed. Helmut T. Lehmann (St. Louis: Concordia Publishing House), "Concerning the Ministry (1523)," 34–6.

indeed in its educational development and at times even its very language, German Jews absorbed – both consciously and unconsciously – the major shifts in society around them, combining them with changes taking place within their own communities. Reformation-era Jews may have been marginalized, but, as recent discussions of marginalization have taught us, the very act of marginalization places the marginalized in direct conversation with the heart of society.

Jewish developments in the Reformation era – as in every other period – ought to be considered in light of the development of interactions with the external world. And yet, it would be a mistake to think that Jews unreflectively adopted what was unfolding around them. As discussions of the rabbinate indicate, while there were indeed significant similarities in the approach to religious functionaries and while the rabbinate was 'professionalized' in some important ways, the foci of the position and its role in a community could be vastly different from that of clergy in Christian society. Jewish discussions of rabbinic authority, therefore, must also be understood within the context of earlier Jewish communal developments and discussions, which drew both from Jewish texts and traditions and their own broader milieux. The notion that Reformation-era Jews were free from rubbish or that they were somehow hermetically separated from the non-Jewish world in which they lived may be safely put to rest. At the same time, however, and, to some extent, countering recent scholarship, one notes that early modern German Jewish society differed from that which surrounded it in important ways. The Reformation affected Jews directly in some ways and less directly in others, and its impact was inflected by Jewish sensibilities and internal concerns – as was true as well for diverse Christian communities across Europe. As a construct, the Reformation is invaluable for framing and grappling with central early modern Jewish developments – for both the ideas and practices that affected Jews and those that lacked resonance because of unique Jewish communal and historical concerns.

EDOM VERSUS EDOM
Echoes of the Lutheran Reformation in Early Modern Jewish Writings
By Markéta Kabůrková

Five hundred years have passed since Martin Luther stepped out publicly with his Ninety-five Theses and launched the Reformation.[1] This move carried farreaching consequences not only within Christian circles but also for European Jewry. It was only natural that the Jews of the period evinced a "great interest in Luther, who seemed to wield the shovel digging the grave of Christianity's burial"[2] Jewish authors were interested in the Protestant Reformation, in the person and teachings of Martin Luther, and in the theological schism within Christendom as well. Unsurprisingly, they judged the religious struggle between the new sect and the Catholic Church from their own frame of reference and no single 'Jewish' view manifested itself, but a variety of perspectives selectively favoring different groups and religious doctrines instead emerged.

This topic has rather escaped scholarly attention. Some important exceptions include Hillel Ben-Sasson's study from half a century ago,[3] several articles by Jerome Friedman[4] and Abraham David,[5] and few monographs focusing on particular cases of Jewish-Christian

---

1. It is perhaps an oversimplification to use the term 'Reformation' in singular as most scholars agree that no unified reformatory movement existed but rather a variety of 'reformations' of which the appearance of Martin Luther was neither the first nor the last. Jewish authors commenting on activities of Martin Luther and his followers were well aware of such diversity, as it will be shown further.

2. Jerome Friedman, "The Reformation in Alien Eyes: Jewish Perception of Christian Troubles," The Sixteenth Century Journal 14 (1983): 23–40, here 26.

3. Haim Hillel Ben-Sasson, "The Reformation in Contemporary Jewish Eyes," The Israel Academy of Sciences and Humanities Proceedings, vol. 4, 12 (1970). Of the same author see also "Jewish-Christian Disputation in the Setting of Humanism and Reformation in the German Empire," Harvard Theological Review 59 (1966): 369–90.

4. Friedman, "The Reformation in Alien Eyes," and also idem, "The Reformation and Jewish Antichristian Polemics," Bibliotheque d'Humanisme et Renaissance 41, 1 (1979): 83–97.

5. Abraham David, "The Lutheran Reformation in Sixteenth-Century Jewish Historiography," Jewish Studies Quarterly 10 (2003): 124–39.

encounters during the Reformation period.⁶ The present article aims to expand the discussion by presenting a wide scope of Jewish reactions to the developments in Christian society and theology that took place in sixteenth-century Europe. The corpus of examined sources ranges from stark descriptive accounts to more elaborate reflections of theological innovations to texts that used major themes of the Lutheran Reformation in highly creative ways. Jewish authors recognized the doctrinal conflict as well as the social and political ramifications of the reform within Western Christendom, and some incorporated insight from the Reformation into Jewish apocalyptic writings of the sixteenth century.

One may classify the Hebrew sources dealing with the Reformation by temporal and physical provenance. Sources contemporaneous with Luther were mostly descriptive attempts to characterize the new face of Christianity. Jews perceived the breakup of the monolithic Catholic framework as auguring better relations between Jews and Christians in the future. The reformer's appearance and his initial call to abandon traditional Christian hostility towards Jews[7] aroused a twofold reaction among Jews. On the one hand, it bolstered their hopes for a new, more tolerant world order; on the other, the idea that the great Catholic Church was not impregnable afforded them significant satisfaction.

Sources originating in Germany and its environs, where Jews encountered Protestantism first-hand, expressed different opinions about Luther than, for example, Italian ones, whose authors were acquainted with the papacy. And both groups of writings differed from texts written by authors living in the Polish-Lithuanian Commonwealth, which at that time enjoyed extraordinary religious tolerance, and in the Ottoman Empire, whose Jewish inhabitants had to rely on hearsay for news of the Reformation's effects. A double-edged wordplay on Luther's name gives us a glimpse of this variation in viewpoint: Joseph (Josel) of Rosheim (c. 1478–1554), Eliezer Eilburg (c. 1530–c. 1580) and other Jews living in the German area referred to

---

6. Hava Fraenkel-Goldschmidt, The Historical Writings of Joseph of Rosheim in Early Modern Germany (Leiden: Brill, 2006); Debra Kaplan, Beyond Expulsion: Jews, Christians, and Reformation Strasbourg (Stanford, CA: Stanford University Press, 2011); Selma Stern, Josel of Rosheim: Commander of Jewry in the Holy Roman Empire of the German Nation, trans. Gertrude Hirschler (Philadelphia: Jewish Publication Society of America, 1965).

7. Though, philosemitic hints of early Luther, expressed in That Jesus Christ Was Born a Jew (1523), were directed solely at fostering conversion, and intended primarily as a polemic against Catholicism. See e. g. Thomas Kaufmann, Luther's Jews: A Journey into Anti-Semitism, trans. Lesley Sharpe and Jeremy Noakes (Oxford: Oxford University Press, 2017), esp. 54–75.

Luther in Hebrew as "lo-tahor" (impure), while Jewish authors beyond the reach of Luther's activity referred to him as "Lauter" German word for "pure." In the kabbalistic writings of Abraham ben Eliezer Ha-Levi (1460 –1528), we even find the following tribute: "For this man who is called Martin Luther has done away with idolatry, may he and his portion be blessed."[8]

Additionally, one can identify various genres among the Jewish texts under discussion. Many, of course, are chronicles, as follows from the nature of the narrative genre.[9] Nonetheless, one encounters passages mentioning Luther and Lutheranism in other types of literature as well, such as polemical treatises and prophetic writings.

In his chronicle *Chain of Tradition* (Šalšelet ha-kabalah), Gedaliah Ibn Yahya (c. 1526–1587) refers to the event of 1517 in rather terse terms: "In the year 1449 to the destruction of the Second Temple Martin Luther began to express his arguments."[10] Other early modern Jewish historiographers, however, offer less succinct reports. David Gans (c. 1541–1592), for example, wrote in the second volume of his *Sprout of David* (Tsemach David), with respect to the year when the Diet of Worms took place:

> Martin Luther, a great scholar and expert in Christian books, studied scrupulously and examined and created a lot of writings, following Johannes Huss who was mentioned above to year 5174/1413. He stood up against the pope and divided the hearts of Christians. He told them to burn all images and statues and no longer offer their prayers to Miriam, mother of their Messiah, and to the Twelve Apostles, and [instructed] bishops, priests and nuns to get married, and [introduced] many other novelties. A lot of people agreed with him immediately and with him lined up the most important princes and burghers in Germany, namely the dukes of Saxony, Silesia, Hessen, Mecklenburg, Brandenburg, Pomerania, Baden, from Switzerland and from Austrian towns, from [Augsburg], Ulm, Nuremberg, Frankfurt, Basel, Strasbourg and many others.
> His teaching was made public at the Diet of Worms in 5282, 1522

---

8. From a letter of Abraham ben Eliezer Ha-Levi, see Ira Robinson, "Two Letters of Abraham Eliezer Halevi," in Studies in Medieval Jewish History and Literature (vol. II), ed. Isadore Twersky (Cambridge: Harvard University Press, 1984), 412; and Gershom Scholem, "Perakim me-toldot ha-kabalah," Kiryat Sefer 7 (1930 –1931): 446.

9. On Jewish attitudes towards historiography, see Robert Bonfil, "Jewish Attitude toward History and Historical Writing in Pre-Modern Times," Jewish History 11, 1 (1997): 7–40; and "How Golden Was the Age of Renaissance in Jewish Historiography?" History and Theory 27, 4 (1988): 78–102. The already mentioned article by Abraham David also discussed in particular historiographic writings mentioning Luther; see David, "The Lutheran Reformation."

10. Gedaliah Ibn Yahya, Šalšelet ha-kabalah (Venice: Giovanni di Gara, 1587), 116v.

according to the Christian calendar, and then great wars broke up in a majority of European lands, greater and heavier year by year, and so more than thousands of thousands Christians perished and were killed for his teaching up to our present time.[11]

First and foremost, we notice that Gans was able to identify Luther, whom he esteemed as a well-read scholar and prolific author in Christian doctrine,[12] as a follower of an earlier reform movement, namely, that of Jan Hus (1369–1415). Hus, after whom the eponymous Hussite movement was named, was a priest active in late medieval Prague. A well-known representative of the Bohemian Reformation, Hus preached against indulgencies, a theme of acute interest in Luther's Ninety-five Theses. Gans' mention of Hus was highly related to his place of residence; the Utraquists had a strong presence in Rudolfine Prague.[13]

Furthermore, David Gans acknowledged the impact of Luther's appearance in the religious strife and highlighted some of its relevant points characterizing the theological conflict between the Catholics and the Reformed. After mentioning Luther's rejection of papal authority, Gans noted the movement's fierce iconoclasm. This negative stance towards images and the veneration of saints was, to a greater or lesser degree, shared by all reformers;[14] moreover, it was easy to observe its actual manifestations in Protestant towns. Other Jewish authors writing about Luther and Christian Reformation also mentioned iconoclastic riots. Abraham ben Eliezer Ha-Levi,[15] whose knowledge of the European religious conflict must have been only indirect, wrote that: "Protestants destroy and burn images of their gods and their idols

---

11. David Gans, Tsemach David (Prague: 1592), vol. II, 103v.

12. Also Joseph of Rosheim acknowledged that Luther "wrote many books," yet these were "books of heresy [that] used to fall out of his lap"; Fraenkel-Goldschmidt, The Historical Writings, 301.

13. During the reign of Rudolf II Habsburg (1552–1612), Prague represented one of the leading centres of the arts and sciences in Europe, and a religiously tolerant milieu, guranteed by the Czech Confession and the Majestätsbrief. Eliska Fucíková, Prague in the Reign of Rudolph II (Prague: Karolinum, 2015).

14. See e. g. Carlos M. N. Eire, War against Idols: The Reformation of Worship from Erasmus to Calvin (Cambridge: Cambridge University Press, 1986); Willem Van Asselt, "The Prohibition of Images and Protestant Identity," in Iconoclasm and Iconoclash: Struggle for Religious Identity, eds. Willem Van Asselt, Paul van Geest, Daniela Mueller and Theo Salemink (Leiden and Boston: Brill, 2007), 299–311.

15. On Abraham ben Eliezer Ha-Levi and his works, see Abraham David, To Come to the Land: Immigration and Settlement in Sixteenth-Century Eretz-Israel (Tuscaloosa and London: University of Alabama Press, 1999), 138–39 and 223; Ben-Sasson, "The Reformation," 260–69; Robinson, "Two Letters," 403–22; and Scholem, "Perakim," 242–48. See also introduction to an edition of Ha-Levi's writings, Abraham Ha-Levi, Maamar meshare kitrin, eds. Gershom Scholem and Malachi Beit-Arié (Jerusalem: Jewish National and University Library Press, 1978).

are cut down in all parts of his [Luther's] dominion,"[16] and similarly, Joseph ben Joshua Ha-Kohen (1496–1575) states in the *History of Kings of France and Ottoman* (Divrey ha-yamim le-malkhei Zarfat u-veyt Ottoman ha-Tugar):[17] "No longer were graven images set up or homage paid to the saints as before."[18] Even remote observers like Abraham Ibn Migash (active in the second half of the sixteenth century),[19] who settled in Constantinople and served as personal physician to Sultan Suleiman the Magnificent, was impressed with this position on images: "This congregation has cast off all faith in icons and priests and has discarded the form of this worthless creed [of Catholicism]."[20]

Luther's followers, among them "the most important princes and burghers in Germany," rejected papal authority, the adoration of the Virgin Mary and the saints, some religious festivities and fasts, and celibacy; "so their religion resolved itself into two religions to this very day," recapitulates Ha-Kohen.[21] Later, the author of the *Anonymous Prague Chronicle*[22] summarized the new religious customs:

---

16. Ben-Sasson, "The Reformation in Contemporary Jewish Eyes," 266.

17. Divrey ha-yamim was divided into three parts. I and II were published together in Sabbioneta in 1554. From the third part only half has been published, ed. D. A. Gross (Jerusalem: Mosad Bialik, 1955). The entire part is preserved in two Mss., housed in the British Library: Or. 3656, Or. 10387. Currently, Robert Bonfil is preparing a critical edition. On the life and intellectual activity of Joseph Ha-Kohen see Martin Jacobs, "Joseph ha-Kohen, Paolo Giovio, and Sixteenth-Century Historiography," in Cultural Intermediaries: Jewish Intellectuals in Early Modern Italy, eds. David Ruderman and Giuseppe Veltri (Philadelphia: University of Pennsylvania Press, 2004), 67–85; Yosef Haim Yerushalmi, Zakhor: Jewish History and Jewish Memory (Seattle: University of Washington Press, 1983), 460–81; Abraham David, "Igrono shel Josef ha-Kohen baal Emek ha-bakha," Italia 5 (1985): 7–105.

18. Ha-Kohen, Divrey, vol. II, 262v.

19. On Abraham Ibn Migash, see Encyclopedia Judaica (New York: MacMillan, 1971–1972), vol. 6, 95 and vol. 14, 21. He came from a dynasty of physicians; his father Isaac Migash or Megas was mentioned in a list of court physicians from 1548–1549, see Uriel Heyd, "Moses Hamon: Chief Jewish Physician to Sultan Suleiman the Magnifiecent," Oriens 16 (1963): 158. The philosophical-religious treatise Kevod Elohim is the only extant of his numerous works; it was published in Constantinople in 1585–1586, and reprinted by Ben-Sasson in Jerusalem in 1977, Abraham Ibn Migash, Kevod Elohim, cd. Haim Hillel Ben-Sasson (Jerusalem: Jewish National and University Library Press, 1977). See also Shaul Regev, "Secular and Jewish Studies among Jewish Scholars of the Ottoman Empire in the Sixteenth Century," in Frontiers of Ottoman Studies, eds. Colin Imber and Keiko Kiyotaki (London and New York: I. B. Tauris, 2005), 241–250; and Friedman, "The Reformation in Alien Eyes," 23–40, esp. 27.

20. Ibn Migash, Kevod Elohim, 127v.

21. Ha-Kohen, Divrey, vol. I, 150v.

22. A Hebrew Chronicle from Prague, c. 1615, ed. Abraham David, Engl. trans. Leon J.Weinberger and Dena Ordan (Tuscaloosa and London: University of Alabama Press, 1993).

A priest named Martinus Luther created turmoil in the Catholic religion, deriding and repudiating its customs. At the same time, the peasants rose up against the priests, seeking to expel them, and the priests were much afraid. There were others among the clergy who sympathized with Luther, despising their dogmas. Subsequently they agreed that priests could marry, that meat could be eaten on Fridays, that certain holy days should be abolished, that the Eucharist is false, and that crucifixes have no substance.[23]

Both Gans and the Prague Chronicle author, together with many others, remarked on the violent character of the religious struggle. Luther's teaching divided not only the "hearts of Christians" but also their lands and dominion. The chronicler of French history, Joseph ben Joshua Ha-Kohen,[24] who held a rather favorable view of the Reformation and strong anti-Catholic sentiment, observed: "Thus, Martin grew wise, probing and investigating and amending many works and matters concerning their faith and cause, and discredited papal practices throughout Germany."[25]

Some Jewish texts distinguished sharply between Martin Luther's initial view on Jews and Judaism and the fierce anti-Semitic tone of his later writings.[26] An anonymous Hebrew anti-Lutheran polemic portrays this turn as follows:

> In the year 280 according to the small counting (1520), a priest named Martin arose and his name proves that he is a bitter material for Jews.[27]

23. Ibid., 28–29.

24. He was born in Avignon, the papal enclave; however he descended from a family of expellees from Spain. He spent most of his life in Genoa. Encyclopedia Judaica vol 11, 595 and vol. 10, 241–42.

25. Ha-Kohen, Divrey, vol. I, 104v. English translation according to Friedman, "The Reformation in Alien Eyes," 30.

26. Literature on Luther's attitude to Jews and Judaism is vast, e.g. Kaufmann, Luther's Jews; idem., "Luther and the Jews," in Jews, Judaism, and the Reformation in the Sixteenth-Century Germany, eds. Dean Phillip Bell and Stephen G. Burnett (Leiden and Boston, 2006), 69–104; Martin Stöhr, "Martin Luther und die Juden," in Die Juden und Martin Luther. Martin Luther und die Juden: Geschichte, Wirkungsgeschichte, Herausforderung, eds. Heinz Kremers, Leonore Siegele-Wenschkewitz and Bertold Klappert (Neukirchen: Neukirchener Verlag, 1985); Heiko Oberman, "Three Sixteenth-Century Attitudes to Judaism: Reuchlin, Erasmus and Luther," in Jewish Thought in the Sixteenth Century, ed. Bernard Dov Cooperman (Cambridge, Mass., and London: Harvard University Press, 1983), 326–64; idem., "Luthers Stellung zu den Juden: Ahnen und Geahndete," in Leben und Werk Martin Luthers von 1526 bis 1546, ed. Helmar Junghans (Berlin: Evangelische Verlag, 1985), 519–30 and 894–904; Robert Michael, Holy Hatred: Christianity, Antisemitism, and the Holocaust (New York: Palgrave Macmillan, 2006); Mark U. Edwards, Luther's Last Battles: Politics and Polemics, 1531–46 (Ithaca and New York: Cornell University Press, 1983); and Gordon Rupp, Martin Luther and the Jews (London: The Council of Christians and Jews, 1972).

27. A word play on the word komer (priest, monk), the name Martin and the

He attracted dukes, lords and noblemen[28] from among his people, and scholars from his faith. He and his faction said that [one should] not place a heavy burden on the Jews, and that [one should] treat them in a respectful and loving manner in order to attract them. And he brought proof and composed a book 'Jesus from the family of Hebrews'.[29] And they mocked him, [saying] that he was a little bit like a Jew, and he regretted it. In order to divert suspicion, since they were complaining about him and saying that his faith tended towards Judaism, when he heard all of this, he changed his words, and wrote to all the nations to act badly towards them [the Jews]. And he said that he did what he had done previously only to draw them [the Jews] to his [Protestant] faith, but once he saw that they did not turn to him, and they were stiff-necked, and did not listen to him, he wrote libels about them, fulfilling the Scripture "he that uttered a slander is a fool" (Prov. 10:18). All sorts of false accusations and lies he could find he put into books, and he gave them [the Jews] a name, calling them Sabbatarians, which comes from the word Sabbath, meaning that they observed Sabbath.[30]

Accusations of Judaizing were hurled from the Catholics to the Reformed and back again. Luther himself was labelled 'semi-Judaeus' by ecclesiastical authorities. For his part, Luther criticized the sect of Sabbatarians in his book, *Against the Sabbatarians* (Wider die Sabbather), written in 1538. The Jewish author of the above-cited passage was clearly familiar with at least some of the content of Luther's treatise *That Jesus Christ Was Born a Jew* (Dass Jesus Christus ein geborener Jude sei),[31] written in 1523. Furthermore, he was able to grasp the turn in Luther's attitude toward Jews. In the early phase of his career – until around 1536, – the reformer voiced concern over their precarious situation in Europe and enthusiastically greeted the prospect of converting them to reformed Christianity.[32] Finding himself unsuccessful

---

phrase "khomer mar le-yisrael" meaning "bitter material for Jews." Also a word play on Martina, when combination of "mar" (bitter) and Aramaic word "tina" (clay, mud) repeats the meaning. Abraham David translates the phrase: "and his name proves that he is common clay"; A Hebrew Chronicle, 129.

28. "Pricim" may denote both noble men and violent men. Kaplan translates as "law-breakers"; Debra Kaplan, "Sharing Conversations: A Jewish Polemic against Martin Luther," Archiv für Reformationsgeschichte 103 (2012), 48. It is also a term used in some Hebrew version of Toledot Yeshu to denote Jesus' followers.

29. Meaning the tract That Jesus Christ Was Born a Jew.

30. MS Mich. 121 (Bodleian), 270v. Versions of this paragraph were published in Ben-Sasson, "The Reformation in Contemporary Jewish Eyes," 289; concerning this MS see Kaplan, "Sharing Conversations," 41–63.

31. Martin Luther, Luther's Works, trans.Walther I. Brandt, vol. 45 (Philadelphia: Fortress Press, 1900–1986), 195–229. Against the Sabbatarians may be found in Luther, Luther's Works, trans. Martin H. Bertram, vol. 47, 64–98.

32. See Ernst L. Ehrlich, "Luther und die Juden," in Antisemitism: Von der Judenfeindschaft zum Holocaust, eds. Herbert A. Strauss and Norbert Kampe (Frankfurt am Main: Campus, 1988), 47–65, here 50.

in that endeavor, he soon became a strong opponent of Judaism, and in his later career called for the harsh persecution of its adherents. Luther's later books, *On the Jews and Their Lies* (Von den Juden und ihren Lügen) and *On the Holy Name and the Lineage of Christ* (Vom Schem Hamphoras und vom Geschlecht Christi), constitute a treasury of anti-Semitic arguments, and he personally campaigned against the Jews in Saxony, Brandenburg, and Silesia. An outstanding example of his success in this effort is the mandate that Luther's prince, Elector of Saxony John Frederick, issued in 1536, prohibiting Jews from inhabiting, engaging in business in, or passing through his realm. In his account of the expulsion of Jews from the city of Braunschweig in 1546, Eliezer Eilburg[33] depicted a particularly adverse impact of Lutheran persecution:

> We were all suddenly expelled [...] on the advice of the foul priest vile Mart[in] and other heretical scoundrels, and due to our iniquities, those prince[s] came before the Council of Braunschweig of accursed memory causing the expulsion with their libellous accusations and temptations. They annulled and broke our charter of many days and years which our fathers bought from them, and even though we had recently renewed our privileges for a great fortune, they did not honour them.[34]

The writings of Josel of Rosheim disclose Luther's increasing malice towards the Jews.[35] Josel served as a representative of German Jewry during the reign of the emperors Maximilian I and Charles V, and he, along with his German-Jewish brethren, were directly exposed to the turmoil of the Lutheran Reformation. Unlike those living in the safety of foreign shores, they did not have the luxury of a distant view of the conflict. Jerome Friedman has characterized their approach to Luther and Lutheranism as non-ideological and pragmatic, expressing a "political position predicated upon concerns removed from esoteric messianism or other conceptual approaches."[36]

33. For a brief biography of the author, see Joseph Davis, "The Ten Questions of Eliezer Eilburg and the Problem of Jewish Unbelief in the 16th Century," Jewish Quarterly Review 41, 3–4 (2001): 293–336, esp. 295–300.

34. The text is part of the author's introduction to his work Machberet ha-measef, extant only in manuscript (located in New York, Jewish Theological Seminary, Mic. 2324). English translation according to David, "The Lutheran Reformation," 128–129. For a slightly different version of this paragraph, see Ben-Sasson, "The Reformation in Contemporary Jewish Eyes," 289.

35. For the biographical survey of the German rabbi, see Marcus Lehmann, Rabbi Joselmann von Rosheim (Frankfurt am Main: Verlag H. Bergman, 1879); Ludwig Feilchenfeld, Rabbi Josel von Rosheim: Ein Beitrag zur Geschichte der Deutschen Juden im Reformationszeitalter (Strasburg: J. H. E. Heitz, 1898); Stern, Josel of Rosheim; Fraenkel-Goldschmidt, The Historical Writings.

36. Friedman, "The Reformation in Alien Eyes," 26, and 34–40 for further details.

Josel met Luther on several occasions, knew Martin Bucer (1491–1551), and was close with Wolfgang Capito (c. 1478–1541). In 1530, in the presence of the emperor and his court at the Imperial Diet in Augsburg, Josel had a public disputation with the baptized Jew Antonius Margaritha (1492–1542), who had published a pamphlet, *The Whole Jewish Faith* (Der gantze Jüdisch Glaub),[37] full of libelous accusations against Judaism. The disputation terminated in a decided victory for Josel, who obtained Margaritha's expulsion from the realm.[38] Josel of Rosheim intervened on behalf of various Jewish communities throughout the Holy Roman Empire and he substantially improved their legal status due to the favorable attitude of Charles V – whom he even described as God's angel sent to protect Jews from the Lutherans:

> We have now beheld it with our own eyes. A nation which founded a new faith with all sorts of modifications attempted to cast off every yoke and plotted to attack us and destroy the Jewish nation by many oppressive decrees and abuses so that it might cease to be a people. He [God] sent his angels in the persons of compassionate kings who gave power and strength to the Emperor Charles to defeat the enemies over and over again, to frustrate their alliances and conspiracies, to subdue them, and to conquer their cities and provinces without effort. He [Charles] won the battle in a miraculous manner and saved the Jewish nation from the might of this new faith which had been founded by a monk called Martin Luther, who is impure, and who planned to wipe out all the Jews, young and old, and to slay them.[39]

Returning to our earlier polemical fragment, we note a striking ref-

---

37. Concerning Margaritha's text see Maria Diemling, "Anthonius Margaritha on the Whole Jewish Faith: A Sixteenth-Century Convert from Judaism and his Depiction of the Jewish Religion," in Jews, Judaism, and the Reformation in the Sixteenth-Century Germany, eds. Dean Phillip Bell and Stephen G. Burnett (Leiden and Boston, 2006), 303–334; Stephen G. Burnett, "Luther's Chief Witness: Anthonius Margaritha's Der ganz jüdisch Glaub (1530/1531)," in Revealing the Secrets of the Jews: Johannes Pfefferkorn and Christian Writings about Jewish Life and Literature in Early Modern Europe, eds. Jonathan Adams and Cornelia Heß (Berlin and Boston: De Gruyter, 2016), 183–200; Idem, "Distorted Mirrors: Anthonius Margaritha, Johann Buxtorf der Ältere and Christian Ethnographies of the Jews," Sixteenth Century Journal 25 (1994): 275–87.

38. Despite this decision, this work would be repeatedly reprinted and cited by anti-Semites over the coming centuries. Martin Luther read *The Whole Jewish Faith* in 1539 before writing his own anti-Semitic tract *On the Jews and Their Lies* in 1543. Josel himself acknowledged the fact that Luther was inspired by Margaritha in a letter to the Strasbourg city council; see Fraenkel-Goldschmidt, The Historical Writings, 388. For Josel of Rosheim's controversy with Margaritha see Elisheva Carlebach, "Jewish Responses to Christianity in Reformation Germany," in Jews, Judaism, and the Reformation in Sixteenth-Century Germany, 451–80, esp. 455 and 460–61.

39. Stern, Josel of Rosheim, 223–24.

erence to the Jews as "Sabbatarians." This mention indicates that the author's familiarity with – or understanding of – the tract *Against the Sabbatarians*[40] was, at best, incomplete. Although *Against the Sabbatarians* was largely dedicated to anti-Jewish polemic, what prompted Luther to write it was his concern with the Sabbatarians, Christians who observed the day of rest on Saturday rather than on Sunday. In the work, Luther clearly distinguished between the Sabbatarians and Jews, whom he blamed for this Christian practice.

Despite the partiality in his comprehension of Luther's writings and various reformation movements' theologies, the author of the aforementioned fragment demonstrates an impressive awareness of detailed distinctions within them. Debra Kaplan has rightly noted that it is likely that he had acquired this knowledge either orally or from a pamphlet detailing Luther's teachings, given what we know about the spread of the Reformation among Christians living in the Empire. Not only were Luther's works printed in pamphlet form in the vernacular to facilitate their circulation among laity, but digests of his writings were also published with great success.[41] These were also read aloud to those who were illiterate, diffusing Luther's teaching beyond those who could read.[42] It is thus likely that the Jewish author had either read such a text, or heard about it from a Christian neighbor who had read or heard these pamphlets.[43]

Our polemical fragment may attest to continuous contact between Christians and Jews living in Europe from medieval times to the early modern period, including both formal and imposed interaction, and informal and voluntary encounters which could have occurred on an everyday basis. Moreover, not only elite authors debated religion; lay people were well acquainted with one another's teachings and rituals.[44] The fact of informal conversations about religion intensified the

---

40. Luther, Luther's Works, vol. 47, 89–92 and 94–95.

41. See, for example, Louise W. Holborn, "Printing and the Growth of a Protestant Movement in Germany from 1517–1524," Church History 11, 2 (1942): 123–37; Richard G. Cole, "Reformation Printers: Unsung Heroes," Sixteenth Century Journal 15, 3 (1984): 327–39.

42. See, for example, Miriam Usher Chrisman, Lay Culture. Learned Culture. Books and Social change in Strasbourgh, 1480–1599 (New Haven: Yale University Press, 1982); Robert W. Scribner, For Sake of Simple Folk: Popular Propaganda for the German Propaganda (Oxford: Claredon Press, 1994).

43. Kaplan, "Sharing Conversations," 51.

44. For medieval times see Israel Jacob Yuval, Two nations in Your Womb: Perceptions of Jews and Christians in Late Antiquity and the Middle Ages, trans. Barbara Harshav and Jonathan Chipman (Berkeley, Los Angeles and London: University of California Press, 2006); Ivan G. Marcus, "A Jewish-Christian Symbiosis: the Culture of early Ashkenaz," in Cultures of the Jews: A New History, ed. David Biale (New York: Schocken Books, 2006), 449–516; and Jonathan Elukin, Living Together,

motivation to compose polemical literature, especially that which was accessible to non-elite Jews:

> And sometimes, the tricksters wish to argue with us about matters of faith, and in order to protect ourselves, for the law requires that we remain steadfast in our faith, I composed this, and it is not lengthy, and its language is clear, so that everyone who comes to read it can understand it, a youth and a small child can lead them (Is 11:6), all who understand the holy tongue.[45]

The polemicist here defined the new threat that Lutheranism posed to Jews, that is, the emphasis on *Sola scriptura*, the centrality of the Scripture in the creed of Martin Luther: "Their faith is based on our prophets and holy writings, and if we did not have prophets, then they would have no proof or anything to say."[46] The anonymous Jewish polemicist even warned his readers to refrain from discussing biblical verses while in conversation with Lutherans:

> And at first, do not begin and talk to them [using references] from the Torah, the Prophets and the Writings. And it is only through the way of nature, and with heart and mind, that one should believe. For it is apparent that there is a unity governing the entire world, ruling over below and above. And this is what you must do to purify and cleanse them, speak to them as if there were no book in the world.[47]

It seems that neighborly discussions about faith, then, may have prompted the composition of the polemic. Interestingly, the author did not instruct his readers to cease speaking with their neighbors. Rather, he recommended that in these conversations Jews avoid discussing the Bible, and instead, that they focus on demonstrating the rational nature of Judaism. In this vein, we may recall an earlier Ashkenazi polemicist, Yom Tov Lipmann Mülhausen (d. 1421), who also defined the necessity to develop rationally and philosophically oriented arguments and thus to equip Jews with more sophistic resources to hold their own in the face of the increasingly sophisticated polemical tools of the rival faith.[48]

Living Apart: Rethinking Jewish-Christian Relations in the Middle Ages (Princeton: Princeton University Press, 2007).

    45. Ms 121, 173r. English translation according to Kaplan, "Sharing Conversations," 48.

    46. Ibid., 57.

    47. Ibid.

    48. Ora Limor and Israel Jacob Yuval, "Scepticism and Conversion: Jews, Christians, and Doubters in Sefer ha-Nizzahon," in Hebraica Veritas? Christian Hebraists and the Study of Judaism in Early Modern Europe, eds. Alison Coudert and Jeffrey S. Shoulson (Philadelphia: University of Pennsylvania Press, 2004), 159–79, esp. 175–76.

The anonymous author of our anti-Lutheran polemic sensed the seductiveness of the Lutheran idea of *Sola scriptura*; the next author we shall consider, this time a representative of Italian Jewry, scrutinized the problematic idea of Sola fide, justification by faith alone. Several passages in *Offering of Zeal* (Minhat kenaot), an acerbic polemic against Jewish Aristotelianism[49] written by Yehiel Nissim (Vitale) ben Samuel of Pisa[50] (c. 1493–before 1572), deal with the difference between Protestants and Catholics in respect to predestination and free will:

> [Fundamental] is the principle of free choice [...] as opposed to the mockers who claim that man neither prospers nor suffers perdition by his works unless divine sanction has so determined... In our generation we have seen the sages of the gentiles divided into sects... Some maintain this view [that man neither prospers nor suffers perdition by his works unless divine sanction has so determined] which is more bitter than wormwood and destructive to the very foundations of faith. But others maintain the principle of free will in a simple and straightforward manner, branding their coreligionists as heretics and apostates [...].[51]

Yehiel rejected the fideistic position opposing belief in free will and the merit of good deeds, doctrines which were held up as common to Judaism and the Catholic Church.

> The new sect that has emerged among Christians who fail to understand the meaning of Scripture, may their souls be damned. In their opinion all the actions of man are of necessity subject to God's determination in the absence of which man can do neither good nor bad. The same is also the case with punishment [...].[52]

At this point, we will leave aside specific examples of doctrinal issues and turn to the next theme which preoccupied the majority of Jewish authors reflecting upon the religious battle within Western Christendom. Reformation ferment had brought about religious uncertainty.

---

49. On this belated battle against philosophy and conflict with Azariah de' Rossi, see Israel Zinberg, A History of Jewish Literature: Italian Jewry in the Renaissance Era (Cincinnati and New York: Hebrew Union College Press and Ktav Publishing House, 1974), 89–95.

50. On him, see Alessandro Guetta, Italian Jewry in the Early Modern Era: Essays in Intellectual History (Boston: Academic Studies Press, 2014), 12–28; Bonfil, Rabbis and Jewish Communities in Renaissance Italy (Oxford: Oxford University Press, 1990), esp. 284–89 and 292–93.

51. Yehiel of Pisa, Minhat kenaot, ed. David Kaufmann (Jerusalem: Mekitze nirdamim, 1970), 11. English translation according to Friedman, "The Reformation in Alien Eyes," 27–28.

52. Yehiel of Pisa, Minhat kenaot, 46. English translation according to Friedman, "The Reformation in Alien Eyes," 28. See also Ben-Sasson, "The Reformation in Contemporary Jewish Eyes," 294.

Not everyone, however, understood in a negative light the religious chaos and even violence of those times, when "Edom turned against Edom."[53] Abraham Ibn Migash, for example, saw in the formlessness of doctrinal opinion a chance to attract Gentiles to Judaism and thus realize the next step towards the Messianic redemption:

> God has aroused the spirit of the Lutherans – who originally belonged to them, but now rejected their views [...]. So they abrogated and devastated much of the unworthy faith they possessed. And each day passes, this people is gaining in strength, so that it waxes exceedingly great – 'And the Lord shall be King over the earth' (Zech. 14:9).
>
> Now behold, this congregation has cast off all faith in icons and priests, and has discarded the form of this worthless creed. So their faith has reverted to a state of primeval flux. Where there are a thousand of them one cannot find ten men willing to rely upon a single doctrine or consent to a given line of reasoning. Thus they are in a state of formlessness, ready to take shape, since faith has departed and no longer finds expression in their utterances. But they have been made ready to assume form when they will find favour with God, after being scourged for their sins and the sins of their fathers, for all that they and their fathers have perpetrated against Israel. And when they find favour with God they will be ready to accept the faith.[54]

Disunity and non-dogmatism, "the return to the state of primeval flux," as Ibn Migash called it, could be perceived positively as well as negatively. In his view, the reformation movement that had originated in the midst of Christianity was an instrument of God's will, designed to destroy the old Christianity which was now afflicted by internal fragmentation. The Lutheran rejection of traditional Catholic beliefs, especially the veneration of saints and images, indeed seemed destined to bring the Gentiles closer to the true monotheism.

In his *Works of God* (Maase ha-Shem), a commentary on the Pentateuch, Eliezer Ashkenazi (1513–1585)[55] expressed an optimistic view of the dynamic changes and voiced sanguine expectations stemming from the prevailing religious nonconformity. Ashkenazi, who lived an itinerant life – residing in Salonika, Egypt, Italy, Prague and Poland – interpreted "Dor Babel" – the generation of dispersion ("Dor ha-ha-

---

53. An Expression from A Hebrew Chronicle, 55.
54. Ibn Migash, Kevod Elohim, 127v-128r. For a shortened version, see Ben-Sasson, "The Reformation in Contemporary Jewish Eyes," appendix I.
55. Little has been written about this thinker and his work. For scattered references, see Ben-Sasson, Hagut ve-hanhagah (Jerusalem: Mosad Bialik, 1959); and Byron L. Sherwin, Mystical Theology and Social Dissent (London: Littman Library of Jewish Civilization, 2006), 58–69, especially for his conflict with Yehudah ben Bezalel of Prague. The first and only comprehensive study of Ashkenazi is N. Ecker-Rozinger Universalistic Tendencies in Rabbi Eliezer Ashkenazi's Teachings [Hebrew] (Ph.D. dissertation, University of Haifa, 2010).

flagah") – as mirroring the times he lived in.⁵⁶ Among those Jewish authors who reflected the Christian Reformation in their writings, both Ashkenazi and Ibn Migash evaluated religious pluralism positively, demonstrating a divine design. For them, pluralism was a sign of the absence of intellectual and religious repression and a necessary prerequisite for the free performance of religious inquiry.

We have seen that the Jews appraised the Reformation not only as an historical event, but also as an act in apocalyptic history. The Lutheran schism appeared at a time when Jews were in particular need of encouragement. Let us recall that in 1517, a mere generation after the expulsion from Spain and forced conversions in Portugal had elapsed. Hence, some Jews, especially the writers of Sephardi origin, perceived this phenomenon as retribution for the suffering brought upon them by the Catholic Church. Abraham Ibn Migash, fascinated by the fundamental rivalry between Edom and Edom, anticipated the ultimate collapse of Christianity and return to Judaism: "[…] they will find favor with God after being scourged for their sins and the sins of their fathers for all that they and their fathers have perpetrated against Israel."⁵⁷

Moreover, the idea emerged that the Lutherans were, in fact, Jews – or at least of Jewish lineage. Solomon Usque (c. 1500 –after 1555)⁵⁸ in *Consolation for Tribulations of Israel* (Consolação ás Tribulações de Israel), from 1553, wrote in reference to forced conversions in Toulouse, in 5106/1346:

> In this way that province was sown with this feed, and many of the descendants of these Jews are probably still uncomfortable in the faith which their ancestors accepted so reluctantly. It would not be implausible to assume that from these people stem the Lutherans,⁵⁹ who have sprung up everywhere in Christendom. For since throughout Christendom Christians have forced Jews to change their religion, it seems to be divine retribution that the Jews should strike back with the weapons that were put into their hands; to punish those who compelled them to change their faith, and as a judgment upon the new faith, the Jews break out of the circle of Christian unity, and by such actions seek to re-enter the road of their faith, which they abandoned so long ago.⁶⁰

---

56. Byron L. Sherwin, "The Tower of Babel in Eliezer Ashkenazi's Sefer maase ha-Shem," Jewish Bible Quarterly 42, 2 (2014): 83–8.

57. Ibn Migash, Kevod Elohim, 127v–128r.

58. Concerning Usque see Abraham A. Neumann, Samuel Usque. Marrano Historian of the 16th Century, Landmarks and Goals (Philadelphia: Jewish Publication Society, 1953), 105–132; and Juan Berajano Guitierez, "Samuel Usque and the Consolation for the Tribulation of Israel," Halapid 21–22 (2011–2012): 34–66.

59. He used this name to denote all reformed groups.

60. Samuel Usque, Consolation for the Tribulations of Israel, trans. Martin A. Cohen (Philadelphia: Jewish Publication Society, 1965), 193.

A similar understanding of Luther as a double agent acting in favour of Jews and Judaism is found in the aforementioned *Kevod Elohim* of Abraham Ibn Migash. The third chapter of the third book contains various anti-Christian tales and remarks, among them, on folio 127a, a passage from the *Toledot Yeshu* narrative. Of particular relevance is the part following the death of Jesus when the land of Palestine witnessed persistent violence between Jesus' followers and adherents of Rabbinic Judaism. The story, representing a core of the so-called Acts narrative of *Toledot Yeshu*, depicted a wise and righteous scholar selected by the rabbis to save the purity of Judaism at the expense of living a life of pretense. Eliyahu, as the sage is named in the version quoted by Abraham Ibn Migash, pretended to be authorized by Jesus himself to teach his followers – "the lawless ones who desecrate Shabbats and holy festivals and slay one another" as they were called by the rabbis – the new law and to separate them from the people of Israel.[61]

On the following page Ibn Migash adds his own experience, framing the story from *Toledot Yeshu* in a personal context:

> One day, when I was in the royal courtyard, the Chamberlain, whose name was Mustafa Aga, said to me: 'Come, I will show you how you [Jews] destroyed human lives.' He brought one book from the royal collections and on reading it, I found that it stated that the Jews worked to destroy the Christian community,

writes Ibn Migash. The following narrative resembles that of *Toledot Yeshu*: the story of a Jewish sage who pretended to be a Christian in order to deceive Christians and divide them. Making contradictory statements to seventy priests regarding their faith, he thus split them into seventy sects. He then told them that in a few days he would ascend bodily to heaven. The method he employed both argues against the belief in Jesus' ascension to heaven and explains the testimony of the empty tomb using a motif from medicine without denying the possibility of the fact itself: the sage drowned himself in a barrel full of quicksilver, a substance which melted all his bones and flesh. The consequences were the following:

> And they slashed one another according to their practice, with swords and spears, until they were covered in blood, because they quarrelled so much, for they were divided into many groups and the disputes multi-

---

61. The quotation of Toledot Yeshu in Kevod Elohim is very similar to the version preserved in MS Strasbourg, one of the most known versions of Toledot Yeshu which, according to William Horbury, was written down in the seventeenth-century Galician Karaite milieu, however the identical text circulated earlier in France and Spain; see William Horbury, "The Strasbourg Text of the Toledot," in Toledot Yeshu ("The Life Story of Jesus") Revisited, eds. Peter Schäfer, Michael Meerson and Yaakov Deutsch (Tübingen: Mohr Siebeck, 2011), 49–59, esp. 55.

plied. This destroyed their habitations, and there were strife and fighting in their tents [...] And I, too, have heard evil reports spread by many, for this matter [that the division in Christianity was induced by Jews] is known but kept secret among the gentiles [...] Be it as it may, it is consensus of opinion among all prophets that our people were the cause of it.[62]

Christians facing the hardships of the sixteenth-century religious wars were thus punished for the sins of their fathers who had persecuted the people of Israel throughout the history, just as Jesus's followers were led to confusion and eclipse by Eliyahu at the beginning of the Common Era. The passage ends with an abbreviated quotation from the *Mishneh Torah*, and Ibn Migash declared that:

Had this [the clash within Christianity] happened in the days of Maimonides [...] he would have danced ecstatically for sheer joy [...] for he has raised up from among them and within them, of their own flesh and bone, of their kin and religion, a phenomenon that destroys them [...] it incites them, fraction against fraction, to destroy their faith; and they burn the statues of their gods in fire, and their asherot they cut down, and their icons they break in pieces [...] This He does unto them by means of leaders and their friends, their brethren Lutherans. For the sword of every man is against his brother, and each man is against his friend and his relative, against his son and his brother, city against city, kingdom against kingdom.[63]

Clearly, then, Ibn Migash adopted the idea of Jewish responsibility for developments within Christian religion. Like Eliyahu – the righteous and learned Jew sent by the rabbis to take charge of the Christian hierarchy and institute new rules in the *Toledot Yeshu* Act narrative – Martin Luther in Ibn Migash's reading is a counter-character: a man who, from within Christian circles, works to bring conflict and collapse to Christianity.

Our Jewish authors were aware that the Catholics charged Luther with the heresy of Judaizing. After all, they themselves perceived some aspects of the new religion as close to Judaism, the original, true, and pure belief. When Gershom Scholem summarized Abraham ben Eliezer's view of Luther, he even used words like "crypto-Jew, a proselyte whose revolt was not limited to the pope but extended to Christianity as a whole, so as gradually to draw the gentiles near to the Jewish religion and its laws."[64] Passages from *Kevod Elohim* stress Lutheran iconoclasm, and also for other Jewish thinkers dealing with

---

62. Ibn Migash, Kevod Elohim, 127v–128r; translation according to Ben-Sasson, "The Reformation in Contemporary Jewish Eyes," 85–87.
63. Ibn Migash, Kevod Elohim, 128r.
64. Scholem, "Perakim," 161.

the Reformation the rejection of images and the veneration of saints represented the first thing they noticed about the new Christian sect. Ibn Migash goes one step further in his presentation of Luther – the one who ignited a conflagration within Christianity – as part of God's plan working in favor of the congregation of Israel.

The above-discussed selection of Jewish texts does not offer a systematic view of the German Reformation, both because no unified Jewish assessment of this development in Christian history ever emerged and because the Reformation itself manifested in various forms. Jewish historiographic works of the early modern period treated the Reformation as an external event, often assessing it in a brief and dispassionate manner. Following a short period of curiosity and cautious hope, Jewish authors living in the area of the Holy Roman Empire reacted to the changing political realities and novel religious forms with a bitter grasp of the negative ramifications of Luther's activities. In Germany, Luther was unequivocally "impure," one who "sought to destroy and to kill all of the Jews, both young and old" – the newest embodiment of the archetypal villain Haman.[65] Texts written by authors living beyond the areas directly affected by Luther's policy, by contrast, display a significantly more creative approach to the Reformation. The scholarship on the Christian uses of Jewish history, Jewish literature, and Jewish figures for internal needs, be they theological, sociological, or political, is vast. It ought to come as little surprise, then, that the Jews engaged in similar exploits of expropriation.

---

65. As expressed by Josel of Rosheim in Sefer ha-Miknah; compare Ben-Sasson, "The Reformation in Contemporary Jewish Eyes," 272 and 288.

Eschatology and Conversion in the Sperling Letters[1]
By Alexander van der Haven

When conversion and eschatology joined forces during Europe's long Reformation period, it was usually to underscore religiously exclusivist claims. Eschatological expectations heightened the sense that those who adhered to the wrong beliefs, did not follow the correct practices, and did not belong to God's sole favored religious community, should convert before it was too late. Thus, eschatologies of this period, also known as the Age of Conversion, tended to ground demands for conversion in exclusivist terms.[2] This was the case for Christian communities in the Reformation, but it was also characteristic of contemporary Jewish eschatologies, which abandoned older traditions that had allowed for righteous Gentile 'Sons of Noah' to find salvation outside the Jewish community. Elisheva Carlebach, among other scholars, portrays early modern eschatologies – Christian as well as Jewish – in these terms:

> Jews knew that if Christian expectations materialized, their own millennial hopes would prove vain; Christians understood that messianic redemption for the Jews would undermine the foundation principles of the Christian religion. Each group remained certain that their own prophetic vision of the endtime would ultimately materialize. Each sought to assure its members that the signs of the endtime identified by the other were fraudulent, products of deliberate deception.[3]

---

1. This research has been supported by the I-CORE Program of the Planning and Budgeting Committee and The Israel Science Foundation (grant no. 1754/12), the European Research Council's Starting Grant TCCECJ headed by Dr Pawel Maciejko of the Hebrew University of Jerusalem, and a Research Fellowship from the Department of Jewish History at Haifa University. I thank also Mike Zuber and both anonymous reviewers for their useful comments.

2. For the use of the term 'Age of Conversion', see Dieter Breuer, "Konversionen im konfessionellen Zeitalter," in Konversionen im Mittelalter und in der Frühen Neuzeit, eds. Friedrich Niewohner and Fide Rädle (Hildesheim, 1999): 59–69.

3. Elisheva Carlebach, "Jews, Christians, and the End time in Early Modern Germany," Jewish History 14:3 (2000): 331–44, here 331.

The fact that religious rapprochement was generally regarded in a negative light confirms this image of Christians and Jews during the long Reformation. A Lutheran woodcarving from the 1550s illustrates this point. Its subject is the Augsburg Interim agreement, in which Emperor Charles V made important concessions to the Protestants. The carving depicts the Interim as one of three demonic characters (alongside the pope and the Turkish sultan) being trampled by a muscular risen Christ. A caption beside the demon's head reads, "*Der Teuffel kumpt in einer gstalt eins Engels*" – the devil comes in the guise of an angel. Beneath the angelic appearance of religious peace, suggests the print, a demonic actor lurks. The Savior's return forebodes disaster for those who make religious concessions to the wrong religions or denominations.[4]

The reactions of writers and artists to the Peace of Westphalia in 1648, which brought an end to the bloody Thirty Years War, demonstrate that such attitudes continued into the seventeenth century. What today is upheld as an example of religious peace-making was portrayed at that time by artists and authors on both sides in eschatological exclusivist terms, as the victory of their own denomination.[5] In this Christian eschatological exclusivism, converts and the phenomenon of conversion were generally taken to signify that, with the end imminent, there was only one road to salvation.

Many of the Christians who converted to Judaism in the Calvinist-dominated Dutch Republic maintained this attitude, and accepted those contemporary Jewish claims that salvation can only be attained through living fully in the Law of Moses.[6] For instance, while in Amsterdam visiting a fellow German who had recently converted to Judaism, a traveler encountered another convert. This was a former Catholic priest, now named Daniel ben Abraham, who expected the messiah to come in 1703. While the traveler was talking with his host, this Daniel ben Abraham:

> [...] sat quiet for a while, but finally talked, saying: "Dear friends, it happens now like it happened at the days of Noah, when the good and pious man was ridiculed, and he and his ark were mocked until the

---

4. Erasmus Alber, Also spricht Gott: Dis ist mein lieber Son an welchem ich wolgefallen hab Den Sollt Ihr Hören (s. l., n.p.: c. 1550).

5. For an overview, see Hartmut Laufhütte, "Der gebändigte Mars: Kriegsallegorie und Kriegsverständnis im deutschen Schauspiel um 1648," in Ares und Dionysos: Das Furchtbare und das Lächerliche in der europäischen Literatur, eds. Hans-Jürgen Horn and Hartmut Laufhütte (Heidelberg: Winter, 1981): 121–35.

6. For such exclusivist Jewish views in the Dutch Republic see, for instance, the writings of the polemicist Isaac Orobio de Castro described in Yosef Kaplan, From Christianity to Judaism: The Story of Isaac Orobio de Castro (Oxford and New York: Published for The Littman Library by Oxford University Press, 1989), 353–59.

Flood, and those who had mocked him begged he would take them in his ark, but in vain. Also the People of God have been laughed at with their hope and waiting for the messiah, which many for certain to their own damage all too late will regret [...]."[7]

Typical of the kind of wide-scope conversion narrative that relied on eschatological expectation, the aforementioned converted priest's combination of promise (for the Jews) and threat (to the Christians), and expectation that the fortunes of the two religious communities would be reversed, mirrored as well as legitimized Ben Abraham's own religious change.

Yet, not all early modern converts thought of their religious affiliation in exclusivist terms, or at least did not express this exclusivism in practice. As recent studies of early modern interreligious relations such as that of Benjamin Kaplan show, converts did not necessarily demand their unconverted family members' conversion or sever ties with relations who remained in their old faith.[8] Moreover, as is amply demonstrated by the rich recent scholarship on Iberian New Christians, the religious self-perception of early modern converts was complex. To continue with the example of Iberian Jewish converts to Christianity, whereas older scholarship assumed that Jewish converts to Christianity either fully embraced their new religion or clandestinely remained loyal to the religion they had publicly been forced to abandon, more recent scholarship such as that of David Graizbord has shown that for these converts, the "threshold" between the Jewish and Christian worlds was "at once a boundary and a crossroads."[9] In other words, early modern converts were markers of religious difference

---

7. "niedergesetzt und ihren Discours in der Stille fleißig zugehöret, endlich aber darein geredet und gesagt, geliebte Freunde, es gehet jetzo, wie zu den Zeiten Noae, da man den guten frommen Mann wohl wird verlacht, und mit seiner Arche verspottet haben, biß die Sünd-Fluth eingebrochen, da ihrer gar viele die ihn zuvor verspottet, werden angeflehet haben, daß er sie doch auch zu sich in seine Arche nehmen mögte, aber vergeblich; Also ist das Volck Gottes Israel jetzo mit seiner Hoffnung und Warten des Messiae verlachet und verspottet, welches gewißlich aber viele mit ihrem Schaden allzuspäth dereinstens [b]ereuen werden;" Johann Jacob Schudt, Jü dische Merckwürdigkeiten: vorstellend, was sich Denkwürdiges in den neuen Zeiten bey einigen Jahrhunderten mit den in alle 4 Theile der Welt, sonderlich durch Teutschland zerstreuten Juden zugetragen. Sammt einer vollständigen Franckfurter Juden-Chronick, Darinnen der zu Franckfurt am Mayn wohnenden Juden, von einigen Jahr-Hunderten, biß auff unsere Zeiten, Merckwürdigste Begebenheiten enthalten, vol. 1 (Frankfurt and Leipzig: s.n., 1714), 275–76.

8. Benjamin J. Kaplan, Divided by Faith: Religious Conflict and the Practice of Toleration in Early Modern Europe (Cambridge, MA: Belknap Press of Harvard University Press, 2007), esp. 266–93.

9. David L. Graizbord, Souls in Dispute: Converso Identities in Iberia and the Jewish Diaspora, 1580–1700 (Philadelphia: University of Pennsylvania Press, 2004), 2.

and exclusivity as they embodied the possibility to dwell in two religious worlds simultaneously.

Likewise, the demand for exclusive commitment in the face of an impending separation of the wheat from the chaff was not endemic to the Age of Conversion's eschatological expectations. Augustine Bader (c. 1495–1530), Quirinus Kuhlmann (1651–1689), Menasseh ben Israel (1604–1657), and Oliger Paulli (1644–1714), for instance, offered another possibility, namely, that the Last Days called the believer to resolve inter-religious strife – albeit mostly without giving up at least one religious denomination in the role of adversary – rather than to unequivocally choose sides. Put differently, early modern eschatology, although predominantly exclusivist, also had the potential to bring different religious groups together.

The present article will explore this side of early modern conversion and eschatology by analyzing two extraordinary letters written in Amsterdam in 1682, and their immediate and broader religious *Umwelt* such as Bader, Kuhlmann, Menasseh ben Israel, and Paulli.[10] The letters are found today in a collection of miscellaneous documents in Hamburg's State Archive, and were formerly held in the archive of the Hamburger *Geistesministerium*, an institution that served as the highest authority of the Lutheran Church in Hamburg and functioned as an advisory body to the city government in the early modern period. They were written by a certain Benedictus Sebastian Sperling to his mother, to explain his conversion from Christianity (presumably the Lutheran faith) to Judaism. Sperling, who by then also used the name Israel Benedeti Ger (*ger* meaning 'proselyte'), tried to comfort his mother who apparently had been greatly upset by the news of his conversion, by presenting her with a scenario of the imminent eschaton that allowed for the salvation of people of different religions.

What is striking about Sperling's letters is the lack of religious exclusivism they convey. This is not what we would expect from an early modern convert in the confessional age of the Reformation, particularly not from a convert in expectation of imminent eschatological events. Nevertheless, as I will show, Sperling recognized Christian scripture as authoritative scripture, claimed that good Calvinists and Lutherans would also be saved, hinted at universal salvation, and depicted the eschaton as a cooperative effort of Protestantism and Islam to return the Jews to their promised land.

It is important to mention that each of these elements – scriptural promiscuity, the claim of multiple paths to salvation, and an escha-

---

10. Staatsarchiv Hamburg 511–1 Ministerium III A 1 d Band 2 (1553–1686), further as "Sperling letters." Translations are mine, and the original German is found in the footnotes.

tology that attributes positive roles to more than one religious group – has, at various times, been exploited to serve exclusivist claims. Sperling's letters can indeed be read in that way: as with many Jewish polemicists before and after him, he used Christian scripture to undermine the dogmas of Christian churches. Furthermore, while Sperling envisioned hosts of Calvinists, Lutherans, and Muslims gathering and aiding Israel to return to its promised land, he also imagined Roman Catholics as their common enemy. As in most eschatologies, Sperling's scenario drew a clear line between the forces of light and darkness.

Yet, to focus on this feature is to ignore the spirit of the letters, in which dualism between the Catholics and the Protestant-Muslim-Jewish alliance plays a minor role relative to the positive elaboration of that alliance. In the following, I explore Sperling's remarkable combination of (on the one hand) personal conversion and thus commitment to a particular religion, and (on the other hand) commitment to a non-exclusive attitude toward different religions. Before addressing Sperling's inclusivist eschatology in the letters themselves, however, I will first briefly explore the historical Sperling as well as the religious environments of Hamburg, whence he came, and Amsterdam, where he converted and wrote his letters.

The Historical Sperling

Benedictus Sebastian Sperling as a historical person has thus far been somewhat of a mystery. The absence of documentation on Sperling's life should have raised the question of whether the letters were perhaps, rather than correspondence written by a son to his mother, literary artifacts: fictive missives composed to further the agenda of a specific religious group somehow associated with the Jewish community of Amsterdam. Neither Wolfgang Philipp, who published Sperling's letters in their original German in 1958, nor Gerald Strauss, who published an English translation in 1974, ever considered this option, and took the letters as authentic.[11] Moreover, because the letters ended up

---

11. Wolfgang Philipp, "Der Philosemitismus im geistesgeschichtlichen Feld: Bericht über eine neue Quelle und Orientierungsversuch," Zeitschrift für Religions- und Geistesgeschichte 10:3 (1958): 220 –30. Philipp published the letters also in idem, ed. Das Zeitalter der Aufklärung, Klassiker des Protestantismus (Bremen: C. Schönemann, 1963), 106–10; and see idem, "Spätbarock und Frühe Aufklärung: Das Zeitalter des Philosemitismus," in Kirche und Synagoge: Handbuch zur Geschichte von Christen und Juden: Darstellung mit Quellen, eds. Karl Heinrich Rengstorf and Siegfried von Kortzfleisch (Munich: Deutscher Taschenbuch Verlag, 1988), 54–7; Gerald Strauss, "A Seventeenth-Century Conversion to Judaism: Two Letters from Benedictus Sperling to his Mother, 1682," Jewish Social Studies 36:2 (1974): 166– 74. Strauss claims that, based on the handwriting, the archived letters must be eigh-

in a governmental archive in Hamburg, Philipp and Strauss presumed that Sperling was from Hamburg. The letters themselves, however, do not indicate their destination.[12]

But Sperling did exist, and the records of the Portuguese Jewish congregation in Amsterdam document that he was indeed from Hamburg. It is not known whether Sperling arrived in Amsterdam already intent on converting, or whether he traveled to Amsterdam for other reasons and found Judaism once there.[13] The former is more likely, though, because in his second letter he claims to be in possession of a bequest from his father to his children, stating that his ancestors had been Jews forcibly converted to Christianity "during wars." His only two appearances in Amsterdam's records are in the Portuguese congregation's *Livro Longo*, where the charity donations, among others, were registered. It lists that on 15 Adar I, 5442 (23 February 1682), thus, six weeks after sending his first letter, two florins were given to "Israel Benedito guer de Hambo": Israel Benedito the proselyte from Hamburg. Three and a half months later, on the first of Sivan (Sunday, 7 June), "Israel Benedito" – this time it is not mentioned that he is a convert – is again given charity, specifically, 3: 3 florins.[14] This is the last we hear of Sperling in the annals of Jewish Amsterdam.

Thus, it seems that Sperling arrived in Amsterdam at the latest in early January 1682, the date of his first letter, and remained there,

teenth-century copies. The archival locations Philipp and Strauss noted are not accurate anymore. Sperling is also mentioned in other research, often merely as a convert to Judaism. The most detailed discussions are by Elisheva Carlebach, who argued that Sperling's claim to be of Jewish descent served to legitimize his conversion, and Paul Thraugh, who used Sperling as a 'Jewish' perspective on Luther; Elisheva Carlebach, "'Ich will dich nach Holland schicken …' Amsterdam and the Reversion to Judaism of German-Jewish Converts," in Secret Conversions to Judaism in Early Modern Europe, eds. Martin Mulsow and Richard H. Popkin, Brill's Studies in Intellectual History 122 (Leiden and Boston: Brill, 2004): 51–70, here 61; eadem, "Converts and their Narratives in Early Modern Germany: The Case of Friedrich Albrecht Christiani," The Leo Baeck Institute Year Book 40:1 (1995): 65–83, here 79; Paul Pitchlynn Traugh, "The Image of Martin Luther in German-Jewish Literature: From Israel Benedeti to Leo Baeck" (PhD Dissertation, University of California, 1972).

12. My own inquiry with Hamburg's archives had no result. Sperling was never registered as a citizen of Hamburg, nor was he listed in its registers of inhabitants without citizenship and strangers. E-mail communication from Anke Hönnig, Staatsarchiv Hamburg, 9 April 2015.

13. The fact that he does not surface in the records of Amsterdam's Christian churches, such as Amsterdam's Lutheran congregation, might be an indication that he was already interested in converting when he arrived. E. g. Stadsarchief Amsterdam (further as SAA) 213 (Archief van de Evangelisch-Lutherse Gemeente te Amsterdam; Kerkenraad en Ouderlingen), 520 –5 (Communicanten registers, 1677–1682).

14. SAA 334 (Archief van de Portugees-Israëlietische Gemeente), 217 (Livro Longo: Kasboek betreffende salarissen, lijfrenten en andere periodieke uitkeringen, 1676–1685), 310 and 339.

receiving financial support from the city's prosperous Portuguese community, at least until June of that year. His subsequent fate is unknown, but additional clues about his social and religious environment in Amsterdam can be found in his letters. Having received charity from the Portuguese congregation does not mean that he had joined the Sephardic community, for the Portuguese provided charity to both Sephardic as well as Ashkenazi Jews. In fact, the name Sperling adopted in Amsterdam, Israel Benedeti, and his chosen term of address, "signor," suggest contact with Italian Ashkenazi Jews rather than, as Philipp assumed, the Sephardic community.[15] The hypothesis that he joined the Ashkenazi community rather than Amsterdam's Portuguese Sephardic congregation is further supported by his postal address, namely, the residence of "Rabbi Gaim Lubbeliner" on the Uilenburg. This was Haim Lubliner, a well-respected rabbi in the Ashkenazi congregation.[16] Unfortunately, too few of the Ashkenazi congregation's records of this period survived World War II to reveal more about Sperling's identity. If, after June, Sperling remained in Amsterdam's Jewish community and died there, he was not buried under the name he had chosen for himself and under which he had received charity, but under a generic proselyte name such as "Abraham Ger of Hamburg."[17]

Sperling and Lutheran Hamburg

The background of Sperling's eschatological beliefs, then, should be sought in both Hamburg and Amsterdam. Philipp in particular, and Strauss while offering a more general contemporary context, only considered Hamburg. Philipp suggested that Sperling's beliefs ought to be understood in view of late Baroque philosemitism in Lutheran Ham-

15. Philipp, "Der Philosemitismus," 224.

16. Sperling letters, p. 1529; Hindle S. Hes, Jewish Physicians in the Netherlands, 1600–1940 (Assen: Van Gorcum, 1980), 66.

17. The Askhenazi burial society buried a proselyte Abraham in 1707 and the "old man" Abraham Ger in 1733; see Jits Van Straten, De begraafboeken van Zeeburg: indexen van personen begraven op de joodse begraafplaats Zeeburg tussen 11 oktober 1714 en 21 juni 1811 = The Burial books of Zeeburg: Indexes of Persons Buried at the Jewish Cemetery Zeeburg Between 11 October 1714 and 21 June 1811 (s.l.: Stichting Bevordering Onderzoek Joodse Historische Bronnen, 1997), 16, 24. Although it would be most likely that he would be buried in one of the Ashkenazi cemeteries, occasionally converts to the Askhenazi community, such as the well-known convert Moses Germanus, were buried at the Portuguese cemetery at Ouderkerk. There are several proselytes buried in the Portuguese cemetery who might be him, such as Abraham Guer in June of 1682 (in his letter, Sperling wrote that he was severely ill), and in 1705 Abraham Ger of Hamburg (Stadsarchief Amsterdam 334 (Archief van de Portugees-Israëlietische Gemeente) 916 (Livro de Bet Haim. Register van besluiten van de maamad betreffende de begraafplaats 1703–1722; journaal van begraven 1680–1716; grafboek 1691–1733), 34, 160.

burg (an idea adopted by later studies such as those of Hans-Joachim Schoeps).[18] Noting the presence in Sperling's letters of millenarian Paul Felgenhauer's (1593–1677) philosemitic ideas, Philipp sketched a broad image of philosemitic culture in Hamburg. Its components included the influence of the Swede Andress Pederson Kempe, the presence of a flourishing Sephardic Jewish community and the messianic Sabbatian movement that had seduced many of this community's members, close contacts with English philosemites, and (later in the seventeenth century), a group of scholars centered around the theologian Johann Friedrich Mayer (1650 –1712).[19]

Like Philipp, Strauss too placed the letters in the context of scholarly interest in the Jewish roots of Christianity and the attraction to Judaism by Christians grown weary of Christendom's internal divisions. Moreover, Strauss regarded Sperling's letters as an example of the late seventeenth-century rapprochement between spiritual Christian messianic expectations and more earthly Jewish ones. Strauss also identified specific eschatological beliefs which were in circulation when the letters were written – for instance, a series of claims focused on the comets that had appeared in the three years preceding Sperling's letters and on the rare astrological conjunctions expected for the years immediately to come.[20] When describing Hamburg's religious climate, Strauss, in contrast to Philipp, emphasized the hostile Christian environment by which it was marked in the second half of the seventeenth century, rather than its philosemitic intellectual milieu.

How might one account for the difference between Philipp's positive and Strauss's negative characterizations of Hamburg? In this regard, it might be useful to recall Hamburg's political division, that is, its relatively tolerant civil leadership on the one hand, and its clerical opposition on the other.[21] The city magistrates' economic interests and distrust of clerical ambitions enabled the Sephardic Jewish community to prosper and reach a peak in the 1660s.[22] The philosemitism evinced by a select group of intellectuals described by Philipp further fueled

18. Hans-Joachim Schoeps, Barocke Juden, Christen, Judenchristen (Bern and Munich: Francke, 1965), 88; Lutz Greisiger, "Chiliasten und 'Judentzer' – Eschatologie und Judenmission im Protestantischen Deutschland des 17. und 18. Jahrhunderts," Kwartalnik HistoriiŻydo´ w, no. 4 (2006): 535–75, here 564–5.
19. Philipp, "Philosemitismus," 224–7.
20. Strauss, "A Seventeenth-Century Conversion to Judaism," 166–9.
21. For a detailed analysis of this conflict in the period that Sperling converted to the end of the century, see Hermann Rückleben, Die Niederwerfung der hamburgischen Ratsgewalt: Kirchliche Bewegungen und bürgerliche Unruhen im ausgehenden 17. Jahrhundert, Beiträge zur Geschichte Hamburgs herausgegeben vom Verein für hamburgische Geschichte (Hamburg: Hans Christians, 1970).
22. Joachim Whaley, Religious Toleration and Social Change in Hamburg, 1529–1819 (Cambridge and New York: Cambridge University Press, 2002), 79.

this cooperative attitude. Nonetheless, the city's Lutheran clergy, generally in opposition to the city's leadership, tended to be hostile towards a non-Lutheran presence in Hamburg, including that of Jews.[23] The second half of the century saw an increase in this hostility following the arrival of Jewish refugees (which may have included Sperling's own paternal ancestors), who were fleeing the Khmelnytsky massacres and other pogroms in the East.[24] This antipathy towards Jews was reinforced by aggressive missionary efforts including the foundation of the Edzardische Proselyten Anstalt in 1667, one year after the conversion to Islam of the Jewish messianic claimant Sabbatai Tsevi (1626–1676), who had many adherents among Hamburg's Jews. Exploiting the Jewish messianic disappointment to convince Jews that Jesus Christ was the true messiah, this missionary institute attracted a great number of converts.[25]

Particularly if his claims about his father are true, Sperling was likely already in contact with Jews when still in Hamburg, making Philipp's suggestion that public interest in Sabbatianism may have contributed to Sperling's conversion highly significant.[26] Pawel Maciejko has recently shown how in the Sabbatian movement "fusing interreligious elements became a positive, and possibly even a supreme, value."[27] Following their messiah, who, in contrast to the historiographic tradition, seems to have sincerely embraced Islam while continuing to observe a number of Jewish practices, Sabbatians became

> […] the most ecumenical of early modern Jews. While mainstream Jewish discourse habitually bundled all 'nations of the world' and their faiths together, Sabbatianism carefully distinguished between different creeds and denominations, often drawing lines not only between large religious formations such as Islam and Christianity, but also between different sects and subgroups, such as different Protestant churches or different Sufi orders.[28]

---

23. Jutta Braden, "Die Hamburger Judenpolitik und die lutherisch-orthodoxe Geistlichkeit im 17. Jahrhundert," Zeitschrift des Vereins für Hamburgische Geschichte 89 (2003): 1–40, here 3–4.

24. Whaley, Religious Toleration, 76; Braden, "Hamburger Judenpolitik," 26.

25. On the institution, see Whaley, Religious Toleration, 86–7. On its conversion successes, see Braden, "Hamburger Judenpolitik," 29.

26. Philipp, "Der Philosemitismus," 225. These contacts would have been likely with Ashkenazi Jews, who from a mere forty to fifty families in the early 1660s had rapidly grown in numbers by the time of Sperling's conversion; see Whaley, Religious Toleration, 81.

27. Pawel Maciejko, ed., Sabbatian Heresy: Writings on Mysticism, Messianism, and the Origins of Jewish Modernity (Waltham, MA: Brandeis University Press, 2017), xxiv.

28. Ibid., xxv.

Hamburg, where Sabbatianism survived the demise of the Sabbatian mass movement, thus offered a Jewish subculture that combined religious conversion and an ecumenical attitude, breathing the same spirit of Sperling's eschatological beliefs described below.

Hence, Hamburg was home to two attitudinal extremes. Whereas a strong Lutheran exclusivist sector tried to either aggressively bar Jews from Hamburg or convert them to Christianity, several subcultures sheltered by Hamburg's magistrates that ranged from philosemitic Lutherans to Sabbatian Jews explored more ecumenical connections between Christianity and Judaism. Sperling's journey to Amsterdam epitomized his own preference for the latter, since these inclusivist attitudes could also be found in Amsterdam.

Sperling's Amsterdam: German Boehmists and International Proselytes

In his second letter to his mother, when Sperling presents his eschatological scenario, he refers to what he "has also heard in the sermons," in which it was claimed that the first angel of the Apocalypse of John refers to "the great angel, the archangel D. Martin Lutherus."[29] It is unlikely that this phrase came from the mouth of an Ashkenazi rabbi. Possibly, Sperling was alluding to a sermon remembered from a German Lutheran past that he had left behind – after all, he mentions sermons while discussing Luther. Nevertheless, the depiction of Luther as an archangel is an integral part of the eschatological belief system he held after his conversion – suggesting that he may have heard the description in sermons he was still attending at the time he wrote the letter. It is also noteworthy that he uses the definite article in his letter ("the" sermons) and chooses the perfect rather than the past perfect tense.

While Boehmists – followers of the German mystic Jakob Böhme (1575–1624) – might not have had the pulpits necessary to directly spread their message, Boehmist elements in the letters, already noted by Philipp, indicate that these sermons might be linked to the presence of German Boehmists in Amsterdam around 1680, such as Johann Georg Gichtel (1638–1710) and Friedrich Breckling (1629–1711).[30]

29. "Meines Verstandes nun nach, und wie ichs auch woll habe gehört in den [Pred]igten [...] der Mann Gottes der große Engel und Erz Engel der D. Martinus Lutherus"; Sperling letters, 1568.

30. Lucinda Martin, "Jacob Boehme and the Anthropology of German Pietism," in An Introduction to Jacob Boehme: Four Centuries of Thought and Reception, eds. Ariel Hessayon and Sarah Apetrei, Routledge Studies in Religion (New York: Routledge, 2014): 120–41, here 121–5. See also Caspar G. C.Visser, "Die mystisch-pietistische Strömung in der niederländisch-lutherische Kirche in der zweiten Hälfte des 17. Jahrhunderts," in Pietismus und Reveil: Referate der internationalen Tagung:

Other suspects are the chiliasts Johannes Rothe (1628–1702) and Quirinus Kuhlmann. Like Sperling, Kuhlmann wrote about an eschatological alliance among Lutheranism, Calvinism, and the (Muslim) Ottoman Empire.[31] Unlike Sperling, however, Kuhlmann attributed to himself a central role in the upcoming messianic events. These or other German-speaking Boehmists in Amsterdam, some of whom were such fervent Hebraists that they spoke Hebrew at home, were likely instrumental in Sperling's turn to Judaism. Moreover, the fact that the Revelation of John figures prominently in Sperling's eschatology points to some continued connection with this Boehmist milieu after joining the Jewish community.[32]

An important clue about another religious environment in Amsterdam can be found at the end of Sperling's first letter, where he cryptically hints in an underlined sentence: "Please know that I am not the first Christian who has become a Jew, and I will not remain the last."[33] As burial and other records from both Amsterdam's Ashkenazi and Sephardic communities show, Amsterdam numbered many converts at the time.[34] These include converts from Hamburg or those with some other connection to it: in the two years before Sperling's conversion, for instance, the English convert Elias Bar Abraham trav-

---

Der Pietismus in den Niederlanden und seine internationalen Beziehungen, Zeist 18–22. Juni 1974, eds. Jan van den Berg and Jan Pieter van Dooren (Leiden: E. J. Brill, 1978): 169–81; Magdolna Veres, "Johann Amos Comenius und Friedrich Breckling als 'Rufende Stimme aus Mitternacht'," Pietismus und Neuzeit 33 (2007): 71–83.

31. Wilhelm Schmidt-Biggemann, "Salvation through Philology: The Poetical Messianism of Quirinus Kuhlmann (1651–1689)," in Toward the Millennium: Messianic Expectations from the Bible to Waco, eds. Peter Schäfer and Mark R. Cohen (Leiden and Boston: Brill, 1998): 259–98, esp. 267–8.

32. For another possible factor, namely the rich and various scene of Dutch philosemites and their interactions with Jews, such as the Dutch millenarians and their contacts with Jews like Menasseh ben Israel, see Richard H. Popkin, "Christian Jews and Jewish Christians in the 17th century," in Jewish Christians and Christian Jews: From the Renaissance to the Enlightenment, eds. Richard H. Popkin and Gordon M. Weiner, Archives internationales d'histoire des idées = International Archives of the History of Ideas (Dordrecht and Boston: Kluwer Academic Publishers, 1994): 57–72.

33. "wisset daß ich nicht bin der Erste Christ der da ist ein Jude geworden, Ich werde auch der letzte nicht bleiben;" Sperling letters 244/1529.

34. On the Ashkenazi cemeteries, see Jits Van Straten, De herkomst van de Aschkenazische joden: De controverse opgelost (Bennekom: [the author], 2009), 159. The Portuguese burial register from the period in which the Sperling letters were written: Stadsarchief Amsterdam 334 (Archief van de Portugees-Israëlietische Gemeente) 916 (Livro de Bet Haim. Register van besluiten van de mahamad betreffende de begraafplaats 1703–1722; journaal van begraven 1680–1716; grafboek 1691–1733). Two other sources mentioning multiple converts contemporary to Sperling are the aforementioned Livro longo (SAA 334: 217), as well as the Portuguese "Manual" that also reported welfare gifts to converts: SAA 334: 175 (Manual, 1677–1689).

eled to Hamburg twice.³⁵ The Portuguese community's charity lists also include several converts from Hamburg in the years following Sperling's letters, who, like Sperling, had come to Amsterdam.³⁶

Social interactions between converts was common in Amsterdam. The aforementioned Moses Germanus and Daniel ben Avraham interacted with fellow converts, as did Abigail Guer ("Abigail the proselyte"), who in the 1640s stipulated that part of her large donation to the Portuguese Jewish community should be reserved as a yearly allowance for Dinah Guer ("Dina the proselyte").³⁷ In addition, at least some of these converts, as Sperling implies, expected that there would be more conversions to Judaism in the near future.

The use of the Book of Revelation as authoritative prophecy by a Jewish proselyte who received his mail at the address of a renowned rabbi comes as something of a surprise. But proselytes, it might be helpful to recall here, occupied a rather liminal status in the Jewish community. Beginning at the end of the seventeenth century, the Portuguese community required the permission of the *maamad*, the synagogue board, for the burial of proselytes, and one instance in its burial book shows a separate plot for proselytes.³⁸ Thus, the Portuguese community, at least, may have deemed converts as belonging to a socio-religious category distinct from that of born Jews.³⁹ If the Portuguese community perceived proselytes differently, the Ashkenazi

---

35. SAA 334: 217 pp. 212, 274. In 1688, the proselyte Abraham Guer of Tunis traveled from Amsterdam to Hamburg: SAA 334: 218 p. 230.

36. At the end of the decade, the Portuguese community twice gave money to proselytes from Hamburg in the house of Sebatay Coen; ibid. 422, and SAA 334: 219, p. 64. In the fall of 1692, money was given for the burial of a child of Abraham Israel Ger of Hamburg; ibid., 104. Around the same time, proselytes from Hamburg, possibly the same as those at the house of Sabetay Coen, were given money; ibid., 138, and again in 1694–5 (p. 301). In 1694, Rachel Israel the proselyte from Hamburg was buried in Amsterdam: SAA 334: 916, pp. 91 and 258.

37. On Abigail Guer and Dina Guer see, for instance: Stadsarchief Amsterdam 334 (Archief van de Portugees-Israëlietische Gemeente), 172 (Manual, 1639–1646), 178, 309. On Germanus and Clericus, see Schudt, Jüdische Merckwürdigkeiten vol. 1, 275–6.

38. Burial 'segregation' begins in this period, when former slaves began to be buried in the "negroes section." In addition, converts begin to be listed as "buried by the order of the maamad," suggesting that their burial in the Jewish cemetery was not self-evident. For an instance of separate burial, see Sarah Ben Abraham's placement in the "row of the giorets" in 1712: Stadsarchief Amsterdam 334 (Archief van de Portugees-Israëlietische Gemeente) 916 (Livro de Bet Haim. Register van besluiten van de mahamad betreffende de begraafplaats 1703–1722; journaal van begraven 1680 –1716; grafboek 1691–1733), 201.

39. See for this argument also Yosef Kaplan, "The Self-Definition of the Sephardic Jews of Western Europe and their Relation to the Alien and the Stranger," in Crisis and Creativity in the World: 1391–1648, ed. Benjamin R. Gampel (New York: Columbia University Press, 1997), 121–45.

Jewish community, financially dependent on their richer Portuguese brethren, likely followed suit. One of the effects of this *différence* may have been a greater toleration – albeit by virtue of neglect – for the peculiar religious views of proselytes.

While the gradually growing distinction between born Jews and proselytes in Jewish Amsterdam might have afforded a certain degree of doctrinal liberty for the city's converts, there seems to have been a more positive factor at play as well. This was the presence of heterodox tendencies among Amsterdam's Jews themselves, in particular among its Portuguese community. Yosef Kaplan and Yirmiyahu Yovel, among others, have shown how Amsterdam's Jews' converso past resulted in widespread heterodoxy in its community – Spinoza being its most famous example – which included positive engagements with Christianity and Christian-Jewish hybridities.[40]

Sperling's statements about the origins of his prophetic beliefs provide additional evidence about the subculture to which he belonged. Combining the principle of *Sola scriptura* with assertions of their own insights and authority, Protestant non-conformists often claimed that their personal interpretations of scripture were equally, if not more, valid than official doctrinal positions. One of the ways *Sola scriptura* was invoked was to argue that God's eternal commandments to Moses were never, and could never be, nullified.[41] As I will show in due course, Sperling shared both this viewpoint and its *Sola scriptura* justification.

Sperling also gave his own readings of the 12th, 14th, and 19th chapters of the Book of Revelation, of Daniel, and of the traditional Jewish life-saver Zechariah 8:23. To his mother, Sperling stressed the personal nature of his reading of scripture, writing, for instance: "*I believe the woman clothed with the sun is* […];" "*I have read in the book of Daniel.*"[42] Of course, this does not rule out the possibility that these readings were shared within an interpretive community.

A further source for Sperling's interpretations emerges in the more

---

40. See Kaplan, From Christianity to Judaism, 110–78; Yirmiyahu Yovel, Spinoza and Other Heretics: The Marrano of Reason (Princeton, NJ: Princeton University Press, 1992), 20–6. See also Graizbord's revealing description of Iberian renegades in Graizbord, Souls in Dispute, 171–6.

41. There are multiple examples in seventeenth-century Amsterdam of Judaizers appealing to sola scriptura to legitimize their religious claims. For one example, see Alexander van der Haven, "Conversion on Trial: Toleration of Apostasy and the Hoorn Trial of Three Converts to Judaism (1614–15)," in Contesting Inter-Religious Conversion in the Medieval World, eds. Yaniv Fox and Yosi Yisraeli (New York: Routledge, 2017), 41–60, here 47–8.

42. "Den ich vermeine daß Israel daß weib sey daß mit der Sonne bekleydet ist;" "Ich hab gelesen beym Propheten Daniel" Sperling letters, 1569, 1568. My italics.

lyrical passages of his missives. At the end of his second letter, Sperling writes about the "Spirit of Prophecy" (Rev. 19:10).[43] Elsewhere, after a dazzling interpretation of biblical prophecy, Sperling halts – perhaps suspecting that his mother, reading the letter, might have begun to doubt his sanity – and writes:

> Many would ask me: How do you know that? Wisdom, who is the judge of all the arts, has taught me. I want to praise her, make her known, show her clearly so that everybody knows what that wisdom is. For through her one gets to know God and his holiest name, which cannot be uttered and which teaches everything [...] She knows God's will and counsel, for she was there when God created the world [...] Through her we will resurrect from the dead and live in eternity, because she inhabits in all that is, and whoever seeks for her finds her. Whoever seeks her from the heart will receive her.[44]

"Wisdom," who appears in Proverbs 3 and 8 and Ecclesiastes 1, was a particularly popular character in the early modern period. Consequently, the origin of Sperling's loyalty to her is hard to assess. He could have picked her up from the Boehmist tradition already mentioned, from Jewish or Christian kabbalists, or even from Sabbatians (who were present both in Hamburg and in Amsterdam), or possibly, from a combination of these. More importantly, however, Sperling's reading of scriptural prophecies stemmed not only from *Sola scriptura* and the discourses of exegetical communities, but also – so he believed – from divine inspiration. Sperling must have belonged to, or at least have been socialized by, one or more groups that upheld individual divine inspiration.[45]

Wisdom was as "pure," "noble," and "careful" as Sperling portrays her: Sophia was able to do something with Revelation, the prophetic text at the core of Sperling's beliefs, that few others have been able or

---

43. "der Geist der weißagung." Ibid., 1570.

44. "Da möcht mich mancher fragen, wie weißt Du daß. Die Weißheit die aller Kunste richter Ist hat es mich gelehret dieselbe wil ich dermahlen Ein rühmen und kundt machen und sie deutlich zu erkennen geben daß jedermann weiß waß die weißheit sey, den durch sie erkennet man Gott und seynen Allerheylichsten Nahmen, der doch unaussprechlich ist der alles lehret. [...] Sie weiß Gottes willen und Rath, den sie ist dabey gewesen da Gott die Welt gemacht hat. Nach den Worten des weisen Königs Salomons, sie wird auch bleiben in Ewigkeit. Durch sie werden wir wieder aufferstehen von den Todten und leben in Ewigkeit, den sie wohnet bey alles waß da lebet, wer sie suchet der findet Sie, wer sie von Hertzen suchet der erwirbet sie;" Sperling letters 1569–70.

45. On individual revelation in early modern Protestantism: Volkhard Wels, "Unmittelbare göttliche Offenbarung als Gegenstand der Auseinandersetzung in der protestantischen Theologie der Frühen Neuzeit," in Diskurse der Gelehrtenkultur in der Frühen Neuzeit: Ein Handbuch, ed. Herbert Jaumann (Berlin and New York: de Gruyter, 2011): 747–808.

willing to do. Although she left one villain in place (in the person of the pope), the thrust of Wisdom's work was to turn the Book of Revelation into a call for and forecast of inter-religious alliance at the end of times.

Sperling's Eschatology

Sperling was not the first to design eschatological alliances among different religious groups. In the rapidly globalizing early modern world, many sought to make room for different religions in their end-time scenarios. A Jewish example is Menasseh ben Israel's well-known appeal to Oliver Cromwell (1599–1658) that the English Christian readmission of Jews would hasten the arrival of the Messiah.[46] In Christian eschatology, Quirinus Kuhlmann (mentioned above as a possible influence on Sperling) outlined an alliance between Lutheranism and Calvinism. Two similar eschatological proposals to join Jews and Christians under a single religious banner were those of Augustin Bader (c. 1495–1530) from South Germany, and the Dane Oliger Paulli, from Amsterdam. Each claimed to be the messiah, or representing the future messiah, of both Jews and Christians and attempted, unsuccessfully, to forge a Jewish-Christian alliance against the Roman Catholic Church.[47]

Sperling's case, however, is different. Even if his letters are literary artefacts rather than personal documents, they lack the obvious strategic interests of something like Menasseh ben Israel's appeal. Nor did Sperling share the messianic religious ambitions of Bader, Kuhlmann, and Paulli – ambitions that set these religious entrepreneurs apart from, and above, the regular human realm with its various religious commitments. This difference makes Sperling's religious eschatology remarkably gentle. One can hear this in the tone of the letters, which is, as Strauss mentioned, unusually tender and conciliatory for someone who believes himself to be witnessing the last events unfold.

---

46. Menasseh ben Israel and Lucien Wolf, Menasseh ben Israel's Mission to Oliver Cromwell: Being a Reprint of the Pamphlets Published by Menasseh ben Israel to Promote the Re-admission of the Jews to England, 1649–1656 (Cambridge and New York: Cambridge University Press, 2012).

47. On Bader, see Rebekka Voss, Umstrittene Erlöser: Politik, Ideologie und jüdisch-christlicher Messianismus in Deutschland 1500–1600 (Göttingen: Vandenhoeck & Ruprecht, 2007), 138–52; Anselm Schubert, Täufertum und Kabbalah: Augustin Bader und die Grenzen der radikalen Reformation, Quellen und Forschungen zur Reformationsgeschichte 81 (Gütersloh: Gütersloher Verlagshaus, 2008). On Paulli, see Schoeps, Philosemitismus im Barock, 53–67, and Jeannine Kunert, "Der Juden Könige zwei: Zum deutschsprachigen Diskurs über Sabbatai Zwi und Oliger Paulli. Nebst systematischen Betrachtungen zur religionswissenschaftlichen Kategorie Endzeit und sozio-diskursiven Wechselwirkungen" (PhD Dissertation, Erfurt University, 2018), 331–436.

Thus, we read:

> Dearest beloved mother, I cannot neglect to write — my filial love for you, mother, burns constantly — regarding the fact that <u>I have become a Jew</u> because of God and his Holy Name. I know that this is already known to my mother, my friends, and my enemies. I intend also <u>to live and die as a Jew</u> in the name of the Lord of Hosts. I beg my mother, brother, sister, and brother-in-law that they will not be hostile because of religion. For I desire to remain in friendship with my friends and blood relatives. For what good is enmity? At all times we should remember that at one point we will appear in front of God's judgment seat to account for ourselves in order to enjoy God's compassion. So let us practice love, and know, that God is pure compassion.[48]

Sperling's rhetorical question – "For what good is enmity?" – supplies an implicit answer – "nothing at all" – by his claim that we all will be judged individually for our actions rather than our denominational commitments. Indeed, in the second letter, in which Sperling mentions that he had heard how badly his mother had taken his conversion, he writes:

> The question now is why could I not have become saved in the Lutheran faith, or whether the Lutherans [Sperling added initially "and Reformed," but crossed that through] are damned. I answer and declare that the upright Lutherans and Reformed will all achieve salvation. Let my soul stand for yours if I write this out of hypocrisy.[49]

Further on in the second letter, Sperling writes also that the third angel, which "I hope will be the messiah, will bring redemption to all people, and all that is evil will be destroyed." Not only good Lutherans and Calvinists could achieve salvation, then, but salvation could

---

48. "Hertz vielgeliebte Mutter Ich kan nicht unterlassen zu Schreiben den die kindliche liebe von mir brennet alle Zeit gegen der Mutter was anlanget <u>daß ich von Gott und seines Heyligen Namens wegen bin ein Jude geworden</u>. Daß weis ich daß solches der Mutter meinen freünden und feinden schon bekandt ist. Ich gedenke auch im Namen der HERRN der Herrscharen <u>ein Jude zu leben und zu sterben</u>. So gereichet nun meine bitte an der Mutter Bruder und Schwester und Schwager daß sie wegen glaubens halber keine feindschaft ausüben. Den ich habe Lust freündschafft zu halten mit meinen freünden und Bluts Verwandten. Denn was soll uns die feindtschafft [phrase striked through] wir müssen doch alle Zeit gedenken, daß wir alle Zeit ein mahl müssen aufftreten für den Richter Stuhl Gottes und Rechenschafft geben, damit wir nun Gottes Barmhertzigkeit genieSen. So last uns Liebe üben, und wisset, daß Gott von lauter Barmherzigheit Ist"; Sperling letters, 1529.

49. "[So] ist nun die frage ob ich den nicht hette können Selig werden in den Lutherschen glau[ben] Oder ob ander Lutherianer und reformirten verdampt sind. So antworte Ich und [be]kenne daß die auffrichtigen Lutherianer und reformierten alle selig werden und [gro]ße Seeligkeit erlangen. Schreibe ich solches auß Heucheley so stehe meine Seele für die ihrige"; ibid., 1567.

be universal.⁵⁰

Let us now turn to the content of Sperling's eschatological views. Two of the passages from the Book of Revelation that he focused on were Revelation 14:6–11, concerning the three successive angels, and Revelation 12: 1, concerning the woman clothed with the sun. Either Sperling copied Revelation 14:6–11 from Luther's translation, or he remembered it by heart (only a single "and" is missing), and he cites it in full. Notably, he ends his exegesis of verse 12 just before the point at which it commands belief in Jesus.

> According to my understanding, and how I have also heard it in the sermons, the first angel [...] as the man of God, the great angel and archangel Martin Luther. The other angel who followed the first and shouted "She is fallen Babylon the great city" was the man of God the great angel and archangel John Calvin [...]. The third angel, with a great voice will speak, saying: Those who worship the Beast and its idol receives the mark on his forehead and the mark of its name, after which the papacy will perish. This angel, the third one, I think has not come yet. I expect the third angel [and] hope it will be the messiah who will bring redemption to all people, and all that is evil will be destroyed. Now I let you know that these two angels, these two men of God Martin Luther and John Calvin, stand for the Lutheran and Reformed host, they are archangels, from the seven of them who stand there and serve God day and night. They are two peaceful angels of one being and hence the Lutherans and Reformed will not wage war with another over religion.⁵¹

Clearly, Sperling, like those who preached the sermons he had attended, believed himself to be witnessing the fulfillment of the very prophecies described in Revelation. The first two phases, in which the first

---

50. "verhoffe daß soll Messias sein und al[ler] Menschen Erlösung soll zu der Zeit kommen und alles übels soll außgerot[tet] werden können"; ibid., 1568.

51. "Meines Verstandes nun nach, und wie ichs auch woll habe gehört in den [Pred]igten, So ist der Erste Engel [...] das ist gewesen der Mann Gottes der große Engel und Ertz Engel der D. Martinus Lutherus. Der andere Engel aber der dem ersten ist nachgefolget und hat geschrie[en Sie] ist gefallen Babilon die große Stadt. daß ist gewesen der Mann Gottes der große Engel und Ertz Engel der D. Johannes Calvinus.

Der dritte Engel aber der mit große Stimme soll sagen. So jemandt [daß] Thier anbetet und sein Bilde und nimpt an sein Mahl Zeichen an seiner [Stirn] und das mahl Zeichen seines Namens, worauff daß Pabstthum wird vergehen. Dieser Engel, nemlich der Dritte meine ich der sey noch nicht gekommen. [Ich] Erwarte den dritten Engel, verhoffe daß soll Messias sein und al[ler] Menschen Erlösung soll zu der Zeit kommen und alles übels soll außgerot[tet] werden können. Nun thue ich auch zu wissen, namelich daß die Zween Engeln der Zween Män[ner] Gottes deß Doctor Martinus Lutherus und deß D. Johannes Calvi[nus] ihre Engeln welche stehen für daß Luthersche und Reformitische Herr, d[aß] sind Ertz Engeln, und sind von den Sieben, die da stehen zu dienen für Gott [Tag] und nacht. Und sindt Zween friedtsahme Engeln in einem wesent [da]rumb werden die Lutherianer und Reformierten keinen Krieg mit einand[er] führen wegen religion"; ibid., 1568–9.

two angels appeared, had already been completed by the arrival of the Lutheran and Calvinist churches. Sperling was waiting for the third angel to come.

God has placed his judgment seat in these two religions, Sperling wrote, and will judge the entire world when the third angel appears. At this point, the Jewish people become part of the eschatological scenario. According to Sperling, the woman clothed in the sun of Revelation 12:14 is not, as in traditional Christian interpretation, the true (Christian) church. Rather, she stands for the Jewish people who, pursued by the great dragon, will be saved by being given the two wings of a great eagle. These wings are the Lutheran and Reformed communities:

> So the two communities, namely the Lutherans and Reformed, will be to the Jews as the two wings of a great eagle. And they will bring them to the barren land, to their place, namely the promised land. That the holy city Jerusalem and the temple of God and the land that has so long lain in ruins will be rebuilt.[52]

This Protestant alliance will help the Jews return to their land in order to rebuild it and its Temple. Failing to predict the appearance of the Ottoman army at Vienna's gates the coming year, Sperling foretold that the Turkish sultan, the caliph of Sunni Islam, would build a "neat road" so the Jews could travel to their promised land.[53]

With the important exception of Roman Catholicism, Sperling described eschatological cooperation among different religions. Together, they would bring about universal redemption by enabling the restoration of the Jews to the land promised to them by God. To support his view, Sperling offered an astrological interpretation of the passage about the woman who is clothed with the sun, has the moon under her feet, and on her head a crown of twelve stars. In so doing, he drew on a traditional identification of the different heavenly bodies with the different religions that stretched back to the illustrious eighth-century astrologers Al Kindi (c. 800–873) and Abu Mashar (c. 787–886). The latter's *De magnis coniunctibus* was a standard item in learned households of the early modern period.[54] Sperling wrote this part of his exegesis in an inspired style:

---

52. "So werden die zween gemeinen, nemblich die Lutherianer und Reformirten. denen Jüden sein wie Zween flügel eines großen Adelers. Und werden sie bringen in daß verwüst landt an ihren Orth. Nemlich ins gelobte Landt. Daß die heylige Stadt Jerusalem. Und der Tempel Gottes und daß Landt so lange wüßte gehele gelegen Izt wieder gebauet wird"; ibid., 1569.

53. "ein Reinlich straßen;" ibid.

54. Robin Bruce Barnes, Astrology and Reformation (New York and Oxford: Oxford University Press, 2016), 23, 55, 72.

You should know that the Lutherans are the mother from whom everything good is born. Luther, you are the clear morning star that heralds every good, oh power of Venus.

The Reformed are a strengthening of the good, prepared to fight against the dark power of the papacy. They are the evening star. Mars, guard Venus with your sword so that she will not become a whore. The Turks are the upholders of the good and archenemies of everything evil, namely the darkness of the papacy. Mahomet, your power is in the moon.

And the three communities, namely the Turks, Lutherans and Reformed are trusted friends of Israel.

The pope with his cardinals, bishops, abbots, prelates, monsignors and whatever belongs to that which is the dark night, the mother of all evil and all whoredom and idolatry. Yes, the dark night that is friend to no-one, pope, your power is fickle. Mercury is [your] star.[55]

Here, with the papacy as the sole negative force, the different religions/heavenly bodies play complementary roles. Like the first angel, Venus/Luther – standing for the Lutheran faith – heralds the good news. Calvin takes over from there with a sterner, more martial role, making sure to keep in line the ex-monk who once proclaimed that "He who loves not wine, women and song remains a fool his whole life long." The sultan, who keeps the pope at bay, is also assigned a disciplinary duty.

Conversion and Universal Salvation

Sperling's inclusivist eschatology raises the question of his conversion. Why did Sperling convert to Judaism when he did not regard Judaism as the sole road to salvation? The explanations Sperling himself provides suggest an interesting model, one that couples religious pluralism with commitment to one religion alone.

Sperling gives two reasons for his conversion. The first is that he had arrived at a personal conviction that God had never abolished the law given to Israel. Sperling supported this claim with, among other texts, Christian scripture, namely, Matthew 5:17–20 and Luke 16:17,

---

55. "Zu wißen die Lutherianer daß ist die Mutter da alles guts ausgebohren wird Luther. Du bist der Helle Morgen Stern, der alles gutes ankündigt O Venus Gewalt.

Die Reformirten sind eine verstärkung deß guten bereit zu fechten wider die finstere Macht des Pabstthumb, der Abend Stern Ist ihr Mars bewache mit deinem Schwerdt daß Venus nicht zur Huren werde, die Türken daß sind Erhalter deß guten, und Erbfeinde alles übels Nemlich der finsternis deß Pabstthumb. Mahomet deine Gewalt bestehet in dem Mondt.

Und die drey gemeinen nemlich die Türken, Lutherianer und Reformirten sindt vertraute Freunde Israel. Der Pabst mit seinen Cardinälen, Bischöfen, Abten, Prelaten, Monsigniors und waß darzu gehört daß ist die finsternacht die Mutter alles Übels aller Hurerey und Abgötterey. Ja die finsternacht die keines Menschen freundt ist, Pabst dein Gewalt ist leichtfertig, Mercurius daß ist Stern;" Sperling letters 1569.

in which Jesus states that he has not come to abolish the Law. Christians who denied that the law of Moses had been abolished were not an infrequent phenomenon in the Dutch Republic. This can be seen in the complaints recorded throughout the seventeenth century by Amsterdam's Reformed Church, which kept a watchful eye on what happened in other religious communities as well.[56] Although 'Judaizing' was often limited to insistence on a specific commandment – most often the observance of the Jewish Shabbat – it occasionally resulted, as in Sperling's case, in conversion to Judaism.[57]

Although Sperling thus maintained that Scripture, correctly interpreted, proved Judaism to be the only true religion, and although he himself converted to Judaism as result of this conviction, he did not hold that adhering to another religion would automatically preclude salvation. This "salvific pluralism" has roots in the Jewish tradition itself, from which the aforementioned attitudes of the proselyte Daniel ben Abraham and many members of Amsterdam's Portuguese community had deviated. Sperling's pluralistic attitude could also be found in seventeenth-century Dutch Jewish discussions of Noahites (initiated by Christian Hebraists such as John Selden (1584–1654), as Miriam Bodian has recently shown), in which the possibility of multiple paths to salvation also appears.[58]

Sperling's views also echo tolerant Christian philosophies, such as those of the influences discussed above, as well as those popular in the Dutch Republic since its early days. For instance, in criticizing Calvin's execution of Michael Servetus (c. 1509–1553), Sebastian Castellio (1515–1563) had argued that "the truth is to say what one thinks, even when one is wrong." And Dirck Volckertsz Coornhert (1522–1590) had written that pagans, too, could attain salvation as long as they followed the "spirit."[59]

The second reason Sperling gave for deciding that he should

---

56. One example is a schoolmaster insisting on observing the Shabbat. Stadsarchief Amsterdam 376 (Archief van de Hervormde Gemeente): 5 (Notulen kerkeraad Amsterdam, 1621–1627), 225, 228.

57. This seems to have been the case with a certain glass maker, whom the consistory for several years tried to discipline: Stadsarchief Amsterdam 376 (Archief van de Hervormde Gemeente): 7 (Notulen kerkeraad Amsterdam, 1633–1644), 196, 202, 206, 300, 301, 339, 341.

58. Miriam Bodian, "The Geography of Conscience: A Seventeenth-Century Atlantic Jew and the Inquisition," The Journal of Modern History 89 (2017): 247–81, esp. 267–72. For a broader discussion of Jewish views on Christians in Seventeenth-Century Amsterdam, see eadem, "The Portuguese Jews of Amsterdam and the Status of Christians," in New Perspectives on Jewish-Christian Relations: In Honor of David Berger, eds. Elisheva Carlebach, Jacob J. Schacter, and David Berger (Leiden and Boston: Brill, 2012): 329–58.

59. Bodian, "Geography of Conscience," 265.

"live and die as a Jew" was that, as mentioned above, he had Jewish ancestry. In his second letter, he wrote:

> I desire to live according to such a wonderful law, all the more so since I descend from the Jewish race, just as my brother and sister, because we come from one father. This will seem quite strange to mother because she knows nothing of it, nor do my brother and my sister. I, however, know it and I let mother know that my father has left behind in writing a bequest and declaration to us children so that we will know from what kind of tribe we are. Because my father's forefathers have been forced [to convert] in wars. They wanted to save their lives. This report I have in the document of my father and can give testimony of it under oath.[60]

Sperling thus claimed that, unbeknownst to his mother and siblings, his father had given him documents proving his and his siblings' Jewish ancestry. Whether Sperling possessed such documents or whether this was a case of invented Jewish ancestry, we will never know.[61] What we do know is that Sperling believed he was of the seed of Abraham through patrilineal descent, and that he was thus called upon to observe other commandments than those of the gentiles.

Eschatology and conversion often accentuated the differences among religious communities. The Sperling letters in their Amsterdam context show that the opposite was also possible. The convert who sought to preserve his or her social and familial ties to a religious past could serve as a bridge between different communities, and even as a guide for them to fulfill – together – their respective roles at the end of time.

---

60. "Habe ich Lust nach solchem Herrlichen Gesetz [zu] leben, über daß weil ich doch von Jüdischem geschlecht bin hergekommen Ingleichen meine Brüder und Schwester weil wir von einem Vater sind hergekommen. Solches wird der Mutter seltzam vorkommen, nach demmahlen sie nichts davon [we]iß auch mein Bruder nicht noch auch meine Schwester nicht. daß ichs aber weiß [thu]e ich der Mutter zu wißen daß mein Vater es in schrifft hat nachgelaßen, [und] zum Erbgut und uns Kindern Zurnachricht auff daß wir wißen solten [von] waß vor geschlecht wir sind Den meines Vaters vor Väter sind durch Kriegswesen gezwungen worden. haben sie anders Ihr lebent wollen salviren Diese nachricht habe [ich] durch die Schrifft meines Vaters und kan es Eydlich außsagen;" ibid., 1567.

61. A great number of victims of the anti-Semitic Chmielnicki massacres of 1648–1649 and subsequent persecutions settled in and near Hamburg, and among these were also Jews who had been forced to convert during these persecutions, and thus arrived as Christians. A famous example is the wife of the Jewish messiah Sabbatai Tsevi, Sarah the Ashkenazi; see Alexander van der Haven, From Lowly Metaphor to Divine Flesh: Sarah the Ashkenazi, Sabbatai Tsevi's Messianic Queen and the Sabbatian Movement (Amsterdam: Menasseh ben Israel Instituut, 2012), 25–30. For a source that appears to be inventing Jewish ancestry to legitimize conversion, see the Graanboom chronicle: Lajb Fuks and R. G. Fuks-Mansfeld, "The Hebrew Chronicle of the Swedish Family Graanboom," in Aspects of Jewish life in the Netherlands: A Selection From the Writings of Leo Fuks (Assen: Van Gorcum, 1995): 100–30.

THE LEGACY OF ANTI-JUDAISM IN BACH'S SACRED CANTATAS
By Lars Fischer

No personal documents have survived in which Johann Sebastian Bach (1685–1750) has anything explicit to say about Judaism or Jews, nor do we have any reason to assume that Bach ever had any personal contact with Jews. There are some who would be only too pleased to let the matter rest right there. Yet what we can say quite a lot about is how Judaism, Jewish-Christian relations and, by extension, Jews were represented in Bach's musical output. It is frequently argued, sometimes with surprising vehemence, that any such issues were surely the responsibility of the librettists and not the composer. Yet it should be instantly obvious that this line of argument hardly holds. In this particular case, it is clear that Bach not only chose the librettos he set but in fact "preferred to work directly with an author rather than use already published collections" of libretti for his cantatas.[1] Moreover, while his peers frequently composed entire annual cycles of cantatas based on the texts of just one librettist, Bach never did so and rarely drew on texts by one and the same librettist for more than three consecutive cantatas.[2] But whatever his level of input into the librettos he chose, he certainly had considerable leeway when it came to the deployment of musical means to de/emphasize certain elements in relation to others; he could go out of his way to highlight or elaborate upon certain ideas and concepts, say, or present them in a relatively dispassionate manner; whether a particular textual element was presented in a chaste or triumphalist manner, for instance, depended in high measure on the musical setting.

Given his education and training, Bach was steeped in the Lutheran orthodoxy of his day and his knowledge of, and commitment to, that orthodoxy was carefully examined before he was appointed to his position as cantor in Leipzig. In that role, he was beholden to provide

---

1. Robin A. Leaver, "Oper in der Kirche: Bach und der Kantatenstreit im frühen 18. Jahrhundert," Bach-Jahrbuch 99 (2013): 171–203, here at 194.

2. Ibid., 193.

a constant flow of church music for the city's main churches, especially St Thomas and St Nikolai. The express purpose of this church music was the utilization of musical means to render the congregants more receptive to the Lutheran orthodoxy of the day and thus intensify its articulation in ways that the spoken word alone, it was assumed, could not. In implementing this agenda, Bach presumably thought of himself not so much as a great artist but primarily as a consummate artisan.[3] Against this backdrop it is ultimately more or less irrelevant what he may have thought or felt in his heart of hearts about certain tenets of the Lutheran orthodoxy of his day. He had a task to perform and we have reason to assume that he was determined to perform that task to the best of his abilities.

Taking into account the interpretations of issues relevant to Jewish-Christian relations prevalent at the time, we can reconstruct with a high measure of plausibility the way in which their reflection in Bach's sacred cantatas is likely to have been understood by most of Bach's congregants, given their own religious education and the extensive religious instruction they received in church each week. In his discussion of Bach's Cantata 46,[4] Michael Marissen – the scholar who has made the most sustained effort to date to discuss constructions of Judaism and Jewishness in Bach's works and specific expressions of anti-Judaism within them – has demonstrated how this reconstruction can be undertaken. If we want to understand what Bach's congregants, as a general rule, would have taken away from any given cantata we need to take into account not only the cantata on its own terms but also the liturgical context within which it was performed, the specific themes and readings assigned to that particular day, contemporaneous exegetical and homiletic literature either in wide circulation at the time or known to have been in Bach's library or that of his immediate peers – and, far from least, images in the churches in which the cantatas were performed. These images were, after all, intended to prompt the congregants to think in certain directions and emphatically not in others. It should also be borne in mind that the biblical and theological knowledge of Bach's congregants, as a general rule, would have far outstripped that of current churchgoers. The meaning of a range of allusions, associations and cross-references would have been

---

3. For an interesting recent discussion of Lydia Goehr's provocative claim that "Bach did not intend to compose musical works," see Gavin Steingo, "The Musical Work Reconsidered, In Hindsight," Current Musicology 97 (2014): 81–112.

4. Michael Marissen, "The Character and Sources of the Anti-Judaism in Bach's Cantata 46," Harvard Theological Review 94 (2003): 63–99; now also in Michael Marissen, Bach & God (New York: Oxford University Press, 2016), 63–121 (chapter 3).

immediately obvious to them. A wealth of inter-textual references, in other words, to which many of us are oblivious today, helped shape their perceptions of the "message" propagated by a particular cantata. This includes, as Eric Chafe has demonstrated with great sophistication, cross-references, both textual and musical, between cantatas that Bach's congregants would have heard within weeks of each other.[5] Moreover, congregants were able to buy the cantata librettos in advance, allowing for a more sustained engagement of the cantatas' theological meaning than might otherwise have been possible.

In my characterization of Marissen's work on this topic, I referred to "constructions of Judaism and Jewishness in Bach's works and specific expressions of anti-Judaism within them." Marissen and I, I should point out, do not necessarily agree on the issue of where legitimate religious polemic directed at Judaism ends and outright anti-Judaism begins. In this discussion, I will rely on an intentionally inclusive definition of anti-Judaism. To my mind, supersessionist (or, as it is sometimes called, substitution) theology – that is, theology based on the claim that the new covenant on which Christianity is predicated has replaced God's earlier covenant with the Jews, and that there are consequently no legitimate grounds for post-biblical Judaism – is, on principle, anti-Judaic. Consequently, I would likewise insist that the claim that the Christian version of the Tanakh, the Old Testament, primarily or exclusively prefigures the New Testament narrative, not to mention the attempt to exploit the vast corpus of post-biblical rabbinic writings to demonstrate the validity of Christian truth claims, are inherently anti-Judaic. Moreover, a number of core juxtapositions integral to Lutheranism – law vs. grace, true faith vs. mere outward adherence to rules, the letter vs. the spirit of scripture – have historically been saturated with anti-Judaic connotations that would have been instantly obvious to early modern Protestants and are likely still to resonate with many Protestants today.[6] Growing up (on and off) in a Lutheran family in Germany in the 1970s and early 1980s, I was certainly still taught these juxtapositions with their anti-Jewish connotations and I would be surprised if they had simply evaporated since. To be sure, in their more lucid moments, at least some professional theologians have not been entirely oblivious to the fact that these juxtapositions actually reflect complicated dialectical tensions within Christianity. If, however, one looks, for instance, at the multitude of

---

5. See especially Eric Chafe, J. S. Bach's Johannine Theology: The St. John Passion and the Cantatas for Spring 1725 (New York: Oxford University Press, 2014).

6. On the history and polemical uses of these juxtapositions in the "longue durée," see David Nirenberg, Anti-Judaism: The History of a Way of Thinking (London: Head of Zeus, 2013).

early modern images that didactically contrasted law and grace, the old and the new covenant, one would have been hard-pressed, even as an educated and well informed congregant, to detect a trace of these dialectical tensions and associate the negative pole in each case not just with Catholicism and Judaism but also with Lutheranism itself.

Eighteenth-century Lutheranism, then, was fundamentally anti-Judaic. To be sure, positions regarding Judaism and the Jews among early modern Protestants varied. This concerned two principal questions. First, there was some controversy as to whether "the Jews" had been damned eternally for their failure to acknowledge the divinity of Christ or might yet be redeemed if they converted at the end of days. Second, some felt that individual Jews were more likely to convert if they were treated with some measure of respect and that an unduly polemical approach would only antagonize them. Even when Christian attitudes towards Judaism were at their most benevolent and relations between Christians and Jews at their most amicable, however, the suggestion that the Jews might be appreciated – to borrow the apt phrase Gershom Scholem coined for a later period – for what they had to *give* rather than what they had to *give up*, remained inconceivable to early modern Christians of any stripe.

In short: Bach would have been entirely out of step with his education and training, the assumptions taken for granted by everyone around him, and the requirements of his professional position, had he been entirely free of anti-Judaic convictions and sentiments. The punch line, then, is hardly that Bach stood out in this respect. If anything, the notion that he might not have subscribed to the prevalent anti-Judaic attitudes would be perplexing and inexplicable. As so often, the really interesting question therefore lies not in the 'did he/didn't he?' but instead concerns the extent to, and the ways in, which the anti-Judaic consensus of his time found expression in his output. In a context in which anti-Judaism went without saying, we can still draw distinctions between those for whom anti-Judaism quite literally went without saying and those for whom it was a major preoccupation – and the various gradations in between these two positions. The vehemence with which Bach chose to accentuate anti-Judaic notions seems to have varied, and his approach was certainly more nuanced than that of, say, Georg Philipp Telemann (1681–1767).[7] Deploy musical

---

7. See Jeanne Swack, "Antijudaismus in Telemanns Kantate zum Sonntag Judica 'Der Kern verdammter Sünder' TWV 1:303," in Telemann und die Kirchenmusik, eds. Carsten Lange and Brit Reipsch (Hildesheim: Olms, 2011): 256–78; "Anti-Judaism and Lutheran Sacred Music in Hamburg in the Early Eighteenth Century," in Constructions of Judaism and Jewishness in Baroque Music, ed. Lars Fischer (forthcoming).

means to lend additional affective force to the propagation of anti-Judaic notions he nevertheless did.

In this context, we also need to bear in mind that, insofar as the existence and legitimacy of Christianity hinges fundamentally on its relationship to, and delineation from, the religion of the biblical Jews, every Christian theological statement is implicitly also a statement about Jewish-Christian relations. When it comes to discerning anti-Judaism in Bach's sacred cantatas, then, we need to focus not only on obvious thematic 'flashpoints' or explicit anti-Judaic/anti-Jewish statements.[8] An inordinate amount of ink has now been spilled over Bach's two Passions. Some work has also been done specifically on Bach's cantatas for the Tenth Sunday after Trinity – known in the Lutheran church as "Israel Sunday" because it is the day on which Lutheran congregations traditionally commemorate(d) the destruction of the Temple in Jerusalem in 70 CE – of which the aforementioned Cantata 46 is one; and on a handful of cantatas with librettos that make explicit anti-Jewish references. Yet the bulk of Bach's 200 surviving sacred cantatas have not been scrutinized from this perspective – on the understanding that there can be no anti-Judaism where the actual words "Judaism" or "Jew" do not feature.

This was certainly the position of leading members of the now-defunct *Internationale Arbeitsgemeinschaft für theologische Bachforschung* [International Working Group for Theological Bach Research], established in 1976, who made (and some of whom continue to make) a sustained effort to discredit any discussion of possible anti-Judaism in Bach's works.[9] As Robin Leaver recently recalled, the working group's "conferences in the early years were generally effective and productive." Yet subsequently "the non-scientific speculations of some of the members" increasingly gained traction in the working group and, following the death of its principal founder, Walter Blankenburg, in 1986, "many in the wider Bach world" became convinced "that the old image of Bach the supreme Lutheran Cantor was being repristinated. Ultimately when it became clear that the wider cultural religious issues such as those pursued by Tanya Kevorkian, or the

---

8. It is worth noting that, as cantor in Leipzig, Bach was spared the temptation, should he have been susceptible to it, of capitalizing on some of the particularly obvious 'flash points,' since cantatas were not performed in Leipzig during Advent and Lent – parts of the church year that had the potential to throw the question of what was qualitatively new about Christianity and why the 'old' had supposedly ceased to serve its purpose into particularly sharp relief. I thank Jeanne Swack for pointing this out to me.

9. I have discussed this in greater detail in Lars Fischer, "Bach Matters," in Constructions of Judaism and Jewishness in Baroque Music, ed. Lars Fischer (forthcoming).

Anti-Judaism explored by Michael Marissen, were not being encouraged, a few of the established members of the Arbeitsgemeinschaft took action that eventually led to the demise of the working group."[10]

Michael Marissen has described his own chequered encounters with this group. Having argued that Bach's music "sometimes puts a spin on the text in a way that is readily explainable as orthodox Lutheran in its orientation" and demonstrated that the librettist and composer of Bach's *St John Passion* could have done a whole lot more to emphasize the anti-Judaic implications of the passion narrative (as Bach's peers frequently did), he was initially the Working Group's "golden boy."[11] But then

> Many in the *Arbeitsgemeinschaft* were sorely disappointed, and indeed violently angry [...] when I went on to write a detailed conference paper on theological anti-Judaism in Bach's cantata *Schauet doch und sehet* (BWV 46) [...] and a subsequent conference paper on Bach's St. Matthew Passion that included a detailed exposé of Luther's heightening in his translation whatever degree of anti-Judaic tendencies there might be in the Greek source text of the Gospel of Matthew [...] What struck my *Arbeitsgemeinschaft* colleagues as further scandal was the fact that my research for these projects had been supported by an *Alexander von Humboldt-Stiftung* research fellowship at the (large and overwhelmingly Lutheran) Theology Faculty of the University of Leipzig. It happened that senior theologians at the university during my year in Leipzig [2001] had likewise strongly disapproved of the research, repeatedly telling me, several times via purple-faced screaming, that it was absolutely impossible for Luther or for Bach's Lutheran liturgy to have said such and such a thing about Jews. They were utterly unmoved by the historical texts I showed them that obviously did say precisely those very things that they had declared impossible. It was a frustrating year.[12]

Somewhat counter-intuitively, given my earlier remarks about the need to move beyond the obvious 'flash points,' in this chapter I will focus principally on the one surviving cantata by Bach in which 'the Jews' are mentioned explicitly and of which one might be forgiven for assuming that its problematic nature would be instantly obvious. And yet, especially in the sort of handbooks likely to appeal to 'practitioners' – pastors, cantors, singers and instrumentalists – their audiences, be they congregants or concertgoers, and, not least, the authors of program notes, the problem simply does not seem to exist. If not even this explicit negative reference to 'the Jews' raises any concerns,

---

10. Robin A. Leaver, "Introduction," in The Routledge Companion to Johann Sebastian, ed. Robin A. Leaver (Abingdon: Routledge, 2017): 1–22, here at 17–8.

11. Marissen, Bach & God, xii.

12. Ibid., xiii.

we can hardly hope for widespread sensitivity regarding the more subtle articulation of anti-Judaic assumptions in Bach's cantatas. Why all this matters rather more than may meet the eye I will address in the final section where I discuss the troubling implications of the neo-traditionalist notion that cantatas are musical sermons that render their message 'real in the present.'

Cantata 42: Am Abend aber desselbigen Sabbats

Cantata 42, *Am Abend aber desselbigen Sabbats* [*But in the evening of the same Sabbath*] was composed for the Sunday after Easter in 1725. It begins with a sinfonia, followed by a recitative setting of a quotation from John 20:19: "But in the evening of the same Sabbath/When the disciples were assembled and the doors closed for fear of the Jews/Jesus came and stood in their midst."[13] The disciples' "fear of the Jews" is subsequently reiterated in a second recitative (no. 5):

> One can see a fine example/In what happened at Jerusalem: For when the disciples had gathered together/In dark shadows/For Fear of the Jews/My Saviour entered in their midst/As a witness that He will be the defence of His Church/Therefore let the enemies rage!

Eric Chafe has recently offered a highly sophisticated discussion of this cantata in the context of the cantatas Bach composed in 1725 for the Sundays between Easter and Trinity against the backdrop of the version of his St John Passion performed that year. Chafe situates the "fear of the Jews" "in the context of the long-established practice of drawing an analogy between the situation of the disciples in first-century Jerusalem and the place of the Christian church in the world." This trope, he argues, "dictated much of what follows in the remainder of the 1725 cantata sequence, which further alludes to the interaction of Jews and Christians in the first century."[14] He draws a line from the final recitative of Bach's St John Passion, via Cantata 42 to the cantata composed for Trinity of that same year, Cantata 176, *Es ist ein trotzig und verzagt Ding* [*There is something contrary and despairing*]. The reference to the disciples' "fear of the Jews" in Cantata 42, he explains, echoed the final recitative of the St John Passion, "where we are told that Joseph of Arimathea kept his discipleship secret 'from

---

13. This "evening of the same Sabbath" is the evening of the day of the resurrection, that is, it is actually a Sunday evening – which already represents a blatantly supersessionist move on the part of the gospel text. The official translation was changed to "Am Abend aber desselben ersten Tages der Woche" ["But in the evening of the same first day of the week"] in the Luther Bible of 1912 and since 1984 reads "Am Abend aber dieses ersten Tages der Woche" ["But in the evening of this first day of the week"].

14. Chafe, Johannine Theology, 12.

fear of the Jews'." The first recitative of Cantata 176, in turn, refers to Nicodemus, "described earlier in the Gospel as a 'high official among the Jews' [...] who was also a 'secret' disciple, coming forth only by night."[15] Nicodemus was widely seen as "a symbol for early Christianity in his eventual emergence from the 'darkness'" and, as Chafe points out, "in Bach's time the memory of such ancient associations bound up with the very origins of the church, was still very much alive."[16] Cantata 42 may be Bach's only surviving cantata expressly to mention the Jews. Yet the disciples' "fear of the Jews" clearly reverberated, and was meant to reverberate, throughout that entire liturgical season stretching from Good Friday to Trinity in 1725.

Marissen discusses Cantata 42 under the heading, "Fearing the Jews, Then and Now."[17] In the cantata, he argues, "Jews are the persecuting enemies of the disciples of Jesus, and 'the Jews' of the Gospel of John are emblematic of the true church's persecutors ever since." Not least, Bach "would have encountered similar statements about Jews as the archenemies of Christians in Johannes Müllers *Judaismus oder Jüdenthumb*,"[18] a standard work of anti-Jewish polemic.[19] Chafe disagrees with this assessment. "The text does not say", he insists, "that the enemies in question would still be the Jews, even in eighteenth-century Leipzig; and it would be a misinterpretation to so understand it." Even so, Chafe does concede that "they [i. e., the Jews] were certainly viewed as among the opponents of Christianity" and "following soon after the *St. John Passion* [...] it seems likely that the librettist intended as much."[20]

Cantata 42 is the only one from this series of cantatas "beginning with an instrumental movement rather than with the *dictum* itself" – suggesting that, to Bach's mind, there was something special about this work. Bach "preceded the opening *dictum* of Cantata 42 with an extended instrumental sinfonia [...] and followed it by an even more extended aria [...] This decision, which must have been Bach's alone, places a great deal of emphasis on the dramatic situation," Chafe explains. For him, the drama lies in "Jesus's appearing 'in the midst'

---

15. Ibid., 414.
16. Ibid., 12–3.
17. Marissen, Bach & God, 134.
18. Ibid., 136–7.
19. The Professor of Church History at Erlangen and zealous Nazi, Hans Preuss, in his pamphlet on Johann Sebastian Bach, der Lutheraner [Johann Sebastian Bach the Lutheran], first published in 1935 and reissued by the Martin Luther Verlag in Erlangen in 1950, rather quaintly described Müller's polemic as "a defence of Christianity against the Jews"; Hans Preuss, Johann Sebastian Bach, der Lutheraner (Erlangen: Martin Luther-Verlag, 1950), 15.
20. Chafe, Johannine Theology, 414–5.

of the fearful disciples, calming their fear."[21] Indeed, he suggests that "the motto [i. e., the quotation from John 20:19] is virtually swallowed up by two extended movements," that is, the preceding sinfonia and subsequent aria.[22]

I would suggest the exact opposite. There can be little doubt that Bach's setting of the first recitative does a good job of conveying a sense of fear and apprehension. Hans-Joachim Schulze, in his one-volume commentary on Bach's cantatas of 2006, emphasizes that Bach's setting gives a sense of "the sort of trepidation where one's heart is in one's mouth."[23] The grand old man of Bach cantata commentary, the late Alfred Dürr, noted the "throbbing continuo semi-quavers, which are no doubt designed to depict the disciples' fear of 'the Jews'", and stressed the "stark contrast" between the recitative and the aria that follows it. His characterization of that aria as radiating "heavenly calm" has repeatedly been cited in the literature.[24] Chafe refers to it as "an oasis of Trost [consolation]." This, I would suggest, is spot-on: the luxuriant nature of the aria that follows the first recitative – which, in recordings, runs to somewhere between ten (Philippe Herreweghe) and more than thirteen minutes (Masaaki Suzuki) – indicates the measure of consolation required following the disciples' traumatic experience of having to lock themselves away "for fear of the Jews." Schulze adds to this the notion that the shift from the D major of the introductory sinfonia – which itself runs to another six (Elliot Gardiner) to seven minutes (Herreweghe) – to the corresponding b minor of the first recitative "effects an abrupt shift from bucolic tranquility straight to an actually or apparently dangerous situation,"[25] suggesting that the recitative indeed necessitated consolation of considerable proportions both before and after. In his older two-volume commentary, William Gillies Whittaker – the first incumbent of the Gardiner Professorship in Music at Glasgow currently held by John Butt – characterized the aria following the reiteration of the disciples' "fear of the Jews" in the second recitative as "almost extravagantly joyful," likewise suggesting a heightened need for consolation to deal with the "fear of the Jews" – about which Whittaker has nothing to say, despite quoting both recitatives in full.[26]

21. Ibid., 415.
22. Ibid., 417.
23. Hans-Joachim Schulze, Die Bach-Kantaten. Einführungen zu sämtlichen Kantaten Johann Sebastian Bachs (Leipzig: Evangelische Verlagsanstalt, 2006), 202.
24. Alfred Dürr, The Cantatas of J. S. Bach, trans. Richard D. P. Jones (New York: Oxford University Press, 2005), 297. Jones's translation of "überirdisch" as supraterrestrial rather than heavenly seems quite odd.
25. Schulze, Bach-Kantaten, 202.
26. W. Gillies Whittaker, The Cantatas of Johann Sebastian Bach: Sacred and

Schulze, as we saw, was evidently trying to soften the blow. He wrote of "an abrupt shift from bucolic tranquility straight to an actually or *apparently* dangerous situation" (emphasis added).[27] He also claimed that the "fear of the Jews" is really only "mentioned in passing" in the gospel text.[28] About the reiteration of the "fear of the Jews" in the second recitative, he has nothing to say. Ultimately, this all looks more like an attempt to evade rather than confront the problem, but at least he does not ignore it entirely. The late Martin Petzoldt, in the relevant volume of his big commentary on Bach's cantatas, published in 2007, did just that. He noted that the recitative quotes John 20,19 without Jesus's assurance of peace at the end, hence placing "the thematic emphasis on the assembly of fearful disciples." This, he points out, was certainly at odds with the interpretation presented in the widely read contemporaneous Bible commentary by Johannes Andreas Olearius (1639–1684). Olearius paid little attention to the disciples' fear and instead stressed the fact of Jesus's miraculous entry despite the locked doors.[29] The fifth movement, in which the introductory narrative is repeated and its meaning spelled out, Petzoldt characterizes as an expression of "profound Biblical thinking."[30] At this point, the fear of the disciples is no longer even mentioned, and nowhere does Petzold comment on the ostensible cause of that fear identified so explicitly (and twice) in the cantata.

Petzoldt is in good company. In the two-volume Bach cantata handbook edited by Reinmar Emans and Sven Hiemke and published by Laaber in 2012, Christina Blanken merely points out that Bach, with simple musical means "illustrates the fear of the disciples of persecution by the Jews" and has nothing more to say on the matter.[31] Most recently, Konrad Klek, a Professor of church music at Erlangen, in the third and final volume of his Bach cantata commentary, has shown himself entirely untroubled by the disciples' "fear of the Jews." He notes that "the librettist accentuates the *fear of the Jews* and, by analogy, perceives of the Christian congregation as a 'little band' (movement 4) that is threatened by 'enemies' (movement 5) and 'persecution' (movement 6). But the liturgical presence of Christ

---

Secular, vol. 1 (London: Oxford University Press, 1959), 299.

27. Schulze, Bach-Kantaten, 202.

28. Ibid., 201.

29. Martin Petzoldt, Bach-Kommentar, vol. 2: Die Geistlichen Kantaten vom 1. Advent bis zum Trinitatisfest (Kassel and Stuttgart: Bärenreiter, Internationale Bachakademie, 2007), 779.

30. Ibid., 783.

31. Christine Blanken, "Der sogenannte 'Dritte Jahrgang'," in Bachs Kantaten: Das Handbuch, vol. 2, eds. Reinmar Emans and Sven Hiemke (Laaber: Laaber, 2012): 1–88, here at 63.

serves as a protective shield." Bach, he adds, implemented the libretto's "accentuation of fear" with the appropriate musical means. Klek also emphasizes the stark contrast between the recitative and the "uniquely calming music" of the subsequent "overly long" aria, music to which one could chill ("*Musik zum 'Chillen'*"). All he has to say about the second recitative, in which the disciples' "fear of the Jews" is reiterated and interpreted, is that it assures the congregation of Christ's protection.[32]

Ever since Alfred Dürr did so back in the 1950s,[33] far from showing any concern, authors have repeatedly singled out Cantata 42 as a particularly apt case in point for Bach's superlative ability to compose cantatas that really are musical sermons and render their message "real in the present." The erstwhile Professor (in various combinations) of Comparative Religion, Old Testament, and Hebrew at the Protestant theological faculties in Brussels, Bochum, and Marburg, and prominent interfaith activist (though with a greater interest in Islam than Judaism), Johan Bouman, for instance, wrote in a text republished in 2000:

> following the reading on Jesus's appearance and encounter with the doubting Thomas, in the Cantata *But in the Evening of the Same Sabbath* (John 20: 19–29) the *applicatio* sounds as follows: 'One can see a fine example in this, from what took place in Jerusalem; for when the disciples had gathered in the dark shadow, out of fear of the Jews, at that my Saviour entered amongst them, as testimony that he wants to be his Church's protection. So let the enemies rage!' This convergence of cantata and sermon has the task of actualizing the exegetical message and stimulating one's own faith and piety.[34]

We will shortly encounter another fan of the cantata's qualities as a musical sermon.

Exceptions to this enduring pattern of oblivion to the disciples' "fear of the Jews" are few and far between. Unsurprisingly, Dagmar Hoffmann-Axthelm, who first pioneered the study of anti-Judaism in Bach's works,[35] is one of them. In program notes for Cantata 42

---

32. Konrad Klek, Dein ist allein die Ehre: Johann Sebastian Bachs geistliche Kantaten erklärt vol. 3 (Leipzig: Evangelische Verlagsanstalt, 2017), 39–40.

33. Alfred Dürr, "Johann Sebastian Bachs Kirchenmusik in seiner Zeit und Heute," [originally published in 1957] in Johann Sebastian Bach, ed. Walter Blankenburg (Darmstadt: wbg, 1970): 290–303, here at 296–7.

34. Johan Bouman, Musik zur Ehre Gottes: Die Musik als Gabe Gottes und Verkündigung des Evangeliums bei Johann Sebastian Bach, 2nd ed. (Gießen: Brunnen Verlag, 2000), 29–30.

35. Dagmar Hoffmann-Axthelm, "Bach und die Perfidia Iudaica: Zur Symmetrie der Juden-Turbae in der Johannes-Passion," Basler Jahrbuch für Historische Musikpraxis 13 (1989): 31–54; eadem, "Bach und die 'perfidia iudaica': Zur Symmetrie

published in 2012, she describes as "depressing from today's viewpoint" the fact that anti-Judaism went without saying for Bach and his peers and congregants.[36] The Emmanuel Music ensemble, which is affiliated with the Emmanuel Episcopal Church in Boston and has "a 46-year tradition of presenting weekly Bach cantatas in a liturgical setting,"[37] is another noteworthy exception. They suggest two ways of dealing with the disciples' "fear of the Jews" in the two recitatives. In the first instance, they pick up on a remarkably popular yet nonsensical exegetical claim that the gospel verse, in fact, refers not to the Jews but to the Judaeans, that is, not to "the Jews" *per se* but merely to those from the Roman province of Judaea (which covered roughly the area of the erstwhile southern kingdom of Judah).[38] As a second, more radical solution, they propose that one might omit the reference to 'the Jews' altogether and refer instead to "*Verfolgung/persecution.*"[39] The latter is certainly a suggestion worthy of consideration though it, in turn, raises the question of whether simple erasure is really an appropriate way of dealing with this legacy. There in fact seems to have been some controversy on this matter within the ensemble. Its founding director, Craig Smith, in his program notes for Cantata 42, while being rather reticent in his commentary on the first recitative, when discussing the second recitative, in which the disciples' "fear of the Jews" is reiterated and interpreted, characterized it as presenting "one of the most distasteful examples of a kind of knee-jerk anti-Semitism in all of Bach." The ensemble's longstanding principal guest conductor John Harbison, in 2004, appended remarks specifically on this "uncomfortable" issue. "It has been often the practice at Emmanuel to change this text and similar reference in the final bass recitative," he explains, and continues:

> Here are some reasons not to do so: 1) the text of any musical work represents its original sources, the artist's conception, and the histor-

---

der Judenchöre in der Johannespassion," Neue Zürcher Zeitung, 2 April 2004: 63; eadem, "Die Judenchöre in Bachs Johannes-Passion: Der Thomaskantor als Gestalter lutherischer Judenpolemik," Freiburger Rundbrief New Series 5 (1998): 103–11, http://www.freiburger-rundbrief.de/de/?item=569 (8 November 2017).

36. Dagmar Hoffmann-Axthelm, "'Am Abend aber desselbigen Sabbats' (BWV 42). 'Nun danket alle Gott' (BWV 192)," in Wie schön leuchtet der Morgenstern: Johann Sebastian Bachs geistliche Kantaten. Werkeinführungen und Dokumente der Basler Gesamtaufführung, eds. Albert Jan Becking, Jörg-Andreas Bötticher, and Anselm Hartinger (Basel: Schwabe, 2012): 200–4, here at 201.

37. http://www.emmanuelmusic.org/who/who_history_mission.htm#pab1_2 (8 November 2017).

38. On the illogical nature of this suggestion, see Marissen, Bach & God, 128–9.

39. http://emmanuelmusic.org/notes_translations/translations_cantata/t_bwv042.htm (8 November 2017).

ical moment of its creation. Witnesses to the work must be trusted to interpret it according to their own belief and culture. 2) The mention of the Jews is at the least paradoxical, since every person in that room, including Jesus, soon to appear, lived and died as devout, practicing Jews. 3) Throughout the book of John, to magnify the significance of the message, the author downplays what is (merely) factional or doctrinal, among Jews. Still it is helpful to remember how many specific enemies are identified as money-changers, chief priests, or Pharisees.[40]

What makes these comments somewhat disconcerting is the fact that they are, at least in part, mutually attenuating. Suffice it to say that, were there not a serious problem at stake, one would not need to emphasize one's trust in the ability of the audience/congregation to interpret that problem away. The subsequent attempt to minimize the measure or substance of the problem in the first place seems rather at odds with that emphasis.

The Cantata as a Sermon in its Own Right

That the congregation should, as Harbison suggests, "be trusted to interpret" the disciples' "fear of the Jews" "according to their own belief and culture" is a plausible suggestion within the remit of liberal theology. Yet, among neo-traditionalists, the notion that cantatas are musical sermons that render their theological message "real in the present" is still (or again) in rude good health and, if anything, advancing. From this point of view, one might just as well say that it does not really matter what is preached from the pulpits today because the congregation can also "be trusted to interpret" the sermons they hear "according to their own belief and culture."[41]

It is by no means just people like the late Renate Steiger, Blankenburg's longstanding and starkly doctrinaire successor at the helm of the International Working Group for Theological Bach Research, who stress this crucial homiletic function of the cantata. She discussed this, for instance, in connection with the complex penultimate movement of Cantata 67, composed a year earlier (1724) for the same Sunday as Cantata 42. Technically speaking a bass aria, the movement combines two distinct elements. On the one hand, there is a deeply calming setting of Jesus's words at the very end of John 20:19 – the aforementioned verse in which the disciples have locked themselves away "for fear of the Jews" – "Peace be unto you." The other element, in stark contrast, is the rather frantic grappling, in the first instance presum-

---

40. http://www.emmanuelmusic.org/notes_translations/notes_cantata/n_ bwv042.htm (8 November 2017).

41. http://www.emmanuelmusic.org/notes_translations/notes_cantata/n_bwv042.htm (8 November 2017).

ably of the disciples but ultimately of all those in need of divine grace, buffeted as they are (or feel) by adversity, with the news of Jesus's resurrection, sung by the sopranos, altos and tenors of the choir. "The resurrected Lord appears to them – today in this cantata," Steiger explained, "in his word and assures them – i. e., us, the listeners – of his peace. The musical depiction of the event represents not a report but a sermon, that is, it renders that of which it speaks real in the present and dispenses it."[42]

Jochen Arnold, one of the most senior officials responsible for church music in Germany's mainstream Protestant church, the EKD, makes the same argument in his post-doctoral thesis (*Habilitation*), *Von Gott poetisch-musikalisch reden. Gottes verborgenes und offenbares Handeln in Bachs Kantaten* [*Speaking of God with Poetical and Musical Means. God's Hidden and Revealed Action in Bach's Cantatas*], arguably the most important recent work on the theology and contemporary liturgical context of Bach's sacred cantatas. Arnold is clearly not interested in, and feels no need to display sensitivity towards, concerns in the realm of Jewish-Christian relations. Tellingly, neither Dagmar Hoffmann-Axthelm nor Michael Marissen feature in his bibliography (which in any case includes only 6 non-German titles). To be sure, he claims that "the aesthetics of affect characteristic of Bach's music [...] *render real in the present Jewish, Reformation and Protestant-Baroque forms of experience of God and the world* that can open up for us a personal encounter with God."[43] Yet, by 'Jewish,' he principally means the Old Testament, and his understanding of the Christian relationship to the Old Testament constitutes a textbook case not just of supersessionist appropriation but of comprehensive expropriation of the Tanakh. Not only does the Old Testament in general, and the Psalter in particular, "prefigure" the New Testament narrative.[44] In the cantatas that begin with a psalm setting, the subsequent movements "realize the lead of the psalm," rendering the "performative quality of the divine word" open to experience with poetic and musical means.[45] Discussing the psalm setting at the beginning of Cantata 110, composed for Christmas Day 1725, for instance, Arnold explains that the librettist "effectively blocked out the promise to Israel of a return from exile in order to transfer it in a generalized

---

42. Renate Steiger, *Gnadengegenwart: Johann Sebastian Bach im Kontext lutherischer Orthodoxie und Frömmigkeit* (Stuttgart–Bad Cannstatt: frommann-holzboog, 2002), 19.

43. Jochen Arnold, *Von Gott poetisch-musikalisch reden: Gottes verborgenes und offenbares Handeln in Bachs Kantaten* (Göttingen: Vandenhoeck & Ruprecht, 2009), 427.

44. Ibid., 424.

45. Ibid., 427–8.

form to the Christian church. The 'we' of the early post-exilic Israel becomes the 'we' of the Christian congregation at Christmas."⁴⁶ As he subsequently reiterates:

> The promise associated with the return from Babylonian exile: "our mouths shall be filled with laughter" (Ps 126,2) is moved to the liturgical presence of salvation at Christmas, that is, it is resolutely rendered real in the present: *May our mouth be full of laughter* means: at Christmas may our mouth be 'full of laughter' *now, here and today*.

And yet, given that there is no explicit Christological reference in this movement, Arnold suggests this psalm setting could be performed separately "at any Christian or even Jewish celebration."⁴⁷ Psalm settings in Bach cantatas, Arnold argues, are "nearly always [...] *performative milestones*." They ensure "that at the end nothing is as it was at the beginning."⁴⁸

Perhaps Arnold also assumes he is dealing with Jewish tradition when he emphasizes representations of the law in Bach's cantatas. This would amount to a sort of black-face approach to Jewish-Christian relations: an attempt to reintegrate Christianity's Jewish roots by dressing up as one's own cliché of what Jewish religion is supposedly about. On this issue, Arnold seems determined to have his cake and eat it. On the one hand, he insists that the marvel of divine grace cannot be fully appreciated unless contrasted to the burden of the law. Consequently, the prevailing one-sided emphasis on God's love to the detriment of his wrath dilutes the message of the gospel. The law, then, is not extraneous to Christianity but integral to it – and consequently not, as widespread conventional wisdom would have it, a tenet exclusive to Judaism. Yet the crucial point is still the "shift from the accusatory voice of the law to the acquittal of the gospel."⁴⁹

Much as Augustine insisted that God had ordained the abjection of the Jews to show others what lay in store for those who refused to acknowledge the divinity of Christ, Arnold insists that the law – and its representation in Bach's cantatas – is there to throw all the more sharply into relief the marvel of the divine grace that renders the law obsolete. To be sure, Arnold pays lip service to the actual dialectic of law and gospel in Christianity but, as we will see, what prevails in his account is not that dialectic but the "objection to [divine] judgment in Bach's cantatas."⁵⁰

---

46. Ibid., 317.
47. Ibid., 424.
48. Ibid., 430.
49. Ibid., 235.
50. Ibid.

For Arnold, then, Bach's cantatas have a transformative capacity; indeed, they "*preach and proclaim the Gospel in their own right.*" To illustrate this, the example that immediately springs to Arnold's mind is none other than Cantata 42, *But in the Evening of the Same Sabbath*. It opens, he explains,

> with a Biblical quotation from John 20 (tenor recitative) and then expands through the text of the following aria, which paraphrases the promise of Mt 18,20:
> Aria (alto)
> Where two or three are gathered together, In Jesus's precious Name, There Jesus appears in their midst, And says to them "Amen".
> With the musicalization of the text by Bach the presence of Christ announced in the Biblical quotation [...] transpires in the here and now: "heavenly calm" prevails.[51]

The latter ("heavenly calm"), as we saw, is a quotation from Dürr. Note that Arnold has elegantly refrained from quoting the text of the recitative or even paraphrasing its content, apart from its final clause: "Jesus came and stood in their midst."

Now, here is my problem: the likes of Steiger and Arnold credit cantata movements with the ability to make manifest in the here and now, in this case, the consolation those in fear of the Jews draw from Jesus – or, on a more general level, the victory of the gospel over the law, of faith over outward adherence to the law, of the spirit over the letter of scripture. But then it must surely follow that the cantata movements providing the foil for that victory also make the burden of the law or the threat of the Jews "real in the present." Readers may be tempted to think (or hope) that I am making this up. Yet Jochen Arnold is very clear about this. None too surprisingly perhaps, for Arnold, the problem becomes most virulent in the context of one of Bach's cantatas for Israel Sunday, specifically Cantata 102, *Herr, deine Augen sehen nach dem Glauben* [*Lord, Your Eyes Look for Faith*].

To add a little historical depth: when this cantata was performed at the opening concert of the 13th German Bach Festival in Essen in July 1925, the musicologist Alfred Heuß (1877–1934) noted in his program notes that "the bedrock of the concert and the entire festival is one of the works that shows Bach unrelentingly preaching repentance with harsh old-testamentarian [*alttestamentarische*] fervor."[52] In it, Heuß went on, Bach "applies a forge hammer to a rock", the music is of a "downright demonic savagery" and "executed with steely

---

51. Ibid., 92.
52. Alfred Heuß, "Zu den Werken des dreizehnten Deutschen Bachfestes," in *Dreizehntes Deutsches Bachfest. Vom 11. bis 13. Juli 1925 in Essen: Bach-Fest-Buch*, ed. Neue Bachgesellschaft (Leipzig: Breitkopf & Härtel, 1925): 3–10, here at 3.

artistry."[53] There can be little doubt that these remarks were meant to be complimentary, which is all the more intriguing, given that Heuß was a notorious antisemite. In October of that same year, he characterized Arnold Schoenberg's appointment to the Prussian Academy of the Arts as "a setback for the cause of German music," which pitted "Germanness against [...] the specifically Jewish spirit of music. This is clear to anyone who knows about racial distinctions [*Rassenunterschiede*]." To be sure, there were assimilated Jews who could make a valuable contribution, but Schoenberg's "personal and racial [*rassenmäßig*]" development had led in a different direction. He was a rootless fanatic who consciously disavowed tradition. The Germanness of German music was already weakened, and Schoenberg's appointment would set the recovery back by decades. Evidently, then, it was entirely possible for one and the same musicologist to admire Bach's "harsh old-testamentarian fervour" and the works of "rooted" Jewish composers and yet engage in antisemitic polemics against Schoenberg – a good indication of some of the complexities that can be involved in understanding non-Jews' attitudes to Judaism, the Old Testament and the Jews.

Arnold, too, seems impressed – albeit negatively – by Bach's "harsh old-testamentarian fervour" in Cantata 102. It "immediately raises the question," he explains: "does its central message lie primarily in the threatening word of the law or the beckoning word of the gospel?"[54] For Arnold, the cantata highlights the need to repent before one's death, that is, before it is too late, but it fails to reflect the promise that awaits those who do repent in time. It thus addresses a genuine empirical affliction of the sinful believer. Though not directly referenced in the libretto, the connection to the destruction of Jerusalem lies in the fact that it serves as an example of that affliction, of what awaits the sinful if they fail to repent in time. How, then, should one deal with this "cantata's sustained propagation of the law"? "Under no circumstances," Arnold stipulates, "should Part II be performed *sub communione* since the propagation of the law could become superimposed on the promise of the Eucharist."[55] The law, in other words, could become real in the here and now at a point where only grace ought to reverberate.

Maybe Arnold has sound empirical evidence to demonstrate defin-

---

53. Ibid., 4.
54. Arnold, Von Gott poetisch-musikalisch reden, 221.
55. Ibid., 227. When Bach composed two-part cantatas, the first part would be performed before, the second after the sermon. It would therefore be highly unusual to consider performing the first part during the Eucharist, rather than before the sermon, hence Arnold's reference to Part II (rather than the whole cantata) in this instance.

itively that Lutheran congregants who associate, say, the juxtaposition of law and gospel with the juxtaposition of Christianity and Judaism no longer exist. If so, this would reflect a fairly groundbreaking turn of events, and his decision not to publish the relevant research would be astonishing in the extreme. If not, one can only assume that he considers it both useful and desirable for today's Lutherans to be exposed to the horrors inflicted by the (Jewish) God of the Old Testament and 'the Jews' to help them understand fully the superiority of Christianity. Given Arnold's status in the EKD, this, surely, is deeply troubling.

A New Model of Christian Interaction with the Jews
Pietist and Evangelical Missions to the Jews
By Yaakov Ariel

The turn of the eighteenth century saw the rise of a new movement in the landscape of Western Christianity and Christian-Jewish relations – German Pietism, which provided an alternative means for Protestants to relate to Jews.[1] The Halle Pietists thus became one of the important movements in the Protestant world, and their pioneering mission, the *Institutum Judaicum*, influenced other groups of Pietists in Central and Northern Europe, as well as English-speaking evangelicals, making a lasting impression on the Protestant scene, modifying, and at times transforming, prevailing attitudes towards the Jews. An exploration of the agenda of this movement, then, may unveil a rich picture of this highly complicated relationship.

The Roots and Origins of Pietist Attitudes Towards the Jews

To a certain extent, Pietist attitudes towards the Jews recall those of the early Martin Luther.[2] Like the father of the Protestant Reforma-

---

1. On the rise, nature, and impact of German Pietism, see Peter E. Erb, ed., The Pietists: Selected Writings (New York: Paulist Press, 1983); Jonathan Storm, Hartmut Lehmann, and James Van Horn, eds., Pietism in Germany and North America, 1680–1820 (Aldershot: Ashgate, 2009); Douglas Shantz, An Introduction to German Pietism: Protestant Renewal at the Dawn of Modern Europe (Baltimore: Johns Hopkins University Press, 2013); Douglas Shantz, A Companion to German Pietism, 1680 –1800 (Leiden: Brill, 2014).

2. Luther's complicated and changing attitudes towards the Jews have received considerable scholarly attention. For an updated comprehensive study of the subject, see Thomas Kaufmann, "Luther and the Jews," in Jews, Judaism, and the Reformation in Sixteenth Century Germany, eds. Dean Philip Bell and Stephen G. Burnett (Leiden and Boston: Brill, 2006), 69–104; Peter von der Osten-Sacken, Martin Luther und die Juden: neu untersucht anhand von Anton Margarithas "Der gantz Jüdisch glaub" (1530/31) (Stuttgart: W. Kohlhammer, 2002); Thomas Kaufmann, Luther's Jews: A Journey into Antisemitism (Oxford and New York: Oxford University Press, 2017).

tion, the Pietists believed that Jews ought to be open to Christianity in its Protestant form. Pietists, however, carried Luther's theological and practical positions a few steps further. In his early career as a reformer, Luther held hopes for the conversion of the Jews to Christianity, but stopped short of establishing a mission or formulating specific means of approaching them. Pietists institutionalized and systematized the agenda outlined by the young reformer. But, unlike Luther, who was disappointed that the Jews did not join his new Protestant church en masse, Pietists, and later on, evangelical missionaries, accepted that most Jews were not interested in converting to Christianity. Content to convert only a limited number of Jews, Pietists set their sights on those individuals who were thus inclined.

Pietist agendas were strongly shaped by the ideas of Philip Jacob Spener (1635–1705), founder of Halle Pietism. In his *Pia Desideria*, the most influential work of German Pietism, Spener promoted an alternative attitude towards the Jews.[3] There, the Pietist thinker expressed appreciation for the longstanding Jewish rejection of Christianity. He blamed Christian societies for mistreating the Jews, and called upon his readers to show good will towards them. Promoting a messianic outlook, Spener, and the Halle Pietists whom he inspired, as well as a number of other Pietist groups that followed them, were convinced that the Jews would again play a decisive role in the events that would lead to the materialization of the Kingdom of God on earth.

Although Pietism developed mostly in Lutheran lands, the Reformed (often labelled 'Calvinist') wing of the Reformation influenced Pietist positions towards the Jews.[4] Reformers of that school, such as Martin Bucer (1491–1551), John Calvin (1509–1564), and Theodore Beza (1519–1605), took with utter seriousness the messages conveyed in the Hebrew Bible, including the idea that their communities were in covenant with God.[5] Unlike Luther, who believed that the place of the Jewish people in history, as an entity distinct from Christianity, had come to an end, Calvin held that while God was angry with Jews as individuals, Jews might still be redeemed as a nation.[6]

---

3. Philip Jacob Spener, Pia Desideria or Heartfelt Desire for a God-Pleasing Reform of the True Evangelical Church, trans. Theodore G. Tappert (Philadelphia: Fortress Press, 1964). The original text appeared in Frankfurt am Main in 1675.

4. Walter Beltz, "Gemeinsame kulturelle Codes in koexistierenden Religionsgemeinschaften, dargestellt und untersucht an Beispielen der Messiasdiskurse in den Reisetagebüchern des Institutum Judaicum et Muhammediacum J. H. Callenbergs," in Sprache und Geist: Peter Nagel zum 65. Geburtstag, eds. Walter Beltz, Ute Pietruschka, and Jürgen Tubach (Halle: Martin-Luther-Univ. Halle-Wittenberg, 2003): 1–29.

5. Cf. G. Sujin Pak, The Judaizing Calvin: Sixteenth-Century Debates Over the Messianic Psalms (Oxford and New York: Oxford University Press, 2010).

6. John Calvin, Commentary on a Harmony of the Evangelists, Matthew, Mark,

Reformed thinkers in England, Holland, France, and Switzerland, as well as in those parts of the New World where Reformed theology gained ground, expressed hope for the Jews' prospect of national restoration and conversion to Christianity.[7] Pietism found parallels and support in Reformed communities, including the Puritan movement that developed in England and New England.[8] Many Pietists and Puritans viewed the Jews as heirs of historical Israel, and focused on the prospect of the return of the Jews to the Holy Land and their conversion to Christianity.[9] Puritans and Pietists adhering to a Christian messianic faith insisted that the biblical references to Israel, Judah, Zion, and Jerusalem should be read literally, and that the Old

---

Luke, translated from the original Latin by the Rev.William Fringle, volume 3, Christian Classics Ethereal Library (Grand Rapids, MI: Baker Books, 2003), here 27:25–26. Calvin starts the commentary along traditional Christian lines, but then moves to promote the idea that God still upholds his promises to Israel and a remnant of the Jews shall be redeemed. http://www.ccel.org/ccel/calvin/calcom33.ii.xxxix.html?scrBook=Matt&scrCh=27&scrV=25#ii.xxxix-p11.1

7. Cf. Myriam Yardeni, Huguenots and Jews (Jerusalem: The Zalman Shazar Center for Jewish History, 1998), 83–112; J. Van den Berg, "Eschatological Expectations concerning the Conversion of the Jews in the Netherlands during the Seventeenth Century," in Puritans, the Millennium and the Future of Israel: Puritan Eschatology, 1600–1660, ed. Peter Toon (Cambridge: James Clarke, 1970): 137–53, esp. 137–9; Frank E. Manuel, The Broken Staff: Judaism through Christian Eyes (Cambridge, MA: Harvard University Press, 1992), 92–8.

8. Richard F. Lovelace, The American Pietism of Cotton Mather: Origins of American Evangelicalism (Grand Rapids, MI: Christian University Press, 1979), 32–5, 65–6.

9. Franz Kobler, The Vision was There: A History of the British Movement for the Restoration of the Jews to Palestine (London: Lincolns-Prager, 1956); Peter Toon, "The Latter Day Glory," in idem, ed., Puritans, the Millennium and the Future of Israel, 23–41; Carl F. Ehle, "Prolegomena to Christian Zionism in America: The Views of Increase Mather and William E. Blackstone Concerning the Doctrine of the Restoration of Israel" (Ph.D. Diss., New York University, 1977), 47–61; Mel Scult, Millennial Expectations and Jewish Liberties: A Study of the Efforts to Convert the Jews in Britain up to the Mid-Nineteenth Century (Leiden: Brill, 1978); Robert M. Healers "The Jews in Seventeenth Century Protestant Thought," Church History 46:1 (1979): 63–79; David S. Katz, Philo-Semitism and the Readmission of the Jews to England, 1603–1655 (Oxford: Clarendon Press, 1982); Barbara W. Tuchman, Bible and Sword: England and Palestine from the Bronze Age to Balfour (London: Macmillan, 1983), 80–101; Christopher Hill, The English Bible and the Seventeenth Century Revolution (London and New York: Penguin, 1994); Christopher Hill, "Till the Conversion of the Jews," in idem, Religion and Politics in Seventeenth Century England (Brighton, Harvester Press, 1986), 269–300; Mayir Verete, From Palmerstone to Balfour: Collected Essays, ed. Norman A. Rose (London and Portland, OR: Frank Cass, 1992); Avihu Zakai, "The Poetics of History and the Destiny of Israel. The Role of the Jews in English Apocalyptic Thought during the Sixteenth and Seventeenth Centuries," Journal of Jewish Thought and Philosophy 5 (1996): 313–50; Eitan Bar-Yosef, The Holy Land in English Culture 1799–1917: Palestine and the Question of Orientalism (Oxford and New York: Clarendon Press and Oxford University Press, 2005).

Testament prophecies about the rejuvenation of Israel were meant for the Jews.[10] With this ideological backdrop, these Christians were keen to seek out Jews for interaction.

Pietists' faith in the imminent return of Jesus to earth rendered their work among Jews pivotal to the unfolding of their notion of the divine plan for salvation. They sought to educate Christians about the messianic role of the Jews and to instruct the latter as to what was, from the Pietist point of view, their true historical mission. In their eyes, Jews were poised to return to the Holy Land to prepare the ground for Jesus' return and the eventual establishment of the Kingdom of God on earth. This theme became a central *topos* in Pietist literature intended for dissemination among Jews.[11] Other Protestant missions to the Jews that emerged in the wake of the Halle Pietist mission, such as the London Society for Promoting Christianity among the Jews, adopted or produced similar literature.[12]

The Halle Pietists and the Evangelization of the Jews

If the Jewish people were tasked with a special mission in God's plans for the messianic times, they merited time and resources: as such, many Pietist groups prioritized their evangelization. Wishing to approach Jews effectively, Pietists equipped their evangelists with knowledge of Jews, Judaism, and Jewish culture. Eighteenth-century German Protestants took an increasing interest in the Jews, their language, culture, and beliefs, as well as their economic and civic status.[13] Halle offered an excellent infrastructure for training and supporting informed missionaries. Among other opportunities, the university, which Spener and other Pietists had established in that city, offered a range of courses in Jewish languages, including Hebrew, Aramaic, and Yiddish. In time, the University of Halle became an important center of research and teaching on Semitic languages, and Biblical and Near Eastern studies. Moreover, the town possessed printing presses that published books in those languages. Headed by Johann Heinrich Callenberg (1694–1760), the new mission started at the University of

---

10. Toon, "The Latter Day Glory," 26–34.

11. Miktav ahavah el kol asire ha-tiqwah ha-meyuhalim an ale bene goles Yisroel di oyf di geule vartn ihertslikher libshaft geshribn/D. Jo. Mulleri Ecclesiastæ Gothani Ad Judæos plena caritatis epistola. recudi curavit ... Jo. Henr. Callenbergius, Johann Müller (Halle: Institutum Judaicum, 1747).

12. Yaakov S. Ariel, Evangelizing the Chosen People (Chapel Hill: University of North Carolina Press, 2000), 9–21.

13. Yaacov Deutsch, Judaism in Christian Eyes: Ethnographic Descriptions of Jews and Judaism in Early Modern Europe (Oxford and New York: Oxford University Press, 2012); Aya Elyada, A Goy Who Speaks Yiddish: Christians and the Jewish Language in Early Modern Germany (Stanford, CA: Stanford University Press, 2012).

Halle, where Callenberg began teaching courses for prospective missionaries in 1724, four years before the official founding date of the mission. The Pietist leader would hold a dual position as a university instructor and head of the mission. Callenberg was in charge of the production of books that enhanced extensive missionary fieldwork that aimed to reach Jews in Central and Eastern Europe, as well as in other parts of the Jewish world.[14]

The Institute yielded an impressive legacy: the comprehensive study of Jewish traditions, customs, and languages, as well as a proliferation of texts on and for Jews. It helped shape dozens of other missions, including in Britain, Scandinavia, Holland, America, Eastern Europe and Palestine. Many of these missions emulated the Halle-mission tactics and produced similar publications.[15]

The novelty of this approach merits a moment of appreciation. Traditional Christian theology and popular opinion had long perceived the Jews as a people frozen in time, practicing a uniform and static tradition. Little attention had ever been paid to the actual customs of the Jews, including their synagogue rites, home-based rituals, religious paraphernalia, and rites of passage. Interest would arise mostly when rumors spread of Jewish disrespect in texts and prayers towards Christianity.[16] Likewise, Christians had previously taken scant notice of the diversity of Judaism and the differing ethnic groups and languages of the Jews. In addition to the study of the Jews, their languages and cultures, the Institutum Judaicum took upon itself to carry out itinerant visits and discussions with thousands of Jews in dozens of different locales in Central and Eastern Europe. Institute missionaries would regularly dispatch reports on routine life in the Jewish communities they visited.[17]

Those representatives of the Institute acted as ethnographers, touring Jewish communities and recording their impressions.[18] The Halle Pietists' trademark was to enter Jewish spaces, including syna-

---

14. Christoph Rymatzki, Hallischer Pietismus und Judenmission: Johann Heinrich Callenbergs Institutum Judaicum und dessen Freundeskreis 1728–1736 (Tübingen: Niemeyer, 2004).

15. Christopher Clark, The Politics of Conversion: Missionary Protestantism and the Jews in Prussia, 1728–1941 (Oxford: Clarendon Press, 1995); Albert E. Thompson, A Century of Jewish Missions (Chicago: Fenning H. Revell, 1902).

16. Isak Nethanel Gath, The Sorcerer from Schwabach: The Process of the Chief Rabbi of the-Ansback Principality, Hirsch Fränkel [hebr.] (Tel Aviv: Ha-kibbutz ha-meuchad, 2013).

17. Rymatzki, Hallischer Pietismus und Judenmission; Thomas Müller-Bahlke, "Die Reisetagebücher des Institutum Judaicum et Muhammedicum der Reisen durch Polen 1730/31," Kwartalnik Historii Żydów (Jewish History Quarterly) 4 (2006): 504–8.

18. Ibid.

gogues, private homes, and markets, and engage in conversations with individuals and groups, soliciting their opinions and eliciting their everyday concerns.[19] Among other discoveries, Pietists found rampant poverty among Jews, a reality that stood in stark contrast to the prevailing stereotypes about them held by contemporary Christians. The rise of Pietism and the early activity of the Institutum Judaicum took place during the heyday of 'court Jews,' a handful of entrepreneurial Jews who served as aides, advisors and managers to local rulers, including Moses Benjamin Wulff (1661–1729), who acted as the lieutenant of the Duke of Anhalt-Dessau, in whose territory the Halle Pietists operated. The Pietist missionaries soon discovered, however, that the Jewish masses were far removed from court life. In fact, most Jews lived in deprivation in comparison to Christian burghers, with no access to higher education, the professions, the military, or other economic opportunities.[20]

Jewish historians have given somewhat short shrift to protective attitudes evinced by German Protestants, such as Pietist activists, towards Jews.[21] Pietists have even been portrayed as hostile towards them.[22] However, while not shying away from criticism of Jews, Pietists defended them against what they considered unfair condemnations, such as blood libels, which were still prevalent in Central and Eastern Europe. Moreover, they advocated improving the civil and economic conditions of the Jews. Pietists and, later, evangelical missionaries, would militate against harassment of Jews all around the world, claiming good will towards the Jews as a Christian virtue, and condemning physical and legal attacks against them.

While expressing sympathy with Jews and protecting them in the public arena, Pietist methods of evangelism did not share twenty-first century standards of tolerance towards other people's faiths. Moving from one Jewish community to the next, missionaries used aggressive tactics and did not hesitate to make provocative statements. In that

---

19. Christoph Bochinger, "Die Dialoge zwischen reisenden Studiosi und Juden in religionswissenschaftlicher Perspektive," Kwartalnik Historii Żydów (Jewish History Quarterly) 4 (2006): 509–20.

20. On Jews in Central Europe in the Early Modern Era, see Elisheva Carlebach, "The Death of Simon Abeles: Jewish-Christian Tension in 17th Century Prague." The 3rd annual Herbert Berman memorial lecture, Center for Jewish Studies, Queens College (New York, CUNY, 2001); Dean Philip Bell, Jews in the Early Modern World (Lanham, MD.: Rowman & Littlefield, 2008).

21. Among the exceptions are Baruch Mevorach, "Messianic Hopes within the Discourse on the Emancipation of Jews and Early Reform" (Ph.D. Diss., Hebrew University of Jerusalem, 1966); Alan T. Levinson, Between Philosemitism and Antisemitism: Defenses of Jews and Judaism in Germany, 1871–1932 (Lincoln and London: University of Nebraska Press, 2004).

22. Gath, Sorcerer from Schwabach.

manner, itinerant evangelists engaged Jews in debates on the appropriate manner of reading Jewish sacred texts, and discussed with them whether the Messiah had already come once before or not. There was certainly an 'exchange' between Pietists and Jews, but hardly in any contemporary sense of interfaith dialogue.

Pietist missionaries also did not always present themselves as what they were. The diaries of two *studiosi*, the itinerant missionaries Georg Widmann (1693–1753) and Johann Andreas Manitius (1707–1758), reveal that, relying on their remarkable knowledge of Jewish languages, culture, and teachings, sometimes the missionaries were able to conceal their Christian identities.[23] In the Widmann and Manitius cases, the Jews suspected that the visitors might not have been Jewish, but were nevertheless curious and therefore gave them the benefit of the doubt. Some wanted to learn more about the Pietist movement, and a number of young Jews contemplated conversion.

Pietist evangelists, as well as evangelical missionaries who came on the scene in the Anglo-Saxon world of the nineteenth century, were certain that their versions of Protestantism would be palatable to the Jews. It was, they believed, a purist, fully reformed Protestantism, which Jews should be able to relate to more easily than other forms of Christianity. By the eighteenth century, the Protestant Old Testament had come to resemble the Jewish *Tanakh*. Protestants mostly printed their bibles without the Apocrypha, those parts of the Roman Old Testament that the Jews had not canonized, such as the books of Judith and the Maccabees.[24] This process, in which the Pietists played a crucial role, would prove vital to the messages of the Pietist missions. When approaching Jews, Pietist missionaries and their successors pointed to chapters and verses in the Hebrew Bible as a basis for theological discussions. Pietists and, later, evangelicals who engaged in missionizing Jews, presented their church environments, liturgies, and ministry as non-offensive to Jewish sensibilities, suiting Jewish styles and concepts. Their houses of worship were empty of iconography; they did not perform the rite of the Eucharist, and their ministers, conducting services without vestments and preaching about biblical passages, were not priests.[25]

While sharing a similar corpus of sacred scriptures with the Jews,

---

23. Bochinger, "Dialoge," 514–8.

24. Luther removed a number of texts from the canon and placed them under the rubric of Apocrypha, included in the Bible, but not carrying a canonical status.

25. Promotion of Protestantism as embodying the purity and authenticity of both Judaism and Christianity appear in a number of the Institute's publications; See [Institutum Judaicum et Mohammedaicum], Catalogus 1748, was zum Gebrauch der Juden [Muhammedaner ... alten orientalischen Christenheit ... Abendländer ... Abendländischen Christen] herausgegeben (Halle: Institutum Judaicum, 1748).

Pietist missionaries were certain that theirs was the correct manner of reading the Bible. For Pietists, their version of the Christian faith, which emphasized regeneration, would lead to salvation and eternal life, while Judaism lacked the ability to offer spiritual guidelines and eternal salvation. Despite their ardent desire to interact with Jews, from the Pietists' point of view, such meetings took place between non-equals.[26] They alone possessed the correct understanding of God's plans for human history, and it was their mission to share it with Jews. While Pietists, like many Puritans and Reformed thinkers, and later on evangelical ones, developed hopes for the revival of the Jews in a restored Davidic kingdom, they agreed with the traditional Christian understanding that observance of the commandments was purposeless after the sacrifice of Jesus on the cross. Only faith in Jesus could redeem the Jews.[27]

Rather expectedly, Jews did not always welcome encounters with Pietist *studiosi*. Jewish leaders experienced Pietist overtures as intrusive, a violation of their integrity as people upholding their ancestral faith.[28] Often, however, the missionaries could rely on individual Jews – particularly young ones – to lend an ear. In their distance from majority-Christian groups, Pietists had greater emotional access to Jews than their more established Christian brethren. Most Jews lived at that time among Catholic, Uniate, or Orthodox Christians, with the patterns of immigration giving growing preference to Protestant lands, where previously Jews had been forbidden to settle. Jews often related to Christian authorities as alien, but some of them felt that the Pietists were different, friendlier and more well-meaning.

While Jewish leaders considered missionaries a threat, they could not always grasp the ideas that motivated the Pietists and evangelicals to take an interest in the Jews. Jewish activists would approach Pietist or evangelical missionaries, such as Franz Delitzsch (1813–1890), who considered the mission he established in Leipzig to be a continuation of the Institutum Judaicum; or William Blackstone (1840 –1935), founder of the Chicago Hebrew Mission, asking for their help in combating anti-Jewish accusations or, later on, promoting Zionist activities. Both Delitzsch and Blackstone militated, in books and articles, against the Blood Libel and other forms of discrimination

---

26. Bochinger, "Dialoge," 509–20.

27. Preferring to emphasize certain elements of the Pietist views and activities, David Dowdey claims that Pietists such as Callenberg re-humanized the Jews; see David Dowdey, Jewish-Christian Relations in Eighteenth-Century Germany: Textual Studies on German Archival Holdings, 1729–1742 (Lewiston, NY.: Edwin Mellen Press, 2006), especially introduction and chapters IV and V.

28. Ariel, Evangelizing the Chosen People, 55–68.

or harassment of Jews.[29] Delitzsch cooperated with Jewish scholars, such as Moritz Steinschneider (1813–1897), on literary projects, while Blackstone worked in tandem with Zionist leaders, such as Stephen Wise (1874–1949).[30]

While promoting the idea of the Jews' centrality in God's plans and developing protective attitudes towards them, Pietists often held stereotypical images of Jews as a people. Contemporary historians who have examined Pietist and early evangelical views of Jews have sometimes been taken aback by these beliefs.[31] Yet such sentiments ought to be analyzed within the context of their time and place, which often held opinions of Jews that had been percolating in European societies for centuries. Considering the Jews as God's first – albeit temporarily cast-aside – nation, Pietists related to the Jews with more goodwill than many other Christians of the period.[32] Concurrent with the Halle Pietists' activities, some non-Pietist German writers, such as Johann Andreas Eisenmenger (1654–1704), wrote very different tracts, conveying outright hostility towards the Jews.[33] Naturally, one finds variation in Pietist attitudes towards Jews. Wuerttemberg Pietists related to them in a different way than Halle Pietists did. Some Wuerttemberg Pietists were not eschatologically oriented and did not envision a special role for the Jews in history. Still, for the most part, Pietist missionaries held to eschatological hopes and considered the Jews a special people, even if they did not always express positive views about Jewish ways. Although communicated in very different political, cultural, and ecclesiastical settings, the attitudes of nineteenth-century English-speaking evangelical missionaries resembled those of eighteenth-century Pietists, a resemblance that was evident in their literature.[34]

---

29. See, for example, Franz Delitzsch's contribution in Christliche Zeugnisse gegen die Blutbeschuldigung der Juden, ed. Alois Müller (Berlin: Walther & Apolant, 1882): 12–8; on Franz Delitzsch's publications in support of Jews and their culture, see Franz Curtiss, Franz Delitzsch: A Memorial Tribute (Edinburgh: T&T Clark, 1891), 70–80; on Blackstone, see Yaakov S. Ariel, On Behalf of: American Attitudes Towards the Jewish People, Judaism and Zionism (Brooklyn, NY: Carlson, 1991), 55–96.

30. For example, Franz Delitzsch and Moritz Steinschneider, Ez Hayyim (Leipzig: J. A. Barth, 1841).

31. Giuseppe Veltri, "Die Diarii des Callenberg-Instituts: Eine Quelle zur Jüdischen Kulturgeschichte in der ersten Hälfte des 18. Jahrhunderts," in Kwartalnik Historii Żydów (Jewish History Quarterly) 4 (2006): 652–61.

32. Peter Vogt, ed., Zwischen Bekehrungseifer und Philosemitismus: Texte zur Stellung des Pietismus zum Judentum (Leipzig: Evangelische Verlagsanstalt, 2007).

33. Cf. Dowdey, Jewish-Christian Relations in Eighteenth-Century Germany, chapters IV and V.

34. Yaakov S. Ariel, An Unusual Relationship: Evangelical Christians and Jews

Literature for and about Jews

The Pietist mission produced books for Jews as prospective converts. Likewise, the missionaries disseminated literature intended to increase knowledge of Judaism and Jews among Christian audiences and interested laypersons.[35] The leaders of the Institutum Judaicum wished to present Jewish life, culture, and languages in a manner that would stir up sympathy and support. Pietist missions in continental Europe and evangelical missions would adopt, adapt, and increase the volume of publications and readers of such tracks.[36] These books and instruction manuals pointed to an acute interest on the part of Pietists in the Jews and their culture, and a wish to engage with and influence them.[37] The publications also allowed missionaries to give expression to their literary ambitions, including in the realms of translation and editing, demonstrating their knowledge of Jewish languages and texts.[38]

In the eighteenth century, Yiddish (or rather Western Yiddish, as it is called today) was still the language of the German Jews, and hence a powerful tool in the missionary endeavors of the German Pietists.[39] The Institute's publications included a manual for the study of Yiddish (1733) and a Yiddish-German lexicon (1736).[40] Christians had written similar manuals before, mostly to assist merchants who wished to trade with Jews. This, however, was the first time such a publication had been designed to convert Jews,[41] and was the precursor of several Protestant manuals, mostly Pietist and evangelical, promoting knowledge of Jewish languages and cultures. Remarkably, the University of Halle, established in 1698, was the first to offer courses on Yiddish in its curriculum. By the same token, evangelical institutions

(New York: New York University Press, 2013).

35. [Johann Heinrich Callenberg,] Catalogus 1739. Was zum Gebrauch der Juden [...] Muhammedaner [...] Christen] herausgegeben Halle, gedruckt in der Buchdruckerey des jüdischen Instituti, den 8. October. 1739 (Halle: Institutum Judaicum, 1739). The titles of the Institute's publications appear in different languages.

36. For example, Christopher Clark, The Politics of Conversion; Albert E. Thompson, ACentury of Jewish Missions.

37. Manuel, The Broken Staff, 249–92; Deutsch, Judaism in Christian Eyes.

38. Elyada, A Goy Who Speaks Yiddish.

39. Ibid., Ch. 1: "Yiddish in the Judenmission."

40. A facsimile of both texts is included in Hans Peter Althaus, ed., Schriften zur jiddischen Sprache [von] Johann Heinrich Callenberg [und] Wilhelm Christian Just Chrysander. Faksimiledruck nach den Ausgaben von 1733, 1736 und 1750 (Marburg: Elwert, 1966).

41. With one sixteenth-century exception: Elias Schadäus (c. 1541–1593), was also the first to explicitly promote the usage of Yiddish as part of a 'friendly' missionary approach. See his Mysterium, Das ist Geheimnis S. Pauli Röm. am II. Von bekehrung der Juden (Straßburg: s.n., 1592), esp. in the introduction. On early modern Yiddish manuals intended for Christian merchants and businessmen, see Elyada, A Goy Who Speaks Yiddish, Ch. 5.

would become the first schools in the English-speaking world to teach Yiddish. Secular or liberal institutions of higher learning, including Jewish schools, would introduce Yiddish to their curricula only in the later decades of the twentieth century.[42]

The Institute published a diverse selection of books in Western Yiddish, ranging from translations of books from the Bible and the New Testament to polemical tracts and Christian catechisms.[43] Many of the writings intended for the Jews were on prophetic themes. Pietists, and evangelical missionaries who followed in their footsteps, considered the messianic hope to be a meeting point between Pietist convictions and Jewish yearnings for the realization of the messianic times. From this common ground, Pietists set out to convince Jews that the Messiah had already come once before and was about to return.[44] Pietists, and in the nineteenth century evangelical missions, thus tried to bring Jews to accept the truth of the Gospel by utilizing Old Testament texts, which Jews knew and respected, and which pointed, so Protestants believed, to the appearance and ministry of Jesus.[45]

Pietists peppered their arguments with rabbinical idioms in order to heighten their credibility in Jewish eyes. At the same time, they repudiated the Talmud as an unacceptable authority. In this respect, Pietists followed the traditional, mainline, Christian understanding of the Jewish Oral Law. They considered Jews to be in need of Christianity for their self-fulfillment as human beings and as Jews, and saw Jews who adopted Pietist Protestant Christianity as true Christians as well as 'fulfilled' Jews, a theme that later Pietist and evangelical missionaries and converts would further pursue. They were willing to utilize rabbinical wisdom to achieve that goal. At least on some level, they treated the office of the rabbinate and those holding the title with respect. They quoted rabbis when doing so suited their line of thought, and took pride in rabbis who converted to Christianity, highlighting their rabbinical credentials. At times, the missions promoted views that corresponded to the ideas of Jewish thinkers of their time. In his work on the mission's writings, including those of Halle convert Immanuel Frommann, Elliot Wolfson has alerted us to similarities between these and the writings of eighteenth-century Sabbateans. The towering Jewish rabbinical figure, Jonathan Eibeschütz (1690–1764),

---

42. Ariel, Evangelizing the Chosen People, 93–100.

43. On the missionary translations of biblical texts into Yiddish, see Aya Elyada's article in the present volume.

44. Miktav ahavah el kol asire ha-tiqwah ha-meyuhalim an ale bene goles Yisroel di oyf di geule vartn ihertslikher libshaft geshribn.

45. Arno C. Gaebelein, The Prophet Daniel (New York: London and New York: Marshall Bros, 1905).

for example, suggested a loosening of the boundaries between Christianity and Judaism in his *Ve-avo Hayom El-haAyin*.[46]

From the Institutum Judaicum to Evangelicals

The Institutum Judaicum inspired Pietists in other German locales.[47] Societies in Switzerland, Holland, Denmark, Sweden, and Norway followed suit, creating their own missionary organizations, which adopted similar theologies, texts, and modes of operation.[48] While the Halle Pietists directed much of their attention to the Jewish populations in Central and Eastern Europe, younger Pietist and evangelical missions in the nineteenth century carried out many of their operations in Western Europe and North America. If previously there were not large communities of Jews in those areas, matters now began to change. The rise of new missions in the New World paralleled patterns of Jewish migration. Pietist, and later evangelical missions, targeted these cohorts.

Pietism had a notable effect on the evangelical missions that sprung up in English-speaking countries at the beginning of the nineteenth century. Like Pietists, evangelical Christians have emphasized the centrality of the Christian sacred scriptures, both the Old and New Testaments, and propagated a more literal reading of the Bible. And, similar to Pietists, many evangelical Christians adhere to a messianic faith, which has often assumed the restoration of Israel to its ancestral land.[49] Finally, similar to Pietists, evangelicals found mission an effective avenue of approach to the Jews.[50] Evangelical missions further systematized and globalized the existing Pietist missionary networks. Evangelical groups that came after the Pietists built storefront missionary centers, which included reading rooms and book stores. Much of their literature was in Yiddish, the native language of most Jews, both in Eastern Europe and among immigrants to the New World, and in addition to books, they printed journals and distributed flyers. Missions recruited Yiddish-speaking evangelists, and at times

---

46. Elliot R. Wolfson, "Immanuel Frommann's Commentary on Luke and the Christianizing of Kabbalah: Some Sabbatean and Ḥasidic Affinities," in Holy Dissent: Jewish and Christian Mystics in Eastern Europe, ed. Glenn Dynner (Detroit: Wayne State University Press, 2011): 171–222.

47. On the mission in Berlin, see Clark, The Politics of Conversion.

48. Thompson, A Century of Jewish Missions.

49. Timothy P. Weber, Living in the Shadow of the Second Coming: American Premillenialism, 1875–1982 (Chicago and London: University of Chicago Press, 1988).

50. Ernest R. Sandeen, The Roots of Fundamentalism: British and American Millenarianism, 1800–1930 (Chicago and London: University of Chicago Press, 1970), 36–9, 53–60, 62–4; Weber, Living in the Shadow, 9–10.

included the teaching of Yiddish in training courses. In that, too, they followed the Institute's example, attempting to reach Jews in their own languages, and utilizing Jewish texts, hopes, and imagery.[51]

As impressive as the Halle Pietist literary ventures were, evangelical missionaries would challenge them, seeing a need to replace early Pietist literature. While the Halle translations were more than adequate in the eighteenth century, evangelical missionaries in the nineteenth century, and even more so in the twentieth, found them unsatisfactory.[52] By the time evangelicals were preparing tracts and copies of the sacred scriptures for the Yiddish-reading audience, the Yiddish that the Institutum Judaicum labored with, namely Western Yiddish, was in rapid decline. In the early nineteenth century, German, Dutch, Alsatian, and Swiss Jews abandoned their Yiddish in favor of High German, or Dutch, or French. Eastern Yiddish thrived among East European Jews who, by the end of the nineteenth century, established new, often secular, venues of creativity in that language. These creative outlets included journals and belles-lettres, political and ideological tracts, as well as a lively theatrical scene. With Eastern European Yiddish alive and well, the gap between it and the by-now defunct Yiddish of eighteenth-century Central and Western European Jews grew even greater. Despite the exquisite quality of the eighteenth-century translations and the knowledge of Jewish texts that they conveyed, they seemed archaic to later generations of Yiddish-reading missionaries and potential converts, who felt that disseminating these early missionary tracts was counterproductive.[53] So, while the literary initiatives of the Institutum Judaicum served as a model for dozens of missions that came after it, its actual publications were later cast aside. It is perhaps symbolic of the shifting map of Pietist and evangelical missionary hubs that the most comprehensive collection of materials from the Institutum Judaicum is currently housed in the Library of Congress in Washington, DC.[54]

Conclusion

Pietists represented a new development in the realm of Protestant interactions with the Jews. While some Pietist opinions on Judaism and

---

51. On the program at the Moody Bible Institute, see Ariel, Evangelizing the Chosen People, 93–100.

52. Henry Einspruch, "Literature for the Christian Approach to the Jews," in Christians and Jews: Report of the Atlantic City Conference on the Christian Approach to the Jews, ed. John S. Conning (New York: s.n. 1931): 97–102.

53. Einspruch, "Literature for the Christian Approach to the Jews"; Ariel, An Unusual Relationship, 126–41.

54. Naomi Seidman, "A Gift for the Jewish People: Henry Einspruch's Der Bris Khadoshe, Poetics Today 35 (2014): 303–23.

Jews followed older Christian paradigms, the attitudes as a whole were innovative, if not revolutionary. Proposing a non-supercessionist understanding of the Jews and their role in history, Pietists have mostly perceived the Jews as a people carrying a special mission. They were willing to invest heavily in sharing with Jews the Pietist reading of the scriptures and messianic vision for the End-Times – regardless of the number of converts they could recruit. While they considered their version of Christianity to be superior to the Jewish faith, they were also protective of Jews and argued for improvement in the Christian treatment of Jewish minorities. Pietists, and many evangelicals whom they influenced by their example, encouraged borderline Christian-Jewish expressions, resulting in individuals, communities and literatures that bridge the two faiths.

Evangelicals have expanded various ideas and attitudes that made their debut with the Pietists. Frommann's vision of blurring the boundaries between Christianity and Judaism found heirs in evangelical writers and leaders such as Arno Gaebelein (1861–1945) and Ernest Ströter (1846–1922), Germans who labored in Germany and the United States in the late nineteenth century. By the turn of the twentieth century, attempts at creating borderline bodies of faith and culture that transformed older divisions between Judaism and Christianity had become more normative among evangelicals, resulting in hybrid communities that sought to combine the two traditions. A new, postmodern spirit of inclusivity and choice allowed for the rise of Hebrew Christians, Messianic Jews, and Jewish Believers in Jesus, groups that attempt to meld Jewish identity and rites with Christian evangelical tenets of faith. This phenomenon traces its roots directly to the theology, agenda, and literature of Pietists and evangelicals.

THE VERNACULAR BIBLE BETWEEN JEWS AND PROTESTANTS
Translation and Polemics in Early Modern Germany
By Aya Elyada

The longstanding Christian ambition to convert the Jews to Christianity received a new impetus with the Reformation and the beginning of the Protestant movement. Responding to Luther's call from the early 1520s regarding the need to deal kindly with the Jews and to instruct them carefully from the Holy Scriptures to encourage their conversion,[1] Protestant theologians and missionaries in the German lands sought suitable methods for successful mission. After realizing that anti-Jewish polemics in Latin, German, or even Hebrew, proved useless among the wider segments of the German-Jewish population, they decided to address the Jews in the Jewish vernacular, that is, in Yiddish. During the Middle Ages and the early modern period, Yiddish served the Jewish communities in the German-speaking lands as the spoken language and, alongside Hebrew, also as a written language. Known today as 'Old' or 'Western' Yiddish (as opposed to Modern Yiddish, which evolved in Eastern Europe), the early modern German-Jewish vernacular was composed almost exclusively from German and Hebrew components, so that – at least from a linguistic perspective – it was much closer to German than modern Yiddish.[2]

The ambition of Protestant theologians and missionaries to use Yiddish as part of an assertive and competent mission among the Jews

---

1. Martin Luther, "Daß Jesus Christus ein geborner Jude sei" (1523), in D. Martin Luthers Werke, Kritische Gesamtausgabe. 120 vols. (Weimar: Böhlau, 1883–2009), vol. 11: 307–36 (henceforth: WA).

2. Modern Yiddish includes an additional Slavic component, absent from early modern Western Yiddish. On the history of Yiddish and the divide between Western and Eastern Yiddish see, in particular, Max Weinreich, History of the Yiddish Language, trans. Shlomo Noble, ed. Paul Glasser, 2 vols. (New Haven and London: Yale University Press, 2008) [originally published in Yiddish, New York: YIVO, 1973]. Throughout this paper, the term 'Yiddish' is used to designate Western Yiddish, the German-Jewish vernacular of the early modern period.

resulted in numerous missionary writings in the language, written and published in the German lands between the mid-sixteenth century and the second half of the eighteenth century. These included Yiddish translations of the Old and New Testaments (either in part or complete, and often after Luther's German Bible), the Catechisms, and various anti-Jewish (and pro-Christian) polemical writings. After initial publications of this kind during the latter half of the sixteenth century,[3] the publication of missionary tracts in Yiddish reached its high point in the first decades of the eighteenth century, with the rise of the Pietist movement within Lutheranism and its renewed emphasis on Jewish conversion. In 1728, the devoted pietist and professor of philosophy and oriental languages at the University of Halle, Johann Heinrich Callenberg (1694–1760), established in the city the *Institutum Judaicum et Muhammedicum*, with the outright aim of spreading Christianity among Jews and Muslims. In addition to the training of professional missionaries, the Institute also had its own printing shop, dedicated to the publication and distribution of missionary writings; first and foremost, in the German-Jewish vernacular.[4]

The missionary initiative of translating the New Testament and other Christian works into Yiddish in order to make them accessible to a Jewish readership seems perfectly reasonable. Less clear, however, are the attempts of Protestant missionaries to translate the Old Testament (i. e. the Hebrew Bible) into Yiddish for the benefit of *Jewish* readers. After all, the Jews had not exactly been waiting for the Chris-

---

3. Most notably, the Yiddish Pentateuch (with *Haftarot* and *Megillot*) of the Protestant Reformer Paulus Fagius and the Yiddish versions of the New Testament published by the convert Paul Helic (c. 1500–c. 1560) and the Protestant theologian Elias Schadeus (c. 1541–1593). See: Paulus Fagius, ed., and [Michael Adam (?)], trans., Hamishah Humshei Torah imHamesh Megillot veha-Haftarot / Die fünff bücher Mosis sampt dem Hohen lied Salomonis ... (Constance: Fagius, 1544) (this translation appeared in two different editions: one with a Yiddish title and introduction, addressed to the Jewish reader, and one with a German title and introduction, addressed to the Christian reader); Paul Helic, ed., and [Johann Harzuge (?)], trans., Das noyay Testyment das da wert ginent Evani[g]elyun ... das ist ... Besurah Toyveh (Cracow: Helic, 1540); Elias Schadeus, ed. and trans, Fünff Bücher des Newen Testaments (Strasbourg: Schadeus, 1592).

4. On the missionary activity of the Institute, see, especially, Christoph Rymatzki, Hallischer Pietismus und Judenmission: Johann Heinrich Callenbergs Institutum Judaicum und dessen Freundeskreis (1728–1736) (Tübingen: Niemeyer, 2004); Christopher Clark, The Politics of Conversion: Missionary Protestantism and the Jews in Prussia 1728–1941 (Oxford: Clarendon Press, 1995), Ch. 2. For an elaborated discussion and analysis of the Institute activities in Yiddish, see Aya Elyada, "Yiddish – Language of Conversion? Linguistic Adaptation and Its Limits in Early Modern *Judenmission*," Leo Baeck Institute Year Book 53 (2008): 3–29, and eadem, A Goy Who Speaks Yiddish: Christians and the Jewish Language in Early Modern Germany (Stanford, CA: Stanford University Press, 2012), Ch. 1.

tians to produce for them Yiddish translations of the Bible. At least from the fifteenth century, Ashkenazi Jews had in their possession Yiddish versions of biblical books: first in the form of manuscripts, and, since the mid-sixteenth century, also in print.[5]

The literary tradition of translating biblical texts from Hebrew into Yiddish, culminating in the publication of two complete Yiddish bibles in Amsterdam in the late seventeenth century,[6] originated from the traditional study of the Bible in the Ashkenazi *kheyder*, the religious primary school for Jewish boys. Since Hebrew was no longer the children's mother tongue, the Bible lessons in the *kheyder* were mainly comprised of the oral translation of each successive word from Hebrew into Yiddish. The *melamed*, or teacher, recited with the children every Hebrew word of the text, followed by its Yiddish equivalent. From the Middle Ages onwards, an entire corpus of supporting literature developed to assist in this form of Bible study. In the first stage, Yiddish glosses were added to Hebrew manuscripts, intended to clarify difficult terms in the biblical text and the commentaries. In the course of the sixteenth century, this medieval tradition further developed with the publication of printed glossaries, concordances, and biblical lexicons.[7]

---

5. On pre-modern Yiddish biblical translations, see, especially, Chone Shmeruk, Sifrut Yidish – Prakim le'Toldoteha (Tel Aviv: Tel Aviv University, 1978), Ch. 4, and Jean Baumgarten, Introduction to Old Yiddish Literature, ed. and trans. Jerold C. Frakes (Oxford and New York: Oxford University Press, 2005), Ch. 5, with further references. See also Chava Turniansky, "Reception and Rejection of Yiddish Renderings of the Bible," in The Bible in/and Yiddish, ed. Shlomo Berger (Amsterdam: Menasseh ben Israel Institute, 2007): 7–20.

6. Yekuti'el b. Yitzhak Blitz, trans., Hamisha humshe tora nevi'im u-ketuvim bileshon ashkenaz ... (Amsterdam: Uri Phoebus, 1678) and Yosef bar Alexander Witzenhausen, trans., Tora nevi'im u-ketuvim mi-leshon ha-kodesh ... (Amsterdam: Yosef Athias, 1679) (2nd ed. 1687). On these Yiddish bibles, see, especially, Marion Aptroot, "'In *galkhes* they do not say so, but the taytsh is as it stands here': Notes on the Amsterdam Yiddish Bible translations by Blitz and Witzenhausen," Studia Rosenthaliana 27 (1993): 136–58, and eadem, "Yiddish Bibles in Amsterdam," in Berger, ed., Bible in/and Yiddish, 42–60.

7. Here one should mention *Mirkeves ha-mishne* of Rabbi Anshel, a Hebrew-Yiddish biblical concordance published in Cracow in 1534, which is the first-known Yiddish printed book, and the two biblical dictionaries from the beginning of the seventeenth century: Moses ben Issachar Sertels, Seyfer beeyr Moushe (Prague: Moses ben Bezalel, 1604–5), which includes terms from the Pentateuch, and idem, Seyfer lekakh tov (Prague: Moses ben Bezalel, 1604), which includes terms from the Prophets and Hagiographa. See Baumgarten, Old Yiddish Literature, 22–3. For an elaborate discussion on the teaching method in the *kheyder* and its close relations to the Yiddish lexicographical tradition see Chava Turniansky, "Halimud baheder ba'et ha'hadasha hamukdemet," in Haheder: mehkarim, te'udot, pirkey sifrut vezihronot, eds. Emanuel Etkes and David Assaf (Tel Aviv: Tel Aviv University, 2010), 3–35, esp. 22 ff.; and see also Walter Röll, "Die Bibelübersetzung ins Jiddische im 14. und 15. Jahrhundert," in

The gloss tradition also gave rise to the so-called *taytsh-khumesh*, a literal translation of the Bible in which every word or phrase in the Hebrew original is replaced with a corresponding Yiddish one. These verbatim translations were intended for use not only in the *kheyder*, but also in the synagogue, as a means for achieving a better understanding of the Hebrew text, and in the Jewish home, as reading material for the women and uneducated men.[8]

Protestant scholars, especially theologians, Hebraists, and Orientalists, were well acquainted with the Yiddish biblical translations that circulated in the Jewish communities. Bibliographical works of prominent theologians in which Jewish literature or different versions of the Old Testament are discussed often feature information on Yiddish bibles, sometimes even entire reviews.[9] Missionaries also read the Yiddish biblical translations – together with other Yiddish works that were popular among the Jews at the time, such as the *Tsene-rene* and the *Mayse-bukh* – mining them for information about contemporary Jewish beliefs (the famous 'know your enemy' stratagem). The idea, of course, was that familiarity with popular Yiddish literature, including biblical translations and adaptations, would achieve a more effective mission.[10] Perhaps more surprisingly, Protestant theologians

---

Die Vermittlung geistlicher Inhalte im deutschen Mittelalter, eds. Timothy R. Jackson, Nigel F. Palmer, and Almut Suerbaum (Tübingen: Niemeyer, 1996), 183–95.

8. On the taytsh-khumesh tradition, see, especially, Chava Turniansky, "Letoldot ha-'taytsh-khumesh': 'khumesh mit khibur'," in Iyunim besifrut: dvarim shene'emru be'erev likhvod Dov Sadan bimlot lo shmonim ve'khamesh shana, ed. Chone Shmeruk (Jerusalem: Israel National Science Academy, 1988), 21–51; eadem, "Halimud baheder," esp. 22 ff.; eadem, "Reception and Rejection"; Erika Timm, Historische jiddische Semantik: Bibelübersetzungssprache als Faktor der Auseinanderentwicklung des jiddischen und des deutschen Wortschatzes (Tübingen: Niemeyer, 2005); and Baumgarten, Old Yiddish Literature, Ch. 5.

9. See, e. g., Christian Kortholt, De variis scripturae editionibus tractatus theologico-historicophilologicus (Kiel: Richelius, 1686); Jacob Le Long, Bibliothecae sacrae pars altera (Leipzig: Gleditsch and Weidmann, 1709); Johann Christoph Wolf, Bibliotheca Hebraea, 4 vols. (Hamburg and Leipzig: Liebezeit, 1715–33), here: vol. II, 1721; Johann Gottlob Carpzov, Critica Sacra Veteris Testamenti (Leipzig: Martin, 1728); Wilhelm Christian Just Chrysander, Unterricht vom Nutzen des Juden-Teutschen (Wolfenbüttel: Meißner, 1750).

10. As the ardent advocate of Jewish mission in Yiddish, Wilhelm Christian Just Chrysander (1718–1788), noted, reading Yiddish literature would be beneficial for Christians in that "one makes for oneself, from their own books, a more accurate and complete notion of the condition of present-day Jews, [...] their teachings, [...] customs, prevalent prejudices, motivations, most common/base sins, blasphemies [...] etc. Consequently, one would be more skilled to missionize them [...] and would be able to better choose the most convenient means for winning them over" (Chrysander, Unterricht vom Nutzen, 20; unless mentioned otherwise, all translations throughout the paper are my own). With regard to specific Yiddish works see, for instance, ibid., 7–8; Christoph Helvicus, ed. and trans., Jüdischer Historien oder Thalmuhdischer /

and Hebraists even used such Yiddish translations, originally prepared by Jewish authors for the Jewish reading public, for intra-Christian purposes; specifically, as a means of assistance, or *Hilfsmittel*, for achieving an accurate reading and understanding of the Hebrew Bible. In some cases, where nothing better could be found, the Yiddish translations were even used by Christians as substitutes for Hebrew dictionaries and lexicons.[11]

So far, we have seen that the Jews of the Holy Roman Empire enjoyed a long and substantial tradition of Yiddish biblical translations and that contemporary Christian theologians and missionaries were well aware of this tradition. So why did the latter consider it necessary to produce additional Yiddish translations of biblical texts for distribution among the Jews? One possible answer is that the Christian missionaries were aware of the fact that the plain Yiddish biblical translations (according to the *pshat*) were not particularly popular among the Jews, especially in comparison to other genres of biblical literature in the Jewish vernacular, such as the *Tsene-rene*, which contained large portions of *aggadot* and *midrashim*.[12] Hence, in the spirit of *sola scriptura*, they wished to enhance the dissemination of plain versions of the Bible in Yiddish among the Jews. Another possibility, which stands at the focus of this essay, is that the Protestant theologians and missionaries were simply not content with the existing Yiddish versions of the Bible, prepared for the Jews by Jewish Rabbinischer / wunderbarlicher Legenden .... 2 vols. (Gießen: Chemlein, 1612), vol. 1, intro., n.p.; vol. 2, intro., n.p.; Johann Christoph Wagenseil, "Rabbi Mose Stendels nach Jüdisch-Teutscher Red-Art vorlängst in Reimen gebrachte Psalmen Davids," in idem, Benachrichtigungen wegen einiger die Judenschafft angehenden wichtigen Sachen (Leipzig: Heinichen, 1705), n.p. (here: intro., n.p.).

    11. Thus, for example, the influential theologian and Hebraist Johann Christoph Wagenseil explained that,whenever he encounters an obscure passage in the Hebrew Bible, he examines biblical translations and interpretations in Yiddish and other languages, such as Aramaic, Greek and Latin, so as to achieve an accurate literal understanding of the text. But, he notes, it is usually the case "that the Jewish-German [i. e. Yiddish] translation of the words and interpretation of a saying is more beneficial for me than all remaining aids, and that I remain with this [translation]: how it then gives word for word, as clear as it can only be, regardless whether it sounds well or foul in the German language"; Johann Christoph Wagenseil, Belehrung der Jüdisch-Teutschen Red- und Schreibart (Königsberg: Rhode, 1699), intro., n.p. And see also idem, "Rabbi Mose Stendels," intro., n.p.; Johann Buxtorf, Thesaurus grammaticus linguae sanctae hebraeae (Basel: Waldkirch, 1609), 652; Chrysander, Unterricht vom Nutzen, 6, 19; and the editor's introduction to the Biblia Pentapla, Das ist: Die Bücher der Heiligen Schrift ..., Nach Fünf-facher Deutscher Verdolmetschung, 3 vols. (Wandsbeck and Schiffbeck: Holle, 1710 –12), vol. 1, intro., n.p.; vol. 2, intro., n.p.

    12. On the popularity of the various genres of biblical literature in Yiddish see, e. g., Turniansky, "Reception and Rejection"; see also Baumgarten, Old Yiddish Literature, Ch. 5.

translators. In their eyes, the Jewish Yiddish bibles were inadequate as media for the transmission of religious truth: instead of serving the Jews as a means to draw nearer to the Word of God, these translations were perceived as preventing the Jews from comprehending and accepting the divine message.

Protestant Criticism of Jewish Biblical Translations

What was it, then, in the Yiddish biblical translations, that aroused the ire of the Protestant scholars? A central motif in the Christian criticism was the Jewish practice of translating biblical works from Hebrew into Yiddish in a strictly wordforword manner. Emerging from a point of deep respect for the sanctity of the biblical text, the Yiddish bibles aimed to keep the translation as close as possible to the literal meaning of the Hebrew original, leaving aside the syntactic and lexical rules of spoken Yiddish, which were closer to German. For Christian scholars, the Jewish custom of translating verbatim from Hebrew into Yiddish, *"unangesehen wie übel es im deutschen lautet"* (regardless of how bad it sounds in German), rendered the Yiddish translations of the Bible stylistically inferior and barely intelligible.[13] Moreover, this method of translation was commonly seen as indicative of 'Jewish superstition.' These severe condemnations appear clearly in the words of Johannes Buxtorf (1564–1629), the most influential Christian Hebraist and Yiddishist of the seventeenth century. Discussing the Jewish custom of translating from Hebrew into Yiddish, Buxtorf opined that

> this is, however, a flaw common to them [the Jews] all: that what they translate from Hebrew, they translate too literally. The Hebraisms are so persistent that they obscure the German idiom. They superstitiously (*superstitiose*) hold so closely to preserving the extraneous and literal word that they sometimes leave no sense at all; sometimes the sense is obscure, sometimes disagreeable. The more ignorant a person is, the more superstitious he is in this regard.[14]

One frequently finds such disparagement of verbatim translation (*verbum pro verbo*) as 'superstitious' and inferior to translating the sense of a given text (*sensum de sensu*) in early modern discussions on the art of translation.[15] In the Jewish context, however, this notion also alluded to an enduring motif in Christian anti-Jewish polemics regarding the Jews' 'superstitious' adherence to the literal meaning of the

---

13. Quote from Fagius, ed., Die fünff bücher Mosis, intro., n.p. On this point see also below.

14. Buxtorf, Thesaurus grammaticus, 652.

15. See Peter Burke, "Cultures of Translation in Early Modern Europe," in Cultural Translation in Early Modern Europe, eds. Peter Burke and R. Po-chia Hsia (Cambridge: Cambridge University Press, 2007), 7–38, here at 24ff.

biblical text at the expense of a deeper and more spiritual understanding. The claim that the Jews were captives of the letter of the Bible and disregarded its spirit goes back to the Church fathers, but it became especially evident in Protestant circles. As an unshakeable expression of the Jews' literal-mindedness, the Jewish practice of translating the Bible in a word-for-word manner was presented in sharp contrast to the 'spiritual' interpretation of the Bible in Christian, mainly Protestant, tradition.

But Jewish superstition and 'servitude of the letter' (*Buchstabendienst*) accounted only partially, according to the Protestant authors, for the literal translation of the Bible into Yiddish. A second reason, from their perspective, was that the Jews were simply not capable of producing better translations. Since the Jews read the Bible according to rabbinic interpretations, so ran the argument, they cannot truly understand the text, let alone correctly translate it. As Jewish versions of the holy text, the Yiddish biblical translations were, as one eighteenth-century Protestant scholar formulated it, "*noch mit der Decke Mosis beleget*" (still covered with Moses' veil), and therefore surely false and mistaken.[16] In this regard, some authors quote from Martin Luther's *Sendbrief vom Dolmetschen* (*An Open Letter on Translating*, 1530), in which Luther criticizes a German translation of the Prophets that was published in Worms in 1527. About this translation, which was prepared by Christians with the assistance of Jewish scholars, Luther writes:

> the art of translation is not a simple craft like any other [...]; It calls for a righteous, pious, true, hard-working, God-fearing, Christian [...] heart. For that reason, I believe that no false Christian or divisive spirit (*rottengeist*) can translate faithfully, as is clear from the Prophets that translated into German and published in Worms. There is no doubt that much effort was put in it, and it closely follows my own German; but there were Jews involved, who did not show much respect for Christ; apart from that, it shows sufficient skill and hard work.[17]

Closely related to the idea that the Jews, by virtue of being Jews, were unable to correctly translate the Bible, was the claim of many Protestant Hebraists and Yiddishists that the Jews could not translate in a correct manner because they had lost their mastery of the Hebrew language. "The Jews of our time are ignorant of the Hebrew tongue," lamented the famous Hebraist Johann Christoph Wagenseil (1633–

---

16. See the editor's introduction to the Biblia Pentapla, vol. 1, intro., n.p.; and vol. 2, intro., n.p.

17. Martin Luther, "Sendbrief vom Dolmetschen" (1530), in WA 30 (2), 632–46, here at 640. This quote appears, for example, in Kortholt, De variis scripturae, 341–2; and Wolf, Bibliotheca Hebraea, vol. II, 455–6.

1705) in 1705,

> and because of that, among other things, the veil hangs in front of their eyes, which prevents them from truly understanding the writings of Moses and the prophets; and so, among many hundreds of Jews, not a single one can be found, who can clearly explain even one chapter of the [Five Books of] Moses, not to mention from the Psalms, Job, or the Prophets, and render it in a comprehensible and correct manner.[18]

This association between the Jews' lack of proficiency in Hebrew and their insufficient knowledge of the Bible already appeared in the writings of the sixteenth-century reformer Paulus Fagius (1504–1549), who interpreted both disadvantages as God's punishment of the Jewish people: "They are called the Hebrews (*Hebreer*), and yet there is no other people under the sun that has less understanding of the true, proper Hebrew language." And he adds: "And so we can see how dreadfully the Lord has punished and afflicted them, in that he took from them not only the correct and true understanding of the Holy Scripture, but also the means by which they could have attained such understanding."[19]

Even worse than the Jewish practice of translating word-for-word from Hebrew into Yiddish were the passages in the Yiddish biblical translations that, from a Christian perspective, deviated from the literal meaning of the Hebrew source text. According to the Protestant authors, the Jews aimed in this way to deliberately falsify and pervert the Hebrew text, and especially the *optima de Messia oracula*, or the places that bear witness to the expected coming of Christ. Moreover, the Jewish translators were accused of shamelessly integrating extensive passages of Jewish apologetics and anti-Christian polemic in the Yiddish texts, "by which the reader is led away from the beneficial use

---

18. Johann Christoph Wagenseil, "Die Hoffnung der Erlösung Israelis," in idem, Benachrichtigungen, 1–125, here at 41.
19. Fagius, Die fünff bücher Mosis, intro., n.p. Similar statements regarding the loss of Hebrew among the German Jews appear in the writings of Protestant Hebraists and Yiddishists throughout the early modern period. See, for example, Sebastian Münster, Chaldaica grammatica (Basel: Froben, 1527), 4; Johann Jacob Schudt, Jüdische Merckwürdigkeiten, 4 vols. (Frankfurt a.M. and Leipzig: Hocker, 1714–18), here vol. 2, 281–2; Wagenseil, "Rabbi Mose Stendels," intro., n.p.; Johann Christoph Bodenschatz, Kirchliche Verfassung der heutigen Juden sonderlich derer in Deutschland (Frankfurt and Leipzig: Selbstverl., 1749), pt 4, 94; Johann Heinrich Callenberg, Neue summarische Nachricht von einem Versuch, das arme jüdische Volck zur Erkäntniss und Annehmung der christlichen Wahrheit anzuleiten (Halle: Buchdruckerey des jüdischen Instituti, 1735), 65–6; and idem, Bericht an einige Christliche Freunde von einem Versuch, das arme Jüdische Volck zur Erkäntniß und Annehmung der Christlichen Wahrheit anzuleiten (Halle: Krottendorff, 1730), esp. Dreyzehnte Fortsetzung (1735), 36, 54–5.

of the divine Word (*a salutari verbi coelestis usu*),"²⁰ and especially from the acknowledgment of Christ.

Accusations of anti-Christian propaganda were often levelled at the first complete Yiddish version of the Bible, translated by Jekuthiel ben Isaac Blitz (c. 1634–1684) and published in Amsterdam in 1678. The Lutheran theologian and Hebraist from Frankfurt am Main, Johann Jacob Schudt (1664–1722), was one such indicter. In his extensive ethnographic work, *Jüdische Merckwürdigkeiten* (*Jewish curiosities*) from the year 1714, Schudt related to this "foolish, tasteless, vicious Jewish-German translation of the Old Testament" (*alber[n]e / abgeschmackte / boßhafftige Juden-Teutsche Übersetzung des Alten Testaments*) as part of his discussion of Jewish life in Holland. Vehemently attacking Amsterdam's authorities for the lack of adequate censorship in their city, Schudt considered this Yiddish bible decisive proof of the unwelcome results of the overly extensive freedom enjoyed by the Jews in Holland, as he formulates it, where "the Jews have their own printing shops, and there they may freely publish their blasphemous books at their liking [...], in which they blaspheme and disgrace Jesus and our faith." As an example of the way the Jewish translator allegedly falsified and misinterpreted "the clearest prophecies of the Lord Messiah" (*die klahreste Weissagungen vom Herrn Messia*), Schudt cites Blitz's translation of Isaiah 7:14, a central point of controversy between Jews and Christians over the centuries. Relating to the second part of the verse, "*hine ha'alma hara ve-yoledet ben*" (The virgin will be with child and will give birth to a son), Schudt sharply criticizes Blitz for translating the word *alma* not as a *Jungfrau* (virgin), but rather as a junge Frau (יונגי פרויא; young woman), thus deliberately pulling the rug out from under a fundamental Christian tenet.²¹

According to this and many other examples,²² the 'problematic' places in Yiddish bibles were not simply viewed as the outcome of some translation fallacy, and certainly not as a legitimate alternative to their own interpretation, but as a strategic mistranslation, ideologically motivated by anti-Christian impulses. The old Italian adage, *traduttore, traditore* (a translator is a traitor), is thus imbued in this

---

20. Quote from Johann Heinrich Callenberg, ed. and trans., Genesis germanice litteris judaicogermanicis (Halle: Institutum Judaicum, 1737), intro., n.p.

21. Schudt, Jüdische Merckwürdigkeiten, vol. 1, 284–5. For more attacks on Blitz's Yiddish bible, see, for example, Kortholt, De variis scripturae, 343–4; Carpzov, Critica Sacra, 759–78; Chrysander, Unterricht vom Nutzen, 7–9; Anon., Nachrichten von einer Hallischen Bibliothek, vol. 3 (Halle: Gebauer, 1749), 106–8.

22. For denunciations of Jewish 'blasphemies' and anti-Christian expressions in other Yiddish prayer books and biblical translations see Kortholt, De variis scripturae, 342; Carpzov, Critica Sacra, 753–6; Wagenseil, "Rabbi Mose Stendels," intro., n.p.; Chrysander, Unterricht vom Nutzen, 14.

case with additional meanings, taken not from the world of literary criticism but from that of Christian-Jewish polemics. The Jews, on this view, used the medium of translation to manipulate the holy text and hence as a weapon in the war they waged against Christian tenets in their Jewish vernacular.

Protestant Criticism of the German-Jewish Vernacular

The Christian charges discussed thus far, namely, that the Jews were incapable of fathoming the Bible correctly, that they translated the holy text too literally, and that they falsified biblical verses in order to conceal the places referring to Christ were, of course, ancient in origin. Rooted in the teachings of the Church Fathers, they constituted central motifs in anti-Jewish polemics during the Middle Ages and the early modern period, where they also came forward in Christian, mainly Protestant, discussions on the Yiddish Bible. Other points of critique, however, were directed specifically at the Yiddish biblical translations, or, more precisely, at the language and style of these texts.

As far as the Christian authors were concerned, Yiddish was basically a kind of German. Thus, in their eyes, the Yiddish biblical translations were in fact German translations. The other characteristics of Yiddish – most notably that Yiddish had a considerable Hebraic component, that many of the German words were pronounced differently, and that the Jews also used 'peculiar words' (*sonderliche Wörter*), namely, words from other languages as well as older German words – were usually perceived by the Christian authors as mere deviations from or, indeed, a corruption of their own German language.[23]

The prevailing assumption among Christian scholars, that Yiddish was no more than "incorrect, corrupted, unreadable, and incomprehensible German" (*ein gantz falsches / corruptes / unleserliches unverständliches Teutsch*),[24] influenced their perceptions of the Yiddish biblical translations. Thus, for instance, we read in the works of early modern Protestant theologians like Christian Kortholt (1633–1694) and Johann Gottlob Carpzov (1679–1767) that the Yiddish bibles of the Jews, "[have] an unrefined and barbaric style, [...] highly unsatisfactory for either Christian or for German ears."[25] Depreciations of this

---

23. For an elaborate discussion on this point see Aya Elyada, "'Eigentlich Teutsch'? Depictions of Yiddish and Its Relations to German in Early Modern Christian Writings," European Journal of Jewish Studies 4 (2010): 23–42, and eadem, A Goy Who Speaks Yiddish, Ch 7.

24. Quote from Caspar Calvör, Gloria Christi, oder Herrligkeit Jesu Christi (Leipzig: Göze, 1710), intro., n.p.

25. Carpzov, Critica Sacra, 751–3 (quote from 751), referring to the translation

kind appear in later works as well. In 1784, the professor of theology in Altdorf and Jena, Johann Christoph Doederlein (1745–1792), criticized the language of Yiddish biblical translations in earlier periods, denouncing it as "utterly impure, barbaric, [...] often ridiculous, and conducive to the maintenance of the language-barbarism (*Sprachbarbarey*) among the Jews."[26]

More egregious than the aesthetical problem was, from the vantage point of the Protestant authors, the problem of understanding, or rather misunderstanding, caused by the corrupted Yiddish language. The Lutheran theologian and Superintendant Caspar Calvör (1650 –1725), for example, argued at the beginning of the eighteenth century that since Yiddish has no proper grammar or accurate orthography, readers of Yiddish works, even the German Jews themselves, are unable to reach a true understanding of such texts.[27] The assertion that the Yiddish bibles were incomprehensible even to Yiddish-speaking Jews had, of course, serious theological implications: if the language of these bibles blocked the transmission of the holy truth, how would the Jews ever acquire it?

The Christian notion that the adulterated language of the Yiddish bibles yielded texts that lacked both clarity and purity was reinforced by the aforementioned Jewish practice of translating the Bible in a word-for-word manner. Since this translation method further contributed to the deviation of the language of translation (the so-called *khumesh-taytsh*) from the syntactic structure of German, it was viewed as largely responsible for the fact that, "when one reads or hears it, one might think it is gibberish rather than German" (*billicher Kauderwelsch als Teutsch*).[28] Jewish translators, argued the theologians,

> regard the character and true essence of the German language as completely unimportant, corrupting and falsifying it, that it is sometimes difficult to understand the meaning of the text [...] sometimes they cling so firmly to the Hebrew letters, so that it becomes completely unintelligible in German.[29]

---

of Witzenhausen (1679); on p. 759 he directs the same criticism towards the translation of Blitz (1678).

26. Johann Christoph Doederlein, Theologische Bibliothek, vol. 3 (Leipzig: Breitkopf, 1784), pt 1, 3.

27. Calvör, Gloria Christi, intro., n.p.

28. Fagius, Die fünff bücher Mosis, intro., n.p.; for similar notions see also Wagenseil, Belehrung der Jüdisch-Teutschen, intro., n.p. In 1705 Wagenseil referred to Mose Stendel's Yiddish translation of the psalms as a work that, "to tell the truth, should be called gibberish rather than German"; idem, "Rabbi Mose Stendels," intro., n.p.

29. Quote from Carpzov, Critica Sacra, 752–3, who also provides lengthy examples.

At this point, it is interesting to note that translating according to the sense of the text and into *idiomatic German*, in order to make Scripture as clear and comprehensible as possible to the broader population of German speakers, was a hallmark of Luther's own vernacular Bible. This characteristic clearly distinguished his translation from Catholic, pre-Reformation German versions of the Bible. These pre-Reformation German bibles were, in fact, translations of the Latin Vulgate, and followed the Latin text in a verbatim fashion, adapting the German language of translation to the Latin source. In his own translation of the Bible, Luther not only attempts to 'purge' the holy text from Catholic interpretations and theological influences; he also rejects wholesale the accepted method of translation, famously asserting that "one does not have to ask the literal Latin how one is to speak German." Instead, Luther advocates an idiomatic, even colloquial translation, explaining that "I wanted to speak German, not Latin or Greek, since it was German I had undertaken to speak in the translation."[30]

In their criticism of the Jewish biblical texts in Yiddish, then, it seems that the Protestant authors followed Luther's approach regarding the desirable style and method for biblical translation. Yet the shifting of the discussion from the context of Protestant-Catholic polemics to that of a Protestant-Jewish one brought to the foreground a new factor: the complete and utter rejection of Yiddish, the Jewish vernacular, by the Protestant scholars and missionaries, as discussed above. Thus, in their own Yiddish biblical translations, such as those produced in the Pietist institute in Halle during the eighteenth century, Protestant missionaries were not satisfied with merely modifying the method of translation. Rather, they also attempted to 'improve' the Yiddish language by Germanizing it, that is, by reducing the Hebraic component of Yiddish to a minimum, or even eliminating it altogether, while retaining solely the Germanic component of the Jewish language. The outcome was that some 'Yiddish' biblical translations, as well as other missionary works, were in fact written in German with Hebrew letters, or in a highly 'Germanized' version of Yiddish. Whether this was the most appropriate medium for missionizing among the Jews is, of course, open to debate.[31]

---

30. See Luther, "Sendbrief vom Dolmetschen" (1530), quotes from WA 30 (2), 637. On Luther's translation of the Bible see, for example, Stephan Füssel, "Introduction," in The Bible in Pictures: Illustrations from the Workshop of Lucas Cranach (1534) (Cologne: Taschen, 2009), 4–32; Mark U. Edwards, Printing, Propaganda and Martin Luther (Berkeley, CA: University of California Press, 1994), Ch. 5; Eric W. Gritsch, "Luther as Bible Translator," in The Cambridge Companion to Martin Luther, ed. Donald K. McKim (Cambridge: Cambridge University Press, 2003), 62–72.

31. On this point see, especially, Elyada, "Yiddish – Language of Conversion?"; eadem, A Goy Who Speaks Yiddish, Ch. 8.

Conclusion: The Vernacular Bible Between Jews and Protestants

The vernacular Bible was arguably one of the greatest achievements of the Protestant Reformation, and a major force behind its success. Luther's teachings of *sola scriptura* and the 'priesthood of all believers,' as formulated in his early writings, inevitably led to the Protestant assertion that the Holy Scripture should be made accessible to every man and woman, who would be able to read and understand the holy text in his or her native tongue. It is no surprise, therefore, that translating the Bible into German was one of the first and most important tasks of Luther as a reformer. Thus, while the Latin Vulgate remained – at least officially – the ultimate Bible of the Catholic Church, the vernacular Bible became the staple of the Protestant movements, resulting in the rapid translation of the holy book into the various European vernaculars from the sixteenth century onwards.

Within the Jewish-Ashkenazi world, vernacular – that is, Yiddish – translations of the Hebrew Bible existed already before the Protestant Reformation. These Jewish, Yiddish translations shared an important characteristic with Luther's and the other Protestant vernacular bibles: they, too, were meant to make the Bible accessible to the broader population, beyond the narrow religious and intellectual elite. In other respects, however, the early modern Yiddish translations of the Hebrew Bible resembled the Catholic, pre-Lutheran German translations of the Latin Vulgate: they produced a verbatim translation of the text, following closely the grammatical rules of the source language, at the expense of an idiomatic translation. Moreover, unlike the Protestant vernacular bibles, which were meant to replace the Vulgate as the canonical text, neither the Catholic nor the Jewish vernacular translations were intended to present an alternative to the hegemonic, sacred text – either in Hebrew or in Latin. Instead, they were seen mainly as inferior substitutes, auxiliary tools to better understand the one and only canonized text.

As this essay aimed to show, Protestant Hebraists and theologians disparaged the Jewish vernacular bibles precisely because of these 'Catholic' characteristics, in addition to their antagonism towards the Jewish religion and the Yiddish language and culture of their Jewish neighbors. Loyal to the Protestant teaching that an individual reading and understanding of the Bible is indispensable for gaining access to religious truth, they sought to provide contemporary Ashkenazi Jews with 'improved' texts of the Holy Scriptures: texts in which rabbinic interpretations were replaced by Christian ones and in which the Yiddish language underwent a process of Germanization; a true 'kosher' Christian Bible – in language, style, and content.

Epilogue: Yiddish Bibles, Protestant Criticism, and the German-Jewish Haskalah

The early modern Protestant mission to the Jews failed to achieve its goal. Despite the diligent publication and distribution of Yiddish missionary writings, including new, Protestant versions of Yiddish biblical texts, the Jews did not convert *en masse* to Christianity. Yet it seems that the Protestant theologians' and missionaries' critique of the Jewish vernacular Bible, and their attempts to 'improve' it, did have a certain impact – if not a religious or theological one, then at least in the linguistic and cultural domain.

In 1783, Moses Mendelssohn (1729–1786), the leading figure of the German-Jewish *Haskalah* (Jewish Enlightenment), published his own translation of the Pentateuch under the title *Sefer Netivot Hashalom*.[32] As was the case with earlier Yiddish translations, Mendelssohn, too, designated his translation language as *leshon Ashkenaz*. By this, however, Mendelssohn did not mean the Yiddish language of his predecessors, but indeed a pure, clear *Hochdeutsch*, transliterated with Hebrew characters.[33]

In the introduction to his Pentateuch, *Or Lintivah*, Mendelssohn criticized earlier Yiddish translations of the Bible, such as the two seventeenth-century Amsterdam bibles of Yekutiel Blitz and Josel (Joseph) Witzenhausen (c. 1616–c. 1686), both for their method of verbatim translation which Mendelssohn vehemently rejected, and for the 'bad German' in which they were written. Referring to Blitz, for example, Mendelssohn claimed:

> Even if his intention was good [...] his actions are not welcome at all, for he did not know the nature of the holy language, nor the depth of its idiom. What he garnered from it, he translated into a stammering, distorted and corrupt language, loathsome to the soul of the reader who knows how to speak [German] correctly (תגעל בה נפש הקורא לדבר עחגת). And since from then until now nobody has endeavoured to straighten the crooked and to translate the holy Torah into the refined language [i. e. German], the way it is spoken in our generation, [...] I took it upon myself to translate the Five Books of the Torah into decorous and re-

---

32. Moses Mendelssohn, Sefer netivot hashalom: ve-hu hibur kolel hameshet humshei ha-tora im tikun sofrim ve-targum Ashkenazi u-be'ur (Berlin: Starcke, 1783).

33. On Mendelssohn's Bible translation see, e. g.,Werner Weinberg, "Language Questions Relating to Moses Mendelssohn's Pentateuch Translation," Hebrew Union College Annual 55 (1984): 197–242; Nils Römer, Tradition und Akkulturation: Zum Sprachwandel der Juden in Deutschland zur Zeit der Haskalah (Münster and New York:Waxmann, 1995), Ch. 8; and, recently, Abigail Gillman, A History of German Jewish Bible Translation (Chicago, IL: University of Chicago Press, 2017), pt 1.

fined German (בלשון אשכנז המסולסל והמתוקן), such as that spoken in our time, [...] sometimes after the word and sometimes after the sense, to educate [the children] in the correctness of the text and in the idiom of the tongue.³⁴

This sort of assessment of the traditional Yiddish translations of the Bible and other religious texts was quite common among the German-Jewish *maskilim*, who attempted to provide the Jewish community with 'decent' (i. e. *maskilic*) substitutes in pure *Hochdeutsch*.³⁵

What motivated Mendelssohn and his followers to offer the Jews pure German biblical translations has been debated intensively in historical research over the past two centuries: did the *maskilim* expect the German Jews of their time to understand the German language of their translations? Did they hope to utilize these translations to promote the learning of *Hochdeutsch* among their correligionists? Or did they simply wish to establish a model of the Jewish Bible in the German vernacular? In light of the present essay, it seems that some additional, related questions are warranted: Were Mendelssohn and his *maskilic* disciples influenced in their translation project not only by previous Jewish criticism on the Yiddish biblical translations³⁶ but

---

34.

"ואם אולי כוונתו הייתה רצויה / ולדרך ולדרך הסכימו חכמי הדור ההוא / אבל מעשיו בלתי רצויים כלל / כי לא ידע בטיב לשון הקודש / ולא הבין עומק מליצותיה / ומה שהשיג ממנה תרגם בלשון עלגים מקולקל ומשחתד מאוד. תגעל בה נפש הקירא היודע לדבר צחות. ומאז יעד עתה אין איש שם על לב אתקן המעוות / ולתרגם את התורה הקדושה בלשון המתוקן הנהוג ומורגל בדורנו / ... האלתי לתרגז המסולסל והמתוקן / כפי אשר הוא נהוג בימינו / ... פעם תיבה בתיבה / ופעם כפי הכוונה והמשך העניין / לחנכם [את הילדים] נכונת הכתוב ובמליצות הלשון"

Moses Mendelssohn, Or lintivah: ve-hu hakdama lahibur netivot hashalom ... (Berlin: [s.n.], 1783), n.p. English translation largely after Weinberg, "Language Questions," 222, 229. And see also the introduction by Mendelssohn and Solomon Dubno to *Alim litrufah* (1778): "[...] the books of the Bible have been translated into German by Yekutiel ben Isaac Blitz of Witmundt [...] but the translator, though motivated by good intentions, did a poor job, for not only was he ignorant in Hebrew, he did not know German either, and so 'with stammering lips did he speak to his people'!" (English quote from Weinberg, "Language Questions," 229).

35. On the maskilic discourse on Yiddish language and literature in late eighteenth-century Germany, including the maskilic German translations of biblical and other Jewish religious texts, such as the Passover Haggada or the Jewish prayer-book, see, especially, Shmeruk, Sifrut Yidish, Ch. 5; Römer, Tradition und Akkulturation, Ch.8. And see also Jeffrey A. Grossman, The Discourse on Yiddish in Germany: From the Enlightenment to the Second Empire (Rochester, NY: Camden House, 2000), Ch. 2.

36. This internal Jewish criticism appears, for example, very clearly in the introduction of Yekutiel Blitz to his own Yiddish Bible from 1678, where he completely rejects the entire Ashkenazi tradition of biblical translations that preceded him, presenting his own translation as a new and improved Yiddish Bible in both language and style. Although present-day research confirms the novelty and modernizing tendencies of Blitz's translation, it was not perceived this way either by Christian scholars or

also by early modern Christian discussions on the Yiddish Bible? Did the *maskilim* wish to present an alternative not only to the Protestant, German Bible, but also to the Yiddish versions produced by the Protestant missionaries? Did they internalize the centuries-long Christian criticism on the Yiddish Bible, sympathize with it, or respond to it in any way? Did they wish to prove the Christians wrong and show that Jews were, in fact, capable of producing a decent Ashkenazi Bible? To date, these remain open questions. Yet there is no doubt that the mere possibility of such an influence can shed new light on the extent and dynamics of Protestant-Jewish cultural transfer in the realm of the vernacular Bible, and the translation of religious texts, on the very threshold of modernity.

---

by late eighteenth-century maskilim, as was demonstrated in this essay.

CHRISTIAN IMAGES OF THE JEWISH STATE
The Hebrew Republic as a Political Model in the German Protestant Enlightenment
By Ofri Ilany

The past two decades have witnessed a burgeoning interest in political Hebraism, namely, Christian, and especially Protestant, scholarship on the political model of the Old Testament.[1] While Greek democracy and the Roman Republic have long been considered the main sources for modern political thought, recent research has highlighted the crucial role that "the Hebrew republic" played in European thinking. This inquiry has awarded a great deal of attention to philosophical and political writings dealing with the alleged Hebrew constitution and state as they are portrayed in the Hebrew Bible. The bulk of these studies have treated early modern Hebraist texts by Dutch, English, and American writers. In this article, I present the Hebrew state as it appears in the works of several writers of the German Protestant Enlightenment, first and foremost among them the renowned Bible scholar Johann David Michaelis (1717–1791). In what follows, I identify the political themes and ideological contrasts in these descriptions of the Hebrew regime, after which I demonstrate their relation to the mid-to-late eighteenth-century German-European political agenda.

Writings on the Hebrew republic [*respublica Hebraeorum*] drew on an ancient tradition, inaugurated with Josephus's reference to "Moses' politeia" already in the first century CE and continuing with Renaissance and Baroque political philosophy. The rise of German Enlightenment historical criticism, however, refashioned the political portrait of the Hebrew state, imbuing it with additional hues. Unlike

---

1. See, especially, Stephen G. Burnett, Christian Hebraism in the Reformation Era (1500–1660): Authors, Books, and the Transmission of Jewish Learning (Leiden and Boston: Brill, 2012); Allison Coudert and Jeffrey S. Shoulson, eds., Hebraica Veritas?: Christian Hebraists and the Study of Judaism in Early Modern Europe (Philadelphia, PA: University of Pennsylvania Press, 2004); Christoph Bultmann and Lutz Danneberg, eds., Hebraistik – Hermeneutik – Homiletik: Die "Philologia Sacra" im frühneuzeitlichen Bibelstudium (Berlin and Boston: de Gruyter, 2011).

earlier depictions, which tended to abstract the Hebrew regime into a political-philosophical model, Michaelis and his students foregrounded the historical dynamics of the Hebrew state's coming-into-being, focusing on relations between regime, society, and culture.

Hebraism and the Protestant Tradition

Many forms of collective identity that developed in the Christian world took inspiration from the Hebrew model – a political phenomenon that Hans Kohn has termed *Hebraic nationalism*.[2] Adrian Hastings has suggested that the Bible, by supplying an early and influential model of the divine chosenness of a particular people, was "a mirror allowing the imagination and creation of Christian nations."[3] Political use of the Old Testament was expressed as early as the Middle Ages in Ethiopia, Byzantium and the Frankish kingdoms, among many other regions. It was in Protestant Christianity, however, that the biblical idea of divine chosenness became especially dominant.

Martin Luther's (1483–1546) relation to political ideas in the Bible contained several fundamental features that influenced the development of later German Hebraism. Unlike contemporary humanists such as Erasmus (ca. 1466–1536), Luther granted real significance to the Old Testament, particularly the Psalms and the Prophets, as well as – albeit to a lesser extent – the Mosaic law.[4] Luther also went further than Catholic theologians in ridding Christianity of the element of the "law," as embodied in Moses, in favor of "revelation," as embodied in Jesus. Diverging from radical reformers who sought to reinstate Mosaic law, Luther insisted that these laws pertain to the Jews alone, unless they accord with natural law. For Luther, Jewish law had no religious or political validity: while Christian rulers should govern "according to Moses' example," they certainly were not beholden to it.

Accordingly, Luther left no real space for political Hebraism, the political use of the idea of the Hebrew state. In his view, the kingdom of the Jews had been supplanted by Jesus' universal kingdom of heaven, and the prophetic promise of a return to Zion had likewise lost its earthly validity. Luther reinterpreted allegorically and in relation to the Christian gospel geographical terms found in Psalms and the Prophets such as 'Zion.' The Jews, then, were mistaken in their

---

2. Hans Kohn, The Idea of Nationalism: A Study in its Origins and Background (New York, NY: Macmillan, 1944), 41–7.

3. Adrian Hastings, The Construction of Nationhood: Ethnicity, Religion, and Nationalism (Cambridge and New York: Cambridge University Press, 1997), 18.

4. See, for example, Siegfried Raeder, "The Exegetical and Hermeneutical Work of Martin Luther," in Hebrew Bible / Old Testament: The History of Its Interpretation – from the Renaissance to the Enlightenment, ed. Magne Sæbø (Göttingen: Vandenhoeck & Ruprecht, 2008): 363–406.

desire to reinstate their kingdom of old rather than to aspire to the new kingdom Jesus gave to the world.[5] Nevertheless, during Luther's lifetime and even more so after his death, German Protestant preachers began attributing biblical significations to local events as well as interpreting the Bible through contemporary political entities.

Political Theory and the Hebrew Model

As previously mentioned, discussions of the "Hebrew republic" were rooted in an ancient tradition that goes back to Josephus's reference to "Moses' politeia" in his Against Apion.[6] Beginning in the Renaissance, and especially following the Reformation, some of Europe's most influential political thinkers, including the seventeenth-century philosophers Thomas Hobbes (1588–1679), Baruch Spinoza (1632–1677), and John Locke (1632–1704), discussed the Hebrew regime. Several jurists even devoted whole books to singing its praises. Both Hugo Grotius (1583–1645), in his *De republica emendada* (1599) and Petrus Cunaeus (1586–1638), in his *De Republica Hebraeorum* (1617) promoted what they termed "the Hebrew theocracy" as an ideally temperate regime: not democratic, oligarchical, or monarchical.[7]

The historian Frank Manuel has claimed that the corpus of Hebrew republic literature in the seventeenth century was marked by a secularization of the discourse on the Hebrew constitution. According to Manuel, during the Renaissance and the Baroque period, forms of humanist reading that had originated in Greek and Roman Classical Antiquity percolated into a realm previously reserved for theologians. He further argued that, since the Renaissance, scholars have turned the Old Testament into a consecutive secular story. The political vocabulary of Aristotle's *Politics*, in this line of thinking, was the seedbed for conceptualizations of the Hebrews' political history.[8] Recent research, however, has undermined Manuel's secularization model. Eric Nelson, for example, has claimed that, quite to the contrary, seventeenth-century Protestant-European political discourse underwent a process of

5. Ibid., 391.
6. Josephus, Against Apion, trans. John Barclay (Leiden and Boston: Brill, 2007), 263; Hubert Cancik, "Theokratie und Priesterherrschaft: Die mosaische Verfassung bei Flavius Josephus, c. Apionem 2, 157–98," in Religionstheorie und Politische Theologie, ed. Jacob Taubes, vol. 3: Theokratie (Munich and Paderborn: Fink, 1987): 65–77.
7. See Guido Bartolucci, "The Influence of Carlo Sigonio's 'De Republica Hebraeorum' on Hugo Grotius' 'De Republica Emendanda,'" Hebraic Political Studies 2 (2007): 193–210.
8. Frank E. Manuel, The Broken Staff: Judaism through Christian Eyes (Cambridge, MA: Harvard University Press, 192), 118–120. And see also Kalman Neuman, "Political Hebraism and the Early Modern 'Respublica Hebraeorum': On Defining the Field," Hebraic Political Studies 1 (2005): 57–70.

sacralization and theologization.[9] In Nelson's view, the Reformation's religious zeal brought theology into the mainstream of political thought. Accordingly, the Bible became increasingly important as an authoritative source of the divine constitution. For Nelson, the biblical model of the Hebrew republic influenced several key aspects of seventeenth-century political theory, not least among them the loss of the legitimacy of the monarchic regime and the promotion of the idea of agrarian reform for the redistribution of wealth.[10] Nelson went so far as to suggest that seventeenth-century political thinkers celebrated the Hebrew regime's theocratic aspect.[11]

It seems to me that readings of the Hebrew Bible facilitated the development of the modern political vocabulary. Political concepts like 'republicanism,' 'theocracy,' 'monarchy,' and 'agrarian reform' shaped the interpretation of biblical history and, in turn, were shaped by it. As Anthony Smith argues, the transition from religious to modern national self-identification was tortuous but continuous, with biblical images resonating in the self-perceptions of modern nationalist movements.[12]

The Debate on "Hebrew Theocracy"

The term "theocracy," one of the most controversial words in early modern political theory, has been tied to the discussion of the Hebrew republic ever since it was coined by Josephus. According to Josephus, rather than choosing to confer governance on a single ruler, as in monarchy, or on a number of rulers, as in oligarchy, Moses chose "ascribing to God the rule and power."[13] It is hard to tell whether Josephus meant a rule of the priests or a regime in which control is, in fact, in the hands of God himself.[14]

The idea of theocracy preoccupied European political philosophy throughout the early modern period. After the Reformation, certain Protestant political writers in England and the Netherlands leveraged the ideal of Hebrew theocracy as a critique of monarchy as well as a desirable model.[15] Other seventeenth-century philosophers analyzed

---

9. Eric Nelson, The Hebrew Republic: Jewish Sources and the Transformation of European Political Thought (Cambridge, MA: Harvard University Press, 2010), 4–5.

10. On this point, please see below.

11. Nelson, The Hebrew Republic, 4–5.

12. Anthony D. Smith, Chosen Peoples: Sacred Sources of National Identity (Oxford and New York: Oxford University Press, 2003), 9–19.

13. Josephus, Against Apion, trans. John Barclay, 263.

14. Cancik, "Theokratie und Priesterherrschaft," in Taubes, ed., Religionstheorie und Politische Theologie, vol. 3: 65–77.

15. See Adam Sutcliffe, "The Philosemitic Moment? Judaism and Republicanism in Seventeenth-Century European Thought," in Philosemitism in History, eds.

Hebrew theocracy politically without positing it as an ideal. John Locke, for example, referred to this regime in his discussion of religious toleration. Locke characterized Judaism as a religion based on submission to law, in contrast to one based on conscience. This feature, he claimed, was an outgrowth of the Hebrews' ancient regime, which knew no separation between state and religion:

> [T]he Commonwealth of the Jews, different in that from all others, was an absolute Theocracy: Nor was there, or could there be, any Difference between that Commonwealth and the Church. The Laws established there concerning the Worship of one Invisible Deity, were the Civil Laws of that People, and a part of their Political Government, in which God himself was the Legislator.[16]

Locke was neutral on the general notion of Hebrew theocracy, only asserting its inapplicability as a political model for Christians: a Christian commonwealth was impossible, as it would counter the separation of church and state inherent to Christianity itself.[17]

At the same time, Enlightenment criticism of organized religion led to much less favorable depictions of Hebrew theocracy. Spinoza's *Tractatus Theologico-Politicus* offers one such expansive analysis of the Hebrew regime. According to Spinoza, Moses' constitution was a worldly political one, with no special religious significance. The Israelites, who were mired in the state of nature following their Egyptian bondage, elected God as their sovereign in a process similar to the signing of a social contract. Thus, God became the Lord of the slaves, and His laws became the statutes of the state.[18] Spinoza went on to enumerate the advantages of the Hebrews' theocratic model but stressed the corrosive influence of the priests and Levites in its actualization, a clear jab at his own country's Calvinist establishment. He even went so far as to claim that God himself established the clerics' rule to chastise His people following the sin of the Golden Calf.[19]

Adam Sutcliffe and Jonathan Karp (Cambridge and New York: Cambridge University Press, 2011): 67–90; Miriam Bodian, "The Biblical 'Jewish Republic' and the Dutch 'New Israel' in Seventeenth-Century Dutch Thought," Hebraic Political Studies 1:2 (2006): 186–202.

16. John Locke, A Letter Concerning Toleration (London: Awnsham Churchill, 1690), 39.

17. Ibid., and see, for example, Allan Arkush, Moses Mendelssohn and the Enlightenment (Albany, NY: SUNY Press, 1994), 252–3; on political Hebraism in Locke, see also Fania Oz-Salzberger, "The Political Thought of John Locke and the Significance of Political Hebraism," Hebraic Political Studies 1 (2006): 568–92.

18. Benedictus Spinoza, Theological-Political Treatise, ed. Jonathan Israel and trans. Michael Silverthorne (Cambridge and New York: Cambridge University Press, 2007), 74.

19. Ibid., 226.

Spinoza's multifarious impact on the Enlightenment's Republic of Letters has been extensively investigated.[20] His twentieth-century commentators are at odds as to whether his account ought to be read as a wholesale negation of Hebrew theocracy or as an ambivalent – or even favorable – one.[21] Be that as it may, in Spinoza's time, Hebrew theocracy was being reevaluated in a way that would sever this term from its earlier meanings within the Christian tradition.[22] In the writings of Deists and radical Enlightenment authors, theocratic rule went from being a vaunted humanistic ideal to being a political slur. As sworn enemies of the clergy on the one hand, and of the Old Testament on the other, these writers considered theocracy the worst of all possible regimes, one in which the state was abandoned to the hands of corrupt clerics.[23]

Following attacks in the 1730s by anti-clerical and Desist writers, European scholars began composing apologies of theocracy.[24] Prominent among these texts was *The Divine Legation of Moses*, published in 1737 by the English bishop William Warburton (1698–1779). In the book, Warburton claims that God himself established theocracy to deter the Israelites from practicing idol worship. Because the Israelites were used to Pharaonic rule in Egypt, he explained, God took on the title of a local deity, ruling over Judah.[25] Theocracy thus transposed

---

20. On German reactions to Spinoza, see Jonathan Israel, Democratic Enlightenment: Philosophy, Revolution, and Human Rights, 1750 –1790 (Oxford and New York: Oxford University Press, 2013), 690–703; Willi Goetschel, Spinoza's Modernity: Mendelssohn, Lessing, and Heine (Madison, WI: University of Wisconsin Press, 2004), 147–69; Menachem Lorberbaum, "Spinoza's Theological-Political Problem," in Political Hebraism: Judaic Sources in Early Modern Political Thought, eds. Gordon J. Schochet, Fania Oz-Salzberger, and Meirav Jones (Jerusalem: Shalem Press: 2008): 167–88; David Bell, Spinoza in Germany from 1670 to the Age of Goethe (London: University of London, 1984).

21. See, for example, Richard Popkin, "Spinoza and the Three Impostures," in Spinoza: Issues and Directions, eds. Edwin Curley and Pierre-François Moreau (Leiden, New York, and København: E.J. Brill, 1991): 347–58; Theo Verbeek, "Spinoza on Theocracy and Democracy," in Everything Connects: In Conference with Richard H. Popkin. Essays in His Honour, eds. James E. Force and David S. Katz (Leiden: Brill, 1999): 325–38; Ronald Beiner, Civil Religion: A Dialogue in the History of Political Philosophy (Cambridge and New York: Cambridge University Press, 2010), 133–40.

22. See Ernst Michael Dörrfuß, Mose in den Chronikbüchern (Berlin: de Gruyter, 1994), 28–29.

23. For a detailed survey, see Reiner Hülsewiesche, "Theokratie," in Historisches Wörterbuch der Philosophie, eds. Joachim Ritter and Karlfried Gründer (Basel: Schwabe & Co., 1984), vol. 10: 1075–80.

24. Wolfgang Hübener, "Die verlorene Unschuld der Theokratie," in Taubes, ed., Religionstheorie und Politische Theologie, vol. 3: 29–64, here at 55–6.

25. William Warburton, Divine Legation of Moses demonstrated on the Principles of a Religious Deist (London: Gyles, 1738), vol. 5: 51; and see also Sorkin, The

paganism: instead of monarchs becoming deities, the deity became a monarch.[26]

Eighteenth-century English texts dealing with the Hebrew state tended to follow the conventions of the Renaissance-Baroque *Respublica Judaica* tradition, the chronological periodization of the different forms of Israelite governance in accordance with a structure originating in Aristotle's *Politics*. This traditional scheme divided the period between the birth of Abraham and the Babylonian exile into four epochs: patriarchy in the pre-Mosaic period; republic or theocracy during the time of Moses and Joshua; aristocracy during the time of the Judges; and monarchy from Saul to the destruction of the First Temple.[27] As I show later in this article, this periodization was maintained in many mid-to-late eighteenth-century texts. The rise of Enlightenment-era historical-ethnographic criticism, however, shifted the political characterization of the Hebrew state, adding new elements to the debate.

The Image of Moses as Lawgiver in Michaelis

Johann David Michaelis was the leading Bible scholar of eighteenth-century Germany. His *Mosaisches Recht* (1775) crystallized a new narrative regarding the Israelites' origins. Michaelis and his followers replaced the typological interpretation of the Old Testament as a symbol or presaging of Jesus' arrival with a historicist interpretation that situated the Hebrew people within the concrete context of an ancient oriental people. Significantly, critical-historical investigation was not meant to undermine the Bible's authority but rather to buttress its authenticity on new grounds.[28]

In Michaelis' work, the juridical-historical analysis of Mosaic law was interwoven with a comprehensive debate on the Hebrew regime and the figure of Moses as a political personage. As David Wisner has noted, the Enlightenment worldview prominently featured "the cult of the legislator," who appears in contemporary essays as a hero and a founder of the nation.[29] During the course of the eighteenth century, however, the debate went from being about laws' rationality and morality to centering on its efficacy. A good legislator was one who

---

Religious Enlightenment, 44–5.

26. Warburton, Divine Legation of Moses, vol. 5: 37.

27. See, for example, Adam Erdmann Mirus, Politica Sacra (Dresden: Zimmermann, 1717).

28. See also Ofri Ilany, In Search of the Hebrew People: Bible and Nation in the German Enlightenment (Bloomington, IN: Indiana University Press, 2018).

29. David A Wisner, The Cult of the Legislator in France, 1750–1830: A Study in the Political Theology of the French Enlightenment (Oxford: Voltaire Foundation, 1997), 36–8.

succeeded in imposing his judicial system upon his people, demonstrating political aptitude.[30]

As noted above, prior to Michaelis, the Hebrew regime was perceived as a stable political-philosophical model. Taking a different approach, Michaelis stressed the coming-into-being and the dynamism of the Hebrew state as well as the narration of the shifting relation between regime, society, and culture. Influenced by the figure of the enlightened legislator in Montesquieu's *Spirit of the Laws*, Michaelis fashioned Moses as a political genius, designing laws that suited his people's national character, customs, and traditions.

Moses himself, however, in Michaelis's description, was not the subject of these national traits. As a legislator, he towered above the limitations of the people's national sentiments. While the Hebrews' beliefs and practices were conditioned by national character as well as by constraints of time and space, Moses formulated his ordinances from an absolute, rational point of view. Moses, we recall, was not a regular Hebrew but one educated in the Egyptian kingdom. The Egyptians were depicted as a mature, prosperous people quite unlike the childish Israelites. Moses' perspective was thus a function of his higher vantage point: he looked over his people from the heights of the largest and most powerful oriental civilization, a culture famed for its sophistication and refinement. Jan Assmann has shown that European scholars of the period presented Egypt as the fount of all oriental wisdom and the birthplace of all other oriental people's political philosophy.[31] Thus, as scholars began to turn away from the Bible and toward the historiographies of other ancient peoples, alternative genealogies that sought different, pre-Mosaic sources for wisdom and religion began to appear. The source of wisdom was identified with, among other peoples, the Chinese, the Indians, and the Chaldeans – and, of course, with the Egyptians.[32]

Michaelis posited two distinct elements as working in tandem within Mosaic law: a higher stratum of Egyptian juridical principles and a lower stratum, originating in customs developed in a state of natural law. Each of these realms required its own interpretive toolkit, and each was to be carefully contextualized. The Egyptian stratum of Mosaic law was an edict imposed upon the Hebrews from without. In contrast, the ancient customs could be construed through the prism of the mindset of the Arabs – who supposedly descended from the ancient

---

30. Ibid., 51–5.

31. Jan Assmann, Moses the Egyptian: The Memory of Egypt in Western Monotheism (Cambridge, MA: Harvard University Press, 1997), 94–111.

32. On this, see Frank E. Manuel, The Eighteenth Century Confronts the Gods (New York, NY: Atheneum, 1967), 70 –1.

Hebrews. Ethnographic reconstruction of the Hebrews' ancient way of life, based on travel descriptions by European travelers, thus served as an aid for understanding the text.

Moses' Farmer Republic

In Michaelis' thought, the constitution of Moses, that Hebrew-born Egyptian scholar, was not rooted in the negation of imperial-universal Egyptian law but rather in its mixing [*Mischung*] with nomadic customs. One further notes this tendency to combine and assimilate opposing political elements in Michaelis's characterization of the Hebrew constitution's content and goals. In his view, the two fundamental elements of the Mosaic constitution, namely, the suppression of contact with other nations and the outlawing of idol worship, represented a wise melding of the ideal and the practical. Moses realized the first principle through agrarian reform and the second through theocratic rule.

The effort to curb mixing with other nations sprang, according to Michaelis, from a fundamental principle of sovereignty: the main goal of the "Israelite state" was to secure the interests and property of its natal citizens. This was coupled by a second goal: ensuring the Israelites' might as a collective. According to Michaelis, the entrance of foreigners into the land hindered the achievement of the first goal, but the main threat to the people's power was the migration of individuals and groups beyond the boundaries of the land.[33]

Michaelis argues that Moses took two steps to stop the Israelites from intermingling with other peoples: first, he legislated a system of laws meant to distinguish the state's citizens' "way of life" [*Lebensart*] from those of the surrounding peoples. To do so, he turned into law many of the Hebrews' distinguishing customs [*Gewohnheiten*]. In Michaelis's understanding, this was the source of the dietary and impurity laws, meant to discourage communal life with other peoples. He supported this idea with the verse "for I the Lord am holy and have severed you from other people" (Leviticus 20:26), which appears in textual proximity to the dietary laws. The second step, which was intended to firmly implant the Hebrews in their land, granted each head of household an estate. For Michaelis, agrarian reform, which aimed to transform the Israelites from migrants to peasants, lay at the very core of Moses' political revolution. It was precisely because the Israelites had been a people without a land that their legislator sought to forge an exclusive, irreversible, and reciprocal bond between them and the land they were about to conquer. In this move, each of the

---

33. Johann David Michaelis, Mosaisches Recht, vol. 1 (Frankfurt a. M.: J. Gottlieb Garbe, 1775), 176–7.

Israelites was to receive an estate that he was barred from selling permanently. According to Michaelis, this land-based constellation was unknown in other states during Moses' time, when sovereigns would regularly invite foreigners to settle uninhabited tracts of land. However, Michaelis pointed out, it was similar to the situation of the Teutonic tribes at their arrival in Germany.[34]

Thus, in Michaelis' work, the itinerant Hebrews become a kind of national precursor of the Germanic tribes. Moreover, Michaelis uses this notion of a primordial political structure as a means to criticize the absolutist state of his own time. In his view, "the goal of the state that Moses established was the happiness of the people [*die Glückligkeit des Volks*], and not the prince's accomplishments." Moses, then, functioned as a real father to his people – recalling the nation's ancient patriarchs, Abraham, Isaac, and Jacob.[35] Absolutist mercantilism, which subjugated the economy and society to the needs of the monarch, was Michaelis' manifest target. As against this policy, he posited the model of an organic-patriarchal economy, in which the society as a whole functions as an extended household and acts for the greater good.[36]

In Enlightenment-era social theory, an agricultural lifestyle was deemed more advanced than that of nomadic herding. One finds in many German essays on the Hebrew state the idea that the course of Hebrew history featured dynamic sociopolitical development.[37] Just as the history of humanity was depicted as a gradual development from barbarism to political and cultural organization, Hebrew history was portrayed as unfolding in a series of stations along the people's *Bildung*. Historical progress took place in the transition between social stages of development, from hunting to herding to agriculture and then to commerce.[38]

Importantly, the discussion of peasants' legal and economic standing within the state also touched on contemporary issues. The question of agrarian reform was on the intellectual agenda in German states as early as the 1760s, becoming a central topic of discus-

---

34. Ibid, 177.
35. Ibid.
36. See for instance Helen Liebel, Enlightened Bureaucracy versus Enlightened Despotism in Baden 1750–1792 (Philadelphia: The American Philosophical Society, 1965), 9.
37. See Ilany, In Search of the Hebrew People, 59–62.
38. Ronald L. Meek, Social Science and the Ignoble Savage (Cambridge: Cambridge University Press, 1976); John Greville Agard Pocock, Barbarism and Religion: Barbarians, Savages and Empires (Cambridge and New York: Cambridge University Press, 2005), 99–110.

sion among the educated classes.[39] Rural poverty and backwardness prompted clerics, bureaucrats, and scholars to discuss the betterment and education of the peasantry. Fierce criticism was levelled at the eastern Junkers, who still employed the infamous policy of peasant smallholding expropriation [*Bauernlegen*].[40]

In the last quarter of the eighteenth century, the idea that only through the modernization of its agricultural farming structure and the acculturation of the peasants could a civil society emerge in the German municipalities began to gain ground among the educated classes. As Rudolf Vierhaus has shown, significant efforts were put into the foundation of commoner and peasant "patriotic societies," meant to transform the peasants into citizens [*Bürger*]. For many educated members of the bourgeoisie, only a well-established class of free citizens would feel patriotic pride and fight for its homeland.[41]

It is against this background that we ought to read the portion of *Mosaisches Recht* dealing with the "ways of life" [*Lebensarten*], upon which the Israelite state was allegedly dependent. In this sizeable section, Michaelis juxtaposed the structure of Hebrew society to that of contemporary Germany. Unlike German society, he stated, the social organization of the Israelites was not based on a class of independent craftsmen [*Handwerker*]. Thus, the Hebrew state had no real citizen class [*Bürgerstand*].[42] Michaelis's analysis of the Mosaic law detected no division of labor among freeborn Israelis. In fact, this was the case in all of the Bible's historical narratives. Such a situation was expressly set up by Moses: by giving every male member of the people a hereditary estate, to be passed on to his descendants, the legislator sought to prevent them from practicing any occupation but agriculture.[43] By the same token, Moses tried to minimize, to the greatest extent possible, commerce with other lands.

The autarkic ideal and opposition to any economy based on foreign commerce were, yet again, a contemporary concern. One notes these themes in essays by other contemporary writers, among them Johann Gottfried Herder (1744–1803).[44] Like Michaelis, Herder claimed that, of necessity, external commerce brought about a growing

---

39. See Werner Troßbach, Bauern, 1648–1806 (Munich: Oldenbourg Verlag, 1993), 47–50.

40. Walther Hubatsch, Das Zeitalter des Absolutismus: 1600–1789 (Braunschweig: Westermann, 1975), 186.

41. Rudolf Vierhaus, Germany in the Age of Absolutism (Cambridge: Cambridge University Press, 1988), 20.

42. Michaelis, Mosaisches Recht, vol. 1: 179.

43. Ibid., 180.

44. See for instance Harold Mah, Enlightenment Phantasies: Cultural Identity in France and Germany, 1750–1914 (Ithaca, NY: Cornell University Press, 2004), 24–5.

influence from abroad, encouraged citizens to leave their lands, and finally accustomed the people to luxuries, thus throttling their bellicose spirit.[45] According to Herder, the citizens of the Israelite state renounced luxury and supplied their own necessities; traders enjoyed no special privileges; and craftsmanship, handled in the houses of the rich by slaves, was deemed a lowly occupation. Therefore, no distinction between peasants, citizens, and nobles existed among the Israelites.

Discussion of Moses' agrarian law [*leges agrariae*] appeared as early as the seventeenth century in Hebraists' work. Cunaeus, who explicitly based his book *De Republica Hebraeorum* (1617) on Maimonides and even praised the medieval Jewish sage, is an excellent example of this trend. Following the Jewish philosopher, the Dutch Hebraist stressed the fact that the law of the Jubilee, which ordered the return of land to its original owner every fifty years, prevented the acquisition of large swaths of land by a single person.[46] He also claimed that the Mosaic constitution managed to distance citizens from trade, laying the groundwork for an agrarian republic. In his opinion, these agrarian laws resulted in stability, thus contributing more than any other regime to the ideal society depicted in the sixth chapter of Aristotle's *Politics*.

While Michaelis made no explicit reference to Cunaeus, it is likely that he was influenced by the latter's take on agrarian law. Michaelis argued that agriculture was the sole basis on which Moses sought to construct the Israelite state, understood by both scholars as a small-landowner peasant republic.[47] Celebrating the model of free peasants loyal to their homeland, Michaelis held that Moses' agrarian state safeguarded not simply its citizens' loyalty but also their equality and social cohesion. The Germans distinguished strongly between the aristocrat and the peasant but, as the Hebrews had no such division, the word 'peasant' [*Bauer*] was not a derogatory one in the Hebrew political culture. The Israelites knew neither lowly peasantry nor high aristocracy: all were of equal stature. Individuals may have experienced stratification by virtue of status and wealth, but there was no estate of hereditary aristocracy that enjoyed privileges above the rest of the people. This structure endowed the Hebrew state with a "tendency to democracy" [*Hang zur Democratie*].[48]

---

45. Michaelis, Mosaisches Recht, vol. 1, 183–9.

46. See Jonathan R. Ziskind, "Petrus Cunaeus on Theocracy, Jubilee and the Latifundia," The Jewish Quarterly Review, New Series, 68:4 (1978): 235–54; Nelson, The Hebrew Republic, 57–87.

47. Michaelis, Mosaisches Recht, vol. 1: 192.

48. Ibid., 163.

Michaelis certainly stopped short of positing Moses' agrarian law as a model for the German state. Throughout his discussion of the matter, and in keeping with his work's general system, he scrupulously distinguished between Moses' and modern legislators' starting points. However, it is hard to overlook the fact that he used Moses' politics to castigate the social institutions of the German principalities. Against the backdrop of the contemporary debate regarding the peasants' civil betterment, he presented a model of a civil society not based on the urban classes but constructed as an agrarian republic.

The depiction of the Hebrew regime as a "peasant republic" [*Ackerbaurepublik*] was assimilated into German political discourse via, among other channels, Michaelis's influence. Moses' agrarian laws also inspired other important political thinkers of the period, especially Justus Möser (1720–1794). In an extensive discussion on the subject of defense, included in his *Patriotische Phantasien* (1775), Möser claimed that Moses, "the great legislator," put in place the best legal system to safeguard liberty and property. Nonetheless, he presented Moses' political model differently than Michaelis did. While the latter saw the distribution of land to citizens as the basis of the Hebrew state, Möser stressed that Moses strove to make all land the property of God, i. e. of the theocratic state.

Hebrew Theocracy in the German Enlightenment

Michaelis identified Egyptian traces in both Moses' agrarian law and other legal fundaments of the Old Testament. He claimed that Egypt was the model of an autarkic state that did not trade with foreign lands. As Jonathan Hess has shown, Michaelis was censuring the imperialism of his contemporary Western European superpowers and preaching an autarkic politics, that is, a self-sustaining state model.[49] Egypt, he claimed, did not seek to conquer foreign lands but rather based its residents' income on the tilling of their own lands. Michaelis, in fact, bemoaned the fact that his contemporaries were unaware of the Egyptians' advanced legal philosophy, which he thought could aid in modern politics.

Michaelis recognized Egyptian influence in Moses' political strategy [*Stratagem*], namely, the methods he used to make his ideas a reality – by which he meant the way Moses combined religion and politics. Harnessing his political know-how, thus Michaelis, Moses used his people's religious beliefs to put them on the road to sustainable freedom.[50] This marked the birth of a regime identified as a

---

49. Jonathan Hess, Germans, Jews and the Claims of Modernity (New Haven and London: Yale University Press, 2002), 64.

50. Michaelis, Mosaisches Recht, vol. 1: 36.

"theocracy" – as already noted, a loaded term in Enlightenment political thought.

Presenting theocracy in *Mosaisches Recht*, Michaelis wrote that the term "has been discussed many times in the past but has never been properly understood."[51] His reading of it fits his general understanding of Mosaic law. More than as a form of regime, Michaelis regarded the establishment of God's rule as the main political move Moses had taken to eradicate idol worship, which had been so deeply rooted in the people. By crowning Jehovah as king over the people, Moses made idol worship a revolt against the monarchy:

> Moses represented this matter to the Israelites in yet another point of view, which gives it peculiar importance in their polity. By their own free consent, he made God their king; and thus idolatry became a direct rebellion against the state. God was the founder of their state, having delivered them out of Egypt and led them by works of wonder into his own sacred land. He thereby acquired all possible right to be their peculiar sovereign that any man could have had.[52]

The invention of theocracy, like Moses' other moves, was intended to overcome the Hebrews' recalcitrance and limited reason. Knowing his people intimately, Moses understood that they would not be able to comprehend the idea of an abstract God.[53] He therefore described Jehovah as the god of the Israelites but never denied the existence of other gods. Michaelis further claimed that the commandment of circumcision aimed to turn the Israelites into Jehovah's "kingdom of priests and holy nation" – like Egyptian priests, who were also circumcised as part of the dedication to their god. Moses even declared Canaan as the land holy to the god Jehovah, taking advantage of the fact that worship of that deity was already being practiced there. The religious characteristics of Mosaic law were thus subjugated to the lawgiver's pragmatic political considerations, and the Hebrew religion was depicted as a kind of state-ideology.

As historian Ernst Michael Dörrfuß has shown, this description of the Hebrew regime was an answer to the Deists' and *Philosophes*' attacks on theocratic rule.[54] For Michaelis, since Josephus, the Jewish state had been incorrectly classified a special priestly regime. The storied *theocracy* was nothing but a camouflage – a national rite or a

---

51. Ibid., 165; and see also: Dörrfuss, Mose in den Chronikbüchern, 30 –32; Rudolf Smend, Die Mitte des Alten Testaments: Exegetische Aufsätze (Tübingen: Mohr-Siebeck, 2002), 57–8.

52. Johann D. Michaelis, Commentaries on the Laws of Moses, trans. Alexander Smith (London: Rivington, 1814), 188.

53. Ibid.

54. Dörrfuss, Mose in den Chronikbücher, 32.

national religion enacted by the legislator to enable the establishment of a unified, autarkic state. By establishing the communal worship of Jehovah, Moses was able to transcend the divisions among the tribes, bringing them together under a single political rubric. In Michaelis's account, the Hebrew republic was made up of twelve tribes, each of which operated in accordance with its own goals but which were unified through a shared covenant. Michaelis compared this structure to the Troglodytes', Arabs', Scots' and ancient Germans' tribal chieftaincies, as well as to the Swiss confederacy, where thirteen cantons were unified into one republic but were allowed to wage war independently. He called the tribes' council a *Landtag* – like the German Reich's representative assembly.[55] And he further stated on the subject:

> Among twelve republics connected with each other, jealousies could not but sometimes arise; and lesser interests thereby stand in the way of the general welfare. The examples of Holland and Switzerland authorize us to believe that such would be the case; and I need not appeal in confirmation of it to the constitution of the German empire, which, from the inequality of its constituent parts, is perpetually distracted by divisions, and often the scene of intestine hostilities. It will then be granted that this jealousy was at any rate politically probable.[56]

Michaelis identifies the main weakness of the federative Hebrew structure as the power imbalance of the different political units, namely, the tribes. This, he held, was well-known to everyone familiar with German Reich politics. A similar comparison appeared in a book by the Helmerstadt historian Julius August Remer (1736–1802), *Handbuch der algemeinen Geschichte*. It contained few original ideas but was published in multiple editions, and it allows us to follow the changing image of the Hebrew regime. In the first editions of his book, published in the 1780s, Remer characterized the Hebrew regime as aristocratic.[57] In later editions, however, basing himself on Michaelis, he portrayed the regime as a union of twelve tribes under Jehovah's rule.[58] It seems that this spotlighting of the Hebrew state's federative structure was not incidental. Juxtaposing the Hebrew theocracy to the political organization of the ancient Germans, Remer claimed that the German nations' [*die Deutschen Nationen*] form of government was identical to that of the Hebrews, the sole distinguishing factor being

---

55. Michaelis, Mosaisches Recht, vol. 1, 258.
56. Michaelis, Commentaries on the Laws of Moses, 237.
57. Julius August Remer, Handbuch der allgemeinen Geschichte vol. 1 (Braunschweig: Fürstl. Waisenhaus-Buchhandlung, 1783), 54.
58. Remer, Handbuch der allgemeinen Geschichte vol. 1 (Braunschweig: Schul, 1802), 102.

that the former did not receive a code of written law from their gods.[59]

The use of the Old Testament as a political model was one of the most important aspects of German Bible reading in the eighteenth century. German historians and political thinkers extracted central elements in the Hebrew Bible to leverage for their purposes a political system integrated with religion; a conservative constitution based on the people's organic traditions; and a federative regime maintaining the liberty of its constituent tribes. Political Hebraism constituted one of the means they employed to integrate and fashion a political identity in the German-speaking space.

Conclusions: Old-New Nation

Eighteenth-century German biblical scholarship pursued a two-pronged project: to reform methods of Bible research, particularly through the historicization of interpretive methods, and to reassert the authority of the Bible in response to attacks by the radical Enlightenment. The power of theology faculties waned, and fields of study that had earlier been under their jurisdiction were taken up by other faculties. From auxiliary subjects in support of theology, history and philology became independent fields of knowledge. Subsequently, even questions pertaining to the Bible were increasingly addressed through the use of historical and juridical tools, whereby biblical events were explained in circumstantial and natural terms.

Michaelis and his students strove to demonstrate that the Hebrews' customs and laws were not unique but rather had developed in a natural manner, in a similar fashion to those of other nomadic peoples. Yet, it is not the case that Michaelis viewed biblical law as having merely archival value and nothing more. In fact, the German scholar's interpretation oscillates between the biblical world and European society of his own time. In the comparisons and analogies he draws, biblical customs are paralleled with European ones. Biblical law is not necessarily interpreted as an "archeological remnant" of a different time and place; the dilemmas raised by biblical law are at times debated as issues on contemporary European and German society's agenda. Biblical exegesis serves here as a medium for debating timely questions; investigation into Mosaic law becomes a sort of debate on social reform in which Moses is construed as siding with enlightened social reformers. In fact, Mosaic law is touted as the model of a legal codex perfectly adapted to the "national concept" of its subjects.

Michaelis's portrait of the Hebrew regime is mainly drawn from earlier texts dealing with this subject – from Josephus to Warburton.

---

59. Ibid.

However, he stands apart from his predecessors in his portrayal of Moses as the quintessential political reformer. In this understanding, Moses undertook to transform the Hebrews from a population of lawless migrants into a sedentary people whose lives are organized around agriculture, autocracy, and monotheism.

Although national identity was not Michaelis's focal point, national and ethnic categories do feature in his writing. As opposed to earlier Enlightenment legal interpreters, he contended that the substance of the state was not the law but rather the *people*. Under the influence of Montesquieu, Michaelis makes ethnographical distinctions between various peoples, taking into account local variables – above all, climate. Yet these distinctions serve to indicate the relativity of all laws and to demonstrate that they are suited to the conditions of their legislation. Every legal system is preceded by the entity that establishes and cultivates it: the people itself. And, as much as he tries to identify the characteristics of an 'Oriental mentality' in the Mosaic law, Michaelis seeks to decipher in this law the signs of national mentality or, more generally, the traces of its people.

STANDARD-BEARERS OF HUSSITISM OR AGENTS OF GERMANIZATION?
Czech Jews and Protestants Competing and Cooperating for the Religion of the Future, 1899–1918
By Johannes Gleixner

Introduction: Czech Jews and Protestants as Political Allies and Avant-garde of Czechness

In 1932, the "*Svaz Čechů-židů v Ceskoslovenské republice*" (Union of Czech-Jews in the Czechoslovak Republic) published a small booklet on the history of its movement. The text opened with the common ground of Jews and Czechs in the Bohemian land: both were heirs of the Czech reformation, struggling against Catholic Habsburg rule and its attempts at Germanization. Even more than the Czechs, the author claimed, the Jews had to overcome German influences to find their place within the nation. In the end, he concluded, they succeeded, and the democratic and tolerant Czechoslovak republic exemplified this successful Czech-Jewish trajectory. It was strikingly obvious to the author that, although heavily referencing the Czech reformation as an overall concept of the national history, this path did not end in the emergence of a Protestant nation, but in an entirely new religious and national entity.[1]

In a similar vein, František Žilka (1871–1944), a prominent Czech Protestant clergyman, praised the republic's founding president, Tomáš Garrigue Masaryk (1850 –1937), calling him the embodiment of the religious foundations of the Czechoslovak state. Guiding Žilka's religious vision was "humanity," an idea at once Protestant and universal.[2] Only by being religious in this way could a nation succeed.[3]

---

1. Dějiny českožidovského hnutí (Prague: Svaz Čechů-židů v Ceskoslovenské republice, 1932), 1–2.

2. The Czech word used for humanity, "humanita" was a neologism, describing a humanitarian political concept.

3. František Žilka, "Masaryk a Protestantism," in Masarykův Sbornik. Časopis pro Studium Života a Díla T. G. Masaryka. Svazek čtvrtý: T. G. Masarykovi k šedesátým narozeninám. Redigovali Edvard Beneš, František Drtina, František Krejčí

In the present article, I do not wish to dwell on the peculiarities of Czech-Jewish assimilation.[4] Taking a different course, I seek to signal the strong parallels between the positions of two influential groups, one consisting of Czech Protestants and one of Czech Jews, when faced with the question of integration or assimilation into a Catholic or secular vision of society without repudiating one's religious and cultural identity. At the turn of the twentieth century, the two communities were similarly pressured to assimilate into mainstream society, and they formulated analogous answers to the question of their place in a future Czech nation. Thus, they were not only allies out of necessity in that they represented religious minorities in an overwhelmingly Catholic society; rather, they successfully shaped a progressive religious counter-narrative of the modern Czech nation, opposing the position that melded traditionalist religion with secular nationalism.[5]

Ultimately, Czech Protestants and Jews drew on a vision of religious progress that could incorporate different identities while remaining Czech in its essence. In doing so, they joined forces with other progressive activists. Given its size, this religious-political coalition was surprisingly successful in the 1907 Austrian election, the first under universal male suffrage. Moreover, it managed to critically shape the discourse of the new Czechoslovak republic in 1918.

The Czech National Narrative in the 19th Century

The Czech national movement of the nineteenth century prided itself on being a large tent. Unlike other contemporary collective narratives, proponents of the Czech "national rebirth" did not tie their national identity to an existing religious denomination, but rather to a historical one. They managed to do so by pitting themselves against a decidedly Catholic monarchy and invoking a unique Czech tradition of re-

---

a Jan Herben, eds. Vasil K. Škrach and Druhé Vydání, Masarykův Sborník 4 (Prague: Čin, 1930): 106–19, here at 108–9. Of course, there is a multitude of similar sources between 1918 and 1938.

4. This had already been done in comprehensive fashion by several scholars. See Hillel Kieval, The Making of Czech Jewry: National Conflict and Jewish Society in Bohemia, 1870–1918 (Oxford and New York: Oxford University Press, 1988); Martin J. Wein, History of the Jews in the Bohemian Lands (Leiden and Boston: Brill, 2015); Michal Frankl, "Prag ist nunmehr antisemitisch": Tschechischer Antisemitismus am Ende des 19. Jahrhunderts, Studien zum Antisemitismus in Europa 1 (Berlin: Metropol, 2011); Kateřina Čapková, Czechs, Germans, Jews? National Identity and the Jews of Bohemia (Oxford and New York: Berghahn Books, 2012); for an earlier account, see also Martina Niedhammer, Nur eine "Geld-Emancipation"? Loyalitäten und Lebenswelten des Prager jüdischen Großbürgertums 1800–1867, Religiöse Kulturen im Europa der Neuzeit 2 (Göttingen: Vandenhoeck & Ruprecht, 2013).

5. To a certain extent, this was an attempt to incorporate the vision of the first Czech awakeners, from a century earlier, into modern society.

ligious tolerance, dating back to the Czech reformation and its martyr Jan Hus (c. 1370–1415). At the same time, there remained an abiding tension between this vision of an historically tolerant nation and more exclusivist notions of the Hussite past, which could at times be virulently anticlerical and anti-Semitic. Still, until the late nineteenth century, nationalist ideology was restricted largely to the upper strata of society, making it a matter of a small elite.

Alongside the Czech language and the historical rights of the Bohemian estates, Hus and the community of Czech brethren, as well as the whole period of the Bohemian reformation through the battle of White Mountain, became symbols of the growing national consciousness. While the Czech national imagery – like many others – had a distinctly religious ring to it, it did not align with a single religious denomination. In the aftermath of the 1848 revolution, members of the reformed Church had seen themselves as the embodiment of a Protestant nation, but Lutherans stayed within a transnational framework up until 1900.[6] And although many of the fathers of the Czech national rebirth had indeed been Protestants of either the reformed or the Lutheran church, the bulk of the Czech-speaking population remained Catholic.[7] The emerging nationalist framework of the late nineteenth century, therefore, was not that of a Protestant, but rather a non-Catholic (and non-German) nation.[8] This allowed not only Czech-speaking Lutherans and reformed Protestants, but also Czech-speaking Jews, to portray themselves as part of the nation and to craft a singular spiritual symbiosis under the banner of a rather vague and purposely ahistorical Hussite tradition.[9]

---

6. The Czech-speaking Lutheran community nationalized itself much later than the reformed church because the latter encompassed most of the Czech Protestants. It was also the reformed church several nationalist intellectuals converted to. Nonetheless, the notion of one existing national denomination never gained much traction. See Ondřej Matějka, "Čeští luteráni 1861–1918: od emancipace k unii," in Luteráni v českých zemích v proměnách staletí, eds. Jiří Just, Zdeněk R. Nešpor, and Ondřej Matějka (Nakladatel: Lutherova Společnost, 2009), 219–309; Zdeněk R. Nešpor, "Evangelické církve," in Náboženství v 19. století: Nejcírkevnější století nebo období zrodu českého ateismu?, eds. Zdeněk R. Nešpor a kol. (Prague: Scriptorium, 2010): 116–68.

7. Patrick Cabanel points out some interesting similarities to French nationalists of the time; see Patrick Cabanel, "Protestantism in the Czech Historical Narrative and Czech Nationalism of the Nineteenth Century," National Identities 11:1 (2009): 31–43.

8. Martin Schulze Wessel, "Die Konfessionalisierung der tschechischen Nation," in Nation und Religion in Europa: Mehrkonfessionelle Gesellschaften im 19. und 20. Jahrhundert, eds. Heinz-Gerhard Haupt and Dieter Langewiesche (Frankfurt am Main: Campus, 2004): 135–50.

9. Kateřina Čapková and Michal Frankl, "Diskussionen über die 'Judenfrage' in den böhmischen Ländern," in Die "Judenfrage" in Ostmitteleuropa: Historische Pfade

The liberal governments in the 1860s had provided legal security and emancipation to both Protestants and Jews in the Habsburg monarchy.[10] Religious communities were strengthened and showed signs of what could be called 'confessionalization,' when attempting to unify (and nationalize) their services in churches and synagogues as well as establishing control over more outlying communities in the Bohemian lands.[11] It was the situation in these smaller towns that might be said to have driven the changes within each community. This was particularly true for the Protestant and Jewish minorities, whose more progressive wings established themselves in towns like Kolín and Pardubice. In both Czech Protestant and Czech Jewish communities, this development originated within similar socio-cultural groups of intellectuals, whose vision was to integrate into the Czech mainstream national identity by retaining their own spiritual identity.

By the late nineteenth century, a modern society with all the signs of social differentiation and a mass public had begun to emerge in the region. Czech elites had long ago emancipated themselves from what they perceived as an effort to Germanize their culture within the Habsburg Empire. By the late 1880s, within an expanding public, a bourgeois liberal national party – *Česká strana svobodmyslná*, referred to as the 'Young Czech Party' – started to dominate the national discourse as well as elections to the Vienna chamber of deputies.[12] Jews and Protestants alike perceived their fate linked to that of liberal nationalism. This integrative nationalist consensus held until the late 1890s, despite the increasingly overt anti-Semitism and anti-clericalism of an influential wing of the Young Czechs.[13]

---

und politisch-soziale Konstellationen, eds. Andreas Reinke et al., Studien zum Antisemitismus in Europa 8 (Berlin: Metropol, 2015): 183–247, here at 184–6.

10. Although the main Protestant churches were recognized by the Austrian state already in the late eighteenth century, it was the "Protestantenpatent" of 1861 which restricted the (renewed) legal influence of the Catholic church in religious matters for good.

11. The use of the term "confessionalization" in this context is rightfully disputed. For the sake of this argument, it should simply define attempts of intensified institutionalization and homogenization of religious communities. See Wolfgang Häusler, "Die österreichischen Juden zwischen Beharrung und Fortschritt," in Die Habsburgermonarchie 1848–1918, vol. IV: Die Konfessionen, eds. Adam Wandruszka and Peter Urbanitsch (Vienna: Verlag der Österreichischen Akademie der Wissenschaften, 1985): 633–69, here at 655; Zdeněk R. Nešpor, "Náboženské oživení v evangelických církvích ve druhé polovině 19. století," in Christianizace českých zemí v středoevropské perspektivě, ed. Jiří Hanuš (Brno: Matice Moravská, 2011): 268–87.

12. See Bruce M. Garver, The Young Czech Party 1874–1901 and the Emergence of a Multi-Party System, Yale Historical Publications, Miscellany 111 (New Haven and London: Yale University Press, 1978), 190–8.

13. Already in 1873, shortly before his death, František Palacký (1798–1876), doyen of the Czech national movement, had to react to growing tensions in the nation-

By the turn of the century, the two Protestant churches found themselves in parallel positions. Although by and large they had nationalized themselves, they remained minority denominations. Moreover, advocating a Protestant nation placed Czech patriots uncomfortably close to pan-German nationalism and its attacks against the Catholic Habsburg monarchy. In response to this political climate, a group of younger clergymen, advocating an independent, unified, and politically active Czech Protestant church, became increasingly influential. In 1919, this unified "Evangelical Church of the Czech Brethren" (*Českobratrská církev evangelická*) became a reality.[14]

Amongst Jews in the Bohemian lands, a Czech-Jewish assimilationist movement appeared during the late 1870s. They likewise appealed to the national symbolism of the Czech nation and condemned anti-Semitism as a German, rather than Czech, trait. Within the Jewish communities, these "Czecho-Jews" called upon others to speak Czech and integrate into the Czech nation, whose historical character was one of tolerance. At the turn of the century, this movement could claim success in turning a growing number of Bohemian and Moravian Jews towards assimilation: the Czech language began to overtake German in virtually all rural and small-town Jewish communities, Prague as the largest city being something of an exception to this trend. According to this assimilationist movement, Jews were indebted to the Czech nation and should strive to be as Czech as possible.[15]

The National Consensus Falls Apart

By the late 1890s, however, the fledgling mass public threatened to outstrip the liberal nationalists themselves. In the Bohemian lands, but also throughout the whole of Cisleithania, the liberal parties were thrown into crisis. Existing discourses on collective identity shattered.

The most visible change was the decline in influence of the Young Czech Party, which had won several landslide victories in elections between 1889 and 1891 and had become the undisputed representative

---

al movement and stressed his Lutheran background against anticlerical attacks from Národní listy, the most influential newspaper of the national movement, which was accusing his denomination of illoyality; see Ondřej Matějka, "Čeští luteráni 1861–1918: od emancipace k unii," in Just, Nešpor, and Matějka, eds., Luteráni v českých zemích v proměnách staletí, 219–309, here at 266.

14. Seeing as several leaders in both churches advocated a unified church long before, I will use the term "Protestant" in a rather indiscriminate way, when speaking of progressive Lutheran and Reformed Protestants alike.

15. Hillel Kieval, Languages of Community: The Jewish Experience in the Czech Lands (Berkeley, CA: University of California Press, 2000), 151–5; Iveta Vondrášková, "The Czech-Jewish Assimilation Movement and its Reflection of Czech National Traditions," Judaica Bohemiae 36 (2000): 143–59, here at 153–5.

of Czech bourgeois nationalism. Its proponents struggled to compete with the rising mass movements of the working class and rural political Catholicism, and the integrative narrative of an anti-Catholic nation started to lose traction. As the Czech public itself grew, so did the realization that most Czechs were, after all, Catholic. At the same time, German liberalism was supplanted by a growing and aggressive pan-German movement, thus making new forms of cooperation in the Vienna chamber of deputies a necessary political move for Czech liberals.[16] The leadership of the Young Czech Club in Vienna had to navigate among Catholics, socialists and pan-Germans. Some concessions to Catholic parties were required, a consequence of the obstructionist politics of the German nationalists and the intransigence of the workers' movement.[17] Beginning in 1891, the Young Czechs had to strike a balance between their integrative position as the dominant Czech party and their need to compromise with the government. This led to criticism of the party from both within and without, and weakened its grip on the Czech intellectual scene as the only option for political action.[18]

In 1897, the political landscape of Bohemia saw several new currents. Mostly originating in the Young Czech Party, these currents were appalled at the latter's compromise position vis-à-vis the monarchy. These "progressives" (*pokrokáři*), mostly young intellectuals from the small towns of Bohemia, never formed a singular party. Instead, they adhered to a common political framework that perceived politics as a general cultural activity beyond elections and parliament, were sharply critical of the Catholic Church, and had a deep interest in the so called social question.[19]

At the same time, the consensus on what defined Czech history

---

16. The anti-Semitic and anti-Habsburg "Alldeutschen" movement led by Georg Ritter von Schönerer (1842–1921) did exceptionally well amongst the Germans in Bohemia, winning a record of 21 seats in the 1901 elections. Although short-lived, its impact on the Czech political public should not be underestimated.

17. See Karel Kramář, Anmerkungen zur böhmischen Politik. Aus dem Böhmischen übersetzt von Josef Penízek (Vienna: Konegen, 1906), 24.

18. For a still relevant overview, see Otto Urban, Die tschechische Gesellschaft 1848–1918, Anton Gindely Reihe zur Geschichte der Donaumonarchie und Mitteleuropas 2 (Vienna, Cologne, and Weimar: Böhlau, 1994), 626–34.

19. See Jan Havránek, "Počátky a kořeny pokrokového hnutí studentského na počátku devdesatých let 19. století," Acta Universitatis Carolinae – Historia Universitatis Carolinae Pragensis. Příspěvky k dějinám Univerzity Karlovy 2:1 (1961): 5–33; Karen J. Freeze, "The Progressive Youth of the 1890s: Children of the December Constitution," in Bildungsgeschichte, Bevölkerungsgeschichte, Gesellschaftsgeschichte in den böhmischen Ländern und in Europa: Festschrift für Jan Havránek zum 60. Geburtstag, eds. Hans Lemberg et al., Schriftenreihe des österreichischen Ost- und Südosteuropa-Instituts 14 (Vienna: Verlag für Geschichte und Politik, 1988): 275–85.

(and therefore Czech identity) was becoming increasingly fragile. Starting with a debate on supposedly historical Czech manuscripts, which proved to be fabrications from the early nineteenth century, the intellectual public contested the historical meaning of the "Czech question." This sparked a discourse that lasted for decades. Basically, the issue boiled down to that of historical truth versus the historical meaning of the Czech nation.[20] Embedded in this controversy was the question who belonged to this nation and who could enter it.[21]

The rural masses, who heretofore had been little more than objects of intellectual nationalist visions, started to enter the public sphere. As the nation grew, so did the pressure on minorities to assimilate. The rise of anti-Semitic movements across the monarchy was one reaction to the crisis of liberalism and political mass mobilization through a gradually expanding electorate.[22] The anti-Semitism was furthered by the peculiar place Jews found themselves in several Bohemian and Moravian cities, where they could tip the electorate to either a German or a Czech majority. At one moment they might be viewed as coveted keys to local majorities, and at the next traitors to the national cause.[23] The Czech nationalist movement, hoping to overcome Austrian-German supremacy, put pressure on Bohemian Jews to fall in line with the national cause and was quick to scapegoat them in case of political defeat.[24] However, these demands allowed only for complete assimilation and neglected the possibility of a Czech-Jewish agency. While the Czech milieu did not see a full-blown racially charged anti-Semitism like the German-Austrian one, it did develop a more exclusive vision of Czechness. Whether the anti-Semitic undertones centered on political accusations of Jews as agents of Germanization or on popular Catholic stereotypes, the effect was the same: a growing number of

---

20. Miloš Havelka, "Spor o smysl českých dějin 1895–1938," in Spor o smysl českých dějin 1895–1938, ed. Miloš Havelka (Prague: Torst, 1995): 7–43, esp. 10–24.

21. Already during the 1850s self-styled Czech patriots had attacked Bohemian Jewish publicists like David Kuh (1819–1879) for casting doubt on the veracity of the manuscripts. See Kieval, Languages of Community, 92–3.

22. Pieter M. Judson, Exclusive Revolutionaries: Liberal Politics, Social Experience, and National Identity in the Austrian Empire, 1848–1914 (Ann Arbor, MI: University of Michigan Press, 1996), 223–25. The period of 1897–1907 was a transitional one, starting with the expansion of the census franchise and ending with the 1907 elections by universal male suffrage.

23. See Markéta Weiglová, "Jews as a Barometer of the National Struggle in Bohemia and Moravia, 1890–1910," Judaica Bohemiae 43 (2007): 93–120, here at 106–8.

24. Hillel Kieval, "Nationalism and Antisemitism: The Czech-Jewish Response," in Living with Antisemitism: The Jewish Response in the Modern World, ed. Jehuda Reinharz (Hanover, N.H.: Brandeis University Press by University Press of New England, 1987): 210–33, esp. 213–5.

Czech elites denied that Jews could be a part of the nation. Consequently, Czech anti-Semitism eventually did develop into a political force of its own.[25] Moreover, several of the parties that emerged in the late 1890s were – like the National Social Party – quite willing to use anti-Semitic slogans as an electoral rallying cry. The rise of political Catholicism dealt another blow to the political influence of traditional liberal nationalism.

Protestants, of course, were in a much stronger position. Still, the quest for the meaning of Czech history started to reframe the narrative of "Hussites vs Catholics." A new generation of historians pointed to the importance of the Catholic phases in Czech history, claiming that one ought to affirm Czech history as a whole or refrain from claiming historical truths about the nation.[26] This approach jeopardized the privileged position of Czech Protestants, who could argue for a Protestant interpretation of history more openly than Czech Jews, but nonetheless had to face a growing Catholic Czech nationalism.

Convergence at the Turn of the Century, 1897–1904

By 1897, some Czech Jews and Protestants had entered a converging trajectory with the progressive movement: they all resisted the emerging alliance between the Young Czech Party and the Catholic rural masses, and countered the vision of an agnostic, but practically Catholic, nation with that of a second Czech spiritual awakening, akin to the national rebirth in the first half of the nineteenth century. Yet, a true political alliance between these groups remained unlikely: Jewish assimilationists were aware of the anti-religious stance of most progressives, including borderline anti-Semitic attacks on "Mosaic clericalism"; Protestants – especially members of the reformed church – still saw themselves as the one and only truly Czech denomination; and, apart from their virulent anticlericalism, most progressives were unconcerned with questions of religion and felt satisfied with a vague need for a cultural renaissance.[27]

A succession of events that took place between 1897 and 1904, however, changed everything. In this period, progressive liberal thought was linked with religion, creating a movement, which – although small in numbers – catered specifically to religious minorities and proved influential. Additionally, a progressive framework and

---

25. Frankl, Prag ist antisemitisch, 16–7.
26. Miloš Havelka, "Spor o smysl," in Spor o smysl českých dějin 1895–1938, 10–24.
27. Under the manifest of "Česká moderna" (Czech modernity), several influential writers of the young generation had decried the lack of culture in the Czech liberal establishment.

its proponents became dominant within each religious community, transcending traditional notions of institutionalized religion.

The Hilsner Affair and the Emergence of a Progressive Czech-Jewish Movement

The first event that rattled traditional political allegiances was the Hilsner affair of 1899. Since the early 1890s, the public mood in Bohemia was prone to anti-Semitic outbursts. Following a broad campaign of nationalists for Czechs to patronize Czech businesses (*svůj k svému*), Jewish businesses were targeted for public violence. The situation in Prague was especially volatile, as the city had become the focal point of the Czech-German conflict. Already early in 1897, the Young Czech Party had fielded an openly anti-Semitic candidate for the upcoming elections to the chamber of deputies, hoping to absorb the expanded electorate.[28] As a consequence of the introduction and subsequent retraction of the language ordinances by the Badeni government in 1897, first Germans, and then Czechs in Prague had rioted. Jewish businesses and buildings bore the brunt of these assaults.[29]

The peak of this anti-Semitic wave was probably the well-known Hilsner affair, which marked a turning point in the relations of Czech Jews and the Czech national movement.[30] In 1899, after a young girl was found dead in the East Bohemian town of Polná, the local authorities arrested a Jewish vagabond, Leopold Hilsner, and accused him of murdering her in line with Jewish rituals. Accusations of ritual murder were still quite common in the region, particularly in rural Catholic areas. What made the Hilsner case special was that the authorities seemed to endorse the blood libel.[31] Subsequently, the whole trial became an anti-Semitic showcase, with not only Hilsner but all Jews on trial, as it were.[32] One of Hilsner's few public defenders was

---

28. Hillel Kieval, "Nationalism and Antisemitism," 216–7. There are, of course, obvious parallels to the rise of Karl Lueger (1844–1910) in Vienna.

29. Kateřina Čapková and Michal Frankl, "Diskussionen über die 'Judenfrage' in den böhmischen Ländern," 224–7.

30. To put it into context, already at the time there was talk of it as the "Austrian Dreyfus affair," with several obvious parallels in how both cases were being treated in the public. As T. G. Masaryk, one of the main protagonists of the affair, noted, it had an international impact that none of the participants foresaw. For a detailed reconstruction as well as the historical context of the affair, see the articles in Miloš Pojar, ed., Hilsnerova aféra a česká společnost 1899–1999. Sborník přednášek z konference na Univerzitě Karlově v Praze ve dnech 24.–26. listopadu 1999 (Prague: Židovské muzeum v Praze, 1999).

31. As Kovtun points out, such cases did show up in court periodically but were usually rejected by the authorities. Jiří Kovtun, "Historická dimenze Hilsnerova případu," in Pojar, ed., Hilsnerova aféra a česká společnost 1899–1999, 17–23, esp. 17–8.

32. Without further proof it was assumed that Hilsner had been helped by two –

a Czech university professor named Tomáš Garrigue Masaryk, who was a well-known public intellectual and supporter of the progressive cause. He intervened after Hilsner was already convicted of the murder, but accomplished the reopening of the case mainly by attacking the idea of ritual murder as scientifically absurd.[33]

As the Young Czech Party showed no sign of reining in its more anti-Semitic members or condemning the affair, the Czecho-Jewish assimilationist movement was thrown into crisis. After its main newspaper, the *Českožidovské listy*, continued to support the nationalist movement even in the face of the latter's support of anti-Semitic tendencies, a group of young Czech Jewish intellectuals, led by Eduard Lederer (1855–1944), Viktor Vohryzek (1864–1918), and Bohdan Klineberger (1859–1928), broke away. The breakaway group called itself "*Rozvoj*" (Advancement) and published a journal of the same name.[34] Based in the Bohemian town of Pardubice, *Rozvoj* still advocated Czech-Jewish assimilation, but reconfigured it by speaking of the acculturation of a separate Jewish identity within a national framework.[35] It also pointed to the need for new and more modern political allies: Czech liberals had betrayed the teachings of Hus and abandoned the path to enlightenment that these teachings had provided. The solution was the strengthening of progressivism: anti-Semitism, after all, was essentially a religious problem, born of reactionary clericalism.[36] As Vohryzek argued in the inaugural edition of the *Rozvoj* journal, the key to assimilation (or rather, acculturation) for Czech Jews was religion.[37]

The "Realist" Party as a Religious-political Project and its Protestant Supporters

Masaryk's defense of Hilsner made him an outcast in most nationalist circles. Apart from the Czech-Jewish movement, only the socialists and a small but determined group of loyalists stood by his side. With the Hilsner affair still in full swing in the spring of 1900, Masaryk and his followers founded yet another progressive party under the name "*Česká strana lidová*" (Czech People's Party), known as "Realists."

supposedly Jewish – accomplices, strengthening the anti-Semitic nature of the case.

33. Tomáš G. Masaryk, Nutnost revidovati process Polenský (Prague: Času, 1899). Masaryk went so far as to actually take some lessons in anatomy, travelling anonymously to Vienna.

34. Vondrášková, "The Czech-Jewish Assimilation Movement and its Reflection of Czech National Traditions," 151–2.

35. Weiglová, "Barometer," 94–5.

36. Kieval, Languages of Community, 168–75.

37. Viktor Vohryzek, "Několik slov úvodem," Rozvoj: Týdenník českých pokrokových židů 1:1 (1904): 1–3.

Although plans for such a party had existed for some years, its founding was inevitably tied to the Hilsner case.[38] Masaryk's prominence in the affair and his leading role in the Realist party earned them the anti-Semitic moniker "the Hilsner Party" among the nationalist press. This was at least true insofar as the progressive Rozvoj group enthusiastically welcomed its arrival.[39]

The Hilsner affair, however, tends to overshadow two other important factors in the founding of the party. There was a distinct Protestant influence present, with progressive Protestant clergy such as the Calvinist Čeněk Dušek (1843–1918) and the Lutheran Ferdinand Hrejsa (1867–1953) instrumental in its inauguration.[40] Several leading members of the Realist party, such as Jan Herben (1857–1936), Žilka, and Masaryk himself, were known to be members of the reformed church.[41]

The party presented an elaborate program which stood out in one main respect: it stressed the need for a unifying, encompassing religious reform that would overcome existing traditional beliefs not only in a scientific but also more moral way. While the program conceded that the party had a certain affinity to the progressive movement and Protestantism, it pointed emphatically to the failure of all positive religions and denominations. Catholicism, Protestantism, and Judaism were all full of "halfness" (*polovičatost*), unfit for modern society. Even more interesting, although the program stressed the religious freedom of the individual, it paradoxically demanded a kind of modern religious politics.[42] Masaryk, who wrote the program himself, had expanded on these ideas in a series of programmatic books published during the 1890s. They all came down to an interpretation of Czech history as an attempt to live according to "humanist" principles. The embodiment of those principles was the Czech reformation; as such,

---

38. Johannes Gleixner, "Menschheitsreligionen": T. G. Masaryk, A. V. Lunačarskij und die religiöse Herausforderung revolutionärer Staaten (Göttingen: Vandenhoeck & Ruprecht, 2016), 79–86.

39. One of the founding fathers of the Czech national movement, František Ladislav Rieger (1818–1903) referred to the Realist party as a Jewish, and therefore destructive, party; see Roland J. Hoffmann, T. G. Masaryk und die tschechische Frage, Veröffentlichungen des Collegium Carolinum 58 (Munich: Oldenbourg, 1988), 221–2, here at 239; Kieval, Languages of Community, 198–203.

40. "The Realists lean towards Protestantism" commented the independent progressive journal Osvěta lidu. "České "Pryč od Říma"?," Osvěta lidu: Pokrokové noviny pro severovýchodní a východní Čechy 6, no. 94 (1901): 4; See also Hoffmann, T. G., 262.

41. Many of them, Masaryk included, left the Catholic church and joined the reformed church. This was a political statement as much as it was a religious one.

42. Rámcový program české strany lidové (realistické) (Prague: Nákladem výkonného výboru české strany lidové, 1900), 77–9.

the Czech question was not only one of language, culture, and political power, but at its heart religious in nature. Czechs, then, should strive to become religiously enlightened. Masaryk's notion of Hus and the reformation was ahistorical and universal.[43] Nonetheless, he claimed to have distilled the scientific core of modern religion. He demanded a Czech version of the "Los von Rom" (Away from Rome) movement, which saw some success in German-speaking areas of Bohemia, insisting that the new church must be religious, albeit not identical to the existing Protestant churches.[44] This paradoxical demand makes sense if it is understood as an attempt to craft a new majority discourse based on religious convictions without referring to existing denominations and religions.

At first, the Realists were a loose collection of groups preoccupied with progressive religious and cultural topics. Apart from the party founders, intellectuals from Prague, this included progressive Jews and Protestants but also Free Thinkers and Atheists. Emanuel Chalupný (1879–1958), a founding member of the party and later its sharp critic, noted how it consisted of three groups, each one of which viewed the party as a vessel of its specific ideas: Protestants, Jews, and "original" Realists with a cultural interest in progress. For Chalupný, the party lacked any consistent ideology, and was united only in mutual interest and an almost religious belief in its own notion of progress.[45] Although his perception of the party's most important wings was accurate, Chalupný was nonetheless motivated by a strong anti-Protestant bias, and underestimated the religious content of the party's program. Early on, Protestant Realists tried to push for an official allegiance to the reformed church, arguing that being a reformed Protestant was the closest one could come to a synthesis of religion and progress in the absence of a true future religion.[46] Echoing the party's program, one Realist argued that simple political parties could not succeed in modern times. Only movements with an "ideal" (like Social Democracy) had a future. The Realist party, then, should work as an avant-garde movement to the "Protestantization" (*poprotes-*

---

43. See, among other sources: Tomáš G. Masaryk, Jan Hus. Naše obrození a naše reformace (Prague: Čas, 1896).
44. See Tomáš G. Masaryk, Ideály humanitní a texty z let 1901–1903, Spisy T. G. Masaryka 25 (Prague: Masarykův ústav a Archiv Akademie věd ČR, 2011), 191. This was a curious demand, as conversions to the Lutheran church were precisely the point of the pan-German "Los von Rom."
45. Emanuel Chalupný, Vznik české strany pokrokové. Historické vzpomínky. Dle původních pramenů (Tábor: St. D. Kubíček, 1911); Zlváštní otisk z "Českého Jihu" 1–2; 54–5.
46. See František Žilka, "Z vývoje a výsledků moderní vědy bohoslovecké," Naše Doba 9 (1902): 349–50.

tantštění) of the people.⁴⁷ Other Protestant Realists opined that party members should at least leave the Catholic church if not outright join one of the Protestant denominations. This idea clashed not only with the Jewish Realists but also with those close to the Czech Free Thought (*Volná myšlenka*), such as Chalupný, who favored the legal status of "without confession" as most closely approximating religious enlightenment.⁴⁸ In turn, Lederer, one of the leading Jewish Realists, pointed out that he and other progressive Jews were perfectly content with conversion to a truly progressive religion, but so should be the Protestants, as their belief was similarly unfit to capture the religious spirit of the Czech nation.⁴⁹ In this remark, Lederer rehearsed the charge made by other progressives who complained about the Protestant goal of transforming every belief but their own.⁵⁰

The Hus Affair of 1903: Protestants as National Outcasts

The year 1903 witnessed the Protestants' own excommunication from the Czech nation, thwarting their self-perception as an avant-garde of Czechness. Being part of an integrative narrative of progress was not the same as dictating it, as the Czech Jews were all too aware. The Protestants, however, had to learn this lesson the hard way by squaring off against the majority discourse of Czech nationalism, which so far had paraded them as progressive paragons of the anti-Catholic nation.

When, on 6 July 1903, the foundation stone of a long-planned statue of Jan Hus on Prague's Old Town square was laid, a Young Czech speaker celebrating the occasion tried to affiliate the Hussite tradition with Catholicism. The statue of Hus was being erected right across the Marian column, the symbol of Catholic reign in Prague – a fact that in his view signaled a mutual belonging. Both the Protestant press and the Realists responded with fury, claiming that the Young Czechs had abused the Czech reformation and made a political pawn

47. "Postavení strany čes. lidové v politické organisací národní (z kruhu rádců české strany lidové)," Přehled 1:21 (1902): 336–7.
48. "O organisaci české strany lidové (Schůze politického klubu 29. dubna)," Přehled 1:22 (1902): 367–77.
49. Eduard Lederer, "Die čechisch-jüdische Assimilation," Čechische Revue 2 (1908): 404–7. Both Lederer and Vohryzek went so far as to put Judaism above the Christian creeds in the ranking of progressive beliefs. See also Vohryzek, "Několik slov úvodem": 2; Interestingly, conversions from Judaism to Protestantism were apparently much more common in Austria (especially Vienna) than in the Czech lands. See Astrid Schweighofer, Religiöse Sucher in der Moderne: Konversionen vom Judentum zum Protestantismus in Wien um 1900, Arbeiten zur Kirchengeschichte 126 (Berlin, Munich, and Boston: de Gruyter, 2015), 64–74.
50. Gustav Tichý: "Etická kultura, náboženství a mravnost," Rozhledy 14 (1904): 966–9.

out of its martyr. A simultaneous celebration of Realists and leading Protestants was lauded as the true embodiment of the spirit of Jan Hus.[51]

Six days later the nationalist press struck back, remarking on the proximity of the Realists to the "Los von Rom," a pan-German Protestant movement led by German nationalists and advocating a greater German empire. "*Národní listy*," the main organ of the Young Czech Party, attacked the Realists as traitors to the national cause. Although the charge itself was ridiculous, Masaryk and especially Dušek had been in close contact with German Protestants from organizations like the "International Committee for the Evangelization of the Bohemian Lands," owing to their prioritization of religious cooperation over national conflict.[52] When a leading Realist Protestant, Jan Herben, was seen entering the German "casino" in Prague to meet with a German Protestant activist, the nationalists finally found him caught in the act: behind the Realists' "religiousness," they alleged, was a plot to lure the Czechs to German Protestantism. Gleefully, they pointed to the hypocrisy of criticizing the Young Czechs' political efforts to compromise with Catholic parties but at the same time embracing a pan-German Protestant plot to subvert the monarchy.[53]

Anti-Protestantism further fueled the already-raging anti-Semitic blaze ignited by several Catholic nationalist authors. In one striking example, the writer Rudolf Vrba (1860 –1939) linked the Protestant "Away from Rome" to an international Jewish plot and saw Austria besieged by both German-Protestant infiltrators and Jewish intellectuals.[54] In the eyes of the Catholic-nationalist consensus, Protestants and Jews alike were excluded from the true Czech nation, although both groups – and especially the progressive Czech-Jewish movement – were clearly working against the Germanization of their communities. Still, the image of Jews as an avant-garde of Germanness in the Bohemian lands, dating back to the middle of the century, persisted. Vrba's exploitation of prejudices against supposedly foreign agents who sought to undermine the Czech nation from within is an interesting example of the fluidity of anti-Semitic stereotypes, with Protestants joining Jews as national traitors.

Although Herben defended himself, the damage was already done

51. Čas, "Husovy oslavy,", July 8, 1903.
52. Lothar Albertin, "Nationalismus und Protestantismus in der österreichischen Los-von-Rom-Bewegung um 1900" (Diss. Phil. University of Cologne: 1953), 123–51.
53. Hoffmann, T. G. Masaryk, 253–5.
54. Rudolf Vrba, Österreichs Bedränger: Die Los-von-Rom-Bewegung. Studien über politische, religiöse und sociale Zustände der Gegenwart (Prague: Selbstverlag, 1903), 632.

and the Realist party struggled to distance itself from the perception of being the political arm of the Protestant churches. An official declaration by the executive committee proclaimed a Czech "Away from Rome" with no association to any existing church. Furthermore, the party stressed its independence from any religion. It repeated its programmatic hostility to any form of "clericalism," explicitly including Protestant, Jewish, and even Orthodox types.[55] This official distancing from organized religions belies its internal discussions, in which the Protestant's overidentification with the party constituted the main problem.

A Political Coalition of Religious Dissent

It came down to Masaryk to settle questions of ideology, as no other Realist matched his authority. Already in 1901, Masaryk seemed keenly aware of the Realist party's position as a political beacon for incompatible religious dissent: when a Protestant supporter complained that the party's official paper, *Čas*, was too "Philo-semitic" and not Protestant enough, Masaryk replied that indeed it was sometimes unbalanced in its polemics, but more importantly, it was the only place in the Bohemian lands where one could talk seriously about religion. Slyly, he added that for Protestants there was no other political newspaper anyway. Even more interestingly, he pointed to the main editor of *Čas*, Herben, a known Protestant Realist, as proof of the paper's religious sincerity, while simultaneously distancing his own conviction from that of Herben.[56]

As the annual Hus celebrations of 1904 approached, Masaryk felt the need to clarify the party's position on religion, lest there be another scandal. Expanding on the paradoxical formula of religion being a private matter but not an individual one, he delivered a speech at a gathering of the Realists' political club (its *de facto* executive committee) on 25 April 1904. In it, he stressed the demand for political freedom as fundamental to the Realist program. Further explaining his own conviction, he affirmed the need for religion, but for the first time openly denied the scientific possibility of Christian revelation.[57] This speech was received with marked ambivalence: while a younger group of activists with a decidedly atheist stance was unsatisfied that Masaryk did not outright advocate atheism,[58] the 'religious' Realists seized the moment to fuse the party's vague religious-political program

---

55. "Řím a Berlin," Přehled 1:33 (1902–1903): 533–6.
56. AÚTGM (Archive of the Masaryk institute Prague), fond TGM Kor I, kr. 29, l. 44.
57. Čas, "Pro svobodu svědomí," June 26, 1904.
58. Hoffmann, T. G. Masaryk, 261–2.

with their own goals, thus completing the party's transformation into a political conduit for religious dissent. Overall, they expressed relief that Masaryk had finally spoken openly on these issues, even if his denunciation of biblical revelation was in no way acceptable to believers.[59]

Interestingly, while the whole Hus affair placed into question the Realist-Protestant alliance, in the long run, the pact was strengthened. Protestants such as Dušek had long realized that Masaryk's inchoate religious convictions were not actually Protestant. Masaryk himself was at times highly critical of Protestantism, once claiming to feel emotionally more like a Catholic.[60] Dušek and other Protestants clergymen sharply disagreed with him from a theological point of view, while stressing that the Realist party remained the only political possibility for Protestants – the culturally "Catholic" Young Czechs and their shallow anti-clericalism were hardly an option.[61] As one progressive (and later Realist) paper commented, the affair led to the "full emancipation of the Czech Protestants from the Young Czechs."[62]

For the progressive Czech Jews, Viktor Vohryzek commented on the speech: he, too, claimed relief that the party's leader had finally spoken up on the "religious question." Although he conceded that Masaryk still had not provided the "promised religious-philosophical thesis, the basis of a new and pure religion, scientifically worked out and reasoned," he nevertheless was optimistic about the matter. In his view, by stripping existing religion of its non-scientific, nonmodern elements, the religious progressives of each denomination, and with them even monists and atheists, would end up together.

Additionally, Vohryzek rightly observed the split between an agnostic notion of progress, which was content to criticize the church and religion in general, and the "truly progressive" Realists, who went beyond simple negativity and for whom traditional beliefs like Christianity and Judaism remained historical, if flawed, vessels of true religiosity. To drive home his point, Vohryzek approvingly quoted the evangelical "*Hlasy ze Siona*" (Voices from Zion) that a future religion still had to include some kind of formal confession (*konfesse*). To be (in a strictly legal sense) "without confession," therefore, was no indication of positive progressiveness; one had to think and act in its spirit as well. And, turning the tables on Protestants and atheists alike, he noted that Judaism, with its lack of clerical structures and its everyday

---

59. Čas, "Pro svobodu svědomí".
60. See Čas, "Prof. Masaryk v Katolických listech," January 30, 1902. Masaryk was born into a devout Catholic family.
61. Matějka, "Čeští luteráni 1861–1918," 283.
62. Hoffmann, T. G. Masaryk, 258.

adherence to moral laws, was already very close to such a religion of the future. For progressives like him, "Mosaism" was neither a belief nor a confession in the accepted sense. "We will defend our Realism against old denominations and new ones, if they are not in agreement with it," he finished.[63]

In this respect, progressive Czech Jews were closer to the core of the Realist movement than many Czech Protestants. Like Masaryk and his disciples, and despite stressing a "positive" spirituality, figures such as Lederer and Vohryzek displayed an intellectual and utilitarian understanding of religion. As Hillel Kieval notes, their pronounced "anti-secularism" came with a distinctly casual attitude toward actual religious practice.[64] This was true for some Realist Protestant intellectuals like Herben as well. In contrast, it was mostly clergymen, like Hrejsa and Dušek, who promoted progressive and political Protestantism. As such, these Protestants had a more ambivalent relationship with the Realists, grasping the need for this cooperation but aware that the religious-political vision of the Realists did not necessarily align with their own vision of a unified Czech Protestant church. Moreover, the progressive wing of the Czech-Jewish movement could not claim to represent the majority of Jews in the Bohemian lands, while the combined Protestant churches' membership did indeed form a majority of Czech Protestants.

In the end, just as Vohryzek observed, those who split from the party were Free Thinkers and atheists such as Chalupný and other so-called "Young Realists," centered around the journal *Přehled*, who were disappointed that religious influences remained strong. Other progressives attacked both the Realists and the Protestants for their purportedly unfounded alliance.[65] Unsatisfied with Masaryk's eternally obscure answers, they demanded to know the specifics of the Realist program of a future religion.

A Future Religion as an Inclusive and Transformative Political Program: Jews and a United Protestantism as Standard-bearers of "Hussitism"

It is worth taking a closer look at why the Realist party program, in all its opacity, was so attractive to religious dissent. The peculiar insistence that societal problems stemmed from religious ones seemed out of place in the other progressive parties, most of which were content

---

63. Viktor Vohryzek, "O svobodě náboženské a volnosti přesvědčení," Rozvoj: Týdenník českých pokrokových židů 1:27 (1904): 1–2.

64. Kieval, Languages of Community, 174.

65. See Karel J. Rohan, "Moderní stoupenci Husovi," Rozhledy. Revue umělecká, sociální a politická 14 (1903–1904): 1–7; 31–40; 59–66.

with aggressive anticlericalism. However, in maintaining that while existing denominations and religious beliefs were flawed, religion itself was not, the Realists extended an irresistible offer to religious minorities to become part of a new religious whole. To frame the Czech question in terms of modern man and religion, as Masaryk did, offered a new option of joining the nation by transforming it. This contrasted with his quite exclusive vision of the nation, as expressed in an interview with Rozvoj, where he declared that the Jews' religious identity was an obstacle in them becoming Czechs.[66] It ought to be borne in mind, however, that the most salient feature of Masaryk's and the Realists' vision of the nation was its exclusion of average Czechs and even the reformed church, thus levelling the playing field for all. As Masaryk himself said, the Realists were not a party of the masses and could never become one; nonetheless, they served as an avant-garde to the whole nation.[67]

At the same time, the fusion of religious convictions with political action allowed the progressive wings of Czech Protestantism and Judaism to surmount traditional institutions, if for conflicting reasons. Progressive Czech Jews and Protestants agreed that the battle for a renewed religiosity was not being fought in the churches and synagogues, but in the political arena. Both felt – albeit for different reasons – the need to overcome institutionalized religion.

The leaders of the Protestant churches, Dušek and Hrejsa, understood that their vision of a unified church which called for the fusion of existing communities did not go far enough. As they aspired to become a true Czech church, they needed to address the non-Protestant masses. The Protestantization of the Czechs would happen, in their view, not through preaching but through political action. Unified Czech Protestantism, then, was at its core a political project that required a political entity. The appeal of the Realists in turning people away from old beliefs and towards a more modern religion seemed to suit the bill.

Similarly, progressive Czech Jews perceived the politicizing of modern religion as a means for Jews to integrate into mainstream society on their own terms. For Vohryzek, it was the Czechs who had strayed from their national ideals of progress as embodied by people like Hus and Comenius. The Christian Czechs needed their Jewish

---

66. See Michael A. Riff, "The Ambiguity of Masaryk's Attitudes on the 'Jewish Question'," in T. G. Masaryk (1850–1937), vol. 2; Thinker and Critic, ed. Robert B. Pynsent, Studies in Russia and East Europe (Basingstoke: Macmillan, 1989): 77–87, here at 83.

67. Česká stráž. Lidové noviny pokrokové, "Z táboru české strany lidové" January 20, 1906, 3.

brethren to complete the journey to their true national character. To reach this stage, a Czech-Jewish accommodation was inevitable.[68] Masaryk seemed to accept this conflation of the historical meaning of the Czech reformation and a Czech-Jewish path towards it. As he wrote Vohryzek, he was particularly pleased to see the progressive Czech Jews propagating the reform movement.[69]

This unique vision of the progressive meaning of the Czech reformation therefore managed to include a progressive Judaism not by accepting Jews as they were but by escalating its demands for Jews and Czechs alike. As Vohryzek and other progressive Jews recognized, the hazy notion of a true Czech reformation could be expressed in terms that conveyed equidistance between Jewish and Protestant (or for that matter, Catholic and Free Thinking) visions of a future religion. Consequently, the Czech-Jewish position went from being indebted to the benevolent and tolerant Czech nation[70] to guiding the very same nation back to its lost ideals.[71]

Last, the notion of a religious avant-garde was a reaction to societal changes. When the rise of political Catholicism threatened to marginalize non-Catholics, the idea that the fundamental social transformation was just the cusp of a fundamental spiritual transformation was particularly attractive to projections of future majorities. Commenting on political Catholicism, Bohdan Klineberger noted, "A change in the war tactics [of the Catholic church, J.G.] has happened. [It points, J.G.] into politics: the abstract fight is cast aside, the fight for political power is happening." And he continued, "The political fight has priority over the scientific. While this uses arguments and reason, that uses feelings and power."[72]

Klineberger here used an argument endorsed by atheist Free Thinkers. This argument exposed how the politicization of progressive religiosity served as an integrating moment for a loose coalition of progressive subgroups. Theological differences aside, they had a common enemy: clericalism, which held the Czech nation back, whether by fomenting anti-Semitism or promoting general backwardness. A strong turnout of Catholic voters was expected in the upcoming elections, thus making the political battle for the spirit of the Czech

68. Vohryzek, "Několik slov úvodem," 3.
69. The Czech term "reformní hnutí" conveys the semantic appeal to the protestant reformation much stronger. See Tomáš G. Masaryk, "Dopis v redakci," Rozvoj: Týdenník českých pokrokových židů 1:1 (1904): 3.
70. Vondrášková, "The Czech-Jewish Assimilation Movement and its Reflection of Czech National Traditions," 154.
71. Kieval, Languages of Community, 171.
72. Bohdan Klineberger, "Otázka antisemitismu," Českožidovské listy 7:2 (1901): 1–5, here at 2–3.

nation a real one indeed. Klineberger also formulated a central insight: the struggle for a new scientific religion was always a political one, if it was to be more than a mere intellectual exercise. Liberalism, for Klineberger, had done more than overlook the real economic damage people in rural areas had experienced: its proponents had neglected to notice how this damage provoked anti-Semitism, particularly among small rural businesses. An anti-liberal movement had arisen by addressing this common feeling of being left behind, and from this common feeling a common ideology followed. Such an anti-liberal party, perforce, had to be an anti-Semitic one as well. It was the Christian Social and Catholic peoples' parties that united these voices and imbued them meaning.

Klineberger made a crucial point: the rural masses, which supported the (anti-Semitic) Catholic parties, sided with these parties because of concrete changes in the structure of society.[73] The question of who would represent the majority of the Czechs in the future was, therefore, still an open one.

Political Success and Demise

When, in 1906, the Realist party merged with another Progressive splinter group to form the *"Česká strana pokroková"* (Czech Progressive Party), the policy of religious progressivism reached its zenith. This time round, the Protestant party members had learned their lesson: several speakers stressed that the reactionary wave (i. e., the political successes of Catholic parties) could only be abated by the progressive elements making common cause. The party's press also spotlighted the mistakes of the Young Czech Party, which had ignored religion as a central topic of contemporary politics.[74] In the 1907 elections to the Vienna chamber of deputies, the party was remarkably successful, given that it represented only a tiny minority of voters. It managed to get two deputies, František Drtina and Masaryk himself, elected. Drtina, however, was elected by a coalition that included Catholic parties. It was mainly Masaryk, the charismatic leader of the Realists, who successfully campaigned on a religious program and managed to defeat his Catholic opponent in his East Moravian voting district. This put an end to the longstanding campaign against the Catholic church that the party had waged almost from its inception. Once elected, Masaryk's attempts to debate religion in politics fell flat. His critique of the Catholic church led once again to an alliance with the pan-German nationalists, which he then quickly abandoned.

Already before the war, during the next elections in 1911, the Real-

73. Ibid., 4–5.
74. Česká stráž. Lidové noviny pokrokové, January 27, 1906.

ists drifted back into mainstream liberalism. An alliance of progressive forces seemed to be a political necessity, thus reducing the importance of religious topics. During the war, the remaining leadership of the party surrounding Herben joined forces with the other bourgeois parties to form a single nationalist block, overlooking the virulent anti-Semitism of several of its proponents. In protest, Lederer left the party, which subsequently split up, disappearing shortly after the end of the war.[75]

Conclusion

The present chapter makes the claim for a simultaneous change in discourses about nation and religion on the one hand, and the structural conditions of the national public on the other. As the focus of Czech politics shifted away from the center and the bourgeois milieu to the smaller towns and their specific socio-cultural environment, its integrative framework changed as well. Although the Bohemian towns had long featured in national mythology as the preservers of Czech culture, it was the actual expansion of the voting franchise that placed them in the midst of a battle for the mobilization of a majority. The Czech-German conflict receded into the background of these debates. The question of who among the Czech speakers was also Czech in a spiritual way became more and more prominent. Not only did the liberal nationalists abandon their tolerant vision in order to woo the Catholic population, but the minority positions also changed. The new direction of the Czech-Jewish assimilation movement, then, was not only a reaction to the anti-Semitic wave of the 1890s. In the Czech context, religiosity became political, as the question of what it meant to be Czech seemed to spark an increasingly diverse range of answers. Masaryk and his followers openly advocated a religious and spiritual reawakening of the nation, something that neither Catholic nor secular nationalists had ever done. The main fault line had been moved from between political Catholicism and the anti-clerical national movement to one between a "religious" and a "non-religious" vision for society. And curiously, the "clerical" parties fell into the latter camp, at least from the perspective of the religious progressives.

Comparison of the Jewish and Protestant positions reveals how both communities were part of a larger shift in Czech society. The motivating factor was the changing national discourse, which had to address a larger public by becoming narrower and more exclusive.

---

75. For Lederer's reaction, see AÚTGM, f. TGM, Republika, Židé, kr. 453. On the final demise of the party, see Josef Harna and Martin Kučera, eds., Politické programy českých "pokrokových" stran 1896–1900, Edice politických programů 6 (Prague: Historický ústav, 2010), 22–4.

Moreover, it was oftentimes unclear who would represent the rural masses that had now entered politics. In this way, religious communities came to see their own identities as increasingly tied to the political discourse, prompting the idea of a political and spiritual awakening within Czech society. They countered the apparent new consensus with an integrative vision of their own, addressing – at least in theory – a different national collective themselves. Even if their vision was narrower from a socio-cultural point of view, it still offered an interesting and alternative discourse that stressed the religious nature of Czechness in order to make it more inclusive. While, by definition, this national religion of the future had to remain indeterminate, it nonetheless displayed political power. To a certain extent, it was a transitional phenomenon on the road to modernity, responding to the question of nationality but also to that of collective identity in modern times.[76] When the (male) mass public finally broke free from restrictions in 1907, this alternative could claim a place for itself. And when the Czechoslovak republic came into existence in 1918, this religious vision loomed large in the republican raison d'être.

Within a small window of opportunity, all these shifts could be brought together by a unifying vision of a progressive religious future. While its immediate political impact was ultimately negligible, it did provide a framework for Czech national discourse that reappeared after the war, again presenting the Czech reformation as a prism of Czech universality.

---

76. With regard to Germany, one should mention Thomas Nipperdey's famous term "vagrating religiosity."

LUTHER'S SHADOW
Jewish and Protestant Interpretations of the Reformer's Writings on the Jews, 1917–1933[1]
By Christian Wiese

The nineteenth- and twentieth-century historiography on the reception of Martin Luther's writings on Jews and Judaism, his *Judenschriften*, is marked by an ongoing contestation concerning the reformer's religious and political views. Did his reflections on the Jews constitute the core of his theology or were they merely a marginal aspect of his thinking? Was the anti-Jewish obsession that emerged ever more clearly at the later stages of his biography rooted in his theological convictions or was it triggered by contemporary social and political circumstances? The issue of continuity or discontinuity between earlier writings such as *Daß Jesus ein geborener Jude sei* (1523) and the viciously anti-Jewish writings published in 1543, too, remains an open question.

In one well-known view, Luther's initial 'tolerant' attitude underwent a dramatic change in response to crises within the Reformation movement, personal disillusionment in the face of Jewish resistance to his missionary intentions, and the insistence of Jewish scholars on the legitimacy of a distinctively Jewish exegesis that opposed the Christian truth claims. An alternative interpretation, which enjoys wide currency today amongst scholars, assumes a continuity between Luther's underlying theological stance on Jews and Judaism and his understanding of the Christological meaning of the Hebrew Bible and his doctrine of justification.[2]

---

1. This article has been written within the context of the Hessian Ministry for Science and Arts funded LOEWE research hub "Religious Positioning: Modalities and Constellations in Jewish, Christian and Muslim Contexts" at the Goethe University Frankfurt am Main and the Justus-Liebig-University in Gießen.

2. For the most recent works, see Thomas Kaufmann, Luthers ‚Judenschriften'. Ein Beitrag zu ihrer historischen Kontextualisierung (Tübingen: Mohr-Siebeck, 2011); idem, Luther's Jews: A Journey into Anti-Semitism (Oxford: Oxford University Press, 2016); Andreas Pangritz, Theologie und Antisemitismus. Das Beispiel Martin Luthers (Frankfurt a. M.: Peter Lang, 2017); for influential earlier works, see Heiko A. Oberman, The Roots of Anti-Semitism: In the Age of Renaissance and Reforma-

First and foremost, Luther's *Judenschriften* must be seen in the context of late medieval perceptions of Judaism and the contemporary socio-political practice vis-à-vis the Jewish minority. It is equally critical, however, to consider them against their reception in the following centuries, from the time of Lutheran Orthodoxy via the emergence of Pietism and the Enlightenment up through the nineteenth-century Jewish emancipation and eventually the Weimar Republic and the Nazi period. As the image of "Luther's Shadow" in the title of this essay suggests, Luther's attitude towards Jews and Judaism strongly influenced – and overshadowed – Jewish-Protestant relations, particularly in the German context, and is part of the complex history of modern anti-Semitism. In different historical and cultural contexts this shadow took manifold, partly contradictory forms, reflecting the specific religious and political perspectives from which Luther's writings were viewed. With regard to the impact of these forms on debates concerning the status of Jews and Judaism in German society, it is important to ask whether and how they were discussed among both Protestants and Jews prior to and after the emergence of modern political, cultural, and racial anti-Semitism.[3] This article examines a crucial stage of those debates, mainly the period 1917–1933. Both bracketing years featured highly symbolic Luther celebrations that lend them-

---

tion (Philadelphia: Fortress, 1984); Peter von der Osten-Sacken, Martin Luther und die Juden – neu untersucht anhand von Anton Margarithas ‚der gantz Jüdisch glaub' (1530/31) (Stuttgart: Kohlhammer, 2002); Dietz Bering, War Luther Antisemit? Das deutsch-jüdische Verhältnis als Tragödie der Nähe (Berlin: Berlin University Press, 2014). Overall, it does not seem plausible to interpret Luther's later writings on the Jews as a lapse from religious tolerance to late medieval hatred. Rather, although the demonization of Judaism and the unpitying recommendation of "sharp mercy" to the authorities in 1543 indeed represented a new element in his thought, the anti-Jewish theological motifs at work here were already present even before 1523. These motifs (among others, the stubbornness of the Jews resulting in God's wrath and rejection of His chosen people; Judaism's tenacious hatred of Jesus Christ and Christianity; a false Jewish and blasphemous understanding of the Bible; Jewish existence as an archetype of the self-glorification of sinful man before God) need to be understood as running consistently through Luther's work, even if they were occasionally tempered by criticism of Christian arrogance and inhumane treatment of Jews. See Ernst Ludwig Ehrlich, "Luther und die Juden," in Die Juden und Martin Luther. Martin Luther und die Juden. Geschichte – Wirkungsgeschichte – Herausforderung, eds. Heinz Kremers et al., 2nd edition (Neukirchen-Vluyn: Neukirchner Verlag, 1987): 72–88. Ehrlich himself diagnoses consistent theological anti-Semitism in Luther; but he also discerns a temporary "new, humane element" (76) of a political nature in Luther's work, inspired by missionary hopes.

3. See Christian Wiese, "'Unheilsspuren'. Zur Rezeption von Martin Luthers 'Judenschriften' im Kontext antisemitischen Denkens vor der Schoah," in Das mißbrauchte Evangelium. Studien zu Theologie und Praxis der Thüringer Deutschen Christen, ed. Peter von der Osten-Sacken (Berlin: Institut für Kirche und Judentum, 2002): 91–135.

selves to an analysis of the theological and political readings of the *Judenschriften* among Jewish and Protestant scholars, as well as those that emerged in anti-Semitic circles.

While the topic of Protestant interpretations of Luther's views vis-à-vis anti-Semitic propaganda has received a great deal of scholarly scrutiny, research on corresponding Jewish perspectives is still a desideratum, both with regard to the *Judenschriften* and to Luther's broader thought. It is worth noting that Heinrich Bornkamm (1901–1977), in his seminal study, *Luther im Spiegel der deutschen Geistesgeschichte* (1955), includes Catholic sources but does not even hint at the existence of Jewish readings of Luther. The failure to do so may be related to an inclination of Protestant church historians at that time to elide the very notion of active and creative Jewish participation in German intellectual discourse.[4] The 1970s and 80s witnessed a change in the perception of Jewish responses to Luther's writings on the Jews.[5] Nonetheless, a broad approach to Jewish readings of Luther in the modern period is still in its nascence.[6]

The present article aims neither to present a systematic account nor even to summarize the multifaceted Jewish interpretations of Luther's significance for German intellectual and political culture during the nineteenth and early twentieth centuries, or to analyse the specifically Jewish character of these readings. Rather, after a brief look at the two dominant trends of that discourse, it will ask to what extent Jewish thinkers took notice of Luther's *Judenschriften*, which strategies they deployed to counter nationalistic and anti-Semitic narratives, and what distinguished these strategies from contemporary Prot-

---

4. Heinrich Bornkamm, Luther im Spiegel der deutschen Geistesgeschichte (Heidelberg: Quelle & Meyer, 1955).

5. See Johannes Brosseder, Luthers Stellung zu den Juden im Spiegel seiner Interpreten. Interpretation und Rezeption von Luthers Schriften und Äußerungen zum Judentum im 19. und 20. Jahrhundert vor allem im deutschsprachigen Raum (Munich: Hueber, 1972); Johannes Wallmann, "The Reception of Luther's Writings on the Jews from the Reformation to the End of the 19th Century," Lutheran Quarterly 1 (1987): 72–97. For a most recent analysis from a Jewish thinker, who presents a historical perspective, see Alon Goshen-Gottstein, Luther the Anti-Semite: A Contemporary Jewish Perspective (Philadelphia: Fortress Press, 2018).

6. See Christian Wiese, "'Auch uns sei sein Andenken heilig!' Symbolisierung, Idealisierung und Kritik in der jüdischen Lutherrezeption des 19. und 20. Jahrhunderts," in Luther zwischen den Kulturen. Zeitgenossenschaft – Weltwirkung, eds. Hans Medick and Peer Schmidt (Göttingen: Vandenhoeck & Ruprecht, 2004): 214–59; Dorothea Wendebourg, "'Gesegnet sei das Andenken Luthers!' Die Juden und Martin Luther im 19. Jahrhundert," Zeitschrift für Religions- und Geistesgeschichte 65 (2013): 235–51; Walter Homolka, "Martin Luther als Symbol geistiger Freiheit? Der Reformator und seine Rezeption im Judentum" in Luther, Rosenzweig und die Schrift. Ein deutsch-jüdischer Dialog, ed. Micha Brumlik (Hamburg: CEP Europäische Verlagsanstalt, 2017): 49–60.

estant ones. The sources indicate that the Jewish readings contained two main features: a critique of the disastrous consequences of the anti-Jewish elements in Luther's theology, and a passionate attempt to oppose the dramatically increasing tendency among German intellectuals since the 1880s to depict Luther as the crown witness for anti-Semitic discrimination by insisting on an idealized counternarrative: that of Luther as a symbolic embodiment of a tradition of tolerance, freedom of conscience, emancipation, and pluralism. In light of the almost complete absence of positive response to this interpretation on the part of Protestant theologians, however, the question of its illusory nature naturally arises.

Between Idealization and Historical Critique: Jewish Readings

Since the early nineteenth century, Jewish readings of Luther have oscillated between two poles: a critique of the reformer as the forefather of political bondage, deference, and spiritual impoverishment, as presented with satirical poignancy by Ludwig Börne (1786–1837) in 1830 in letters from Paris, and an enthusiastic appraisal of Luther as a harbinger of the Enlightenment, as articulated in Heinrich Heine's (1797–1856) essay *Zur Geschichte der Religion und Philosophie in Deutschland* (1834). Jewish intellectuals in the nineteenth and early twentieth centuries favored the latter view, which permitted them to advance the idea that the symbolic figure of Protestant culture in Germany had been a pioneer of religious tolerance, including Jewish emancipation.

Of course, such a reading was far from those that showed Luther as the hero of Germanness, an interpretation that dominated German national historiography in the final decades of the nineteenth century. This tendency to portray Luther as the embodiment of the German national character turned out to be inherently exclusive and – explicitly or implicitly – anti-Jewish. Nationalistic interpretations such as those articulated by the historian Heinrich von Treitschke (1834–1896) in his 1883 essay "Luther und die deutsche Nation"[7] clearly demonstrated that Jewish and non-Jewish readings of Luther were developing in clearly opposite directions.

At the beginning of the twentieth century, Jewish historians offered a compelling counternarrative, and they did so in two distinct ways. Hermann Cohen (1842–1918), who was in constant critical dialogue with cultural Protestantism,[8] held that the Reformation and Protestant

---

7. Heinrich von Treitschke, "Luther und die deutsche Nation," Preußische Jahrbücher 52 (1883): 469–86.

8. For Cohen's relationship to Protestantism, see Wendell S. Dietrich, Cohen and

thinking were not merely constitutive components of Europe's intellectual and political progress but an important link between Jewish tradition and German culture. In a 1917 essay entitled "Zu Martin Luthers Gedächtnis," Cohen referred to the reformer as the "most powerful creator of Germanness" and as a symbol of the intellectual overcoming of the Middle Ages. Luther's translation of the Bible, Cohen argued, had inscribed the Jewish spirit into Western culture, rendering the Hebrew Bible a "tree of life" "for all modern intellectual life, the root from which all the strengths of the newer nations had sprung and have been nourished."[9]

Cohen was well aware that many aspects of both the historical figure of Luther and the Reformation contradicted his conception. He insisted, however, that it was not each and every utterance of Luther, who was a child of his times, that was decisive, but rather the *idea* of the Reformation, the impetus that idea gave to the development of German thought. With the aid of this conceptual abstraction, Cohen was able to appropriate Luther as part of a Biblical-prophetic tradition extending from Plato and Maimonides to Kant and onward, including his own neo-Kantian interpretation of Judaism – the guarantor of Judaism's relevance for the "German spirit." The fulfilment of this interpretation, that is, Luther's significance for a future completion of Jewish emancipation and cultural integration by virtue of a synthesis of "Germanness" and Jewishness, would have required a response from the German Protestant side; in effect, an acknowledgment that Judaism was part of German culture. The absence of such a response was the unstated catalyst for the ensuing debates between German Jewish scholars concerning the historical influence of Luther's writings about the Jews.

A much more critical image of Luther was presented by Leo Baeck (1873–1956), who had emerged as a prominent voice in the polemical controversies between Jewish scholarship and liberal Protestantism about the "essence" of Judaism and Christianity that had taken place since the turn of the century.[10] In Baeck's essay on "Romantische Reli-

---

Troeltsch: Ethical Monotheistic Religion and Theory of Culture (Atlanta, GA: Scholars Press, 1986); Robert Raphael Geis, "Hermann Cohen und die deutsche Reformation," in idem, Gottes Minorität. Beiträge zur jüdischen Theologie und zur Geschichte der Juden in Deutschland (Munich: Kösel, 1971): 136–51; William Kluback, "Friendship without Communication: Wilhelm Herrmann and Hermann Cohen," Leo Baeck Institute Year Book 31 (1986): 317–38; David N. Myers, "Hermann Cohen and the Quest for Protestant Judaism," Leo Baeck Institute Year Book 46 (2001): 195–214.

9. Hermann Cohen, "Zu Martin Luthers Gedächtnis," Neue jüdische Monatshefte 2 (1917/18): 45–9, here 46.

10. See Christian Wiese, "Ein unerhörtes Gesprächsangebot. Leo Baeck, die Wissenschaft des Judentums und das Judentumsbild des liberalen Protestantismus,"

gion" (1922), Luther appears as championing an amoral "romantic" religion, one whose emphasis on the Paulinic and Augustinian sola fide reduces believers to passivity, fixated on the salvation of their own souls.[11] Judaism, by contrast, is presented as embodying the "classical" religion that views human beings as subjects of their own moral actions, endowing them with responsibility for worldly justice. In his lecture "Heimgegangene des Krieges," which Baeck delivered in 1918 at the *Lehranstalt für die Wissenschaft des Judentums* in Berlin, he concurred with his Protestant colleague Ernst Troeltsch (1865–1923) about Luther. According to Troeltsch, Luther, the admirable religious genius, was at the same time a man whose intolerance was rooted in the Middle Ages and whose conservative patriarchal thought had helped to perpetuate both authoritarian rule and political passivity, with disastrous consequences for German political history.[12] Baeck echoed this view, emphasizing that the "Prussian religion," now fortunately rendered obsolete by the revolution of 1918, had been characterized by a "rigid concept of authority and subservience."[13] Baeck's hope was that, with the end of the *Kaiserreich*, Luther's "un-Protestant" attitude,[14] which had moved Lutheranism far from Judaism ("As Jewish as Luther had begun, his subsequent path led him to a point remote from everything Jewish"[15]) might be finally overcome through a fulfilment of the "spirit of Enlightenment" that was so closely related to the "Jewish spirit."[16] Only then would a new culture arise in Germany, a culture more conducive both to the country's Jewish minority and to dialogue between Judaism and Christianity.

Strikingly, the question of Luther's anti-Semitism, which dominated Jewish-Christian debates about the reformer after 1945, was more or less neglected by the majority of aforementioned German-Jewish authors. One reason for this may be that in the Protestant domain, Luther's *Judenschriften* were only rediscovered and discussed in more detail with the late nineteenth-century emergence

in Leo Baeck 1873–1956., Mi gesa rabbanim' – Aus dem Stamme von Rabbinern, eds. Georg Heuberger and Fritz Backhaus (Frankfurt a. M.: Suhrkamp, 2001): 147–71.

11. Leo Baeck, "Romantische Religion," in idem, Aus drei Jahrtausenden – Das Evangelium als Urkunde der jüdischen Glaubensgeschichte, Werke vol. 4 (Gütersloh: Gütersloher Verlagshaus, 2000): 59–120.

12. See Ernst Troeltsch, Die Bedeutung des Protestantismus für die Entstehung der modernen Welt (Munich: Oldenbourg, 1911).

13. Leo Baeck, "Heimgegangene des Krieges," in idem, Wege im Judentum. Aufsätze und Reden (Gütersloh: Gütersloher Verlagshaus, 1997), 285–96, here 288.

14. Ibid., 286.
15. Ibid., 288.
16. Ibid., 289.

of both modern political anti-Semitism and a corresponding nationalist approach to the reformer.[17] Additionally, with their focus on integration into German culture, many Jewish intellectuals – at least those following the line from Heinrich Heine to Hermann Cohen – preferred to perceive Luther as a forerunner of Enlightenment and emancipation. Even those, from Ludwig Börne to Leo Baeck, who portrayed him as an embodiment of Protestant servitude to the authoritarian state, refrained from accentuating his attitude towards Jews and Judaism. The early nineteenth-century German-Jewish historians who could not ignore Luther's writing on Judaism and the Jews, because the period of the Reformation played an important role in their representation of Jewish history, tended to sidestep the anti-Jewish dimension of the reformer's theology. In 1828, for example, Isaak Markus Jost's (1793–1860) *Geschichte der Israeliten* mentioned *Daß Jesus Christus ein geborener Jude sei* only, and omitted any reference to the later writings.[18]

The first Jewish historian to deal explicitly with the topic, thus fundamentally changing Jewish perceptions of Martin Luther, was Heinrich Graetz (1817–1891). In his eleven-volume *Geschichte der Juden von den ältesten Zeiten bis auf die Gegenwart* (1853–1876), Graetz tried to explain why Luther, in contrast to the late medieval politics of discrimination and persecution, "so forcefully administered to the Jews' needs in his first flare of reform" and then suddenly repeated "all the false tales of poisoned wells, the murder of Christian children and the use of human blood" in his later years.[19] For Graetz, the source of this apparent *volte-face* was Luther's bitterness in view of the failure of the majority of the Jews to embrace the Protestant interpretation of the Christian Gospel, combined with his profound misperception of Judaism's moral character. As a consequence, Graetz argued, the reformer poisoned the Protestant world "with his anti-Se-

---

17. For a discussion of the history of the editions of Luther's writings on the Jews before the Nazi rise to power, see Volker Leppin, "Luthers 'Judenschriften' im Spiegel der Editionen bis 1933," in Martin Luthers "Judenschriften". Die Rezeption im 19. und 20. Jahrhundert, eds. Harry Oelke, Wolfgang Kraus et. al. (Göttingen: Vandenhoeck & Ruprecht, 2016): 19–44.

18. Isaak Markus Jost, Geschichte der Israeliten seit der Zeit der Maccabäer bis auf unsere Tage, vol. 8 (Berlin: Schlesinger, 1828), 211–2. On Jost, see Ismar Schorsch, "From Wolfenbüttel to Wissenschaft – The Divergent Paths of Isaak Markus Jost and Leopold Zunz," Leo Baeck Institute Year Book 22 (1977): 109–28.

19. Heinrich Graetz, Geschichte der Juden. Von den ältesten Zeiten bis auf die Gegenwart, vol. 9: Von der Verbannung der Juden aus Spanien und Portugal (1494) bis zur dauernden Ansiedelung der Marranen in Holland, reprint of the 4th edition 1907 (Berlin: Arani, 1998), 300. Graetz described Luther's early writing as a "word such as the Jews had not heard for a thousand years" (ibid., 189).

mitic testament" for centuries to come.[20]

Later scholarship has nuanced this picture, concentrating more on Luther's theological motives and less on his personal ones. Ludwig Geiger (1848–1919), who had ample familiarity with the relevant Renaissance, humanistic, and Reformation sources, mentioned Luther's disappointment at failed missionary efforts but foregrounded something else: a gradual realization on the reformer's part of a fundamental Jewish-Christian disagreement regarding how to read the Hebrew Bible.[21]

It was in the early twentieth century that the question how to understand the discrepancy between Luther's writings from 1523 and 1543 and its significance for contemporary debates on Jewish integration and anti-Semitism came to the fore. At the end of his *Jewish Encyclopedia* article of 1916 on Martin Luther, historian Gotthard Deutsch (1859–1921) observed that "The wholly different attitudes that Luther showed at different times in relation to Jews made him, during the controversies surrounding anti-Semitism at the end of the nineteenth century, an authority who was cited equally by friends and foes of Jews."[22]

Paying close attention to Jewish voices in that period reveals that, for the most part, the German Jewish authors writing on Luther favoured a "two periods" or "disappointment" theory over one that posited a theological continuity between his earlier and later attitudes.[23] In an influential study published in 1911, the historian Reinhold Lewin (1888–1943) concluded that Luther, in his later years, had indeed left his earlier tolerance behind, marking a clear caesura between a 'pro-Jewish' and an 'anti-Jewish' period in his theological development. Even though Lewin argued that the position of the early Luther ought to be relevant for contemporary Protestantism, he had no

---

20. Ibid., 301–2.
21. See Ludwig Geiger, "Zur jüdischen Geschichte. 2. Luther und die Juden," Jüdische Zeitschrift für Wissenschaft und Leben 5 (1867): 23–9; idem, "Die Juden und die deutsche Literatur," Zeitschrift für die Geschichte der Juden in Deutschland 2 (1888): 297–374 (on Luther, 326–8); idem, "Renaissance und Reformation," in Kulturgeschichte in ihrer natürlichen Entwicklung bis zur Gegenwart, ed. Friedrich von Hellwald, 4th edition (Leipzig: Friesenhahn, 1898): 68–217.
22. Gotthard Deutsch, entry on "Luther, Martin," in The Jewish Encyclopedia, vol. 8, 4th edition (New York and London: Funk and Wagnalls, 1916), cols. 213–5. Deutsch was Professor of Jewish History at the Hebrew Union College in Cincinnati; for the most part his article treats the question of Luther's attitude to Judaism.
23. Brosseder, Luthers Stellung zu den Juden, 89–96, 112–4, 148–54, and 303, briefly outlines the position of some Jewish researchers in this respect. He emphasizes their tendency to understand Luther's "late writings" as a break with an earlier, more positive attitude towards the Jews and, once again, as the consequence of disappointed missionary hopes.

doubts regarding the historical impact of his later ideas: "Whoever, for whatever motives, writes against the Jews, believes they have the right to refer triumphantly to Luther."[24]

A decade and a half later, the criticism levelled by Russian-Jewish historian Simon Dubnow (1860 –1941) in his *Weltgeschichte des jüdischen Volkes* is considerably sharper. For Dubnow, Luther's early stance on the Jews, rather than being an expression of true tolerance, reflected a desire "to win them for Christianity of the most recent order." His disillusionment concerning the fulfilment of his naïve missionary hopes then transformed his original goodwill into pathological hatred of Jews and Judaism – a kind of "judeophobia":

> The people of the Bible, from whom Christ and the apostles originated, refuse to join the Lutheran church and thus confirm the divine mission of its founder, so – Luther concluded – they were incorrigible and deserved all the suffering and persecution to which they had been exposed in the Christian countries. This was the logic of the events that caused Luther to swiftly discard the mask of friendliness towards the Jews, and to declare a fight to the death on Judaism.[25]

In light of Dubnow's argument, it is interesting to note that the notion of a rupture in Luther's position appears to have gained acceptance in proportion to the extent to which – starting at the beginning of the twentieth century and then with increased vehemence in the Weimar period – anti-Semitic representatives of German nationalism adopted Luther's anti-Jewish writings. The more anti-Semites declared the latter the crux of his theology and a basis for the political treatment of the Jewish minority in Germany, the more Jewish intellectuals insisted on the primacy of the reformer's 'pro-Jewish' early writings. In his essay "Luther und die Juden," for instance, published for the 1917 commemoration of the Reformation, the historian Samuel Krauss (1866–1948), who taught at the *Israelitisch-Theologische Lehranstalt* in Vienna, thus characterized Luther as one of the worst anti-Semites of his age, his "great, unrestrained hate" for the Jews being the result of both theological intolerance and the naïveté with which he antici-

---

24. Reinhold Lewin, Luthers Stellung zu den Juden. Ein Beitrag zur Geschichte der Juden in Deutschland während des Reformationszeitalters (Berlin: Trowitzsch, 1911), 110. Interestingly, Protestant scholars who shared anti-Semitic sentiments and saw Luther's anti-Semitism as anchored in his theology, attributed Lewin's interpretation to his being a Jew; see Erich Vogelsang, Luthers Kampf gegen die Juden (Tübingen: Mohr, 1933), 8–9 ("The fact that [...] Reinhold Lewin as a rabbi, in spite of an attempt at objectivity and scientific method, was barely able to grasp anything of Luther's actual concerns, should not surprise us"). On Vogelsang, see below.

25. Simon Dubnow, Weltgeschichte des jüdischen Volkes. Von seinen Uranfängen bis zur Gegenwart, vol. 6 (Berlin: Jüdischer Verlag, 1927), 192–217, here at 200 and 202–3.

pated "Judaism merging into Christianity."[26] At the same time, Krauss rendered homage to Luther, depicting him as an advocate of integration and equal rights that had become an inexorable force in modern society:

> The principles that he [Luther] introduced to the whole world at the start of his career, and which were also purer and more just than those put forward in his old age, distorted as they were by hate and bitterness, principles of enlightenment and of the free development of the human intellect, including the demand that the Jews must not be subject to either psychological or physical compulsion, turned out to be powerful factors of the subsequent period, which could not be banished even by Luther's own faults.[27]

Protestant Readings in an Age of Völkisch *Anti-Semitism*

We find an echo of such idealized Jewish interpretations of Luther's early writings in the rare efforts of Weimar Republic Protestant theologians to oppose the usurpation of Luther's anti-Jewish writings in the context of nationalistic and anti-Semitic positions. One such effort was made by the Stuttgart Lutheran theologian Eduard Lamparter (1860–1945), in an extraordinary text published in 1928 under the title *Evangelische Kirche und Judentum. Ein Beitrag zum christlichen Verständnis von Judentum und Antisemitismus*. Lamparter, who was a leading figure in the *Verein zur Abwehr des Antisemitismus* and a proponent of liberal democracy, here lamented Luther's betrayal of his own "just and truly Protestant attitude to the Jewish question," a betrayal that had led the Protestant church in a false direction.[28] He praised the young Luther for his high regard for the "Old Testament" and for having objected out of compassion and a sense of justice to the prevailing late medieval policies towards the Jews. In Lamparter's view, it was "one of the most painful things, that this great German, who previously had found such warm words full of sympathy, justice and love for the Jews," then "developed a hatred for them so blind"

26. Samuel Krauss, "Luther und die Juden," Der Jude 2 (1917/18): 544–7 (reprinted in Kurt Wilhelm, ed., Wissenschaft des Judentums im deutschen Sprachbereich. Ein Querschnitt, vol. 1 (Tübingen: Mohr-Siebeck, 1967), 309–14, here 310 and 312).

27. Ibid., 313. Historian Ismar Elbogen (1874–1943), in his Geschichte der Juden seit dem Untergang des jüdischen Staates (Leipzig and Berlin: Teubner, 1919), 69–71, also confirmed the long-term effect of Luther's anti-Semitic invective, but insisted that he remained "the most important milestone on the road to the civil state and to freedom of thought and conscience" (70).

28. Eduard Lamparter, Evangelische Kirche und Judentum. Ein Beitrag zum christlichen Verständnis von Judentum und Antisemitismus (Stuttgart: Brönner, 1928), 5.

that he condemned them out of hand.²⁹ In so doing, Lamparter asserted, Luther had done violence to his own principles of religious freedom and freedom of conscience and had become the "principal witness for modern anti-Semitism." Contemporary Protestant theology, therefore, needed to be won over for the original and true Luther, "who at the pinnacle of his reforming work for the oppressed, despised and ostracised, stood up for them with such warm words and so urgently commended to Christianity brotherly love as the utmost obligation, including in relation to Jews."³⁰ For Lamparter, this Luther stood aligned with the Lutheran tradition of a 'mission to the Jews' characterized by 'love for Israel' that had been particularly emphasized by Pietism;³¹ with the Enlightenment; and with other theologians who had battled against anti-Semitism.

Lamparter's plea for a positive reception of the young Luther's position was coupled with a strong censure of modern anti-Semitism, an attempt to lay the theological foundation for an appreciation of postbiblical Judaism's religious, ethical, and cultural achievements, and a call to overcome traditional stereotypes as well as to discover and accentuate shared values. His reflections on the Reformation, more than a mere rejection of anti-Jewish implications of Luther's theology, went far beyond what those calling for a friendly 'mission to the Jews' considered possible; and it was certainly beyond what the early Luther had in mind. The wealth of religious and ethical affinities

29. Ibid., 15.
30. Ibid., 17.
31. For the intellectual origins, see Christoph Rymatzky, Hallischer Pietismus und Judenmission. Johann Heinrich Callenbergs Institutum Judaicum und dessen Freundeskreis (1727–1736) (Tübingen: Niemeyer-Verlag, 2004); for the Lutheran 'Mission to the Jews,' see, e. g., Christopher M. Clark, The Politics of Conversion: Missionary Protestantism and the Jews in Prussia, 1728–1941 (London and Oxford: Clarendon Press, 1995). An example for the rather ambivalent attitude of the representatives of the 'Mission to the Jews' with regard to Luther's Judenschriften is Ernst Schaeffer, the director of the Gesellschaft zur Beförderung des Christentums unter den Juden in Berlin, who published a book entitled Luther und die Juden in 1917. In view of the anti-Semitic debates during World War I, he suggested that German society should turn to the young Luther, whose friendly missionary attitude towards the Jews might serve as a model for the present. Even though the reformer's later polemical statements had to be understood historically as a response to Jews' stubbornness, his harsh advice to the authorities needed to be rejected as intolerant. However, Schaeffer seemed strongly irritated by the self-confident insistence of German Jews on Judaism's religious and cultural relevance for modern society and warned against Jewish arrogance as well as the "poisonous" Jewish influence on Christianity. By emphasizing that the main task was to "strengthen Christian self-confidence against the Jews," he made it very clear that a critique of anti-Semitism neither meant acknowledging Judaism as a tradition which deserved an equal status in a pluralistic society, nor excluding religious and political prejudice; Ernst Schaeffer, Luther und die Juden (Gütersloh: Bertelsmann, 1917), 62.

between Judaism and Christianity, Lamparter argued, ought to oblige Christians to maintain a relationship of "peace and mutual respect": "the duty to acknowledge Judaism as a divinely ordained path towards the solution of the most crucial questions of life" was, therefore, at least as important as the task "to hype Christianity amongst the Jews." Without explicitly relinquishing the idea of a missionary testimony for Christianity's truth, he acknowledged Judaism's right to be seen as a valuable religious and cultural tradition and as a legitimate part of a pluralistic German society and culture:

> Amongst the nations which have a share in modernity's intellectual culture, foreign hands may not interfere with the sanctuary of personal religious conviction and decision. Judaism is an awe-inspiring phenomenon of cultural and religious history. We will make the deepest impression on our Jewish fellow Germans when we do not withhold this admission. The easiest way to win over their hearts is to refute anti-Semitism as an attitude that contradicts the true spirit of Christianity.[32]

Lamparter's thoughts on Luther, published a few years before the Nazis seized power, can be characterized as an attempt to overcome the increasingly dark shadow of Luther's anti-Semitism through an idealizing evocation of an enlightened tradition of love and religious freedom: qualities the liberal theologian saw as rooted in the Reformation. We now know that Luther never came close to a truly positive theological acknowledgment of Judaism but rather, despite the more benevolent tones of the early Reformation period, he held a negative image of Jews and the Jewish religion throughout his life. Thus, Lamparter, like his Jewish colleagues, strongly idealized the reformer's position. Just as anti-Semites used the later Luther to legitimize their hatred, both Jewish and Protestant advocates of German Jewish emancipation were determined to wrest as benign a *Weltanschauung* as possible from the early Luther's ideas.[33]

Jewish and Liberal Protestant observers were, of course, painfully aware that, since the end of the nineteenth century, a completely different – nationalistic and *völkisch* – interpretation of Luther had emerged. Furthermore, they understood that much of contemporary Protestant theology, due to its inherent anti-Jewish inclinations, could hardly counteract that trend.[34] The immediate context of that develop-

---

32. Lamparter, Evangelische Kirche und Judentum, 59–60.

33. For the early Nazi period, Dietrich Bonhoeffer (1906–1945) should be mentioned in this context. In 1933, he introduced his essay "Die Kirche vor der Judenfrage" with several quotations from Luther's early work; see Eberhard Bethge, "Dietrich Bonhoeffer und die Juden," in Die Juden und Martin Luther, eds. Kremers et al. 211–48.

34. For other Protestant voices during the Weimar Period, see Gury Schnei-

ment was the amalgamation of modern political anti-Semitism with racist and social Darwinist theories, as well as a critique of modernity rooted in cultural pessimism. More than ever before, the Jewish minority was seen as the embodiment of all the phenomena *völkisch* thinking was fighting against: capitalistic mass society, socialism, liberal democracy, individualism, pluralism, and the notion of humanitarian values. Under the influence of racial theories, anti-Semitic thinking amalgamated into the 'Aryan myth,' including its negative countermyth of a Semitic race.[35] The defining characteristics of this ideology were the conviction that the Jews were a biologically inferior and destructive race, and a dualistic worldview, according to which the course of Western history, including the contemporary social, political, and cultural conflicts of modern society, was to be explained by the profound antagonism between the Germanic and the Jewish race. This radical variant of modern anti-Semitism developed into an ideology that tended to turn also against the Christian religion and her Jewish roots or, as in Houston Stewart Chamberlain's (1855–1927) *Die Grundlagen des neunzehnten Jahrhunderts* (1899), focused on an "Aryanization" and "dejudaization" of Christianity.[36] Such anti-Semitism drew on an abundance of sources providing political, racial, and religious arguments, including Luther's *Judenschriften*.

A paradigmatic example of this increasingly influential phenomenon is Theodor Fritsch (1852–1933), one of the most important and infamous representatives of radical *völkisch* anti-Semitism during the German *Kaiserreich* and the Weimar Republic.[37] Fritsch sought to systematically undermine the position of the Jews within German society by means of a hateful defamation of their religion, character, and mentality. Already in 1887, Fritsch had published his *Antisemiten-Katechismus*, which was later widely disseminated under the title *Handbuch der Judenfrage*. In this pamphlet, Fritsch compiled copious material depicting the Jewish minority as a dangerous enemy of the German people, and called for a "holy war" against Judaism's "evil spirit" as well as for the preservation of the "highest values of Aryan

---

der-Ludorf, "'Luther und die Juden' in den theologischen Bewegungen der Zwischenkriegszeit," in Martin Luthers "Judenschriften", eds. Oelke, Kraus et al, 145–60.

35. See Leon Poliakov, The Aryan Myth: A History of Racist & Nationalistic Ideas in Europe (New York: Basic Books, 1974).

36. See Uriel Tal, Religious and Anti-Religious Roots of Modern Antisemitism (New York: Leo Baeck Institute, 1971).

37. See, e. g., Elisabeth Albanis, "Anleitung zum Hass. Theodor Fritschs antisemitisches Geschichtsbild. Vorbilder, Zusammensetzung und Verbeitung," in Antisemitische Geschichtsbilder, eds. Werner Bergmann and Ulrich Sieg (Essen: Klartext Verlag, 2009): 167–91.

humanity."[38] The struggle against the Jewish religion played a crucial role in his political agitation. The Jewish emancipation, he claimed, had been granted on the basis of the utterly false assumption "that the Jewish religion had the same moral foundations as the Christian [tradition]."[39] He projected his obsessive anti-Semitic fantasies of a "Jewish world domination" onto the allegedly secret contents of rabbinical literature, using the accusation that the Talmud denigrated non-Jews as a class and permitted Jews all manner of criminal acts against them, including economic exploitation and ritual murder. The demonization of Judaism by means of traditional Christian stereotypes served to mobilize and reinforce existing anti-Semitic emotions. Fritsch extended his attacks against the concept of God in the Hebrew Bible, construing an animus between the 'God of Judaism,' a criminal idol, and the 'true God of Christianity.' In his pamphlet, *Der falsche Gott* (1916; first published in 1911 under the title *Beweis-Material gegen Jahwe*), Fritsch referred to Martin Luther, who had "crusaded against the dishonourable strangers with the sharpest weapons," as a model for an appropriate attitude towards the Jews.[40] He quoted extensively from Luther's polemics, emphasizing particularly his insistence on burning the synagogues and expelling the Jews as a means in the battle against the "poisonous, malicious snakes, assassins, and children of the devil."[41] Fritsch slandered Jewish citizens as heinous enemies of the German people, praising the "German Luther" as a savior who had bound Christianity and Germanness together and exposed the Christian opposition to Judaism, which had been covered up by the "Judaized" Catholic church.[42] While he was not in the slightest degree interested in Luther's actual theological arguments, the anti-Semitic demagogue shamelessly exploited the reformer's writings for his own tirades of hate.

As an early representative of a *völkisch* appropriation of Luther's late *Judenschriften*, Fritsch can be seen as a portent of what was to

38. Theodor Fritsch, Handbuch der Judenfrage. Eine Zusammenstellung des wichtigsten Materials zur Beurteilung des jüdischen Volkes, 26th edition (Hamburg: Hanseatische Druck- und Verlagsanstalt, 1907), 415–6.

39. Ibid., 12.

40. Theodor Fritsch, Der falsche Gott. Beweismaterial gegen Jahwe, 10th edition (Leipzig: Hammer-Verlag, 1933), 192.

41. Ibid., 189.

42. Ibid., 190–2. For the response of Jewish and Protestant thinkers to Fritsch's demonization of Judaism and the Jewish concept of God, see Christian Wiese, "Jahwe – ein Gott nur für Juden? Der Disput um das Gottesverständnis zwischen Wissenschaft des Judentums und protestantischer alttestamentlicher Wissenschaft im Kaiserreich", in Christlicher Antijudaismus und Antisemitismus. Theologische und kirchliche Programme deutscher Christen, ed. Leonore Siegele-Wenschkewitz (Frankfurt a. M.: Haag und Herchen, 1994): 27–94.

follow. Another anti-Semitic author, Alfred Falb, who published a pamphlet on Luther *und die Juden* in 1921, was clearly influenced by Fritsch as well as by the infamous book, *Die große Täuschung*, published in the same year by the Assyriologist Friedrich Delitzsch (1850–1922). "Luther the liberator," Delitzsch claimed, even though he was not equipped with modern knowledge about Judaism and the nature of the races, had already intuitively – by virtue of the "indignation of his Germanic character" – taken the path towards the insights of anti-Semitism, but unfortunately had stopped halfway through the journey.[43] However, Falb added, it should be appreciated that Luther had at least developed from a "pronounced friend of the Jews to their sharpest adversary."[44] The innocent Luther of 1523 had been too naïve to perceive the intrusion of the "Jewish spirit" into contemporary Christianity and to grasp the racial origins of Jewish usury. He had falsely assumed that it was possible to explain the shameful activities of the Jews as a religious delusion that could be overcome, rather than recognizing "that all our thinking and feeling, doing and acting [emerges from] the deepest foundations of our innate nature, which arises from our blood."[45] The reformer had, therefore, held onto the belief in Jesus' Jewish descent, whereas modern scholarship had now clearly demonstrated his Galilean-Aryan roots.

In the main section of his vitriolic pamphlet that is devoted to the topic, "Luther as an enemy of the Jews," Falb quotes extensively from Luther's anti-Jewish writings and links them to contemporary anti-Semitic propaganda. The reformer's acerbic attacks against the Jews can be explained by his anticipation of the "future Judaization of Christianity"[46] as well as by his perception of the vindictiveness and bloodthirstiness of the Jewish people. He should have recognized that Israel, rather than being God's chosen people, was the people of an evil demon.[47] At least Luther's followers in the present ought to understand that everything they loved in the "Old Testament" was "in reality merely Luther's poetic word and Luther's soul,"[48] whereas it was in actuality nothing but Jewish idolatry. Despite his naïveté, however, Luther had asked himself why it was even possible that such a "Barbarian people" existed on Earth, and his powerful turning against Judaism was thus highly significant for "Aryan humankind": "as an innermost outrage and abrupt rebellion against the Jewish-ori-

---

43. Alfred Falb, Luther und die Juden (Munich: Boepple, 1921), 4 and 8.
44. Ibid., 11.
45. Ibid., 24.
46. Ibid., 30.
47. Ibid., 47.
48. Ibid., 53.

ental violation of [human] nature, as a first awakening of the Germanic soul to an Aryan knowledge of God and rebirth."[49] While Luther had expressed this on an emotional level rather than as a clear political insight, he had at least sensed in his Germanic soul that the "God of the Jews" was not the God of Christian love, but an abominable idol. Contemporary – "Judaized" –Protestant theology, however, had distorted the reformer's message rather than reinterpreting it in the light of contemporary knowledge. Hence, they had irresponsibly silenced Luther's true theological legacy – "his fear for the future of the German soul, which, as he clearly anticipated, was in danger of being suffocated by the claws of the creeping demon of usury."[50]

Numerous examples of this discourse of hate might be listed: the recurring accusation, for instance in the *völkisch* writings of Mathilde Ludendorff (1877–1966), in Arthur Dinter's (1876–1948) "197 Thesen zur Vollendung der Reformation" (1926), and in the abundance of inflammatory anti-Semitic writings which stated that granting Jews equal rights had been a terrible betrayal of Luther. The church, then, had to get back to his late writings, his "unveiling of the secret goals of the Jews," and his "fiery sermons devoted to the defensive battle against Judaism," as Ludendorf phrased it in 1928.[51] Since 1917 at the latest, *völkisch* as well as German-Christian circles had adopted Luther's anti-Jewish polemics as an integral part of their agenda. The voices that made him a forerunner of racial anti-Semitism range from the *Bund für deutsche Kirche*, founded in 1921, to the *Glaubensbewegung Deutsche Christen* that had emerged in 1932.[52] Their sole objection was that Luther's reformation had not been radical enough, stopping short of eliminating all Jewish traces from Christianity, that is, from abandoning the "Old Testament" and discovering the "Aryan Jesus."[53] During the Nazi period, such attitudes were used to justify anti-Jewish violence; for instance, when the Thuringian bishop Martin Sasse (1890 –1942) portrayed the November pogrom in 1938 as a fulfilment of Luther's political suggestions to the Saxonian authori-

---

49. Ibid., 59.
50. Ibid., 53.
51. Mathilde Ludendorff, Der ungesühnte Frevel an Luther, Lessing. Mozart und Schiller im Dienste des ewigen Baumeisters aller Welten (Munich: Selbstverlag, 1928), 11; for Ludendorff's role in the völkisch movement, see Annika Spilker, Geschlecht, Religion und völkischer Nationalismus. Die Ärztin und Antisemitin Mathilde von Kemnitz-Ludendorff (1877–1966) (Frankfurt and New York: Campus, 2013).
52. For the phenomenon of völkisch theology, see Uwe Puschner and Clemens Vollnhals, eds., Die völkisch-religiöse Bewegung im Nationalsozialismus. Eine Beziehungs- und Konfliktgeschichte (Göttingen: Vandenhoeck & Ruprecht, 2012).
53. See Susannah Heschel, The Aryan Jesus: Christian Theologians and the Bible in Nazi (Princeton, NJ: Princeton University Press, 2010).

ties:

> On 10 November 1938, on Luther's birthday, the synagogues are burning in Germany. [...] In this hour the voice of the man needs to be heard, who, as the prophet of the Germans in the 16th century, once started, due to his ignorance, as a friend of the Jews, and who then, driven by his conscience, his experiences, and reality, became the greatest anti-Semite of his age, the warning voice of his people with regard to the Jews.[54]

In this vein, it might be mentioned that Alfred Rosenberg (1892–1946), whose views strongly influenced those of Hitler,[55] took a completely different direction in his infamous book, *Der Mythus des 20. Jahrhunderts* (1930). In this work, Rosenberg characterized Luther's enterprise and the Reformation as a step towards the "Judaization" of the German people: by translating the Bible, particularly the "Old Testament," into German and making it a Christian *Volksbuch*, Luther had permeated the German people with the "Jewish spirit." Thus, in one of the most influential articulations of Nazi ideology, Luther was not depicted as an anti-Semite but as a "friend of the Jews." By contrast, the German-Christian and *völkisch* circles in the Protestant church were eager to demonstrate the opposite, appropriating Luther's writings for their own anti-Semitic purposes and interpreting the principle of *ecclesia semper reformanda* as a means to "dejudaize" Christianity.

More interesting in this context than the radical racist discourse that instrumentalized Luther in order to justify anti-Semitic slander, demonization, hatred, and violence are the voices of those more moderate Protestant theologians who attempted to offset or limit the radical *völkisch* distortions of Luther's thinking. Most of them, however, did so without refraining from legitimizing their own anti-Semitic thought patterns in theological terms by referring to the reformer's ideas. While they aimed mainly to defend Christianity against the potential anti-Christian implications of anti-Semitism, in only very rare cases was this effort accompanied by genuine solidarity with Jews and Judaism.

How difficult it was for the majority of the German Protestant theologians to dissociate themselves from *völkisch* perspectives can

---

54. Martin Sasse, Martin Luther über die Juden: Weg mit ihnen! (Freiburg: Sturmhut-Verlag, 1938). For the völkisch and National socialist interpretation of Martin Luther, see Brosseder, Luthers Stellung zu den Juden, 156–208; and see Günter B. Ginzel, "Martin Luther: Kronzeuge des Antisemitismus," in Die Juden und Martin Luther, eds. Kremers et al., 189–210.

55. Alfred Rosenberg, Der Mythus des 20. Jahrhunderts. Eine Wertung der seelisch-geistigen Gestaltenkämpfe unserer Zeit (Munich: Hoheneichen-Verlag, 1930); see Ernst Piper, Alfred Rosenberg. Hitlers Chefideologe (Munich: Blessing, 2005).

be appreciated by looking at a series of articles the Rostock Lutheran church historian, Wilhelm Walther (1846–1924), published in 1921 under the title "Luther und die Juden" as a response to the aforementioned pamphlet by Alfred Falb. While rejecting the latter's contempt for the "Old Testament," Walther articulated clearly anti-Semitic views. "The repulsive element of today's anti-Semitism," he argued, was "that, in order to thoroughly denigrate the Jews, it also relentlessly makes the Old Testament contemptible. That way it only wreaks havoc, diminishing the victorious power of its legitimate fight."[56] According to the theologian, it was wrong to project Luther's justified accusations against the Talmud and the Jews of his time onto the "Old Testament." Many Christians were distressed by such attacks as it was undeniable that "the national flaws of the Jewish people" were obvious in the biblical stories, and yet Jesus had been loyal to the "Old Testament" in his message as well as in his deeds.[57] If the anti-Semites thought that "the weapon of ridiculing the Old Testament was indispensable for their battle against the threat emerging from Judaism," they should be aware that "the same Luther who so strongly valued the Old Testament, extracting so many blessings from it for our sake, clearly recognized the Jews' flaws and the threat they represented and warned against them in powerful language."[58] For Walther, the reception of Luther's thinking was supposed to teach Christians to respect the "Old Testament," but to despise postbiblical and contemporary Judaism as well as the Jews as a social group. Everything else about anti-Semitic prejudice and politics was perfectly justified:

> As harshly as the anti-Semites contradict Luther [with regard to his appreciation of the Old Testament], as much they have the right to refer to his sayings as far as their battle against the Jewish spirit is concerned. By referring to Luther they can make a strong impression, particularly since the latter, for a long period, took a much friendlier stance regarding the Jews, i.e. it needed many saddening experiences to prompt his harsh judgment about them.[59]

In the following passages of his lectures, Walther defended the anti-Jewish polemics of Luther's later writings while underscoring their contemporary relevance. The reformer, he argued, had no choice but to change course with respect to his position on the Jews: first, the Jews of his time blinded themselves to the truth of the Gospel, and second, his research into rabbinical literature opened his eyes to the

---

56. Wilhelm Walther, Luther und die Juden (Leipzig: Dörffling & Franke, 1921), 6.
57. Ibid.
58. Ibid., 9.
59. Ibid.

rabbis' acid mockery of Christianity in general and Jesus in particular. This enmity towards Christianity, Walther claimed, was also characteristic of contemporary Jewry. The anti-Semites were right in "pointing to the most recent events as a confirmation of Luther's assertions, since Jewish leaders of the Revolution, particularly in Russia [...], have unscrupulously shed as much Christian blood as they deemed useful in order to gain and secure their rule."[60] Furthermore, Walther implicitly questioned the entire process of Jewish emancipation in the modern period, again pointing to Luther's negative experiences:

> Were the consequences more favourable than those which Luther needed to deal with after having expressed similar thoughts in his writing in 1523 with its positive attitude towards the Jews? He came to the conclusion that the Jews would become the masters, and the Christians their servants.[61]

Walther thus corroborated anti-Semitic resentments and limited himself to cautioning against an exaggeration of anti-Jewish hatred as well as against the consequences of racist concepts; these would ultimately turn against the "Old Testament," denigrating it as "a purely Jewish book" and as a tradition stemming from "the evil Jewish spirit."[62] In this way, perfidious anti-Semites would themselves do the destructive work of the Jews – a popular argument among Protestant theologians at that time which enabled them to express their affinity to anti-Jewish views without abandoning the "Old Testament."

Walther's strategy of making theological and political concessions to anti-Semitic views while trying to prevent them from damaging Christianity's scriptural foundations was not uncommon among Protestant theologians of his day. In this regard, one popular tactic was to differentiate between the "Old Testament" – understood as the preliminary stage of Christianity – and Judaism, thus asserting a fundamental opposition between the two religions. This move was undergirded by a traditional supersessionist theology, which claimed the "Old Testament" (or rather, its 'valuable' parts) for Christianity, and rendered postbiblical Judaism a history of blindness and life under God's curse. Particularly the Luther of the late Judenschriften was seen as a guarantor of this anti-Jewish tradition; his early writings were depicted as an irrelevant error made by an inexperienced youth.

---

60. Ibid., 35.
61. Ibid., 37.
62. Ibid., 39.

1933 and the Failure of a Counternarrative

The effort of Jewish intellectuals to rescue an idealized Luther from anti-Semitic instrumentalization by accentuating the discontinuity between his early and his later writings on the Jews and to create a counternarrative to his appropriation by a nationalistic, anti-Semitic and anti-emancipatory ideology by portraying him as the forerunner and hero of the Enlightenment was doomed to failure. We know this from the reception of Luther's *Judenschriften* at the beginning of the Nazi period. It should be noted that, in the present article, the complex theological context can merely be indicated. Since the late nineteenth century, the "German Luther" had become a figure of German nationalism, and the reformer's later writings on the Jews were drawn on with increased frequency in public discussions of the social position of the Jewish minority in Germany. The 'Luther renaissance,' a programme of renewed historical and theological research on the reformer that had begun shortly before World War I,[63] had elicited a strong response from young Protestant theologians; the response was now intensified, with the numerous academic events on the occasion of Luther's 450th birthday on 10 November 1933 providing the opportunity to promote him as the herald of a new, *völkisch* Germany and the symbol of a revitalized 'Germanness.' Protestant church historians who were close to the renewal of Luther's theology felt compelled to treat the topic "Luther and the Jews" in one way or another and thus contributed to the widespread impact of the theo-political thought patterns of the reformer's anti-Jewish writings. The Jewish lawyer and publicist Ludwig Feuchtwanger (1885–1947) had a good sense of what the celebrations signified:

> This is not an antiquarian curiosity, a peculiar quirk of the dotage of a great man, retold on the occasion of his 450th birthday. The way Martin Luther let loose then against the Jews – that has been heard again and again from the German people for 450 years. In November 1933, we are finding that numerous important representatives of the Protestant church and academia are explicitly adopting this position of Luther, aping him word for word, and insistently citing and recommending his writings on the Jews.[64]

---

63. See, e. g., Christine Helmer and Bo Christian Holm, eds., Lutherrenaissance Past and Present (Göttingen: Vandenhoeck & Ruprecht, 2015). Ludwig Feuchtwanger, "Luthers Kampf gegen die Juden," Bayerisch-Israelitische Gemeindezeitung 9 (1933): 371–3, here 371. Feuchtwanger referred to the following sentence from a lecture by the Berlin liberal church historian Hans Lietzmann (1875–1942) on "Luther als deutscher Christ." "It is a terrible judgement that Luther passes here on the Jews, and we can establish that in the assessment of their harmful influence on Germany, he is fully in accord with the popular view of our present day" (quoted ibid., 371).

64. Ludwig Feuchtwanger, "Luthers Kampf gegen die Juden," Bayerisch-Israel-

Prominent Protestant theologians such as Heinrich Bornkamm, Hanns Rückert (1901–1974), Erich Seeberg (1888–1945) and others devoted much attention in their speeches to Luther's late writings; and while they tended to reject the *völkisch* usurpation of these texts, they were not immune to anti-Semitic prejudices, including racist ideas. Bornkamm, for instance, delivered a lecture titled *Volk und Rasse bei Martin Luther*, in which he indicated that Luther was also motivated by an "instinctive racial aversion to the Jews." The strong ambivalence of his position becomes apparent when he insists that, ultimately, the reformer's accusations against the Jews did not arise from racial difference, but then all the more emphasizes religious enmity: "They [Luther's accusations] were directed at a nation that incessantly offended God with their faithlessness and blasphemy." While there can be no doubt about the essentially religious character of Luther's enmity towards the Jews, Bornkamm argued, it is also true that the "crime" of "blasphemy against Christ," of defiance against the Holy Scripture, and of the "Jewish deprivation of God's honor" cannot account fully for Luther's rage. Rather, his response must have been intensified by the economic damage inflicted upon society by the Jews and their habit of "sucking out Germany."[65] The way in which Bornkamm outlined Luther's position, letting it go completely unchallenged, was more than likely to reinforce anti-Jewish sentiments amongst his audience. As such, it exemplifies the irresponsibility of Protestant theology at that political moment of German history.

Bornkamm is but one among many Protestant theologians who, despite dissociating themselves from blatantly racist readings of Luther, did not refrain from celebrating his hatred of the Jews.[66] A telling example in this regard is the Königsberg Luther scholar Erich Vogelsang (1904–1944), who presented his views in 1933 in a book dedicated to the Protestant Reich Bishop Ludwig Müller (1883–1945)

---

itische Gemeindezeitung 9 (1933): 371–3, here 371. Feuchtwanger referred to the following sentence from a lecture by the Berlin liberal church historian Hans Lietzmann (1875–1942) on "Luther als deutscher Christ." "It is a terrible judgement that Luther passes here on the Jews, and we can establish that in the assessment of their harmful influence on Germany, he is fully in accord with the popular view of our present day" (quoted ibid., 371).

65. Heinrich Bornkamm, "Volk und Rasse bei Martin Luther," in Bornkamm, Volk – Staat – Kirche. Ein Lehrgang der Theolog. Fakultät Gießen (Gießen: Töpelmann, 1933), 15–6.

66. On Nazi-inspired interpretations in the context of German-Christian theologies, see Peter von der Osten-Sacken, "Der nationalsozialistische Lutherforscher Theodor Pauls. Vervollständigung eines fragmentarischen Bildes," Das mißbrauchte Evangelium, ed. idem, 136–66.; Oliver Arnhold, "'Luther und die Juden' bei den Deutschen Christen," in Martin Luthers "Judenschriften", eds. Oelke, Kraus et. al., 191–212.

under the fitting title *Luther's Kampf gegen die Juden*.[67] While citing an "anti-Semitism that is necessary for the people these days"[68] and declaring his agreement with the Aryan paragraph, Vogelsang's main concern was to reject, by way of Luther, any notion of Christian solidarity with Judaism. Rather than eliding the fundamental antagonism between Judaism and Christianity – a tendency he saw at work in liberal theology from the Enlightenment onwards – what was needed in theological terms, he suggested, was an understanding of the fate of the Jews through the categories of "curse and blinding, wrath and the judgement of God" alone.[69] In this respect, he summarized Luther's position as follows: "That is the mysterious curse that has hung over the Jewish people for hundreds of years […], in truth, a self-inflicted curse. On Christ, the bone of contention, they are dashed to pieces, crushed, dispersed."[70] The Lutheran theologian went as far as alluding to the myth of the "eternal Jew," implying that this curse, from which no political emancipation could redeem the Jews, made them a dangerous, demonic element within German society. In theological terms, he was unable to perceive something different in Judaism than a nation damned by God, and even the tradition rooted in Luther's writings from 1523 and then adopted by the 'mission to the Jews', which at least a critical potential against *völkisch* anti-Semitism, played no role whatsoever in his thinking.

Instead, Vogelsang's interpretation of Luther's "battle against the Jews" had a clear political dimension and featured a full range of stereotypes from the arsenal of anti-Semitism – from polemics against the "Jewish-rabbinical morality" to the interpretation of the notion of Israel's chosenness and the faith in the coming of the Messiah as an expression of "Judaism's enormously tenacious claim to world domination."[71] Vogelsang even attributes völkisch categories to Luther by asserting that he had an aversion against "everything foreign to the country," with much of his sentiment against the Jews having a "nationalist tone," being directed against their "un-German slyness and mendacity."[72] Correspondingly, Luther's real strength, Vogelsang suggested, was the "inner agreement and close fit of German-

---

67. For a Jewish response, see Ludwig Feuchtwanger's review in Bayerisch-Israelitische Gemeindezeitung 9 (1933): 380–2.

68. Vogelsang, Luthers Kampf gegen die Juden, 6.

69. Ibid., 18.

70. Ibid., 10.

71. Ibid., 14.

72. Ibid., 31. Judaism should not, according to Vogelsang, be exposed to racial contempt, but "People and peoples and races are not – as the rationalism of the philosemites opines – all of equal value, equal in terms of nobility, intelligence, approval, strength" (ibid., 12).

ness and Christianity."⁷³ He left open – as did many of his Protestant colleagues – the precise nature Luther's "tough mercy" (*scharfe Barmherzigkeit*) was meant to take in the politics of the present, but his emphasis on Luther's idea of a "clean separation between Jews and Christians"⁷⁴ demonstrates that what he had in mind was a politics of separation and of a determined revision of the legal emancipation and social integration of German Jewry. It would be difficult not to understand this attitude as a legitimation of the initial Nazi politics against the Jews. In any case, Vogelsang firmly rejected Eduard Lamparter's liberal position: Luther's solution for the "Jewish Question" was definitely not "mutual understanding" or "rapprochement," let alone the amicable acknowledgment "that [quoting Lamparter] the Jewish religion, too, had been granted a divine right to exist *alongside* the Christian [religion], and a special gift and task within humankind's spiritual life (even today)." Rather, the basic contours of the politics of the church ought to be "separation of the spirits and a determined defensive action against the inner subversion by Jewish ways, against all 'Judaization'."⁷⁵

Vogelsang espoused a classic form of Jew-hatred that combined elements of traditional supersessionist anti-Judaism with obvious socio-cultural enmity towards the Jewish minority and openness to racial concepts⁷⁶ – a widespread Protestant attitude in 1933 and

73. Ibid., 32.
74. Ibid., 23.
75. Ibid., 25.
76. My perspective differs here from that of Brosseder, Luthers Stellung zu den Juden, 131–5, who insists that Vogelsang's work is of "high value" despite its being temporally affected by the situation of 1933. For Brosseder, Vogelsang attempted a "description of the Jewish question in Luther that does justice to the theology of the reformer" (130). He concedes that Vogelsang both lacks the "academically necessary distance" in relation to Luther's later writing (132) and that he isolates the "Jewish question" in Luther from the overall context of his theology. Given Vogelsang's argument, however, it seems obvious that his goal was, in his capacity as an expert on Luther, to legitimize contemporary anti-Semitism on the basis of the writings of the outstanding theological authority within Protestantism and thus to express agreement with the initial political measures of the Nazi regime. Only within that framework Vogelsang's book understands itself also as a contribution to historical and theological research. This is corroborated by a comparison to another book published in 1932 by Walter Holsten (1908–1982) under the title *Christentum und nichtchristliche Religion nach der Auffassung Luthers*. Much stronger than Vogelsang, Holsten aimed at a scholarly understanding of Luther's writings on the Jews and tried to avoid touching on contemporary politics or alluding to racial categories. However, Holsten, too, presents an anti-Jewish theology according to which Christianity was Israel's "continuation and fulfilment," whereas the "legalistic" religion of postbiblical Judaism was the "authentic scion and descendant of the illegitimate religion of Old Israel" which was, in fact, blind with regard to the truth of the Holy Scripture; see Walter Holsten, Christentum und nichtchristliche Religion nach der Auffassung Luthers (Gütersloh:

beyond. Vogelsang might have made the same points without recourse to Luther, who simply served as legitimation for a virulent anti-Semitism obviously in debt to Adolf Stoecker (1835–1909), who had influenced an entire generation of Protestant academic theologians and ministers.[77] The image of the Jews that was disseminated by them was that of an alien and hostile, if not dangerous, race, whose allegedly 'subversive' power imperilled Germany and called for action – a tacit consent to the Nazi's discriminatory measures. The fact that the Lutheran church and Lutheran theologians were also influenced by Luther's "two kingdoms theory," which prompted them to concede the right to act in the political realm completely to the State, further contributed to their policy of leaving the fate of the Jews to the Nazi regime. The same holds true for the Confessing Church, which turned out to be equally impotent and passive – first, because many of its members shared the prevailing anti-Semitic sentiments,[78] and second, because it could not rely on a theological tradition that would have enabled it to foil the defamation of Judaism and the persecution of the Jews.

This impression is corroborated by a brief look at yet another Protestant statement from the 1930s regarding Luther and the Jews. In 1936 and 1937, Hans Georg Schroth, a member of the Confessing Church, who was close to Karl Barth's "dialectical theology" and, after 1945, was part of the *Arbeitsgemeinschaft "Juden und Christen"* at the German Protestant Church Convention, published two pieces, titled "Luther und die Juden" and "Luthers christlicher Antisemi-

---

Bertelsmann, 1932), 101. Holsten's systematized summary of Luther's theological verdict on Judaism, presented with an air of agreement (ibid., 99–116), denies Judaism the theological right to exist; and when the author interprets Luther's "sharp mercy" as an expression of "reformatory depth and acerbity," delineating it from a "soft and thus wrong merci" and depicting it as "a loyal imitation of the merci of God," who "performs his merci by way of his alien act, his annihilating wrath," it seems hard not to read this as an at least potential justification of violence against the Jews. The statement following these words, addressing the anti-Semites and emphasizing that he was talking about an essentially "religious issue" and that "the merci meant by Luther was ultimately merci and not hatred" (ibid., 125–6), is strongly limited by what is said before.

77. See Günter Brakelmann, Martin Greschat and Werner Jochmann, Protestantismus und Politik: Werk und Wirkung Adolf Stoeckers (Hamburg: Christians, 1982).

78. See Wolfgang Gerlach, And the Witnesses Were Silent: The Confessing Church and the Persecution of the Jews (Lincoln: University of Nebraska Press, 1999); for the discussion of Luther's Judenschriften among theologians of the Confessing Church, see Siegfried Hermle, "'Luther und die Juden' in der Bekennenden Kirche," in Martin Luthers "Judenschriften", in eds. Oelke, Kraus et al., 161–90. For receptions within differing groups within the German Protestant church, see Christopher J. Probst, Demonizing the Jews: Luther and the Protestant Church in Nazi Germany (Bloomington and Indianapolis: Indiana University Press, 2012).

tismus". These publications took a courageous stance insofar as the author defended missionary activities amongst the Jews against the views of racial anti-Semitism, insisted on the right of baptized Jews to become Protestant pastors, vigorously rejected the so-called "Aryan paragraph" and repudiated the radical assumptions of *völkisch* theologies. Luther's "Christian anti-Semitism," Schroth argued, clearly contradicted any form of racial thinking; rather, it was based on hope for the salvation of the Jews and aimed for a theological refutation of Judaism. Even though Judaism, from the reformer's view, was part of the diabolical coalition of the Antichrist as it allegedly slandered Christ, Luther knew that the Church, the "new Israel," was continously threatened by the temptation to deny Christ and thus to become "Judaism" itself. In its essence, Schroth emphasized, Judaism was "anti-Christianity," as was racial anti-Semitism due to its attacks against the Christian tradition: "The Jew is always standing in front of the door, and this would even be the case should there no longer be a racially or politically visible Judaism. And who would deny that today we have to fight such an 'anti-Semitic' battle within the Church?"[79] In theory, Schroth even wanted to express a positive thought – namely, that Christians should not abandon the Jews to hatred as they shared with them the solidarity of being sinners before God and because Christians, too, were always tempted to turn against Christ. In addition to this thought, which recalls the attitude of the young Luther, he intended to say that in the present, Luther's "Christian anti-Semitism" could be understood as directed not just against the Jews but also against the *völkisch* movement. Thus, if a nation decides to turn against Christ, it becomes "Jewish," "be it what it may in terms of its race and ethnicity, and even if it is Catholic, Protestant or non-religious. And when a nation, by deciding against Christ, has become a people of Judaism, it will share the fate of racial Judaism: rejection by God."[80] According to Schroth, "the Jew prevails also in anti-Semitism if the latter turns against Christ" – and that is why it is the church's duty to "resist against all forms of anti-Christianity or *völkisch*-national Christianity, as Luther has done with regard to the Jews."[81]

Schroth was apparently unaware of how dangerous and counterproductive Luther's "salvational anti-Semitism" was and that this rather desperate and convoluted argumentation, a belittlement of Luther's anti-Jewish theology, fostered anti-Semitic patterns of thought even if it tried to turn them critically against Nazism. Here,

---

79. Hans Georg Schroth, Luthers christlicher Antisemitismus heute (Witten: Westdeutscher Lutherverlag, 1937), 20.
80. Ibid., 22.
81. Ibid., 22–3.

Judaism becomes the symbol of the "anti-Christ" and of the diabolical, which implies that the diabolical in all of its manifestations is related to Judaism. Jews and Judaism thus appear as a countervailing power poised to undermine what is true and ethically good. It is hardly surprising, then, that while Schroth defended Jews who had converted to Christianity, he had no word of solidarity with the other Jews and did not challenge the regime's right to engage in racial politics. His position is revealing as it demonstrates that – even with the best intentions – it was impossible, on the basis of Luther's theology, to effectively counter the anti-Semitic image of the Jews, let alone the denial of Judaism's theological right to exist. On the contrary, anti-Jewish sentiments were reinforced by such interpretations.

In retrospect, the idealization of Luther on the part of Jewish intellectuals and their belief in the liberating effects of the Reformation on German culture emerges as a tragic illusion, the authors blind to the reformer's true views and the absence of contemporary Protestantism's response to their dialogical approach. The same might be true for their political faith in the Enlightenment principles they strove to see at work in Luther. Nevertheless, it seems worthwhile to note the dignity inherent in the endeavour to invoke – via an idealized Luther – a liberal counter-tradition of freedom of thought, tolerance, and human decency that had, tragically, become widely irrelevant in German politics – and in Protestant theology. By showcasing otherwise hidden implications of Luther's ideas, Jewish scholars protested what they perceived as a catastrophic decline of the liberal tradition that had once guaranteed Jewish emancipation and integration. Ultimately, idealizing Luther in an attempt to offset the inhumane logic of modern anti-Semitism was both a desperate apologetic strategy and an act of intellectual resistance that merits respect.

This seems all the more the case in view of the lack of solidarity on the part of nearly the full gamut of Protestant theologians. Luther's writings on the Jews not only overshadowed Jewish-Christian relations when theologians tolerated or actively promoted the reformer's ideas in order to demonize the Jewish minority or justify anti-Semitic politics. More subtly, even Protestant theologians who rejected the harsh views espoused by Luther in 1543 and tried to oppose anti-Semitism by referring to the more sympathetic elements of his statement in 1523 failed to address the fundamental flaws of the reformer's perception of Judaism and to engage in a radical critique of the inevitable political consequences of his supersessionist theology. Consequently, they did not develop a tradition of respect and dialogue that would have served them in countering the radicalization of anti-Semitic mentalities within the Protestant church and beyond. The handful of hopeful signs for a turn towards an affirmation of Judaism as a valuable religious and cultural force within German society, seen in Eduard Lamparter's rather unique position, were silenced by an overwhelming merging of different anti-Jewish and anti-Semitic convictions that came to the fore in the crucial years which destroyed Weimar democracy.

The challenge in the Jewish discourse on Luther since the Enlightenment, be it characterized by idealization or theo-political critique, remained unheard by German Protestantism before World War II and the Shoah. It was only gradually – and often reluctantly – that Protestant theologians turned their gaze to the shadow Luther's anti-Semitism had cast on Protestant-Jewish relations and on Protestantism itself.[82] The historical and theological questions with which they were confronted were nothing less than radical: was there a direct connection between Luther's writings on the Jews, a specifically German-Protestant variant of anti-Semitism, and the 'eliminationist' anti-Semitism (Daniel J. Goldhagen) that led to an unprecedented genocide? Whatever the historical answer to that question, Protestant self-reflection after the crimes of the twentieth century must face the destructive theological and political traditions that belong to the legacy of Luther and the Reformation. The theological questions emerging from the historical analysis were no less challenging: was it possible to forge a new tradition of respectful dialogue with Judaism on the basis of Luther's theology by reinterpreting his understanding of the Bible and his doctrine of justification, or was it necessary to jettison constitutive elements of his thought?

Albert H. Friedlander (1927–2004), a German-Jewish emigré scholar in London, offered a personal response to such questions in an essay he published in 1987, titled "Martin Luther und wir Juden". As part of his reflections, he presented a vision of Luther in his *feste Burg* – a solid castle with a treasure chamber full of glimmering gold, but also dark vaults and torture chambers. It is in the latter that the tools for pogroms are to be found – the place where the Jews became the menacing antagonists of his own faith. In an imagined interchange, Friedlander asks Luther to lock the doors of the torture chamber and to walk with him to the treasure chamber – his library, which houses the Bible and where they can engage in a dialogue about their differing understanding of this shared book in an atmosphere of mutual respect. With this vision, Friedlander offered Protestant theology a path towards a critical confrontation with Luther's

---

82. For the Protestant discourse after 1945, see Wolfgang Kraus, "'Luther und die Juden' in den kirchenpolitischen Stellungnahmen und Entwicklungen seit 1945," in Martin Luthers "Judenschriften", eds. Oelke, Kraus et al., 289–312.

legacy. In this vision, the dark chamber of Protestant anti-Semitism would be acknowleged and left behind, and a conversation would begin about what unites as well as what separates Judaism and Christianity.[83]

---

83. Albert H. Friedländer, "Martin Luther und wir Juden," in Die Juden und Martin Luther, eds. Kremer et al., 289–300, esp. 297.

Exclusive Space as a Criterion for Salvation in German Protestantism during the Third Reich

By Dirk Schuster

Recent years have witnessed an expansion in the use of spatial conceptions for historical analysis.[1] In the fields of Study of Religion and Theology specifically, researchers such as Kim Knott have introduced 'space' as an analytical category.[2] This term is distinctly polysemic, encompassing, in the religious arena, physical space such as a church, mosque, or synagogue; geographic space such as a region or country; but also social space, perhaps a Baptist women's choir or a Protestant congregation. In a broad sense, the first two areas, that is, physical and geographical, might be perceived as constructed space, and the third by its content. Our Baptist women's choir, for instance, is a space in which women of Baptist belief meet in order to sing together. Thus, we already note a certain exclusivity by which entry into this space is governed: one must be a woman, wish to sing, and adhere to the Baptist faith in order to belong.

Our Baptist women's choir, however, is still not an 'exclusive space,' as its boundaries are permeable. It would be possible for this choir to accept men into its ranks, perhaps because there was no men's choir available for those who would like to sing in a group. It would also be possible that the choir numbers among its members someone who does not sing, but performs administrative duties for the group.

---

1. For a research overview, see Christoph Bernhardt, "Governance, Statehood, and Space in 20th Century Political Struggles. An Introduction," Historical Social Research 42 (2017): 199–217.

2. For example, the articles in Journal of Religion in Europe 9 (2016), issue 4; András Máté-Tóth and Cosima Rughiniş, eds., Spaces and borders: Current Research on Religion in Central and Eastern Europe (Berlin: de Gruyter, 2011); Lise Paulsen Galal et al., "Middle Eastern Christian Spaces in Europe: Multi-sited and Super-diverse," Journal of Religion in Europe 41 (2016): 1–25; Thomas Erne and Peter Schüz, eds., Die Religion des Raumes und die Räumlichkeit der Religion (Göttingen: Vandenhoeck & Ruprecht, 2010).

Furthermore, it would be possible to include non-Baptist members if appropriate, say, for inter-religious projects.

In what follows, the term 'exclusive space' will extend the spatial conception regarding religion to the feature of 'race' (race referring to a racist categorization of humans). For this purpose, 'exclusive space' is to be understood in the sense that only a specific group of individuals ever has access to it. 'Outsiders' can never enter this 'exclusive space.' In this context, then, space becomes a social construction that coheres with the sociological approach of spatial conception, as, for example, Kim Knott has discussed in her work on boundaries in different religious spheres.

For Knott, "it is boundaries – themselves constructed and invested with meaning – that define containers and position people and objects, that generate margins, and encourage, permit or prohibit crossings. Insides and outsides [...] are themselves constituted by boundaries."[3] As such, the boundary is the decisive criterion for constructing spaces.

The interior, or space, then, is not characterized primarily by its content, but rather by its boundaries. This boundary building process features built-in differentiation. To take a simple example, we might consider the insider and the outsider, that is, those who belong within the space – or those permitted to enter it – and those who do not belong within or are not permitted to enter it.[4] Defining space in this way not only makes it possible to clarify who belongs to the ingroup, but also the definition of the actual in-group using this mechanism. By excluding 'others,' criteria are presented to the in-group which must be fulfilled in order to belong. In this indirect way, the in-group is defined by the 'others.'[5]

Recalling our Baptist women's choir, we have an example of a space defined by boundaries (it is, after all, a *Baptist women's* choir) which are somewhat porous. In the present article, I discuss a space

---

3. Kim Knott, "Inside, Outside and the Space in-between: Territories and Boundaries in the Study of Religion," Temenos: Nordic Journal of Contemporary Religion 44 (2008): 41–66, here at 45.

4. Ibid., 44.

5. For this mechanism as expressed in the example of national identities, see Elfie Rembold and Peter Carrier, "Space and Identity: Constructions of National Identities in an Age of Globalization," National Identities 13 (2011): 361–77, esp. 362–5. And see Oliver Zimmer, "Boundary Mechanisms and Symbolic Resources: Towards a Process-oriented Approach to National Identity," Nations and Nationalism 9 (2003): 173–93. During the nineteenth century it was important for Catholics and Protestants for the own identity to refer at the differences between the own confession and the 'other'; see Anthony J. Steinhoff, "Ein zweites konfessionelles Zeitalter? Nachdenken über die Religion im langen 19. Jahrhundert," Geschichte und Gesellschaft 30 (2004): 549–70, here at 561.

that did not evolve naturally,[6] but, like countries or buildings, was constructed intentionally with exclusive entry criteria. In this respect, one might think of a popular club, in which entrance selection is made on the basis of style, appearance, social status, or connections. In the article, I try to connect this mechanism of inclusion – or rather, exclusion – to religion. Specifically, I discuss defining race as the criterion for accessing a particular form of religion which then crafted a distinct pattern of exclusion.

Race as a Boundary for Religious Salvation

Let us begin by clarifying what is meant by a religiously motivated exclusion based on race. For this purpose, I shall define race and racism, and discuss the grounds on which a racial categorization is made.

George Frederickson defined racism by ethno-cultural differences, which he further characterizes as congenital, indelible, and unchangeable. Here, he is referring to features such as language, traditions, and family relations which are regarded as characteristics of an imaginary collective.[7] To this characterization I would add, as a typical feature of racial concepts, the alleged behavioral patterns of such a constructed collective. By this I refer to persisting ideas such as 'Jewish greed' or 'the inability of Africans to accommodate to western standards.' Fredrickson mentions a further feature of racism, relevant in this context: "Racism is expressed in practices, institutions, and structures which find their alleged justification or validation in the recognition of a group as 'the others.'"[8] In what follows, I will not use the term 'racism' in contexts that admit of the possibility of assimilation. It was from this assimilation that the possibility of conversion within the confines of institutionalized religion evolved.

Boundaries are drawn to differentiate oneself from 'the other.' Hence (national) identity is constructed in the process of defining 'the other,' a particularly relevant point with respect to building group identity. One separates from 'the other' to demarcate the features of one's own or in-group-identity.[9] If these identity boundaries are understood as insuperable due to innate characteristics, we are dealing with a racial – or racist – conceptualization.

---

6. For the so-called 'Borderscapes Concept' as a dynamic social process, see Chiara Brambilla, "Exploring the Critical Potential of the Borderscapes Concept," Geopolitics 20 (2015): 14–34. For a critical overview on Borderscapes, see Elena Dell'agnese and Anne-Laure Amilhat Szary, "Introduction. Borderscapes: From Border Landscapes to Border Aesthetics," Geopolitics 20 (2015): 4–13.

7. George M. Fredrickson, Rassismus: Ein historischer Abriß (Hamburg: Hamburger Edition, 2004), 13.

8. Ibid., 13.

9. Rembold and Carrier, "Space and Identity," 361–77.

To take an obvious example, let us consider skin color. If one is denied access to a group because of his/her skin color, this is racist behavior. It rules out the possibility that 'the other' could ever become part of the 'in-group,' One might even call this racial exclusion on the grounds of innate and irreconcilable barriers.

In Nazi Germany, the cohabitation of Germans and Jews was portrayed as impossible. The Jews, here 'the others,' had to be separated from the Germans. These 'racially othered' people were denied access to society: they were actually excluded from being part of society.[10] This concept resurfaced in the apartheid regime in South Africa, and in the former racial restrictions of the U.S. judicial system. Exclusion from social and political participation in the U.S. and South Africa, however, was not directed at religion. The 'racially othered' could participate in the dominant religion of the 'standard culture.' Despite their oppression, American and South African people of color could join the Christian community.

While the American church communities were often in the past divided into Whites and people of color, with separately held services, access to Christianity itself was not denied. Racial exclusion in religion to create an exclusive space, however, is something else again. In what follows, I show that some people in Germany were denied access because of their alleged belonging to a specific race. This meant denial of religious salvation, because such salvation rested on sacraments such as baptism and Communion. Ultimately, this ended in exclusion from the Christian community itself. Only people of the 'right' race were able to receive the holy sacraments and the divine message of the clerical doctrine. There was no avenue for the 'others' to become Christian or to maintain their status. In this way, the space in which religion could be practiced or experienced was defined by race. This racial boundary determined who would partake of religious salvation. The boundary became the distinguishing feature – precisely as Knott presented in her discussion of space in the sphere of religion.[11]

The Creation of an Exclusive Space for Salvation – The German Christian Church Movement and the De-Judaization of Christianity

In the first part of the present article, I drew my examples from Christianity because my empirical case-study, presented below, deals with

10. See for example the 'prophet' of the volkish movement in the nineteenth century, Paul de Lagarde (1827–1891) and his position in Ulrich Sieg, Deutschlands Prophet: Paul de Lagarde und die Ursprünge des modernen Antisemitismus (München: Hanser, 2007).

11. Knott, "Inside, Outside and the Space in-between," 56.

the realization of the aforementioned racial-religious concept in twentieth- century German Protestantism.

In 1927, two young pastors in Thuringia founded a group that later became known as the "German Christian Church Movement" (*Kirchenbewegung Deutsche Christen*). I use the term "German-Christians" to refer specifically to this ideological group, and not to the general population of Christians in Germany. Let me note from the outset that we are not dealing here with an isolated phenomenon mostly found on paper. To be sure, there were several small groups of the so-called *volkisch* movement in Germany in the first half of the twentieth century that counted no more than 1,000 members. For example, the "German Nobility Society" (*Deutsche Adelsgenossenschaft*), established in 1920, featured an "Aryan-paragraph" (*Arier-Paragraph*) that restricted membership in this society to Aryans.[12] But this and similar societies exerted little influence on broader parts of the German society.[13]

The German Christian Church Movement, by contrast, took control of the whole regional church in Thuringia during the church elections in 1933.[14] In the following years, the Movement expanded its ecclesial-political influence to other Protestant regional churches in the Third Reich. By the end of the 1930s, it supervised six Protestant regional churches (*Landeskirchen*) in Nazi Germany, and had forged alliances with other regional churches. The evangelical regional churches, which sympathized with the German Christian Church Movement, adopted its German-Christian conception of religion. This Protestant movement, which was active until 1945, held significant sway over Germany's regional churches.

German-Christian religious doctrine was grounded in the racial subdivision of humankind. Accordingly, it understood the different races as reflecting a divine hierarchical order. This racist doctrine was not only a (scientific) theory; it also formed the basis for German-Christian action:

---

12. Stefan Breuer, "Der Streit um den 'nordischen Gedanken' in der völkischen Bewegung," Zeitschrift für Religions- und Geistesgeschichte 62 (2010), 1–27, here at 17.

13. See Uwe Puschner, Die völkische Bewegung im wilhelminischen Kaiserreich: Sprache – Rasse – Religion (Darmstadt: Wissenschaftliche Buchgesellschaft, 2001). For the so called 'volkisch movement' during the Third Reich, see Uwe Puschner and Clemens Vollnhals, eds., Die völkisch-religiöse Bewegung im Nationalsozialismus. Eine Beziehungs- und Konfliktgeschichte (Göttingen: Vandenhoeck & Ruprecht, 2012).

14. See Oliver Arnhold, "Entjudung" – Kirche im Abgrund, vol. 1: Die Thüringer Kirchenbewegung Deutsche Christen 1928–1939 (Berlin: Institut Kirche und Judentum, 2010).

> First and foremost, the fight against Judaism is an irrevocable command to the German people. This contrast is far-reaching and affects all areas of the German life. For this contrast poses the greatest decision, in religious and ecclesiastical life, within German history. In the question of the possible influence of Judaism or the Jewish spirit on German religious life, and in the question of the elimination of this influence, the indispensable and unavoidable fundamental question of the present German religious situation is posed.[15]

German-Christians believed that they grasped the hierarchical order of the world. 'Miscegenation' and 'Internationalism' were viewed as rebellion against the divine plan. Important factors influencing the effectiveness of the German Christian Church Movement were Protestantism, the interdependence of Christianity (in Germany) and National Socialism, as well as a radical anti-Semitism.

The German Christian Church Movement explicitly sought to impose a second reformation of Protestant Christianity in Germany. As Walter Grundmann (1906–1976), professor of Volkisch Theology and New Testament in Jena/Thuringia and scientific director of the "Institute for the Study and Eradication of Jewish Influence on German Church Life" (*Institut zur Erforschung und Beseitigung des jüdischen Einflusses auf das deutsche kirchliche Leben*),[16] pointed out:

> Let us be clear about this: It seemed impossible to people during Luther's time that one could be Christian without acknowledging the Pope's authority – which for us is a matter of course. Today it seems just as improbable to many of us that one can sustain Christianity and the Church without the sacred-historical reference to the history of the Old Testament [...]. We are convinced that the history of the coming decades will confirm our view [of the German Christians; D.S.].[17]

God often sent holy men to his chosen people – the German-Christians believed these to be Germans. Not surprisingly, they considered Martin Luther to have been the first among these holy men. Protestantism, then, was a German belief system for this church movement. And, rejecting "Jewish influence" on the church, the German-Christians wanted to impose Luther's reformation under the 'Führer' Adolf Hitler, sent by God.

The term 'Germanisation' (*Germanisierung*) refers to a racially

---

15. Walter Grundmann, Die Entjudung des religiösen Lebens als Aufgabe Deutscher Theologie und Kirche (Weimar: Verlag Deutsche Christen, 1939), 9–10.

16. On the Institute, see Susannah Heschel, The Aryan Jesus: Christian Theologians and the Bible in Nazi Germany (Princeton, NJ: Princeton University Press, 2008); Oliver Arnhold, "Entjudung" – Kirche im Abgrund, vol. 2: Das "Institut zur Erforschung und Beseitigung des jüdischen Einflusses auf das deutsche kirchliche Leben" 1939–1945 (Berlin: Institut Kirche und Judentum, 2010).

17. Grundmann, Die Entjudung des religiösen Lebens, 17.

motivated concept of religion with an exclusive character. It was directed against Jewish influences and church members who were not 'ethnically German.' Such racial approaches to Christianity were not new: they had been a feature of German Protestantism since the early twentieth century.[18] In 1914, for example, an evangelical group in Vienna sought to split the Austrian church into a German one and a Slavic one, so that each race would have its own church and organization.[19] But the German Christian Church Movement was the first to connect the idea of a German Christianity with the racist doctrine of a political movement – National Socialism. Hitler was assigned the role of messiah in German-Christian doctrine: "Führer by the grace of God," "Führer, sent by God," "God's instrument," and "German prophet":

> Thus, Adolf Hitler's National Socialism hammers against the last gate, stands in the concealed dark place of every true fighter, stands there – this is completely different and new – as the German people, in order to be forgiven for its sins and to be blessed for its holy world mission. Because his nature is truthful no matter what questions he raises, because he, with an unprecedented passionate fervor, recognizes the eternal Creator's will, he will soon step over the threshold into the kingdom of the last knowledge for the salvation of the world for the next three and four centuries. Then again will be the time when piety is not a disease, not a flight from the world, but health and strength, where one adores and fights and works and sees worship in it. Then history will write: the best National Socialists were also the best Christians, and Adolf Hitler has set the soul of the German people free to meet their Creator and Savior Jesus Christ![20]

This racist doctrine was constitutive of the German-Christians' ideology. "Miscegenation" was seen as a violation of "the order of God." And "biological miscegenation" was just the beginning. Religion, too, was deemed "racially predestined." According to German-Christians, God revealed Himself to people of different nations in different ways, so that every nation would have its own realization of Christianity. As such, for Siegfried Leffler (1900 –1983), the church can "not circumvent the heavy altercation with the new [National Socialism], if it con-

---

18. At this time, this conception was often combined with the idea that Jesus was not a Jew but an Aryan; see Heschel, The Aryan Jesus, 26–66.

19. See Dirk Schuster, Die Lehre vom "arischen" Christentum: Das wissenschaftliche Selbstverständnis im Eisenacher "Entjudungsinstitut" (Göttingen: V&R unipress, 2017), 48. More examples regarding the topic can be found in the following pages.

20. Siegfried Leffler, "Nationalsozialismus und Christentum," Briefe an Deutsche Christen 1 (1932): 2–4, here at 4. On this topic, see Dirk Schuster, ""Führer von Gottes Gnaden" – Das deutsch-christliche Verständnis vom Erlöser Adolf Hitler," Zeitschrift für Religions- und Geistesgeschichte 68 (2016): 277–85.

tinues to aim at spreading the enlightened idea of God from within the people, and at illustrating the eternal power of God as Creator to the nation."[21]

The political agitation of the German-Christians was not particularly aimed at other Christian confessions in Germany, such as Catholicism. In this, we see that the real restriction of religious salvation was based on racial conception. For the German Christian Church Movement, Protestantism was reserved for members of the Nordic, or Germanic, race. With their international scope, other Christian belief systems, such as world Protestantism and a universal papacy,[22] were deemed 'Jewish' ideas in the eyes of the German-Christians, and anathema to divine creation.[23]

While the German-Christians accused the German Catholics of following a falsified doctrine, introduced by foreign racial influences, the latter were still eligible for religious salvation because of their belonging to the allegedly 'right' race. In this way, German-Christians cherished the idea of bridging the schism of the Christian church in Germany and eventually of uniting all Germans in one "national church" (*Nationalkirche*), based on the concept of race. Faith in the Christian God and the racially constructed membership of the German people were of greater significance in the attainment of salvation than singular confessional voices.

The space in which salvation was a possibility, then, was a racial one. That accounts for why Scandinavians, who had such racial affinity to the 'German Aryan race,' were granted access to salvation by the German Christian Church Movement. This spatial orientation becomes patent in the case of the so-called 'Jewish Christians.'

'Jewish Christians' were individuals who were either converts to Christianity, or Christians with Jewish ancestors who converted to Christianity. Church records (*Kirchenbücher*), the same documents used by the Nazis to determine who was Jewish and who was not, made this differentiation an easy matter. This criterion was a central one for the German-Christian religious doctrine. The German people was regarded as God's chosen people and the German-Christians saw the Germans in a contrary position to the outcast Jewry:

---

21. Leffler, "Nationalsozialismus und Christentum," 2.
22. For the problem of Papacy and Catholicism in the view of the German Christians, see Dirk Schuster, "Papst und Papsttum aus der Perspektive der Kirchenbewegung Deutschen Christen," in Die Päpste und die Protestanten: Begegnungen im modernen Europa, eds. Gerulf Hirt, Silke Satjukow, and David Schmiedel (Cologne, Weimar, and Vienna: Böhlau, 2018): 57–78.
23. See, for example, Walter Grundmann, Die Entjudung des religiösen Lebens; Hugo Pich, Frei vom Juden – auch im Glauben! Ein Ruf zur Entjudung von Kirche und Christentum (Sibiu/ Hermannstadt: Krafft & Drotleff, 1943).

> To have made the thought of race an expression of the feeling of the people is the merit of Adolf Hitler. [...] The question of race has arisen for Adolf Hitler in Judaism. Judaism is not first and foremost another religion, but a foreign race that intrudes, that wants racial chaos in order to exercise dominion itself. [24]

No less a figure than Jesus himself, along with the early Christians, were marshalled in the battle against the Jews: according to the German-Christians, it was they who had initiated the struggle in the first place. Furthermore, God revealed Himself in historical figures such as Martin Luther, Frederick the Great, and even Otto von Bismarck. For German-Christians, who saw the revelation of God in historical events, God revealed Himself in German history, which led to the conclusion that Germans were God's chosen people.[25]

For German-Christians, Adolf Hitler had been divinely sent to the German people in their greatest misery. It was the declared goal of this group to complete Luther's unfinished reformation under the God-sent Führer Adolf Hitler. Thus, in 1933, they began to 'liberate' doctrines and liturgy from "alleged Jewish" influences, expanding this practice to the communities under their influence. Immediately after the Nazis dismissed all alleged Jews from the civil service, the German-Christians followed suit in their churches. Importantly, here the term "alleged Jews" does not necessarily refer to an adherent to the Jewish faith. For the most part, people who were thus racially categorized merely had ancestors of Jewish descent. The German-Christians dismissed all such persons, although they were Protestant Christians by confession. They then divided the church community into two groups: Christians and 'Jewish Christians.'[26] They would not permit a 'German' pastor to perform sacred rites such as christen-

---

24. Walter Grundmann, Religion und Rasse: ein Beitrag zur Frage "nationaler Aufbruch" und "lebendiger Christusglaube" (Werdau: Meister, 1933), 7.

25. For this idea, which does not originate from the German-Christians but rather has been part of Protestant thinking since the nineteenth century, see Hartmut Lehmann, "The Germans as a Chosen People: Old Testament Themes in German Nationalism," in Hartmut Lehmann, Religion und Religiosität in der Neuzeit: Historische Beiträge, eds. Manfred Jakubowski-Tiessen and Otto Ulbricht (Göttingen: Vandenhoeck & Ruprecht, 1996), 248–59.

26. For example, the regional church of the Palatinate (Pfalz), which had close connections to the German Christian Church Movement, declined a proposition in March 1939, according to which all Jewish Christians were to be excluded from the church. The background to this, however, was that at that time no Jewish Christians were members of the regional church of the Palatinate. Nevertheless, the church leadership emphasized that Christians of Jewish origin were not welcome in the church. Roland Paul, "Antisemitismus und Haltung zur Judenverfolgung," in Protestanten ohne Protest: Die evangelische Kirche der Pfalz im Nationalsozialismus, vol. 1: Sachbeiträge, eds. Christoph Picker et al. (Speyer: Verlagshaus Speyer, 2016), 359–60.

ings or Communion on the latter. These Jewish Christians could not pay church taxes because they were no longer perceived as part of the Christian community. The separated Jewish Christian communities were later partly dissolved, and the affected people were expelled from church. But expulsion was not always necessary. These 'Jewish Christians' left of their own accord, emigrated, or became victims of the Holocaust. After the end of the war, the exclusion of Jewish Christians from the Christian community during the Third Reich was criticized in an expert report commissioned by the Protestant regional church of Thuringia. However, the same report also stressed that the Jewish community – albeit not Jewish Christians – posed a danger to Christianity as a whole.[27]

The German-Christians created a religious community that was defined on the one hand as Protestant Christian, and on the other as belonging to the Aryan or Nordic race. The 'Jewish Christians' who lived in the area of influence of the German Christian Church Movement stood no chance of rejoining the Protestant church. The border was precisely their 'racial background.' They were banned from church services, baptism, Communion, and religious instruction. Salvation in Christian terms was not possible for these individuals: only those who belonged to the 'right' race were allowed access.

It is at this point that the demarcation described by Kim Knott becomes obvious: access to salvation was about race, pure and simple. Christenings and Communion are sacraments for Protestants, and fundaments of the faith for religious Christians. Access to these essential religious acts was reserved for those belonging to the supposed right race under the leadership of the German Christian Church Movement, regardless of whether the individual could forgo participation in the Holy Communion according to his or her own individual beliefs. The key point is that access was denied to this ritual completely, if one of these individuals was defined as Jewish or partly Jewish.

Thus far, racial theory could be proclaimed as God's overall plan. One could explain, with recourse to German history, why Adolf Hitler was the supposed 'Führer' sent by God. It was even possible to create religious space(s) to which accessibility and in which the attainment of salvation were defined by race. Yet one hurdle remained: the history of Christianity and its traditions. According to the New Testament, Jesus was a Jew. The German Christian Church Movement, as one of the most influential Protestant groups in the Third Reich, needed to legitimize its racialized conception of religion. It had to provide concrete evidence as to why only Aryans were granted

---

27. See Schuster, Die Lehre vom "arischen" Christentum, 256–57.

salvation and not, for example, Jewish Christians. Towards this goal, six Protestant regional churches, led by the German Christian Church Movement, founded the "Institute for the Study and Eradication of Jewish Influence on German Church Life" in 1939. More than fifty academics contributed to this anti-Semitic research institute, which was aimed at the 'de-Judization' of Christianity. The members of the Institute produced purported evidence in genealogical works on Jesus' parents that the latter had been Jewish from a religious point of view, but could not have been so racially. The research tried to demonstrate Aryan origins in these Galileans. Jesus would then have been at least partly of Aryan descent.[28] And Jesus was supposed to have spearheaded the struggle against Judaism. According to their racial ideology, the Aryan and Jewish races have been at each other's throats since antiquity. All biblical and extra-biblical evidence which depicted Jesus as a Jew was considered falsified by Jews. Besides this alleged evidence of Jesus not being Jewish, the Institute produced a 'Jew-free' (*judenrein*) Christianity for contemporary times. This was an active process to fulfill their aim of finishing Luther's Reformation for a 'Jew-free' Christianity in a 'Jew-free' Third Reich.[29] Relying on publications of the Institute penned by well-known scholars such as Johannes Leipoldt (1880 –1965), Carl Schneider (1900 –1977), and Hans Heinrich Schaeder (1896–1957), the German Christian Church Movement was able to construct their Aryan Christianity and adduce evidence that Jesus had not been Jewish. Johannes Leipoldt, Professor of New Testament Studies in Leipzig, for example, attested that ancient Judaism accepted non-Jews within its ranks. However, these converts were only Jews by religion, not by race. And the nature of race cannot be altered, irrespective of the particular religion to which an individual adheres. Following this line of thinking, the New Testament scholar positioned Jesus' declarations and actions in direct contrast to the 'nature of the Jew': Jesus preached Christian charity and acted accordingly. Such Christian charity, however, is supposedly foreign to Jews due to their racially determined 'nature.' This is why, according to the Institute scholars, helpfulness always arises from self-interest in Jews, never from conviction.[30] It was for this very reason that Jesus of

---

28. See, for example, Walter Grundmann, Jesus der Galiläer und das Judentum, 2nd edition (Leipzig: G. Wigand, 1941); Johannes Leipoldt, Jesu Verhältnis zu Griechen und Juden (Leipzig: G. Wigand, 1941).

29. Dirk Schuster: "Die Kirchenbewegung Deutsche Christen und die "Beseitigung des jüdischen Einflusses". Ein aktiver Prozess zur Gestaltung des "Dritten Reiches"," in Judentum und Antisemitismus in Europa, ed. Ulrich A. Wien (Tübingen: Mohr Siebeck, 2017): 247–78.

30. Johannes Leipoldt, "Jesus und das Judentum," in Christentum und Judentum: Studium zur Erforschung ihres gegenseitigen Verhältnisses. Erster Band. Sitzu-

Nazareth had few followers among Jews. Ancient Greece, by contrast, which Leipoldt declared as belonging to the "Aryan race," "feels an intrinsic kinship with Jesus, considers his teachings and develops them further."[31]

Such publications – as well as those by Walter Grundmann, who allegedly found genealogical evidence that Jesus was not a Jew but "Aryan"[32] – formed the basis for the separation of Judaism and Christianity on a racial footing. If Jesus himself was not Jewish but rather struggled against Judaism on the grounds of racial differences between Jews and 'Aryans,' then contemporary Christianity must be cleansed of all Jewish influences and 'elements.' Carl Schneider, Professor of New Testament Studies in Königsberg, even attempted to present anti-Semitism as the central message of early Christianity. According to him, the struggle against Judaism was one of the main motives of Jesus of Nazareth. Schneider explained Jesus' purported animus towards the Jews by resorting once again to race: Jesus was a "full-blooded Aryan" in line with National Socialist racial ideology.[33] Thus, claimed Schneider, Christianity in the 'Third Reich' ought to be at the forefront of the fight against Judaism; after all, it had been involved in a racial conflict against 'the Jews' for the past 2,000 years.

Conclusion

The term 'space' can be used to refer to religion in a geographical or social way – of course there are many more possibilities. Regarding social space, it can be said that this is primarily negotiated by the action of agents, "[…] through the linking of the elements of social commodities and living creatures to each other by memory and perception processes, as well as through abstract notions and specific positioning."[34]

These spaces describe social distances between different positions[35] whereby boundaries define the entry criteria for a given space. Religions and religious institutions typically feature well-defined

---

ngsberichte der ersten Arbeitstagung des Instituts zur Erforschung des jüdischen Einflusses auf das deutsche kirchliche Leben vom 1. bis 3. März 1940 in Wittenberg, ed. Walter Grundmann (Leipzig: G. Wigand, 1940): 45–6.

31. Leipoldt, Jesu Verhältnis zu Griechen und Juden, 221. For more examples on Leipoldt, see Schuster, Die Lehre vom "arischen" Christentum, 148–68.

32. For details of this racial construction see ibid., 169–98.

33. See Carl Schneider, Das Frühchristentum als antisemitische Bewegung (Bremen: Kommende Kirche, 1940).

34. Sergej Stoetzer, "Ort, Identität, Mentalität – soziologische Raumkonzepte," in Die Religion des Raumes und die Räumlichkeit der Religion, eds. Thomas Erne and Peter Schüz (Göttingen: Vandenhoeck & Ruprecht, 2010): 87–103, here at 97.

35. Ibid., 88.

boundaries. Christianity, for instance, is defined by the sacrament of baptism, by which one enters into the Christian congregation. An individual may become part of a religious community and thereby gain access to the space called religion by accepting given entry criteria and rules of behavior. Thus, while boundaries can be rather clear, acceptance of such criteria can serve to render them permeable.

In my case-study, however, something different was afoot. The German Christian Church Movement did not construct geographical or cultural spaces that could be used to breach the borders of salvation. Had they done so, converts who considered themselves 'German' and 'Protestant' could have been invited in. My study shows that, instead, this movement used race to build a space with restricted access to the divine. The racial subdivision was perceived as part of God's creation. Descent, meaning the religion one was born into or the religion of one's ancestry, defined this spatial boundary. It was only within these borders that religion could be accessed. The possibility of belonging to a specific God and a specific religion was thus circumscribed by exclusive racial boundaries. Religious space defined by confession and race excluded the 'other' subjects from salvation in an absolute way that left no possibility of becoming a member of the church. Only members of the 'Aryan race' could inhabit this constructed space, and only they could receive divine salvation. While those who were refused admittance to this space could still self-identify as a Christian, the church denied such individuals access to the holy sacraments because it did not deem them Christians, but rather Jews.

In this way, a religious space was constructed whose accessibility was restricted by race. This demarcation was justified by racist doctrine and legitimized by scientific research that 'demonstrated' the proclaimed contrast between Jews on the one hand, and Germans as the Chosen People, on the other. The last step towards adjustment of the religion with racist ideology and a realization of the German-Christian doctrine was the 'de-Judization' of contemporary Christianity, a step implemented by the Institute for the Study and Eradication of Jewish Influence on German Church Life.

Nazi Racism, American Anti-Semitism, and Christian Duty
U.S. Mainline Protestant Responses to the Jewish Refugee Crisis of 1938
By Kyle Jantzen

Upon seizing power in the winter of 1933, Adolf Hitler and his National Socialist movement began implementing their long-standing plans to oppress Germany's Jews. Economic boycotts, bureaucratic purges, and educational prohibitions marked the first wave of anti-Semitic persecution. In 1935, social segregation dominated, through laws which stripped German Jews of citizenship and prohibited them from having sexual relations with so-called Aryan Germans. By 1938, Jews had largely been driven from the German economy, barred from professional life, and stigmatized in society. This Nazi pre-war victimization of Jews culminated in the *Polenaktion* of October 27–29, 1938, and the Kristallnacht pogrom of November 9–10, 1938.[1]

Scholars have criticized the North American Protestant response to the Nazi regime and its persecution of Jews. According to one well-known study, apathy ruled the day, and "no sustained universal outcry on behalf of the beleaguered refugees ever erupted from [...] the Christian [...] rank and file."[2] Frederick K. Wentz surveyed Prot-

---

1. See Hermann Graml, Reichskristallnacht: Antisemitismus und Judenverfolgung im Dritten Reich (Munich: DTV, 1998), 9–37;Walter Pehle, November 1938: From 'Kristallnacht' to Genocide (New York: Berg, 1990); Martin Gilbert, Kristallnacht: Prelude to Destruction (New York: Harper-Collins, 2006).

2. Irving Abella and Harold Troper, None Is Too Many: Canada and the Jews of Europe 1933–1948 (Toronto: Lester & Orpen Dennys, 1982), 51 and 284. See also Alan Davies and Marilyn F. Nefsky, How Silent Were the Churches?: Canadian Protestantism and the Jewish Plight during the Nazi Era (Waterloo, ON: Wilfred Laurier University Press, 1997), 128, 131; Haim Genizi, The Holocaust, Israel and Canadian Protestant Churches (Montreal: McGill-Queen's University Press, 2002) (which deals primarily with the postwar era); and Norman Erwin, "Hitler's Assault on Civilization: Antisemitism and English Canada's Response to Kristallnacht," in Violence, Memory, and History: Western Perceptions of Kristallnacht, eds. Colin McCullough and Nathan Wilson (New York: Routledge, 2015): 108–29.

estant journals and their response to the rise of Nazism and to the Nazi assault on Christianity. He found liberal journals to have been the most eager among these periodicals to do battle against Nazism, corresponding to their interest in social justice and hatred of totalitarianism. The largest segment of Protestants in the center included those concerned chiefly with religious liberty and the well-being of the German churches, and less likely to fight Nazism directly. Least likely to oppose Nazism were the fundamentalists and millenarians, who condemned many modern developments, among which Nazism was only one.[3] In Frederick Ira Murphy's dissertation, entitled "The American Christian Press and Pre-War Hitler's Germany, 1933–1939," the author contended that the churches had been alarmed about the rise of Nazism (except for its anti-communism), critical of Hitler himself, and equivocal about Jews. Christians had denounced attacks like the Kristallnacht pogrom and rejected blatant anti-Semitism, but accepted Hitler's need to solve a "Jewish problem" and subscribed to prejudicial stereotypes about Jews and their relationship to both capitalism and communism. As for the refugee situation, "attempts to arouse the average American Christian to act to help Christian refugees from Germany had little success," Murphy argued.[4]

Two important studies have assessed the responses of the U.S. religious press to the plight of the Jews under Nazi rule. William Nawyn analyzed the periodical literature of Baptists, Methodists, Presbyterians, Episcopalians, and Congregationalists. He found that liberal Protestants combined theological latitudinarianism and a commitment to Western notions of human dignity to encourage support for Jews and Judaism, while conservatives held three contradictory ideas in tension: the belief that Jews were responsible for the death of Christ; the conviction that Jews were a chosen people of God, the source of Jesus Christ, and the foundation of Christianity; and the view that Jews were a people to be evangelized.[5] Nawyn concluded that, even if liberals were more likely than conservatives to advocate for Jews, none of the leading denominations did much of practical value, such as raising significant funds in aid of Jewish refugees. Rather, the leading Protestant denominational publications "ignored, or perhaps failed

---

3. Frederick K. Wentz, "American Protestant Journals and the Nazi Religious Assault," Church History 23: 4 (1954): 321–38, and Wentz, "The Reaction of the Religious Press in America to the Emergence of Nazism" (PhD diss., Yale University, 1954).

4. Frederick Ira Murphy, "The American Christian Press and Pre-War Hitler's Germany, 1933–1939" (PhD diss., University of Florida, 1970), 353.

5. William E. Nawyn, American Protestantism's Response to Germany's Jews and Refugees 1933–1941 (Ann Arbor, MI: UMI Research Press, 1981), 34–5. Nawyn examines not only the press but also various Protestant ecclesial sources.

to recognize the true nature of, the Jewish problem in Germany and the full implications of the Nazi racial policies."[6] Of note, Nawyn did recognize that the mainline Protestant church press had been attentive to the Nazi persecution of Jews and the consequent Jewish refugee crisis of the later 1930s, but added that even these matters "were not, in general, of continuing and paramount concern."[7]

The historian Robert Ross was even sharper in his critique of the Protestant churches and their publications, characterizing the American religious response to the Nazi persecution and extermination of the Jews as *silence* – the silence of "the failure of information to persuade," of "the failure of concerted effort," and of "the failure of modest actions."[8] Curiously juxtaposed to this negative assessment was Ross's recognition that Protestant journalists and commentators had written widely on the Nazi persecution of the Jews, and that U.S. Protestants had been quite active on behalf of Jews, donating money, organizing rallies, writing protests, commissioning delegations to Germany, petitioning President Roosevelt, the U.S. State Department, and Congress, establishing denominational and interdenominational committees, cooperating periodically with Jewish organizations, and organizing prayer rallies. But after listing all of these activities, Ross dismissed them on the grounds that they had neither deterred Hitler from persecuting Jews nor convinced the U.S. government to intervene in German domestic affairs. Yet, not only was Ross's evaluation naive about the potential of U.S. Protestant church leaders to influence either Hitler or Roosevelt, it concentrated on what Christians and churches had *not* done. Left aside was any analysis of how Protestants understood and interpreted Hitler, Jews, and Judaism, or what actions they had proposed that either the U.S. churches or the U.S. government should have undertaken.[9]

Haim Genizi, for his part, tackled the specific question of American apathy towards *Christian* refugees from Nazism, many of whom were Jews or "non-Aryans" according to the Nazi Nuremberg Laws, even if Christians by religious choice. Genizi noted the efforts of the Federal Council of Churches and other mainline voices to rouse American Protestants to aid refugees, but argued that agencies like the American Committee for Christian German Refugees and dozens of other organizations were basically unable to generate support from either Christian individuals or church bodies. In fact, Jewish organiza-

---

6. Ibid., 46.
7. Ibid., 59–60.
8. Robert W. Ross, So It Was True: The American Protestant Press and the Nazi Persecution of the Jews (Minneapolis: University of Minnesota Press, 1980), 286–8.
9. Ibid., 287–8.

tions provided most of the early funding for the American Committee for Christian German Refugees.[10]

Scholars have continued to reassess U.S. and Canadian Protestant attitudes and actions concerning Jews and Judaism during the Nazi era. For example, various recent studies have discussed the significant protests of American Christians just after the Nazi seizure of power and also, most notably, in the wake of the November 1938 Kristallnacht pogrom.[11]

Examining the convoluted history of evangelical-Jewish relations, Yaakov S. Ariel has mostly agreed with Nawyn that conservative evangelicals found themselves caught between competing ideas. They strongly condemned Nazi anti-Jewish policies and viewed Nazi ideology as "a rebellion against God and a distortion of Christian theology and values."[12] True to their convictions about salvation in Jesus Christ, they also worked to evangelize Jews, expressing particular concern for "non-Aryan" Christians caught in Hitler's persecution. Nevertheless, evangelicals remained under the influence of traditional antipathy towards Jews and Judaism, and were quick to blame Jews for apostasy and conspiracy. They uncritically accepted *The Protocols of the Elders of Zion* as genuine descriptions of Jewish behavior

---

10. Haim Genizi, American Apathy: The Plight of Christian Refugees from Nazism (Ramat Gan: Bar-Ilan University Press, 1983), 112–14. See also Genizi, "American Interfaith Cooperation on Behalf of Refugees from Nazism, 1933–1945," American Jewish History 70:3 (1981): 347–61. See also Peter Ludlow, "The Refugee Problem in the 1930s: The Failures and Successes of Protestant Relief Programmes," English Historical Review 90, no. 356 (1975): 564–603.

11. Victoria J. Barnett, "Christian and Jewish Interfaith Efforts During the Holocaust: The Ecumenical Context," in American Religious Responses to Kristallnacht, ed. Maria Mazzenga (New York: Palgrave, 2009): 13–29; Kyle Jantzen, "'The Fatherhood of God and Brotherhood of Man': Mainline American Protestants and the Kristallnacht Pogrom," in Mazzenga, ed., American Religious Responses to Kristallnacht, 31–55; Maria Mazzenga, "Toward an American Catholic Response to the Holocaust: Catholic Americanism and Kristallnacht," in Mazzenga, ed., American Religious Responses to Kristallnacht, 85–110; Patrick J. Hayes, "American Catholics Respond to Kristallnacht: New Refugee Policy and the Plight of Non-Aryans," in Mazzenga, ed., American Religious Responses to Kristallnacht, 111–44; Barnett, "Track Two Diplomacy, 1933–1939: International Responses from Catholics, Jews, and Ecumenical Protestants to Events in Nazi Germany," Kirchliche Zeitgeschichte 27:1 (2014): 76–86; Kyle Jantzen and Jonathan Durance, "Our Jewish Brethren: Christian Responses to Kristallnacht in Canadian Mass Media," in Crisis and Credibility in the Jewish-Christian World: Remembering Franklin Littel. The Fortieth Annual Scholars' Conference on the Holocaust and the Churches, special issue of Journal of Ecumenical Studies 46:4 (2011): 537–48.

12. Yaakov S. Ariel, An Unusual Relationship: Evangelical Christians and Jews (New York: New York University Press, 2013), 98. See also idem, On Behalf of Israel: American Fundamentalist Attitudes Towards Jews, Judaism, and Zionism, 1865–1945 (Brooklyn, NY: Carlson, 1991).

and intentions throughout the 1930s, only abandoning this view as the Nazi persecution of the Jews deepened.[13] More negatively, Caitlin Carenen has argued that mainline Protestants – convinced of their cultural pre-eminence – were largely intolerant of Jews (and Catholics) in the interwar period. Christian cultural power and rising nationalism fed a growing anti-Semitism. Among fundamentalists, some, like Gerald Winrod's *Defenders of the Christian Faith*, participated in this anti-Semitism and stoked fears of Jewish conspiracies. Others, though, stressed the importance of Jews in Christian eschatology and urged kindness towards them. Particularly after the Kristallnacht pogrom, Carenen claims, sympathy for Jews increased among both liberal and conservative Protestants, as did support for Jewish emigration to Palestine, though not to the United States.[14]

In contrast to the aforementioned emphasis on what U.S. Protestants failed to do in response to Nazism and the Holocaust, this chapter will examine how they perceived Hitler, Nazism, and the persecution of Germany's Jews in the prewar era, and what kinds of responses, if any, they proposed. Basing my inquiry on examples from prominent Protestant publications,[15] I argue five interrelated points: 1) that main-

---

13. Ibid., 121, 142–52.

14. Caitlin Carenen, The Fervent Embrace: Liberal Protestants, Evangelicals, and Israel (New York: New York University Press, 2012), 1–47. Alongside Ariel and Carenen, David Rausch defended fundamentalist journalist Arno C. Gaebelin's reporting on the plight of Jews in Nazi Germany and the Holocaust, arguing it was both anti-Nazi and pro-Zionist. More recently, Timothy Padgett has assessed Gaebelein and his magazine, Our Hope, alongside other conservative publications like Moody Monthly and Christian Herald, finding a mixture of sympathy for and criticism of Nazi Germany, concern about anti-Semitism, calls to evangelize Jews, worries about Nazi attacks on Christianity, and interest in Zionism and its relationship to Christian eschatology. Matthew Bowman argued much the same thing, noting that fundamentalist Protestants remained politically marginalized since the Scopes trial in the 1920s, but followed events in Europe closely, condemning Hitler and searching for eschatological clues in the turmoil surrounding the Jews. Finally, Timothy Weber contended that conservative, premillenialist Christians lined up politically as allies of the Jews, for eschatological reasons, and religiously as enemies of the Jews, because of the Jewish rejection of Christ. David A. Rausch, "Our Hope: An American Fundamentalist Journal and the Holocaust, 1937–1945," Fides et Historia 12:2 (1980): 89–103; idem, Arno C. Gaebelein, 1861–1945: Irenic Fundamentalist and Scholar (New York: Edwin Mellen, 1983); Timothy Padgett, "Warmongers?: Continuity and Complexity in Evangelical Discourse on United States Foreign Policy" (PhD diss., Trinity Evangelical Divinity School, 2016), 28–70; Matthew Bowman, "Persecution, Prophecy, and the Fundamentalist Reconstruction of Germany, 1933–1940," in Mazzenga, ed., American Religious Responses to Kristallnacht, 183–204; and Timothy P. Weber, On the Road to Armageddon: How Evangelicals Became's Best Friend (Grand Rapids, MI: Baker Academic, 2004).

15. Evidence for this study will be drawn from the following periodicals: *Advance*, a liberal Congregational weekly published in Boston and long edited by the

line Protestant spokespersons viewed Nazism with great foreboding, sensing crisis in the air; 2) that they were *primarily* concerned with the Nazi persecution of *Christians*; 3) that they *also* cared about the persecution of Jews; 4) that they both condemned *and* perpetuated forms of anti-Semitism in the United States; and 5) that, above all, they understood the challenge of Nazism in terms of a cosmic battle between Christianity and irreligion – a battle liberals and conservatives understood somewhat differently from one another, as I will show.

Sense of Crisis

First and foremost, what is most striking about the U.S. mainline Protestant periodicals in 1938 is their projection of a sense of crisis. The demagoguery of Hitler, the brutality of his Nazi regime, the dangers of anti-Semitism in Europe and America, and the breakdown of the international order combined to cast a dark shadow over the church press in this study. Here a striking example can be found in a single issue of the Congregational weekly *Advance*, from February 1, 1938. Arthur E. Holt, Congregational church leader and Professor of Christian Social Ethics in Chicago, opened the discussion by lamenting the decline and indeed absence of democracy in the non-Western world and in much of Europe, on account of the rise of communism, fascism, and National Socialism. Next, Henry Smith Leiper, missionary, member of the Federal Council of Churches, and Executive Secretary of the American Section of the Universal Christian Council for Life and Work, worried about racism in America, Bolshevism in Europe, and "the manifold evils which threaten even civilization itself." In this regard, he quoted a commonwealth political leader who declared that politics was failing and "the world is drifting towards catastrophe." Finally, Alfred Schmalz, Congregationalist minister and prominent Christian social activist, asserted that German grievances relating to the Treaty of Versailles had produced Hitler and Nazism. Given similar resentments in Italy and Japan, international tensions were rising, and Schmalz predicted that the outcome of the "economic con-

---

clergyman William E. Gilroy; *Christendom*, a liberal quarterly published in Chicago, edited by Charles Clayton Morrison of *The Christian Century* and enlivened by writers connected with the FCC and the American Sections of the World Conference on Faith and Order and the Universal Christian Council for Life and Work; *The Churchman*, a liberal Episcopal biweekly published in New York and long edited by Guy Emery Shipler; *The Living Church*, a high-church Episcopal weekly edited by Clifford P. Morehouse and published in Milwaukee, WI; *The Presbyterian*, a conservative weekly edited by Dr. Stewart M. Robinson and published in Philadelphia; and *Zion's Herald*, a conservative Methodist weekly published in Boston and edited for over two decades by Lewis Oliver Hartman, who would go on to win election as the American Bishop of the Methodist Church in 1944.

flict between the world's great imperialistic powers," if not checked, would be "world war."[16] Other articles throughout 1938 bemoaned "a world in the grip of violence and the threat of war," "the impression of a strange, demonic, and dangerous power" in Nazi Germany, the "death" of the League of Nations, and the fact that "everyone expects war, many expect it soon."[17] In the wake of the Munich Agreement, which handed the Czech Sudetenland to Hitler, Guy Emery Shipler, editor of *The Churchman*, an Episcopal biweekly, noted the "moral bankruptcy of Hitler" and described the German *Führer* as a "psychopathic individual." Two weeks later, he wondered how "anyone [...] should place any trust in Hitler's word," adding that eventually people would understand that both Hitler and Mussolini were "but ranting pygmies."[18] That same week, Clifford Phelps Morehouse, editor of *The Living Church*, another Episcopal publication, averred that "The main issue is still whether or not the totalitarian heresy is to dominate the world." He went on to describe totalitarianism (whether Nazism, Fascism, or Communism) as "a denial of the individual worth and dignity of man [...] the negation of the liberty for which our forefathers fought and [...] a philosophy of blood and hate as opposed to a religion of mercy and love."[19] News reports and editorials such as these filled the pages of mainline Protestant periodicals, attesting to the dismay with which U.S. Protestant spokespersons – many of them prominent church leaders – viewed the expansion and exercise of Nazi power in the prewar period.

Attacks on Christianity

In their response to Hitler and Nazism, writers and editors in the mainline Protestant periodicals analyzed in this chapter zeroed in most often on the grave danger to Christianity posed by Nazism and the many attacks against Christians and churches, particularly in Germany. In January 1938, *Advance* reported that Hitler had jailed 1300 pastors between 1934 and 1937. Two months later, the editor William E. Gilroy brooded about various totalitarian threats to religion. "In Russia,

---

16. Arthur E. Holt, "Shall Protestantism Implement Democracy?" Advance (February 1, 1938): 57–8; Henry Smith Leiper, "The State of the Church," Advance (February 1, 1938): 62; Alfred Schmalz, "Peaceful Change – The Alternative to War," Advance (February 1, 1938): 63.

17. William E. Gilroy, "The Editorial Outlook," Advance (April 1, 1938): 156; Henry Smith Leiper, "The State of the Church," Advance (June 1, 1938): 253; Hubert C. Herring, "The State of the Nation," Advance (November 1, 1938): 496.

18. Guy Emery Shipler, "Editorial," The Churchman (October 1, 1938): 7–8; Guy Emery Shipler, "Editorial", The Churchman (October 15, 1938): 7–9.

19. Clifford Phelps Morehouse, "The Situation in Europe," The Living Church (October 19, 1938): 374.

Germany and Italy, alike," he wrote, "the Christian is under the heel of pagan dictatorships that flout the Christian faith and idealism and run roughshod over the Christian conscience and the Christian will."[20]

The Churchman also offered regular reports on anti-Christian policies and events in Germany. In March 1938 alone, articles and editorials called the Nazi religious program "neo-pagan" and praised Confessing Church pastor Martin Niemöller as "a champion of religious liberty," claimed that Niemöller's arrest was a sign that he had inspired fear among the Nazis, and drew attention to the fact that many other clergy were also in prison or forbidden to preach.[21] The plight of the German churches was broadcast throughout the year in terms that are well encapsulated in the title of an article that came out in November: "Caesar Presses His Claims in the Reich: The Trappings Change, But the Plot is the Same." Attempts to Nazify the Sermon on the Mount and rewrite John's gospel were depicted as an effort "to bring Christianity into conformity with Nazi nationalism – that absurd and abominable compound of 'race, blood and soil.'" The article's main point was that "The central force in the drive to destroy the Christianity of Germany is in the mind and personality of Hitler. He is the chosen and idolized leader of those who hate the church. He himself has ordered the illegal and violent repression of those who have dared to speak the truth."[22]

Among the most energetic Christian writers commenting on Nazi attacks against Christianity was Henry Smith Leiper, who wrote for several publications. Reporting on the German church scene at the close of 1938 for *The Living Church,* Leiper noted a "clear intention" among National Socialists "to liquidate any Church which does not show itself entirely in agreement with the proposal that it prostitute itself unqualifiedly to the 'positive Christianity' of Mr. Hitler and Mr. Rosenberg." He documented the steady progress towards the subjugation and corruption of the Church "so that it may become merely the ecclesiastical arm of the [Nazi] revolution." In support of this, he claimed the arrest of over 10,000 Christian leaders and "the destruction of the Church educational system," which would, in turn, he asserted, corrupt the future leadership of the church. The banning of Bible teaching in schools, the charging of clergy who prayed for peace

20. Henry Smith Leiper, "The State of the Church," Advance (January 1, 1938): 13, 26; William E. Gilroy, "The Editorial Outlook," Advance (March 1, 1938): 108–10.

21. "Democracy: Dodd Describes Nazism at CLID Annual Meeting," The Churchman (March 1, 1938): 18; Guy Emery Shipler, "Editorial," The Churchman (March 15, 1938): 7.

22. Henry Smith Leiper, "Caesar Presses His Claims in the Reich: The Trappings Change, But the Plot is the Same," The Living Church (November 1, 1938): 12–3.

with treason, and the cutting off of the pay of oppositional clergy were just some of the other measures cited by Leiper as evidence of a full-scale offensive against Christianity in Germany.[23] Many of his fellow writers and editors in these U.S. Protestant periodicals analyzed in this chapter concurred with this assessment, sounding a collective alarm regarding the danger for the Church.

Concern for Jewish Refugees

Though U.S. Protestant spokespersons were primarily concerned with Nazism's impact on the Christian churches of Germany, the plight of Jews did not escape the notice of at least some members of the church press in this study. By 1938, the Jewish refugee crisis had reached a critical level. Between 1933 and the outbreak of war in September 1939, roughly 282,000 of the 523,000 German Jews abandoned their homeland and found refuge abroad, in the United States, Palestine, Great Britain and other Commonwealth countries, Central and South America – even China and Japan.[24] By 1938, Hitler was ratcheting up international tensions through his annexation of Austria in March, his demand for Sudeten Czech territory in the spring and summer, and his occupation of vital Czechoslovak territory in October. This too spurred Jewish emigration. No fewer than 117,000 of the 174,000 Jews in Austria departed between the German annexation in March 1938 and the beginning of war in September 1939.[25] And although 85,000 Jewish refugees reached the United States during this eighteen-month period, many more tried and failed: no fewer than 300,000 Jews applied for the 27,000 visas available under the U.S. immigration quota system.[26]

At first, the mainline periodicals here analyzed were fairly tepid in their response to the refugee crisis. One early article by Hubert C. Herring of *Advance* thanking President Roosevelt and Secretary of State Cordell Hull for proposing an international meeting at Evian-les-Bains, France, where Herring believed "that international action [would] be taken to provide refuge for German and Austrian refugees from Adolf Hitler." He added that, "The United States, the richest nation, can afford to drop the bars and let substantial numbers in. Let

---

23. Henry Smith Leiper, "Discusses Churches' Situation in Germany," The Living Church (December 28, 1938): 699 and 712.

24. "German Jewish Refugees, 1933–1939," United States Holocaust Memorial Museum Holocaust Encyclopedia, https://www.ushmm.org/wlc/en/article.php?ModuleId=10005468 (July 2, 2016).

25. Ibid.

26. "Refugees," United States Holocaust Memorial Museum Holocaust Encyclopedia, https://www.ushmm.org/wlc/en/article.php?ModuleId=10005139 (July 2, 2016).

us urge that this will be done."²⁷

While *Advance* had little else to say about the matter, *The Churchman* advocated strongly on behalf of Jews, covering closely the Nazi persecution and consequent Jewish refugee crisis. On January 1, 1938, in an article entitled, "Anti-Semitism: 24 Christian Faiths Sympathize with Jews," editor Guy Emery Shipler reported on a statement by the Episcopalian Home Missions Council, remarking on the growth of "exaggerated nationalism" and explaining how "the rise of anti-Semitism in many lands has cast a pall of gloom over the Jews of the world." The report went on to reject anti-Semitism, demand its eradication in North America, and call upon Christians to recognize their special obligation to the Jews.²⁸

What is striking about the discourse on Jewish persecution in *The Churchman*, however, was how often it was linked to Christian persecution. Shipler's editorial writing is an excellent case in point. In an editorial from April 1, 1938, Shipler introduced a discussion of Hitler, Jews, and Christians with a quotation from Hanns Kerrl, the Nazi Minister for Religious Affairs: "A new authority has arisen as to what Christ and Christianity are – Adolf Hitler." Shipler explained how "neighbor" had come to mean "blood brother" under Nazi rule, resulting in "such heart-breaking misery that decent people are nauseated as they are forced to confess that Adolf Hitler is technically a human being." He then applied his critique of Nazi racial exclusivity to both Jews and Christians:

> No one who is a follower of Jesus the Jew; no one in whose heart have sung the words of Paul the Jew echoing from the thirteenth chapter of his first letter to the Corinthian Christians; no one who has ever been really touched by the meaning of Christian love can feel anything but revulsion and horror at the monstrous reversion to the jungle represented by Hitler in his treatment of the Jews. Hitler hates Christianity with a maniac's hatred, as he hates the Jew.²⁹

Similarly, in June, as Shipler discussed an American Jewish Congress (AJC) plan to work with Christian clergy to campaign jointly against anti-Semitism, he affirmed his opposition to anti-Semitism: "We will support every constructive effort made against anti-Semitism; our record on that score stands for anyone to read. We have fought against anti-Semitism and shall continue to do so." Immediately thereafter, however, he proceeded to relabel the anti-Semitic attacks as a general human rights crisis affecting both Jews and Christians – no doubt not

---

27. Hubert C. Herring, "The State of the Nation," Advance (May 1, 1938): 205.

28. Guy Emery Shipler, "Anti-Semitism: 24 Christian Faiths Sympathize with Jews," The Churchman (January 1, 1938): 20.

29. Guy Emery Shipler, "Editorial," The Churchman (April 1, 1938): 7.

quite what the AJC had had in mind. He wrote:

> As to the matter of Jewish persecution, we have long held the conviction that our Jewish friends would further their own cause more effectively if they would emphasize that persecution by such totalitarian states as Germany is a Christian as well as a Jewish problem. [...] The American public is still largely under the illusion that refugees from Germany are entirely Jewish [...] though thousands [of Christian refugees] have been forced to leave Germany and are without any means of livelihood. If we are to have a united front let it be not only against anti-Semitism but against persecution of both Jews and Christians.[30]

Shipler's repeated reframing of the Jewish refugee crisis in this way is nowhere more forcefully demonstrated than in the November 1 issue of *The Churchman*. There, a letter to the editor from W. Russell Bowie of the American Committee for Christian German Refugees outlined the dual Jewish-Christian nature of the refugee crisis. Remarking that "the persecution of Christians is growing in extent and severity," Bowie explained how Germany's annexation of Austria had "greatly intensified the refugee problem, especially increasing the percentage of refugees who are 'non-Aryan' Christians." In support of this claim, Bowie cited American industrialist and diplomat Myron C. Taylor's statistics from the Evian Conference, claiming that, of the 660,000 people in Germany and Austria who needed to find homes in other countries, about 285,000 were Protestants, 75,000 Catholics, and 300,000 Jews.[31] As Bowie clarified, the German refugee problem was not exclusively a Jewish problem. It "concerns every Christian throughout the world." Accordingly, Bowie asked clergy to set aside a Sunday offering or congregational benevolent funds to support the American Committee for Christian German Refugees, so they could assist Christians (most of whom, of course, would have been Jewish in terms of Nazi racial law) attempting to flee Hitler's Reich.[32]

Just a few pages later, Shipler dedicated part of his multi-page editorial to affirming Bowie's letter and urging support for his organization. After reiterating the number of *Christians* displaced as refugees, Shipler pointed out that Hitler's seizure of the Sudetenland would only increase the refugee pressure: "Here, surely," he exhorted, "is a challenge to the generosity of the Christian church in the United States." Once more, he restated the refugee crisis as a Christian problem:

---

30. Guy Emery Shipler, "A Jewish-Christian Cause," The Churchman (June 1, 1938): 8.

31. Taylor's estimates only included potential refugees who were under the age of 50.

32. W. Russell Bowie, "Victims of Nazism," The Churchman (November 1, 1938): 3.

> Hundreds of thousands of our fellow-Christians are fleeing before Nazi brutality. It is impossible to exaggerate their suffering. They are victims of the ruthless philosophy of "race, blood and soil"; a philosophy which finds the religion of Jesus a stumbling block which must somehow, if possible, be eliminated. And let us make no mistake about it. The assault of the Nazi on Christianity is a carefully planned program of extermination; it has not stopped short of the fearful barbarism of the concentration camp and all the terrors of exile.[33]

With that, using language we are more accustomed to hearing in the context of the subsequent events of the Holocaust, Shipler recapitulated Bowie's request for American churches to give generously to the American Committee of Christian German Refugees.

Shipler's linking of anti-Semitism and the persecution of Jews to anti-Christianity and the suffering of Christian refugees typified U.S. mainline Protestant efforts to aid Jews. As Haim Genizi has shown, both Jewish and Christian leaders were reluctant to push the Roosevelt Administration to relax immigration quotas in order to save Jewish refugees, because they feared a public discussion would "let loose a flood of bitter, anti-alien and anti-Jewish agitation, which will intensify inter-group antagonism in the United States."[34] Rather, prominent Christian leaders tried to assist Jews in peril by repeatedly attempting to convince American Christians that the refugee crisis was as much a Christian problem as a Jewish one. The failure of this initiative betrays the fact that the broader Protestant public was far more likely to view Shipler's refugees through the lens of Nazi racial ideology – as Jews – than it was to see the refugees through the lens of Christian theology – as brothers and sisters in Christ.

Other Protestant publications were slower to enter the fray, but, like *The Churchman*, the Episcopal weekly *The Living Church* and the more conservative publications like *The Presbyterian* and *Zion's Herald* (Methodist) expressed clear sympathy for the plight of Jewish refugees, especially later in 1938, as conditions in Germany worsened. From time to time – though not often – Protestant sympathy also included the contemplation of Jewish immigration to Africa, Australia, or the United States itself.[35]

---

33. Guy Emery Shipler, "Shall We Help the Persecuted?" The Churchman (November 1, 1938): 7–9.

34. Haim Genizi, "American Interfaith Cooperation on Behalf of Refugees from Nazism, 1933–1945," American Jewish History 70:3 (March 1981): 347–61.

35. In the case of The Living Church, for example, see "Prayer Day Sought by Federal Council," The Living Church (October 5, 1938): 332; "Nazi Oppression of Jewish Christians Creates Serious Problem for Lutherans Here," The Living Church (October 26, 1938): 429; "Churches Called to Fight Anti-Semitism," The Living Church (November 9, 1938): 486; "President Asked by Synod to Help Jews," The

Condemnation and Perpetuation of Anti-Semitism

One important obstacle to U.S. Protestant sympathy for Germany's Jews was the persistent prejudicial stream that ran through American society. Interestingly, Protestant commentators in the church press here analyzed interacted in different ways with the racism and anti-Semitism in U.S. society. It was not uncommon for editorials and articles in mainline Protestant publications to acknowledge, as did William E. Gilroy, the editor of *Advance*, that, "Our protest of Hitler's treatment of the Jews is partly ineffective because the Germans have been well publicized concerning our treatment of the Negro. [...] We cannot speak with the powerful and authoritative moral voice of a clear conscience or a clean record."[36] Gilroy went on to chastise his readers about their lack of love for minorities, proclaiming that "if God's love had been only for white, one-hundred-percent Americans there would be no gospel worth proclaiming."[37] Similarly, *The Churchman* featured condemnations of U.S. racism, such as a February 1, 1938, article which reprinted a Federal Council of Churches' message on race relations. In it, the FCC took issue with racism directed towards Mexicans, Orientals, and Blacks in the United States. "We in America have felt keenly and said much about the treatment of Jews in Germany," the text ran, adding that "Any real solution of race relations requires that each nation face its own problems. Before we in America can tell other nations what to do we must confront our own distressing situation. [...] Each national group has made a lasting contribution to our composite civilization." In particular, the FCC report singled out the "decidedly unchristian and unstatesmanlike" Oriental Exclusion Act, and asserted that "the churches cannot escape responsibility for such living conditions" as were endured by the "poor Mexicans" in their midst.[38]

But if racism was an easy target for these Protestant writers and editors, anti-Semitism proved much more complicated. Like racism, anti-Semitism was widespread in U.S. society, and even when Americans were highly critical of the Hitler regime, they remained anti-

---

Living Church (November 9, 1938): 492; "Terror Over Germany," The Living Church (November 23, 1938): 537–8; "Church Groups Hit Nazi Persecutions," The Living Church (November 23, 1938): 547, 557; "Church Groups Make Nation-Wide Protest," The Living Church (November 30, 1938): 581, 585; "The Future of German Jews," The Living Church (December 7, 1938): 596; William G. Peck, "By the Rivers of Babylon," The Living Church (December 14, 1938): 635–6.

36. William E. Gilroy, "The Editorial Outlook," Advance (April 1, 1938): 156.

37. William E. Gilroy, "The Editorial Outlook," Advance (November 1, 1938): 494.

38. "Race Relations: Federal Council Issues Message for February 13," The Churchman (February 1, 1938): 21.

pathetic towards Jews. Opinion polls confirmed this time and again. For instance, a Roper poll from April 1938 found that 48 percent of United States citizens surveyed believed that the persecution of Jews in Europe was at least partly the fault of the victims, while 10 percent felt it was entirely their fault.[39] In November 1938, just *after* the Kristallnacht pogrom, Roper polls found that one-third of respondents believed that hostility towards Jews in the United States was rising, with many blaming Jewish financial power, business practices, and avarice. Moreover, 77 percent opposed allowing more Jewish exiles from Germany into the United States, while 43 percent even opposed the U.S. government contributing "money to help Jewish and Catholic exiles from Germany settle in lands like Africa and South America." And fully two-thirds of those surveyed rejected the proposed Wagner-Rogers Bill to permit refugee children from Germany to be allowed into the country. A few months later, in April 1939, almost 85 percent of Protestants and Catholics opposed increasing immigration quotas for European refugees. In fact, polls conducted throughout 1938 and 1939 discovered that 12 percent of the Americans surveyed consistently favored a campaign against Jews in America, while another poll taken in July 1939 found that 42 percent of Americans who were asked wanted either to take measures to prevent Jews from gaining too much economic power in America, or (less often) to deport them as fast as humanely possible.[40]

While these members of the Protestant church press frequently criticized American anti-Semitism,[41] their writers and editors often employed a confusing and contradictory discourse about Jews. For instance, in the summer of 1938, Frederick C. Grant perpetuated aspects of traditional Christian anti-Jewish rhetoric in an article he wrote for the journal *Christendom*, which was affiliated with the American Sections of the World Conference on Faith and Order and the Universal Christian Council for Life and Work. Discussing the place of Jews in Christian history, he presented the long history of the Jews as a series of crises, explaining how Jesus had offered the Jewish people a chance to become "the church, a people of God, mixed like leaven among the peoples of the earth, […] the conscience of mankind." This they refused. Grant continued:

> I do not bring charges against our brethren in the synagogue; but I can-

---

39. Hadley Cantril and Mildred Strunk, Public Opinion 1935–1946 (Princeton, NJ: Princeton University Press, 1951), 382–3.

40. Ibid., 382–3, 385, 1081, 1150.

41. For example, Zion's Herald repeatedly condemned the rise of fascist and anti-Semitic speech and groups in the United States, in articles like "Jersey City – Fascist Cell," Zion's Herald (May 25, 1938): 676.

not help feeling that the long tragedy of Israel's wanderings, the bitter persecution even unto this day, might have been averted had […] 'the proposal of Jesus' been adopted rather than rejected by his own people.

While Grant was actually trying to use Judaism as an illustration for a lesson Christians needed to learn, his assessment of the Jewish condition shows how even liberal Protestants intent on acting with good will towards Jews could not quite refrain from placing part of the blame for Jewish suffering squarely on the victims themselves.[42]

Although *The Churchman* was a strong opponent of anti-Semitism in both Europe and the United States, like *Christendom*, it too published material which reinforced traditional anti-Semitic stereotypes. In a case of supremely bad timing, Alfred Artyn Gross, a former cleric, published "Manners and Morals of Anti-Semitism: Why Do We Dislike Our Neighbors?" in the November 15 issue of *The Churchman*. In this extensive article on anti-Semitism in America, Gross argued that Hitler's persecution of Jews – he could not have known about the Kristallnacht pogrom when he wrote – reminded Americans of their own anti-Semitism problem. In an effort to explain contemporary rationalizations for anti-Semitism, however, Gross proceeded to discuss Jewish customs – ways of eating, drinking, and celebrating holidays – which he felt were different, but not immoral. Then, he turned to Jewish business practices. Here he did not entirely reject the ideas that Jews tended towards dishonesty or that they dominated the learned professions, but blamed Christians for putting Jews in these positions:

> What about the responsibility the Christian world must face for making the Jews the sort of people they are? When did a long history of persecution create a people of consistently noble characters? Ought we not to exult in those Jews, who despite their handicaps, have achieved greatness of soul? […] Undoubtedly there are unlovely Jews; it is doubtful that unloveliness is a Jewish monopoly.

Gross then brought up the old accusation that the Jews were the Christ-killers, rejecting it by arguing that first-century Jews acted as any mob might have, stirred up by "the priests and their satellites." Moreover, he objected to the conflation of first- and twentieth-century Jews: "To hold the Jews of 1938 responsible for the sins of the mob of the year 30 is repeating the mentality which brought about the tragedy of Calvary. The world misunderstood Jesus and thought him dangerous. It executed him. There have been Calvaries before and since." In the end, Gross put forward a hopeful solution: the cure for

---

42. Frederick C. Grant, "Our Basic Faith," Christendom 3:3 (Summer 1938): 340.

anti-Semitism "lies in the recognition of our common humanity." As he wrote:

> A man is no better and no worse than his neighbor because he views the eternal verities differently. He becomes better or worse as he translates his insights into action. [...] What is religion? Jesus tells us it is very simple: "Love God. Love your neighbor." Jews fall within the category of neighbours. You can call anti-Semitism a denial to Jews of the status of neighbors. As anti-Semitism succeeds, religion must fail.

To be sure, writers such as Grant and Gross meant well, and sought vigorously to combat anti-Semitic stereotypes. Still, they themselves were unable to avoid these very prejudices in their own writing.

Such mixed responses were not limited to the liberal wing of mainline Protestantism. Take, for example, a guest article on "The Plight of the Jews" penned by Dr. Joseph Taylor Britan, co-publisher of *Israel My Glory*, for the fundamentalist Friends of Israel Gospel Ministry, which appeared in the November 10, 1938, edition of *The Presbyterian*.[43] (This is another case of terrible timing. Published on the day of the Kristallnacht pogrom, the article was quite obviously written beforehand.) Britan's assessment of the Jewish situation begins with compassion for Jews who had suffered persecution, even as it depicts them in a completely undifferentiated manner:

> The Jew stands today in the center of the world's stage. He is frequently in the headlines. What he does not only arouses the interest of the world, but what is done to him is no less important. He is still the man without a country [...]. Persecuted in many nations, deprived of almost every economic, social, cultural and political opportunity, many of the greatest scientists, merchants and professional men are driven from the land of their birth, their property is confiscated and they themselves are reduced to abject poverty and ruthless power.

Britan wrote dramatically of Jewish misery, in terms that both mirrored the Nazi racial image of Jews and grasped the Nazi intent to destroy European Jewry:

> No one knows the number of suicides among this race which have followed their persecution in certain nations in Europe. No one knows the number of innocent men, women and children starved to death or killed by the hostile powers which are determined to remove all Jews from their midst. Reliable authorities have estimated that many millions have been starved and otherwise "liquidated" during recent years in two or three nations in Europe. Thousands, if not millions, of Jews are today being driven from one country to another with no place whereon the

---

43. Joseph Taylor Britan, "The Plight of the Jew," The Presbyterian (November 10, 1938): 11–2. The quotations which follow are all taken from the article.

soles of their feet may permanently rest.

For Britan, these developments were a "reversion to the terrible racial antipathies of the Dark Ages," and he added that there was "every indication that it will continue."

Britan goes on to meld philosemitic sentiment and a bid for support on the one hand, with prejudicial stereotypes and supersessionist theology on the other. Surveying the "alleged reasons" for the present-day persecution of the Jews, he observed that the Nazis believed Jews to be the leaders of the Communist movement, while others believed in a global conspiracy of Jews to establish a dictatorship. While he disparaged these ideas as false propaganda, he further opined that "The Word of God declares that the sufferings of Israel are His judgments for idolatry and for their rejection of His son and their own Messiah." Immediately thereafter, though, Britan pivoted away from the implications of this condemnation: "This, however, gives no nation and no individual the Divine permission to persecute the Jew; and the penalties promised to those who do persecute the Jews are certain to be visited upon offending persons and nations."

From there, Britan turned to the danger of anti-Semitism in the United States and the scapegoating of Jews in U.S. society. Yet even as he defended American Jews from stereotyping under the collective identities as communist or financier, he continued to draw on the very language of collective identity: "Even if it were discovered that all the leaders of Communism are Jews (a supposition contrary to fact), there still would be no reason to persecute the Jews as a race and make the truly patriotic and righteous members of the race to suffer for the economic and political sins of the Jew."

At this point in the article, Britan returned to the "dire need of the Jew" in foreign lands and the "ungodly and un-Christian persecution of innocent Jewish men, women, and children over the face of the earth," commenting that Americans "would surely rise as one man and demand the cessation of persecution […] if the emotions and sympathies of the world had not been deadened by the diabolical deeds of the World War."

Having diagnosed the ills of anti-Semitism and persecution, Britan turned to address the question of cure. First, he maintained, Christians should protest and work to educate Americans so that anti-Semitism "may find no place in American life." Pastors, Bible teachers, and leaders were the key figures Britan claimed could erect "barriers against the evil tides of prejudice and persecution." The second response Britan advanced, and the one he spent the most time discussing, was financial and spiritual support for Jewish missions.

Enumerating different Philadelphia Presbyterian attempts to evangelize Jews, he observed both the eager interest of Jews and their reluctance to convert, which he blamed on Jewish spiritual blindness – "For the veil is still over the eyes of many Jews [...]" – and centuries of prejudicial treatment at the hands of Christians. For Britan, the "278,000 Jews of Philadelphia" constituted "one of the most neglected mission fields for evangelistic work in the city," important to undertake "if the powerful paganism of our day is to be met and our Christian institutions preserved."

While American Christians were supposed to respond with protests against injustice, education for tolerance, and the evangelism of Jews at home, they were not to forget their responsibility to Jews in Europe. Like other Protestant writers, Britan reframed the suffering of Jews as the suffering of Christians and Jews: one and a half million "Hebrew Christians" in Europe required immediate aid, he specified, adding that British churches were already helping "Jews and Jewish Christians." He quoted a Scottish churchman to argue that "the non-Aryan Christians of Germany are a problem side by side with the Jewish problem: or rather they are part of the problem, for no distinction is made on grounds of faith." Jews, Briton declared, were "completely astounded" that Christians were not helping fellow Christians of Jewish origin, and deplored that "hardly any help has been forthcoming from Christian sources" to aid the tens and hundreds of thousands of non-Aryans who have never known of any other faith than Christianity, even as word from Germany was that these people "are slowly and inexorably being annihilated." Britan closed with an appeal for money and prayer, invoking the words of Jesus from the Gospel of Matthew: "In as much [sic] as ye have done it unto one of the least of these my brethren (the Jews), ye have done it unto me."

It is hard to guess the conclusions drawn by readers who made it to the end of Britan's article. Would they have been swayed by the author's passionate defense of Jews from anti-Semitic prejudice and persecution, or, rather, absorbed his many traditional anti-Jewish stereotypes, supersessionist theology, and calls for Jewish conversion? Difficult to categorize, this article illustrates how Protestant publications mirrored the internal tension within 1930s U.S. conservative Protestantism, both condemning and perpetuating anti-Semitism, and the way in which Protestant support for persecuted Jews always took place under the theological and socio-cultural shadows of the long history of Jewish-Protestant relations.[44]

---

44. Among other examples of this mixture of positive and negative responses to Jews and Judaism in the context of Nazi persecution, see James C. Clark, "The Christian Church and the Jew," The Presbyterian (September 15, 1938): 7–8.

The Cosmic Battle of Christianity and Irreligion

Finally, it must be said that although mainline Protestant leaders fought against anti-Semitism, decried the plight of German Jews, and worked to generate financial and practical support for Jewish (and Jewish-Christian) refugees, all of these concerns were subsumed by their broader preoccupation with the cosmic struggle between Christianity and irreligion, which emerged from a profound sense of crisis related to both global political turmoil and religious upheaval. In the Protestant church press analyzed in this chapter, this battle of good and evil took two forms: liberal and conservative.

On the liberal side, these Protestant writers and editors warned their readers about the forces of barbarism, totalitarianism, and war which threatened to destroy civilization, democracy, and freedom. Time and again, they reinforced the link between religion, specifically Christianity, and democracy and civilization. An attack on any one of these institutions was an attack on them all.

Arthur E. Holt captured this idea astutely in his article, "Shall Protestantism Implement Democracy?" published in *Advance* in February 1938:

> It will remain for Protestantism to be the spiritual energizer of these democracies. Catholicism is not interested in the democratic process. [...] If the democracies of the world are to be spiritualized, energized, it will remain for the Protestant churches to carry on the task. There is an interplay between Protestantism on the one hand and the democratic governments on the other. [...] These two movements – democracy in political life and democracy in religious life – reinforce each other or die together. [...] Something terrible will happen to the world if the world gives up on the idea of living by persuasion, by social cohesion, by fellowship, by progress and by mutual exchange of ideas. That is essentially the philosophy, it seems to me, of democracy and Protestantism.[45]

In the same issue, Henry Smith Leiper wrote,

> Efforts to avert war have only been substitutes for religion. Peace must be grounded more deeply that upon anything that has as yet been tried. We must go down deeper. Only religion can save us. The churches must get on with their job. The responsibility rests with them. Religion is peace.[46]

In August, T.W. Graham argued that Christianity elevated individual human worth, which was a significant contribution to the Greek idea

---

45. Arthur E. Holt, "Shall Protestantism Implement Democracy?" Advance (February 1, 1938): 57–8.

46. Henry Smith Leiper, "The State of the Church," Advance (February 1, 1938): 62.

of democracy. "Are you concerned for the opportunity for the ordinary man to make judgments as to the common good?" he asked. "Then the world must be fashioned after the mind of the great democrat of the ages: Jesus Christ. Then we must set ourselves to drive war out of the world. Then must you give yourselves in every area of life to make democracy effective."[47]

If Jesus was Graham's "great democrat of the ages," Wilbur Larremore Caswell of *The Churchman* presented Paul as the originator of a great liberal tradition that carries on into the twentieth century![48] And, as former U.S. ambassador to Germany William Dodd put it in a speech to the Church League for Industrial Democracy, "If we abandon democracy, we cannot help but abandon Christianity, and then we will go into another system which reminds one of the autocratic rule of the late Middle Ages where the government was everything and the individual counted for nothing." Distressed, he described fascism as "the worst situation the world has ever known" and called on "Christians in democratic countries" to cooperate to save democracy, freedom of speech, and freedom of the press.[49]

A letter to the editor on May 1st echoed these sentiments: "At first slowly, now suddenly and dramatically, the world, all who see and understand and hope for order and freedom and the survival of civilization, Christian, Jew and even non-believer, seems to look to the great religions of the world to save it from suicide." After the failure of the League of Nations and its member governments to maintain world peace, the world looks to "Christian or religious concepts of right and wrong, of justice, freedom, peace and – our last and greatest hope – of human brotherhood."[50]

More apocalyptic still was Sturgis Lee Riddle's September article entitled, "Civilization Takes Refuge in the Church," in which he argued:

> Now that self-sufficient humanism has run its course, sown its seed, now that science, undirected by Immortal Mind, is loosing a new barbarism upon us, now that man's five-century-old determination to live unto himself alone is turning the world again into a place of horror, the church of God is once more called upon to assume the trusteeship of civilization.[51]

---

47. T.W. Graham, "Democracy or War," Advance (August 1, 1938): 365.
48. Wilbur Larremore Caswell, "New Orthodoxy and Old Liberalism: Liberalisms May Pass but Liberalism Never," The Churchman (March 1, 1938): 14–5.
49. "Democracy: Dodd Describes Nazism at CLID Annual Meeting," The Churchman (March 1, 1938): 18.
50. Robert R. Reed, "Hull or Hitler?" The Churchman (May 1, 1938): 4.
51. Sturgis Lee Riddle, "Civilization Takes Refuge in the Church," The Churchman (September 1, 1938): 10–1.

If liberals tied the salvation of Western civilization to the strength of Christianity, conservatives honed in on apolitical Christian spiritual renewal and prayer as remedies for the world's ills. For example, in November 1938, *The Living Church* published a public address delivered by U.S. Assistant Secretary of State Francis B. Sayre, in which the politician outlined the task of Christianity in the face of "the increasingly acute human need and the growing world problems which press in upon us from every side." After depicting the collapse of "old institutions, old beliefs, old standards," and "the "prodigious change [which] everywhere affects the very foundations of our life," Sayre urged Christians to "take stock of their own beliefs, to evaluate and formulate their own faith and, if theirs is to be a conquering faith, to reach some kind of agreement on a program for action."[52] For Sayre, this program included faith in God rather than physical force; "the free giving of oneself to other people, irrespective of race, nation, or creed," rather than selfish "material acquisition;" and international human brotherhood rather than national rivalries. What was required was a return to "a revitalized and purified Christianity." Sayre propounded belief in the goodness and love of God at work in the world, and stated, "We believe that actually the world cannot function effectively until men learn to put Christ at the centre of their lives." In terms of a program of action, Sayre called for "a thoroughgoing loyalty to all mankind beyond the narrow confines of class, nation, or race." He went on to petition for the cessation of war, the creation of a just social order, and the elimination of "race, color, or creed discrimination." All of this, though, was an appeal for individual Christian belief and action, not a political buttressing of Western civilization by institutional Christianity.

Prayer as a response to the crises of totalitarianism and irreligion was a recurring theme in *The Living Church*. As a September article on "The Clouds of War" proclaimed: "It is a time for Christians of all nations to pray without ceasing – and to endeavor to raise up a truly Christian generation that may be able to build a better world than that of which the present generation has made such a mess."[53] And in mid-December, the editors printed "A Prayer for the Oppressed" from a minister in Colorado. It read:

> O God, the Creator of men and of nations: we implore Thy fatherly care and protection in behalf of all Thy children everywhere who suffer persecution. In all their trials and tribulations be Thou their refuge and strength. Impart to them Thine own comfort and courage. Turn the

---

52. Francis B. Sayre, "Christianity Faces the World," The Living Church (November 16, 1938): 509–10.

53. "The Clouds of War," The Living Church (September 7, 1938): 209.

hearts of the oppressors from evil to good. Stop the hands and convert the wills of those who would array brother against brother in racial strife. Restore to all men everywhere the blessing of religious freedom. Fill our hearts and inspire our minds with a desire firmly to establish peace and justice, liberty and fraternity, throughout the world; for His sake who suffered for all mankind, Thy Son Jesus Christ, our Lord. Amen.[54]

Similar calls for individual spiritual renewal were to be found in *The Presbyterian*, where pleas for prayer also appeared. In a striking example, Dr. Mark A. Matthews, pastor of the largest Presbyterian church in the United States, asked readers, "Have You Forgotten How to Pray?" He warned of "a world on fire," totalitarian attacks on liberty, individual rights, and democracy, and a coming war for "the preservation of liberty and the right to exist." His response was this question: "Have we forgotten how to pray, why we should pray, and when we should pray?"[55]

One week later, Arthur Burd McCormick reported on the many calls to prayer, prayer meetings, and intercession services which had recently taken place in response to the Czech Crisis and Munich Conference. In this context, he told of the request of a women to her pastor that the ministerial association set aside its meeting to pray, and that churches around the city of Philadelphia be opened to prayer meetings. Within the hour, arrangements had been made, and even city hall and some schools stopped their work for prayer. "Things like this were going on all over the earth," McCormick wrote. "Who dare say that those prayers had nothing to do with the settlement at the eleventh hour and fifty-ninth minute."[56]

For McCormick and others in the conservative wing of mainline Protestantism, spiritual renewal was key to combatting the evils of the current age. As he argued:

> The only remnants of internationalism left in the world are to be found among the churches (including synagogues). This new emphasis on Aryanism, race, blood, nation; this new resort to brute force; this new policy of terrorism; this absolute denial of freedom, justice and love; this disregard of decency and common morality; this setting of governments outside of the idea of law – all this is a return on a world scale to the ruthlessness of the tribal clan or the cry of the wolfish pack. We have witnessed Mussolini's contemptuous indifference to the Church. We have seen the Nazi attempt to create a pagan-Christian church which

---

54. "A Prayer for the Oppressed," The Living Church (December 14, 1938): 636.
55. Mark A. Matthews, "Have You Forgotten How to Pray?" The Presbyterian (October 6, 1938): 3, 6.
56. Arthur Burd McCormick, "The World As I See It," The Presbyterian (October 13, 1938): 5.

will give blind support to the government.

Here McCormick gave examples of Nazi attacks on both Christians and Jews, and asked:

> Is it not therefore evident that the time has come for all who believe in spiritual religion, for all who are opposed to totalitarianism, for all who prize their freedom to get together and present a common front against this new savagery that threatens the destruction of all we hold dear? Jews, Catholics and Protestants face a common foe: why not face it together? [57]

Other conservative appeals for spiritual renewal and devotional activity as the weapon with which to defeat the forces of irreligion appear in the Methodist weekly *Zion's Herald*. For instance, during Easter 1938, an article entitled, "Looking for the Resurrection" explored the meaning of the resurrection of Christ in the context of the modern totalitarian state. When dictatorships dominate the many domains of life, then "Jesus Christ, the living Jesus Christ, has once more been crucified and placed in a tomb whose entrance has been doubly sealed, lest He should escape and once more proclaim hope and freedom and faith to men." As the states make power their god, as they suppress human freedom, "the pagans are having their day." Observing the persecution of Christians in Germany, the author declares: "The scene is not new. Nero – Hitler; catacombs – prison camps; Colosseum – execution grounds. A different year, a few changes in costumes, another location – that is all. History is repeating itself."[58]

Most conspicuous in this article, as in so many other cases, is not so much the emphasis on Christian suffering rather than Jewish suffering as the contest between the spiritual power of Christ over and against the paganism of totalitarianism. As the author continued,

> There are signs that the tomb [...] is beginning to crack. There are evidences of newness of life [...] for the living Christ cannot be bound in the grave-clothes of pagan power. [...] [T]here is a flush in the east, and little streaks of light that proclaim the advent of a new day of love and righteousness. Be of good cheer. Christ shall rise again – here and now in this sin-distracted world.[59]

Two months later, another article, entitled "Witness-Bearing – 1938," advised Christians how to participate in the spiritual subversion of totalitarian irreligion. Witness-bearing, the author counseled, must go beyond personal religious devotion. "In this twentieth century of con-

---

57. Ibid.
58. "Looking for the Resurrection," Zion's Herald (April 13, 1938): 464.
59. Ibid.

fusion when men have gone so far astray in their wider relationships," the author called for witness-bearing right across the world.[60] But what were Christians supposed to bear witness to? The answer: "First of all, to the sovereignty of God. This is not Hitler's world, Mussolini's world, the Mikado's world, the politician's world, the capitalist's world, the labor leader's world. It is God's world. We are to do His will first, last, and always, and let consequences be what they will." Next, Christians were to bear witness to the significance and purpose of life and to the supremacy of love, and to do so through the proclamation of the gospel. "Preach the word! Preach the word – not empty words." And laypeople had a role too, to speak out, work in committees, pass resolutions, and "seek to put the principles of the gospel to work wherever you have the opportunity."[61]

This was a spiritual renewal to defeat the forces of irreligion with spiritual weapons:

> The church cannot and should not attempt to operate governments, settle economic problems, dictate labor policies, pose as an expert in the technique of industry, draw up trade agreements, point out in concrete detail all the proper relationships among the nations. The church's business is to bear witness, to insist upon the application of gospel principles to all life. When it does this it lives in Christ; when it fails to do this it dies, though the empty forms of its organization may survive for years.[62]

In another case, Charles M. Laymon, a prolific writer of biblical commentaries and practical theology, published in August 1938 an article about how pastors should preach apocalyptically. In times of wickedness, preachers ought to proclaim the breakthrough of a new work of God. This he applied to the present time, first noting the economic uncertainty in the United States, after which he turned to the international scene:

> From press and radio come reports of even greater uncertainty abroad. The chess-game of European politics is being speeded up with dizzying rapidity. No one would predict with confidence the national boundary lines of Central Europe twelve months hence. This is the type of soil that grows apocalyptic thinking. Culture seems to have failed. Self-interest has cocained [sic] reason. Man is not sure he can trust himself, and less sure that he can trust his brother. If the world is to be saved, God alone can save it, and because He must, He will![63]

---

60. "Witness-Bearing—1938," Zion's Herald (July 6, 1938): 868.
61. Ibid.
62. Ibid.
63. Charles M. Laymon, "Preaching and Apocalypse: Today's Need for a Triumphant Faith," Zion's Herald (August 3, 1938): 991.

Laymon further explained the elements of what he called an apocalyptic spirit: a conviction of the purpose of history which will be realized in God's ultimate judgment, a sense of urgency, a greater sensitivity to "the reality of the 'Unseen,'" and a triumphant faith that God will ultimately win the day.[64]

Later in the fall, in the wake of the Czech Crisis, *Zion's Herald* published an article entitled "The Four Horsemen" – another reference to the apocalypse, or the end of the world. In the article, however, the four horsemen refer to the four political leaders who negotiated the dismemberment of the Czechoslovak state. Decrying the Munich Agreement as a breaking of agreements and an abandonment of ethics, the writer interpreted the pact as a demonstration that:

> […] the only solution of the world's woes is the practice of Christianity. Not Communism with its shifty ethics and appeal to force, not Nazism [sic]or Fascism with their sword-rattling and their blatant denial of morals, will save the world […]. Turn away from Munich and look at Calvary. In the crucified Christ is the honest word of God, love, truth, integrity, peace, justice, which must prevail not through brute force but by example and persuasion. He can deliver this sin-sick world from destruction. He alone can do it. There is none beside.[65]

Conclusion

In 1938, against the background of German racism, American anti-Semitism, and a growing Jewish refugee crisis, the writers and editors of the mainline Protestant church press examined in this chapter understood their Christian duty as a call to respond to a profound sense of crisis. Democracy, civilization, Christianity, and all religion were under attack from the forces of war, totalitarianism, racism, and paganism. Clergy writing in mainline church periodicals responded by naming the evils of war and totalitarianism, in particular the threat that Hitler and Nazi Germany posed to the civilized world. They also fought against anti-Semitism and tried to aid Jews, though not without slipping into the language of enduring anti-Jewish prejudices, and also not without reframing the persecution of Jews and the Jewish refugee crisis as the persecution of Christians and Jews, and the Christian and Jewish refugee crisis. Of paramount importance to these mainline Protestants, however, was the affirmation that it was Christianity, and Christianity alone, that had the power to rescue civilization, save democracy, and preserve the world from self-destruction.

---

64. Ibid., 991–2.
65. "The Four Horsemen," Zion's Herald (October 12, 1938): 1236.

Lutheran Churches and Luther's Anti-Semitism
Repression, Rejection, and Repudiation
By Ursula Rudnick

Introduction

The commemoration of Martin Luther's quincentenary in 1983 saw the Lutheran World Federation (LWF) tackle, for the first time, the famous theologian's anti-Semitism. In a pioneering move, the LWF organized a meeting with the International Jewish Committee on Interreligious Consultations (IJCIC), a consultation that resulted in a published document. The document is composed of three statements, one made by the meeting's Lutheran participants, a second one made by its Jewish participants, and a third one made jointly.[1] The Lutheran part states unambiguously: "The sins of Luther's anti-Jewish remarks, the violence of his attacks on the Jews, must be acknowledged with deep distress. And all occasions for similar sin in the present or the future must be removed from our churches."[2] Never before had a body of Lutheran churches recognized and condemned Luther's judaeophobia and committed itself to combatting anti-Semitism.

Arguably, we witnessed a watershed. One might well ask: what

---

1. The consultation took place in Stockholm, Sweden, from July 11–13, 1983. Jean Halpérin and Arne Sovik, eds., Luther, Lutheranism and the Jews: A Record of the Second Consultation between Representatives of the International Jewish Committee for Interreligious Consultation and the Lutheran World Federation, held in Stockholm, Sweden, 11–13 July 1983, Lutheran World Federation Studies (Geneva: The Lutheran World Federation, 1984). An earlier consultation had taken place in Bossey, Switzerland, in 1982 and its results were published: The Lutheran World Federation, ed., The Significance of Judaism for the Life and the Mission of the Church (Geneva: The Lutheran World Federation, 1983).

2. Statement from the International Jewish Committee on Interreligious Consultations (IJCIC) and the Lutheran World Federation (LWF) Consultation, Stockholm 1983. Quoted in A Shift in Jewish-Relations?, eds.Wolfgang Greive and Peter N. Prove (Geneva: The Lutheran World Federation, 2003): 196. Available at: https://www.ccjr.us/dialogika-resources/documents-and-statements/interreligious/759-lwfi-jcic1983

prompted the Lutheran Church to make this extraordinary decision? How did it happen that this impulse was taken up and put into practice? This essay examines the question of how the Lutheran churches in Europe – as represented by the Lutheran Commission on the Church and the Jewish People (LEKKJ) – have begun to confront Luther's anti-Semitism, how this move is reflected in official statements, and what steps have been taken towards a new and respectful relationship between the Lutheran Church and the Jewish people.

The European Lutheran Commission on the Church and the Jewish People

The European Lutheran Commission on the Church and the Jewish People (LEKKJ) is a network of Lutheran churches that deals with questions concerning the relationship between the churches and the Jewish people. The only umbrella Protestant institution in Europe that has operated continuously since its establishment in 1976, the LEKKJ was founded in Christiansfeld, Denmark, by eight Lutheran churches and missionary organizations from Scandinavian countries, the Federal Republic of Germany, and the Netherlands. Church delegates meet annually for a conference at the invitation of a member church. The conferences engage with a wide range of topics pertinent to Jewish-Christian relations and theological questions, specifically Lutheran-Jewish relations. A sampling of themes includes: the relevance of Judaism for Christian self-understanding; anti-Judaism and the renewal of Lutheran theology in the face of Judaism; hermeneutics of the Hebrew Bible; as well as the organization of practical work in church communities and schools and the fight against anti-Semitism. Over the decades, the conference discussions have yielded significant output, including official statements, articles, and books.

Luther's Heirs

The book *Luthers Erben: Das Verhältnis lutherischer Kirchen Europas zu den Juden* (*Luther's Heirs: The Relationship of European Lutheran Churches to the Jews*)[3] is one such literary product of the LEKKJ conference circuit. Luther's Heirs emerged from the organization's first study project, started in the second year of its existence. In its early stages, the project was referred to by the general title *Christians Meet Jews – Jews Meet Christians*. During the course of the study process, however, LEKKJ members decided to tackle explicitly Luther's ideas on Jews and Judaism and Lutheran issues within the wider con-

---

3. Arnulf H. Baumann, Käte Mahn, and Magne Saebø, Luthers Erben und die Juden: Das Verhältnis lutherischer Kirchen Europas zu den Juden (Hannover: Lutherisches Verlagshaus, 1984).

text of Jewish-Christian relations.⁴

Published in 1984, *Luther's Heirs* is a collective volume edited by German Lutheran ministers Arnulf H. Baumann and Käte Mahn, along with a Norwegian Lutheran scholar of the Hebrew Bible, Magne Saebø.⁵ The publication, which features Lutheran authors as invited contributors, was funded by the national Lutheran Church office in Hannover, the Norwegian Israel Mission, and the Finnish Lutheran mission.⁶

Luther's Heirs was written for a target readership, namely, "Lutheran Christians across Europe to whom the relationship between Jews and Christians is dear," and with a specific aim, that is, to contribute to the "dismantling of prejudices for a deeper understanding and better coexistence of Christians and Jews in the future."⁷ The book represents a groundbreaking attempt to sketch the history of relations between Jews and the Lutheran churches in Europe, to understand the difficulties of present Lutheran-Jewish relations, and to set forth boldly the relevant theological challenges. Furthermore, it raises the profound question of how "Luther's heirs" have thus far approached Jews and Judaism. In this respect, "It shows how extremely different attitudes and behaviors have manifested themselves at various times in different countries."⁸ The publication, which gathers previously unavailable information and materials from many different churches, is available in a useful handbook form.

The first chapter of *Luther's Heirs* sketches the situation of the Jewish population in Germany at the beginning of the sixteenth century, briefly describes Luther's perception of and relationship with the Jews, and discusses the representation of Judaism in Lutheran confessional writings. The final part of the first chapter is dedicated

---

4. "Bei der Tagung in Hoekelum / Niederlande 1978 wurde Übereinstimmung darüber erzielt, dass es notwendig ist, einen historischen Überblick über die Juden in der Reformationszeit und eine Darstellung der theologischen Anschauungen Luthers und der lutherischen Bekenntnisschriften über die Juden voranzustellen"; Baumann, Mahn, and Saebø, Luther's Erben, 10.

5. Ibid., 11.

6. Ibid., 9

7. Translations from the German are mine. "Die Studie wendet sich an lutherische Christen in ganz Europa, denen das Verhältnis von Juden und Christen am Herzen liegt, insbesondere an solche, die aktiv im kirchlichen Dienst stehen oder sich in der Begegnung mit Juden engagiert haben. Sie kann zur Vertiefung ihrer Kenntnisse über die Entwicklung im eigenen Land helfen, aber auch zur Erkenntnis, wie und warum es in anderen Ländern anders gelaufen ist"; ibid., 11.

8. "Es zeigt, wie außerordentlich unterschiedlich sich die Einstellungen und Verhaltensweisen zu verschiedenen Zeiten und in verschiedenen Ländern ausgeprägt haben. Es bietet Material zur Beantwortung der eingangs gestellten Fragen, wie es sonst nirgends zugänglich ist"; ibid. 9.

to the question of how Judaism features in a specific Lutheran confessional text, namely, the *Confessio Augustana*, a foundational Lutheran work that remains a point of reference for Lutherans today. Additionally, the chapter points to the unique relationship between the Lutheran Church and the Jewish people, stemming from their shared foundation in the Bible: "the prophetic and apostolic writings of the Old and the New Testament."[9]

In the second chapter of the book, one reads of the historical relationship between the Lutheran churches and Jews in some European countries, with a special focus on Germany. The third chapter – the most extensive of the volume – discusses the relationship between the European Lutheran churches and contemporary Jews. The focal point of the fourth chapter is the issue of foundational theological questions from the Lutheran point of view, such as the relationship between Old and New Testaments, the particular relationship between the Church and Judaism, and the testimony of Christ.

The book's brief account of Martin Luther's portrayal of Jews and Judaism follows the established pattern by depicting the early attitude and writings of Luther as friendly towards Jews and Judaism, especially his treatise *Dass Jesus Christus ein geborener Jude sei* ("That Jesus Christ was Born a Jew"), published in 1523. The authors present Luther's early writings as an expression of appreciation, neglecting the fact that Luther's political advice was driven by his hope of the Jews' conversion to Christianity and thus was not an appreciation of Jews and Judaism as such.[10]

The late writings of Luther, *Von den Juden und ihren Lügen* (*On the Jews and Their Lies*) and *Vom Schem Hamphoras und vom Geschlecht Christi* (*Of the Ineffable Name and the Generations of Christ*), written in 1543, are characterized as follows:

> These writings, which have a much sharper tone, arose within the framework of a theological discussion which was characterized by historical and exegetical arguments […]. Thus, from these writings we hear not only venom and indignation, but, above all, fear that his words, which were so clear to him, had no effect on the Jews. This could only be due to their 'blindness' and 'stubbornness.' At the same time, Luther was afraid of the effect of their arguments. Driven by fear that faith in Christ

---

9. "[…] zu den prophetischen und apostolischen Schriften Alten und Neuen Testaments als zu dem reinen, lauteren Brunnen Israels, welcher alleine die einige wahrhaftige Richtschnur ist, nach der alle Lehrer und Lehre zu richten und zu urteilen seien"; ibid., 15.

10. "Das Ziel der Schrift bestand demnach vor allem darin, Christen oder Konvertiten aus dem Judentum, die missionarisch wirkten, eine Orientierungshilfe zu bieten"; Thomas Kaufmann, Luthers Juden (Stuttgart: Reclam, 2014), 66. Towards this end, Luther advocated friendly behavior towards Jews.

might be lost, he would be led to the infamous statements, which Protestant enemies of the Jews later invoked time and again.[11]

Hence, on the one hand, the authors distance themselves from Luther's vitriolic anti-Jewish diatribes. On the other, however, their analysis is marked by apology. Luther's invectives and the demonization of Jews and Judaism, his literal identification of Jews with the devil, are glossed over as 'ugliness' (*Gehässigkeit*) and 'indignation' (*Entrüstung*).[12] His hostility towards Jews and Judaism is explained, in part, via the *Zeitgeist* and his *Weltanschauung*, political circumstances as well as Jewish (re)actions. The text's attempts to analyze, understand, and explain Luther's judaeophobia are, thus, colored by a definite defensive mode.

The authors state the necessity that "[…] theology and the church clearly distance themselves from all Luther's anti-Jewish statements,"[13] since anti-Semites invoked them over and over again during the course of history.[14] Tellingly, however, nowhere does one find the notion that a repudiation of these statements could be necessary for the sake of the church itself: its faith and theology.

In sum, while the authors raise important questions and formulate lucid and laudable goals, they often fall short of achieving these aims. This decidedly partial accomplishment can be variously accounted for. Most prominently, perhaps, the volume would have profited from the inclusion of non-Lutheran perspectives – Jewish scholars, in particular. It might have taken its cue from the Lutheran World Federation, which jointly organized a consultation with the International Jewish Committee on Interreligious Consultations and in which members of LEKKJ participated and were even instrumental in its preparation.[15] Although the depiction of Luther's attitude towards Judaism is char-

---

11. Ibid., 15.
12. Ibid.
13. Ibid., 16.
14. The invocation of Luther's anti-Semitism continues until today. During the federal election campaign in 2017 the NPD (Nationaldemokratische Partei Deutschlands), an extreme right-wing party, put up election posters showing Luther with the caption: "Ich würde NPD wählen – Ich könnte nicht anders" (I would vote NPD – I couldn't do otherwise), alluding to Luther's words, allegedly spoken at the Reichstag in Worms: "Hier stehe ich, ich kann nicht anders" (Here I stand, I cannot help it.) The Evangelische Kirche in Deutschland (EKD) protested this strategy.
15. The Report of the Assembly Committee on the Church and the Jewish People explicitly thanks LEKKJ: "We do not want to leave unspoken our recognition of the very extensive and helpful work in Lutheran / Jewish relations that has taken place in our member churches, particularly in the USA and in Europe. The chief coordinating agencies were the European Lutheran Commission on the Church and the Jewish People in Europe and the Lutheran Council in the USA"; Greive and Prove, A Shift in Jewish Lutheran Relations?, 199.

acterized by defensiveness and an apologetic stance, these shortcomings do not detract from the fact the book represents the first post-1945 Lutheran attempt to deal with these acutely painful topics.[16]

The Declaration of Driebergen

After the Shoah, the awareness of the need for a renewal of Christian-Jewish relations developed slowly in the churches. In this vein, an important Protestant statement, the declaration of the Synod of the Rhineland, Germany, was published in 1980.[17] In the past decades, many Protestant – as well as Catholic – churches in Europe, North and South America, and Australia, have published statements that express a fundamental theological shift. Among these are the condemnation of anti-Semitism, the rejection of anti-Judaism, the insight of God's enduring covenant with the Jewish people based on a re-interpretation of Paul's letters to the Romans, the focus on Jesus' and Paul's Jewishness and consequent perception of them as part of the Jewish people and Jewish culture of the first century CE – and finally, a rejection of the teaching of supersessionism. This theological shift can be seen as the attempt to depart from the "theology of contempt" – as the French historian Jules Isaac termed it – and to establish a new relationship between the churches and the Jewish people.

In 1990, the LEKKJ published a comprehensive theological *Statement on the Encounter between Lutheran Christians and Jews*.[18] This succinct declaration, also known as the *Document of Driebergen*, is composed of four parts. The first section sets forth basic theological insights, such as the enduring chosenness of Israel and the unique relationship between Christians and the Jewish people. The second section reflects on the Shoah and the history of Christian anti-Judaism, condemning Christian triumphalism and calling for repentance: "In order to gain a new relationship with the Jews, we must learn to do penance as a church."[19]

---

16. For a detailed discussion, see Andreas Pangritz. Theologie und Antisemitismus: Das Beispiel Martin Luthers (Frankfurt a.M.: Peter Lang, 2017).

17. Rolf Rendtorff and Hans Hermann Henrix, eds, Die Kirchen und das Judentum: Dokumente von 1945–1980. (Paderborn: Bonifatius, 1988), 593–6.

18. European Lutheran Commission on the Church and the Jewish People, Statement on the Encounter between Lutheran Christians and Jews (Driebergen, The Netherlands, May 8th, 1990). A German version of the text can be found in Hans Hermann Henrix and Wolfgang Kraus, eds., Die Kirchen und das Judentum: Dokumente von 1986–2000 (Paderborn: Bonifatius, 2001), 448–51.

19. "In this context, the extent to which Christians – even after the Holocaust – still have to change their preaching and teaching – as well as their whole practice – has become clear"; "Dabei wurde immer klarer, wieviel die Christen nach der Shoa noch in ihrer Verkündigung. im Unterricht und in ihrer gesamten Praxis ändern müssen." In: Hans Hermann Henrix and Wolfgang Kraus, eds., Die Kirchen und das Judentum:

The question of missionizing among Jews was a highly controversial topic among the members of LEKKJ. This document eschews the term "mission" and instead uses the word "witness," speaking of the role of "mutual witnesses" to which Jews and Christians are called.[20] "He [God] frees [us] from the pressure of having to accomplish everything by oneself. This insight places Christians under the obligation to give witness and render service with due respect to the conviction and the faith of their Jewish partners." Members of the LEKKJ have understood these lines as rejecting any proselytizing attempts of Christians among Jews.[21] However, one finds no consensus among the Lutheran churches in Europe on this topic.

Most significantly, the document calls for an overhaul of Lutheran education and preaching, demanding:

> We also urge that the fundamental patterns of Lutheran theology and teaching such as "Law and Gospel," "faith and works," "promise and fulfilment," and the "two kingdoms/realms" be reconsidered in view of their effects on the relationship between Christians and Jews.[22]

Furthermore, the statement calls for "joint theological work with Jews, especially in the field of Bible."[23] Thus, it understands Jewish exegesis as enriching Christian exegesis of the Bible.

This text is a significant theological articulation of the position of Lutheran churches in Europe on Jews and Judaism. It contains crucial statements such as the recognition of guilt, combined with the call for repentance; the condemnation of anti-Semitism; the emphasis on the unique relationship of Christianity to Judaism; and a continuing relationship with Judaism and the Jewish people. The explanations

---

Dokumente von 1986–2000 (Paderborn: Bonifatius, 2001), 448.

20. "Any encounter between Christians and Jews must be based on the understanding that God Himself is the one who sends out, that is, who is the missionary. This insight into the missio dei helps us to understand one's own possibilities and tasks. God authorizes us to mutually witness our faith, trusting in the independent working of the Holy Spirit; for it is God who alone decides what effect our witness will have; and it is His decision with regard to the eternal salvation of all mankind. He frees us from the pressure of having to accomplish everything by ourselves. This insight places Christians under the obligation to give witness and render service with due respect to the conviction and the faith of their Jewish partners"; Ibid., 450.

21. The synod of the Austrian Protestant Churches quotes these lines and continues understanding it as a clear "no" to any form of missionary activities: "Da der Bund Gottes mit seinem Volk Israel aus lauter Gnade bis ans Ende der Zeit besteht, ist Mission unter den Juden theologisch nicht gerechtfertigt und als kirchliches Programm abzulehnen"; Erklärung der Generalsynode: "Zeit zur Umkehr – Die Evangelischen Kirchen in Österreich und die Juden." November 1998. https://evang.at/wp-content/uploads/2015/07/umkehr_011.pdf

22. http://www.lekkj.eu/dokumente.

23. http://www.lekkj.eu/dokumente.

on mission and testimony are to be understood as a rejection of any Christian missionizing activities among Jews. The distinctive character of this statement lies in its call for a theological examination and reformulation of Lutheran theology, as well as the call to theological collaboration. In a gesture of striking humility, the authors observe: "Great learning tasks lie before the churches, their organizations, their communities and all employees in preaching and teaching."[24]

The impact of the Declaration of Driebergen can be seen in several European Lutheran churches. In Germany[25] and in Austria, for instance, the text is quoted in the 1998 declaration of the *Evangelical Austrian Church* and in a 2015 statement of the synod of the Evangelical Church in Germany (EKD) on Luther's anti-Semitism.[26]

Recent developments

After the Declaration of Driebergen, the LEKKJ continued its work with a number of smaller projects, publishing educational material and briefer statements, such as the text entitled *Martin Luther and Judaism – Challenges for Lutheran Churches of Today* (2011).[27] In this document, the LEKKJ draws attention to the declaration of the Lutheran World Federation of 1984 and points out that the Reformation Jubilee in 2017 ought not to pass without recalling and repudiating Luther's judaeophobia. In this document, reference is made to the core message of the declaration of the Lutheran World Federation from 1983.[28] Furthermore, the central challenge formulated in the statement of Driebergen to "rethink fundamental Lutheran theology" and to bring scholarly insights into the churches and congregations, is restated as a task still not realized.[29] The statement ends by pointing to Luther's appreciation of the entire Bible – not only the New Testament

---

24. http://www.lekkj.eu/dokumente.

25. Lutheran Churches in Germany were asked to formulate an assessment by the VELKD: this was formulated by the Evangelical Lutheran Church in Bavaria and the Lutheran Church of Hanover. VELKD archive (AZ: 17/8–1–4). The Hanovarian church even published a flyer; see Henrix and Kraus, eds., Die Kirchen und das Judentum: Dokumente von 1986–2000, 448.

26. Erklärung der Generalsynode: "Zeit zur Umkehr – Die Evangelischen Kirchen in Österreich und die Juden." November 1998. https://evang.at/wp-content/uploads/2015/07/umkehr_011.pdf und "Martin Luther und die Juden – Notwendige Erinnerungen zum Reformationsjubiläum". https://www.landeskirchehannovers.de/damfiles/default/evlka/frontnews/2015/11/19/EKD-Beschluss-11-11-2015-6da1af-1131c1b4a18be18ced723cd082.pdf

27. http://sakasti.evl.fi/sakasti.nsf/0/9C5E043DDFA43B-10C22579AA00497F54/$FILE/LEKKJ%20zu%20Luther-Helsinki%202011%20-English.pdf and http://www.lekkj.eu/dokumente.

28. http://www.lekkj.eu/dokumente.

29. Ibid.

– and recalling the theological challenge: "We believe it is a primary task of the Lutheran Church today to further Christian hermeneutics of the Hebrew Bible and consider the Jewish interpretation as enrichment to the understanding of our common biblical basis."[30]

Conclusion

The quincentenary of Martin Luther's birth proved to be a crystallization point on an international level for the critical self-reflection of Lutheran churches on the famed theologian's anti-Semitism. In the Lutheran World Federation as well as in the European Lutheran Commission on the Church and the Jewish People (LEKKJ), an awareness arose regarding the urgent need for historical and theological discussion. The ensuing discussion of Luther's anti-Semitism in the LEKKJ took place almost exclusively among Lutheran ministers and scholars, which explains, among other things, the apologetic tone of *Luther's Heirs*. In the study published by LEKKJ members, the anti-Semitism of the late Luther is roundly rejected. Yet, comprehensive scholarly treatment of it and its long-term effects awaits future inquiry.

The Declaration of Driebergen formulates a fundamental theological renewal: this includes ecumenical insights such as the condemnation of anti-Semitism and an affirmation of the unrevoked covenant. Furthermore, the statement makes patent the need for a reconstruction of Lutheran theology and practice. Core elements of Lutheran theology, such as the relationship between Law and Gospel, contain anti-Jewish aspects. Thus far, however, only a handful of theologians, including, notably, Friedrich Wilhelm Marquardt,[31] has tackled these constitutive theological concepts in any serious and systematic fashion.

Nonetheless, it can be said that, to an increasing degree, sober historical and theological analyses are replacing apologetics. The celebration of 500 years of the Reformation in Germany gave rise to important research and discourse. The impact of Luther's judaeophobia on the church and society at large in Germany was debated fiercely,[32]

---

30. Ibid.

31. Friedrich-Wilhelm Marquardt, Von Elend und Heimsuchung der Theologie: Prolegomena zur Dogmatik (Munich: Kaiser, 1988); idem, Das christliche Bekenntnis zu Jesus, dem Juden: Eine Christologie, 2 vols. (Munich: Kaiser, 1990/91); idem, Was dürfen wir hoffen, wenn wir hoffen dürften? Eine Eschatologie, 3 vols. (Munich: Kaiser and Gütersloher Verlagshaus, 1993–1996); idem, Eia, wärn wir da – eine theologische Utopie (Munich: Kaiser and Gütersloher Verlagshaus, 1997).

32. Harry Oelke, Wolfgang Kraus, Gury Schneider-Ludorff, Axel Töllner, and Anselm Schubert, eds., Martin Luthers Judenschriften: Die Rezeption im 19. und 20. Jahrhundert (Göttingen: Vandenhoeck & Ruprecht, 2016); Christopher Ocker, "Martin Luther and Anti-Judaism and Anti-Semitism" http://religion.oxfordre.com/

in the church pews no less than in the hallways of academia.[33] As part of the Lutheran Church's educational project, several exhibitions on this topic were prepared[34] and various ecclesial boards released statements, among them the synod of the Evangelical Church in Germany.[35] And, on November 9, 2015, in Wittenberg – and a year later in other German cities – a poignant public gesture was made: in a reversal of the iconographic Christian image of the blindfolded *synagoga*, the eyes of the statue of Martin Luther were covered with a blindfold, signaling, with this switch, Luther's blindness and that of his heirs.

---

view/10.1093/acrefore/9780199340378.001.0001/acrefore-9780199340378-e-312

33. For an example of a controversial publication, see Johannes Wallmann, "Zum Umgang mit Martin Luthers Judenschriften: Die Evangelische Kirche verleugnet ihre Geschichte," part 1. http://www.pfarrerverband.de/pfarrerblatt/index.php?a=show&id=3621

34. Evangelische Kirche Berlin-Brandenburg-Schlesische Oberlausitz and Touro College Berlin, eds., Martin Luther und das Judentum: Rückblick und Aufbruch (Berlin: Evangelische Kirche Berlin-Brandenburg- Schlesische Oberlausitz, 2016).

35. Synode der Evangelischen Kirche in Deutschland, "Martin Luther und die Juden – Notwendige Erinnerung zum Reformationsjubiläum" 2015; https://r2017.org/fileadmin/downloads/ekd_kundgebung_luther_und_die_juden.pdf

GERMAN GUILT AND HEBREW REDEMPTION
Aktion Sühnezeichen Friedensdienste and the Legacy of Left-Wing Protestant Philozionism
By Johannes Becke

Note: The author would like to thank Bernhard Krane, head of the Israel desk at Aktion Sühnezeichen Friedensdienste, for an interview on the topic and for his generous support in researching material for this chapter. Many thanks also to Jenny Hestermann for her advice on locating the Sühnezeichen diaries from the first cohorts and of course to the anonymous reviewer for the detailed and helpful criticism.

Introduction

The history of *Aktion Sühnezeichen Friedensdienste* (ASF) in Israel constitutes an intriguing point of departure to study the legacy of left-wing Protestant Philozionism within German-Israeli relations. Ever since ASF began sending volunteers to Israel in 1961, the encounter between left-wing Protestant pacifists and the Jewish nation-state produced various forms of converts: converts to Judaism, converts to Zionism, and converts to the Palestinian cause.[1] While many volunteers chose Israel for the sun, the beach,[2] and the promise of romantic encounters in the exotic Levant,[3] few left the

---

1. In the third cohort alone, four volunteers converted to Judaism, "two stayed on in Israel; and all remained strongly pro-Israel"; see Lilach Marom, "'On Guilt and Atonement': Aktion Sühnezeichen Friedensdienste and Its Activity in Israel," Yad Vashem Studies 35 (2007): 187–220, here at 196.

2. Harald Martenstein, "Das volle Utopieprogramm," Tagesspiegel (January 10), 2004, http://www.tagesspiegel.de/kultur/das-volle-utopieprogramm/480722html (last accessed September 28, 2018).

3. The first bashful hint towards romantic encounters between German volunteers and Israelis is contained in the diary of the first cohort, which explains that native-born Israelis are called "sabras" after the prickly pears, which are prickly on the outside but sweet on the inside – "especially the women, 'according to reports'", Evangelisches Zentralarchiv (EZA) 19/735 [all translations by the author]. Later accounts by Aktion Sühnezeichen volunteers are much more explicit. The third issue of the volunteer journal Memrachit (1986) contains practical advice for female German

region unchanged. The graduates of ASF's Israel program frequently moved on to fill Israel-focused (or Middle East-focused) positions in the German media, Protestant churches, political foundations, and academia. Both the current president of the German-Arab Society (and a vocal critic of Israel's foreign policy), Michael Lüders, and the late Eike Geisel, a key inspiration for the left-wing pro-Zionist movement known as 'Anti-Germans' (*Antideutsche*), began their intellectual careers as *Aktion Sühnezeichen* volunteers in Israel.[4] Within the Protestant churches, the impact of pastors who served as volunteers in Israel can be felt in the Protestant Middle East Commission (*Evangelische Mittel-Ost Kommission*),[5] in the Working Group "Jews and Christians" at the Protestant Church Congress (*Evangelischer Kirchentag*),[6] in key policy documents on the Arab-Israeli conflict, including the recent position paper "Promised Land" (*Gelobtes Land*),[7] and in the transformation of Israel Sunday (*Israelsonntag*) from an obscure remainder of supersessionism and the Protestant missions to the Jews into a yearly celebration of Christianity's Jewish roots.[8] When the research field of Israel Studies was strengthened within German universities in 2015 on the occasion of half a century of German-Israeli diplomatic relations,[9] two junior academic positions were created in Heidelberg and Munich – and both were filled with graduates of ASF's Israel program.[10]

The history of ASF,[11] the attitude of German Protestants and the

volunteers on how to escape unwanted male Israeli attention, including "entangling people in political conversations" and "reacting to physical come-ons with a slap in the face," EZA 19/1868.

4. For a number of introductory essays on the "Anti-Germans," see Moshe Zuckermann, ed., Tel Aviver Jahrbuch für Deutsche Geschichte 2005: Antisemitismus, Antizionismus, Israelkritik (Göttingen: Wallstein Verlag, 2005).

5. Kirchenamt der EKD, ed., Israel-Palästina: Eine Positionsbestimmung der Evangelischen Mittelost- Kommission (Hannover: EKD, 2009).

6. Gabriele Kammerer, In die Haare, in die Arme: 40 Jahre Arbeitsgemeinschaft "Juden und Christen" beim Deutschen Evangelischen Kirchentag (Gütersloh: Gütersloher Verlagshaus, 2001).

7. Evangelische Kirche in Deutschland (EKD), Gelobtes Land? Land und Staat Israel in der Diskussion: Eine Orientierungshilfe (Gütersloh: Gütersloher Verlagshaus, 2012).

8. For a detailed theological engagement with Israel Sunday by theologians close to ASF, see Wolfgang Raupach, ed., Weisung fährt von Zion aus, von Jerusalem Seine Rede: Exegesen und Meditationen zum Israel-Sonntag (Berlin: Aktion Sühnezeichen Friedensdienste, 1991).

9. Johannes Becke, "Land and Redemption: The Zionist Project in Comparative Perspective," Trumah 23 (2016): 1–13.

10. This includes Daniel Mahla, the current coordinator of the Center for Israel Studies at the Ludwig Maximilian University in Munich, and the author of this article.

11. Gabriele Kammerer, Aktion Sühnezeichen Friedensdienste: Aber man kann es einfach tun (Göttingen: Lamuv, 2008); Anton Legerer, Tatort: Versöhnung. Aktion Sühnezeichen in der BRD und in der DDR und Gedenkdienst in Österreich (Leipzig:

German Left towards Israel,[12] as well as the embeddedness of ASF volunteers in the politics of post-war reconciliation,[13] have all received ample scholarly attention. Despite its enormous impact on German-Israeli relations, however, the history of *Aktion Sühnezeichen* in Israel awaits its scholarly due.[14] This chapter lays the ground for a systematic examination of ASF in Israel by presenting a framework for the study of Philozionism, atonement, and the politics of German guilt.

Philosemitism and Philozionism: Young Germans playing Israelis?

When it comes to the German-Israeli dimension of the larger Protestant-Jewish encounter, the affinity for Israel is frequently framed as part of the broader phenomenon of Philosemitism.[15] With respect to studying the activity of ASF in Israel, though, a more adequate framework might be Philozionism, a type of affinity for Jewish nationalism which openly sympathizes with the Zionist motif of a radical break with the history, politics, and culture of the Ashkenazi Jewish Diaspora. Liliane Weissberg famously mocked the German Philosemitism of the bygone Klezmer craze as "young Germans […] playing Jews."[16] In examining the phenomenon of German Philozionism (whether within ASF or among the Anti-Germans), we might adapt this phrase to speak of *young Germans playing Israelis* with regard to language,

---

Evangelische Verlagsanstalt, 2011).

12. Martin Kloke, Israel und die deutsche Linke (Frankfurt: Haag und Herchen, 1990); Gerhard Gronauer, Der Staat Israel (Göttingen: Vandenhoeck & Ruprecht, 2013).

13. Christiane Wienand, "From Atonement to Peace? Aktion Sühnezeichen, German-Israeli Relations and the Role of Youth in Reconciliation Discourse and Practice," in Reconciliation, Civil Society, and the Politics of Memory, eds. Birgit Schwelling (Bielefeld: transcript, 2012), 201–35; Christiane Wienand, "Reverberations of a Disturbing Past: Reconciliation Activities of Young West Germans in the 1960s and 1970s," in Reverberations of Nazi Violence in Germany and Beyond, eds. Stephanie Bird et al. (London: Bloomsbury, 2016): 223–50.

14. For an overview, see Jörn Böhme, "Die Arbeit der Aktion Sühnezeichen/Friedensdienste in – Geschichte und Entwicklung," in 20 Jahre Deutsch-Israelische Beziehungen, ed. Karlheinz Schneider (Berlin: Deutsch-Israelischer Arbeitskreis für Frieden im Nahen Osten, 1985: 137–50; Marom, "'On Guilt and Atonement.' Aktion Sühnezeichen Friedensdienste and Its Activity in Israel"; Aktion Sühnezeichen Friedensdienste, 50 Jahre Aktion Sühnezeichen Friedensdienste in (Berlin: Aktion Sühnezeichen Friedensdienste, 2011).

15. Adam Sutcliffe and Jonathan Karp, "Introduction: A Brief History of Philosemitism," in Philosemitism in History, eds. Jonathan Karp and Adam Sutcliffe (Cambridge and New York: Cambridge University Press, 2011): 1–26.

16. Liliane Weissberg, Reflecting on the Past, Emvisioning the Future: Perspectives for German-Jewish Studies (New York: Leo Baeck Institute, New York, and German Historical Institute, Washington, 2003), 12.

habitus, dress code, or an overall perspective on Jewish life and the Arab-Israeli conflict.

While Philosemitism and Philozionism rely on a similar set of textual and historical symbols in their perception of "the Jews as a resolutely distinct people, with distinctively admirable characteristics,"[17] they tend to draw rather different conclusions. At the risk of over-simplification, one might suggest the following typology: Philosemites study the Talmud (through the eyes of Daniel Boyarin), but Philozionists read the Hebrew Bible (through the eyes of David Ben Gurion)[18]; Philosemites admire Diasporic statelessness, but Philozionists celebrate state-making and military prowess; Philosemites learn Aramaic and Yiddish, but Philozionists study modern Hebrew; finally, Philosemites dream of converting to Judaism (the Orthodox stream, to make it more authentic), but Philozionists mimic the traits of Israeliness (secular Ashkenazi Israeliness, to make it more prestigious).

For an organization whose very name carries the loaded term 'atonement,' the salient phenomenon of conversions to Judaism as a form of *Vergangenheitsbewältigung* (overcoming the past)[19] might not be terribly surprising.[20] Conversions to Zionism (or Anti-Zionism, for that matter) have proved to be more problematic, however, both for political and theological reasons. In the context of ASF's activities in Israel, engagement with the question of Philozionism left an enduring impact on the organizational culture of the organization. Countering the romantic Christian Zionism of ASF's founder, Lothar Kreyssig, the Israel volunteers on the ground quickly developed an abiding organizational culture of sarcasm (with significant traces of Israeli humor).

17. Sutcliffe and Karp, "Introduction: A Brief History of Philosemitism," 7.

18. In this context, left-wing German Protestantism developed its own tradition of studying the Talmud, but in a decidedly Jewish-Israeli setting, a close entanglement of Philosemitism and Philozionism. As a critical intervention against Christian Anti-Judaism (often based on distorted readings of the Talmud), the study program Studium in Israel (Studies in Israel) has brought more than 600 German students of Protestant theology to Israel to study Rabbinic literature at the Hebrew University of Jerusalem. Unsurprisingly, the study program has a strong Sühnezeichen connection: Michael Krupp, one of its founders, was the former head of the ASF office in Jerusalem. The study program also produced an influential series of preaching material that deals with Christian-Jewish relations; see Wolfgang Kruse, ed., Predigtmeditationen im christlich-jüdischen Kontext: Zur Perikopenreihe I (Neuhausen: Kruse, 2002).

19. On conversions to Judaism as Vergangenheitsbewältigung see Barbara Steiner, Die Inszenierung des Jüdischen: Konversion von Deutschen zum Judentum nach 1945 (Göttingen: Wallstein Verlag, 2015), chapter 5.

20. For the conversion account of Christel Eckert (Michal Evenari), who belonged to the first cohort of Aktion Sühnezeichen volunteers and was married to an Israeli, see Michal Evenari, "The Story of a Life: From Germany to Israel," Chabad, 2008, http://.www.chabad.org/theJewishWoman/article_cdo/aid/704922/jewish/The-Story-of-a-Life.htm (last accessed September 29, 2017).

Second, in response to the radical critique of ASF's one-sided identification with the Zionist project (both real and imagined) which was voiced by *Aktion Sühnezeichen* volunteers from the New Left, ASF's leadership attempted to promote an ethos of 'critical solidarity' with Israel, based on the writings of the left-wing theologian Helmut Gollwitzer (1908–1993).[21]

ASF's culture of sarcasm may seem somewhat puzzling; after all, the organization is known for its nuanced and theologically complex position towards German memorial culture.[22] In a spirit of camaraderie, former volunteers jokingly refer to one another as "fellow atoners" (*Mitsühner*), and former Israel volunteers are known as "first-class atoners" (*Edelsühner*). Such sarcastic humor seems to have emerged from the gap between the organization's sublime theology of atonement and the mundane reality of difficult volunteer work done in nursing homes, kindergartens and Holocaust memorial sites. Among the Israel volunteers, however, this dark wit, which was already articulated by the very first cohort, might also be understood as backlash to the organization's guilt-driven Philozionism. The letters of Lothar Kreyssig from that period, for instance, depict Israeli state formation from a decidedly Christian Zionist perspective, with German volunteers playing the role of the biblical spies (Numbers 13: 1–33) and the eschatological ingathering of the gentiles (Isiaiah 56: 6–7). Kreyssig portrayed the first cohort of Israel volunteers as the "first reconnaissance patrol, with which we will arrive in Israel after a long and arduous wandering across the mountain ridges of German guilt."[23] When the volunteers had to wait in the Netherlands before being allowed into Israel, Kreyssig likened their journey to the biblical wandering across the desert, "when the People of Israel lived in tents for forty years on the way to the conquest of the Land (*Landnahme*). What a deep reference to the end of all ways, that we can now accompany the People of God on the way to its final conquest of the land!"[24]

---

21. Helmut Gollwitzer, Vietnam, Israel und die Christenheit (Munich: Christian Kaiser Verlag, 1967). On ASF's activities in Israel, see esp. Helmut Gollwitzer, "Zur Israel-Arbeit der Aktion Sühnezeichen" (February 1977), EZA 97/719.

22. Christian Staffa, "Die 'Aktion Sühnezeichen': Eine protestantische Initiative zu einer besonderen Art der Wiedergutmachung," in Nach der Verfolgung: Wiedergutmachung nationalsozialistischen Unrechts in Deutschland?, eds. Hans Günther Hockerts and Christiane Kuller (Göttingen: Wallstein-Verlag, 2003): 139–56.

23. Letter from Lothar Kreyssig to Harald Schlagowski, January 28 1962, EZA 19/735.

24. Letter from Lothar Kreyssig to Eleonore Dannemann, January 10 1962, EZA 19/735. For more examples of Kreyssig's idiosyncratic theology of atonement, see Konrad Weiß, Lothar Kreyssig: Prophet der Versöhnung (Gerlingen: Bleicher Verlag, 1998), chapter 18 – including the idea to have Aktion Sühnezeichen volunteers build a temple for Jews, Christians and Muslims in Jerusalem or to establish a 24/7 prayer

Yet it did not take long for the initial romanticism of encountering the Land of Israel from the deck of a ship in Haifa to be replaced by an acid wit. The first cohort referred to itself as an "atonement team" (*Sühnemannschaft*) and an "atonement family" (*Sühnefamilie*) guided by their "atonement father" (*Sühnevater*, the group's pastor). Volunteers who picked potatoes for up to ten hours each day were said to be engaging in "real atonement" (*echt zu sühnen*) while female volunteers or "atonement girls" (*Sühnemädchen*) who fell ill were described as "incapacitated to atone" (*sühnekampfunfähig*).[25] Many of the terms appear already crossed out in the original manuscript, and none made it into the official publication of parts of the diary of the first cohort in Ansgar Skriver's book on *Aktion Sühnezeichen*.[26] The self-deprecating humor, however, prevailed: decades later, the volunteer journal *Memrachit* would feature mock advertisements poking fun at Israel as the "atonement paradise," pretended to offer T-shirts with the logo "Atone with us. Atoning is fun," and inquired of its readers, "Have you atoned today?"[27]

While such satire might have helped ASF volunteers deal with the disillusionments of romantic Philozionism, it was no match for the ideological battles that came to shape the organization's work in Israel after the Six Day War in 1967. When ASF opened its doors to conscientious objectors in 1969, an increasing number among the volunteers arrived with affiliations to the New Left and were no longer willing to read the "conquest of the Land" (*Landnahme*) in the occupied territories in light of biblical prophecy. Political violence began to affect the organization's activities, and when a Palestinian terrorist attacked an ASF bus in Nablus in 1976 with a nail bomb, two young Germans were killed and many more were injured.[28] The traumatic experience made a strong impression on future generations of volunteers, but the terror attack did not seem to disillusion those volunteers who openly identified with the Palestinian cause. Volunteer projects that focused on the Palestinian Arab minority in Israel, in particular, produced vocal opponents of Israel's settlement policy.[29] In the first issue after the

---

team of volunteers at Yad Vashem.

25. EZA 19/735.

26. Ansgar Skriver, Aktion Sühnezeichen: Brücken über Blut und Asche (Stuttgart: Kreuz-verlag, 1962), 120–38.

27. Memrachit 1–3, EZA 19/1868.

28. Kammerer, Aktion Sühnezeichen, 159–62.

29. For publications by former ASF volunteers on the occupied territories, see Jan Metzger, Martin Orth, and Christian Sterzing, Das ist unser Land: Westbank und Gaza-Streifen unter israelischer Besatzung (Bornheim-Merten: Lamuv, 1980); Dieter Bednarz und Michael Lüders, Palästina Protokolle: Bestandsaufnahme und Perspektive (Hannover: Fackelträger-Verlag, 1981).

outbreak of the First Intifada, the volunteer journal *Memrachit* printed its name in Arabic instead of in Hebrew letters, published legal advice in case of being arrested at demonstrations, and included an angry accusation directed at the Israel desk at ASF headquarters:

> Honestly speaking, I am quite disappointed by ASF's Israel policy. ASF invokes two elements that are important to me: The 'Confessing Church' and the phrase 'learning from history'. You know the situation in Israel. Would you disagree when I say that there is racial discrimination, 'highly arbitrary' 'democratic rights', torture in the prison system and racial prejudice? 'Learning from history': How many people [still] need to be arrested, tortured, shot down before ASF shows its true colors? I'm not calling on you to send us stones or Molotov cocktails. Like almost all the volunteers in the Arab sector, I'm finally calling for more clear-cut statements and a more definitive advocacy for the Palestinian cause.[30]

From Critical Solidarity to a Theology of Israel

No such clear-cut statement would arrive from Berlin. On the contrary, in response to the First Intifada, ASF published a long and carefully worded open letter addressed to "all those in the Federal Republic who follow the news from Israel and the occupied territories with great concern and ask themselves what to do."[31] Framed as a German response to a much more radical statement by Israeli peace organizations (which criticized the "wide-spread unconditional loyalty towards the State of Israel" and called for a struggle against "the moral and physical decay of Israeli society"[32]), ASF's missive showed all the hallmarks of the 'critical solidarity' with Israel which the *Aktion Sühnezeichen* leadership had begun to promote in the 1970s as a response to an influx of New Left volunteers: a conflicted sense of solidarity with *both* sides, a rejection of simplifications, and an ethics of responsibility rooted in both the history of German guilt and leftwing Protestantism.[33]

---

30. Memrachit December 1987, EZA 19/1868.

31. Ulrike Berger et al., Offener Brief an alle, die in der Bundesrepublik die Nachrichten aus Israel und den besetzten Gebieten mit Sorge verfolgen und sich fragen, was sie tun können (Berlin: Aktion Sühnezeichen Friedensdienste, 1988).

32. "Appell an die Freunde Israels," ibid., 8; quoting Jesch Gvul, Ha Schana ha 21, and Dai le Kibusch. "Appell an Die Freunde Israels." In Offener Brief an alle, die in der Bundesrepublik die Nachrichten aus Israel und den besetzten Gebieten mit Sorge verfolgen und sich fragen, was sie tun können, edited by Ulrike Berger, Jörn Böhme, Dietrich Gaede, Bernhard Krane, and Heribert Krane, 8. Berlin: Aktion Sühnezeichen Friedensdienste, 1988.

33. For earlier ASF statements on the topic, see Volkmar Deile, Heiner Holland, and Johannes Müller, "Richtlinien der Arbeit der Aktion Sühnezeichen/Friedensdienste in Israel," Zeichen 2 (1977): 30–1; "Präambel für die Arbeit in Israel," Zeichen, 9:1 (1981): 11–2; "Grundsätze der Israelarbeit," Zeichen, 14:2 (1986): 16–7.

In contrast to the Christian Zionism of Pietist and Evangelical origins (with its own Israel-based volunteer organization),[34] this left-wing Protestant Theology of Israel was decidedly non-messianic, showing a clear sympathy for the socialist ideals of the kibbutz. Thus, in a speech entitled "Israel – and Us" (*Israel – und wir*), held in Berlin in 1958 after returning from a trip to Israel,[35] Helmut Gollwitzer famously identified three "moments" – that is, perspectives – on the State of Israel: from a moral perspective, "[every] German who travels to Israel should be clear: every Jew who lives today lives not because of us, but in spite of us […] in spite of me!" From a theological perspective, the renewal of Jewish life in the Land of Israel/Palestine could lead to a renewal of biblical hermeneutics and Christian-Jewish dialogue; after all, "anyone who deals with Israel must – like it or not – be a theologian." Finally, from a sociological perspective, Gollwitzer argued that Israel (in sharp contrast to the Federal Republic of Germany) represented an example of a "non-restorative social structure," a form of socialist awareness crystallized in the "phenomenon of kibbutzim."[36]

As an expression of this Gollwitzer-style 'critical solidarity,' the ASF open letter from 1988 emphasizes the "specific German background […] of the Shoah" and its consequence of "a strong need for security that is felt by many Jews inside and outside of Israel," only to contrast this with "the need for security by the Palestinians, in whose history the flight and expulsion of 1948 known as 'al-Nakba' (the catastrophe) is a central frame of reference."[37] While underlining the self-understanding of Zionism as "the national liberation movement of the Jewish people" and the "non-colonial character" of the Arab-Israeli conflict, the text sheepishly admits "colonial aspects in Israel's development, concerning, for instance, the appropriation of lands and the economic linkage between the occupied territories and the heartland."[38] In addition, after rejecting the claim that Zionism represents "a form of racism," the letter goes on to acknowledge "racist thought and actions" in Israel, including the "almost total lack of rights and

---

34. Andrea Schneider, "Hagoshrim – Die Brückenbauer: Freiwilligendienst in Israel," www.rundfunk.de, 2016, https://rundfunk.evangelisch.de/kirche-im-radio/am-sonntagmorgen/hagoshrim-die-brueckenbauer-7826 (last accessed August 28, 2018).

35. Helmut Gollwitzer, Israel – und wir (Berlin: Lettner, 1958).

36. All quotations according to W. Travis McMaken, "'Shalom, Shalom, Shalom Israel!' Jews and Judaism in Helmut Gollwitzer's Life and Theology," Studies in Christian-Jewish Relations 10:1 (2015): 1–22, here at 13–5.

37. Ibid., 3.

38. Ibid., 4.

the oppression of the Palestinians in the occupied territories."[39] After strongly condemning the claim to a "special German responsibility towards the Palestinians" as "the victim's victim,"[40] the text also rejects the temptation to "wholeheartedly take a position for one of the two sides. Such wholehearted support could only refer to both peoples' right to exist in Israel/Palestine."[41] Even the text's concluding call for action appears exceedingly well-balanced by criticizing West Germany's "military cooperation with Israel *and* the Arab states, which makes it harder to find a political solution to the conflict."[42]

This carefully constructed equidistance crumbled under the shock of an intense polarization in the German Left during the First Gulf War and the two Palestinian intifadas. DIAK (*Deutsch-Israelischer Arbeitskreis für Frieden im Nahen Osten*), the left-wing offshoot of the more mainstream German-Israeli Society (DIG, *Deutsch-Israelische Gesellschaft*), took a sharp turn towards a more radicalized critique of Israel and the Zionist project.[43] *Aktion Sühnezeichen*, for its part, increasingly returned to its Philozionist roots, not least by abandoning all volunteer projects that centered exclusively on Israel's Palestinian Arab minority in 1994. This ideological shift comes into stark relief when one reads ASF publications dedicated to the celebration of Israel Sunday: in 1995, for instance, the brochure contained an interview with Eliezer Feiler, a member of the Israeli Communist Party who had long been responsible for the party's external relations.[44] In its original form, the interview had been published by two ASF volunteers deployed in the "Arab sector,"[45] preceded by the following tendentious introduction:

> The political activist Feiler […] repeatedly witnessed wrongful Jewish actions against Arabs and had to realize that chauvinism and national arrogance are not typically German characteristics: Ominously, the attitude of many Jews in Israel towards the Arabs resembles in many respects the German position towards the Jews in the time of National

---

39. Ibid., 5.
40. In another example of ASF sarcasm, during the author's stay in Israel (2001–2002), a German Protestant senior volunteer was jokingly referred to as "the victims' victims' victim" after a group of young Palestinians in Jerusalem had stolen his wallet.
41. Ibid., 7.
42. Ibid., 8 [emphasis added].
43. Martin Kloke, "In aller Freundschaft: 50 Jahre Deutsch-Israelische Gesellschaft," haGalil.-com, 2016, http://www.hagalil.com/2016/03/deutsch-israelische-gesellschaft/ (last accessed October 9, 2017).
44. Yossi Melman, "He saw Red," Ha'aretz, 2004, https://www.haaretz.cim/he-saw-red-1.111779 (last accessed October 9, 2017).
45. Dieter Bednarz and Michael Lüders, Blick zurück ohne Hass: Juden aus Israel erinnern sich an Deutschland (Cologne: Bund-Verlag, 1981), 116–39.

Socialism.⁴⁶

In the 1995 ASF brochure for Israel Sunday, this passage disappeared. Nonetheless, while keeping quiet about Eliezer Feiler's affiliation with the Israeli Communist Party, the interview still contains the passage which had attracted the attention of its original publishers: "The Germans uncritically adopted the propaganda depiction [of the Jew], because a majority of Germans had no idea what a Jew was supposed to be. Here [in Israel] the same thing happens when it comes to the Arabs."⁴⁷

ASF's publications for Israel Sunday from recent years are decidedly less open to a radical critique of Israel and the Zionist project. Consider, for example, the content of the Israel Sunday brochures from 2003 until 2017, which discussed the politics of Palestinian nationalism, including BDS⁴⁸ and the Kairos Palestine Document.⁴⁹ However, although the texts featured Jewish-Israeli voices (often from the moderate Israeli left), during the same period only a single Palestinian author appeared in the brochures, tellingly to discuss Jerusalem from a Muslim (not, say, Palestinian) perspective.⁵⁰

While the collections of short texts include highly critical discussions of Evangelical Christian Zionism,⁵¹ the overarching legacy of Protestant Philozionism is unmistakable. For instance, a liturgy suggestion for Israel Sunday from 2008 describes the establishment of the State of Israel as "God's sign of protection (*Gottes Zeichen seiner Bewahrung*) [of his people] after and within a history of homelessness and hardships among the nations, including Christendom."⁵²

---

46. Ibid., 116.
47. Aktion Sühnezeichen Friedensdienste, Wenn die Propheten aufständen …: Handreichung zum Israel-Sonntag 1995 (Göttingen: Aktion Sühnezeichen Friedensdienste 1995), 39.
48. Christian Staffa, "Was tun mit der Kampagne Boykott, Desinvestition, Sanktionen?," in Israelsonntag 2015: Denkt nicht, ich sei gekommen, die Tora und die Propheten außer Kraft zu setzen (Berlin: Aktion Sühnezeichen Friedensdienste, 2015), 25–28.
49. Hanna Lehming, Und es ist doch ein Kairos! (Berlin: Aktion Sühnezeichen Friedensdienste 2011).
50. Abdallah Hajjir, "Jerusalem aus muslimischer Perspektive," in Israelsonntag 2012: Jerusalem – Niemand wird dich noch "Verlassene" nennen (Jesaja 62, 4) (Berlin: Aktion Sühnezeichen Friedensdienste, 2012), 37–38. In contrast to the title, the text itself does contain references to Jerusalem from a Palestinian perspective.
51. Martin Kloke, "Christliche Zionisten – Eine kritische Darstellung," in Israelsonntag 8. August 2010. "Wünschet Jerusalem Segen …" Psalm 122, 77–87 (Berlin: Aktion Sühnezeichen Friedensdienste, 2010).
52. Helmut Ruppel, "Liturgie Für den Gottesdienst am 10. Sonntag nach Trinitatis. 'Israel 1948–2008'." in Israelsonntag 2008 …und so wird ganz Israel gerettet werden, wie geschrieben steht: 'Aus Zion wird kommen der Retter.' (Brief an die Ge-

In the confession of sins, the text recommends asking for forgiveness for the fact that "we failed to recognize it as a sign of your faithfulness when [your people] returned to live within its borders as an independent state."[53] The prayers of intercession ask God to "sharpen our attention for anything which appears as an indignant criticism of Israel (*Israelkritik*), but is in reality anti-Jewish (*judenfeindlich*)." In a somewhat curious phrasing that seems undecided whether the divine promise ends at the Green Line, the prayer concludes by requesting divine protection "for the Jewish communities here and the Israeli cities and settlements over there."[54]

The most recent position paper on ASF's activities in Israel from 2014, written by Bernhard Krane, the head of the ASF Israel desk, aptly captures this return to the left-wing Christian Philozionism of Helmut Gollwitzer and his disciple Friedrich-Wilhelm Marquardt.[55] With clarity that would have been unthinkable throughout *Aktion Sühnezeichen*'s period of anxious equidistance, the position paper notes:

> For theological and political reasons, Aktion Sühnezeichen fights for the belief that a special bond links the People of Israel (AM ISRAEL) and the Land of Israel (EREZ ISRAEL) and that the modern State of Israel has the right to exist as the nation-state of the Jewish People. Such a pro-Zionist position creates both common ground as well as divisions in ASF's cooperation with other civil society groups and parties. [...] ASF's Theology of Israel is based on the continuing relevance of God's covenant with the People of Israel and the Divine Promise of the Land.[56]

Atonement as At-One-Ment: From Christian to Post-Christian Philozionism

How exceptional is the history of ASF in Israel? Zygmunt Bauman reminds us that positive and negative exceptionalism are both fruit of the same tree. He depicts the long history of Western exceptionalism towards the Jewish people as "Allosemitism," "the practice of setting the Jews apart as people radically different from all the others, needing separate concepts to describe and comprehend them and special treatment in all or most social intercourse."[57] Thus, German Protestant

---

meinde in Rom, 11,26) (Berlin: Aktion Sühnezeichen Friedensdienste, 2008), 18–22, here at 18.

53. Ibid., 19.
54. Ibid., 21.
55. Friedrich-Wilhelm Marquardt, Die Juden und ihr Land (Hamburg: Siebenstern-Taschenbuch-Verlag, 1975).
56. Bernhard Krane, Grundsätzliches zur ASF-Israelarbeit (Berlin: Aktion Sühnezeichen Friedensdienste, 2014).
57. Zygmunt Bauman, "Allosemitism: Premodern, Modern, Postmodern," in

Philozionism should not be studied in isolation from its counterimage, namely, a theologically grounded Antizionism within the same milieu: resentment towards Zionism and the State of Israel has a long history within the German Protestant Church, especially within left-wing Protestantism.[58] The level of German Protestant investment (both financially and emotionally) into the community of barely 3,000 Palestinian Arab Lutherans in the Holy Land, for instance, far outstrips their numbers and relevance for the declining minority of Palestinian Arab Christians. Consequently, the study of both Protestant Philozionism and Antizionism needs to be integrated into a broader history of *Allozionism*,[59] an exceptionalist understanding of Jewish nationalism which, in the German case, goes back to Johann Gottfried Herder's fascination with the ancient Hebrews.[60]

Such a historicizing approach ought to be applied as well to the phenomenon of German guilt and *Sündenstolz* (sinner's pride): research on the German-Jewish-Israeli conundrum still tends to be approached as a densely entangled cluster of exceptionalism, demarcated by a sense of Jewish nationhood as an *exceptional* people, the Shoah as an *exceptional* crime perpetrated by the Germans, and finally, the State of Israel as an *exceptional* state. Paradoxically, the recent establishment of separate chairs and research institutes for the study of the State of Israel and the Holocaust in German academia has the potential to further entrench this phenomenon, unless their teaching and research are closely integrated into a comparative research agenda.

In the case of ASF, such an approach might explore, for instance, linkages between transgenerational guilt-driven identification with the victims and similar historical processes. To put it in the sarcastic parlance common among former ASF volunteers: how does German *Edelschuld* (first-class guilt) and German *Edelsühne* (first-class atonement) differ from ordinary white guilt? What distinguishes guilt-driven German converts to Judaism from figures like Rachel Dolezal, the famous "trans-racial" convert to blackness?[61] What are

---

Modernity, Culture and "the Jew," eds. Bryan Cheyette and Laura Marcus (Cambridge: Polity Press, 1998): 143–56, here at 143.

58. For a concise overview, see Martin Kloke, "Deutsche Protestanten und der Sechstagekrieg 1967. Eine Biblanz nach 50 Jahren," Compass-Infodienst, 2017, https://www.compass-infodienst.de/Martin-Kloke-Deutsche Protestanten-und-der-echstagekrieg-1967.15867.0.html (last accessed October 11, 2017).

59. Johannes Becke, "Beyond Allozionism: Exceptionalizing and de-Exceptionalizing the Zionist Project," Israel Studies 23:2 (2018): 168–93.

60. Ofri Ilany, In Search of the Hebrew People: Bible and Nation in the German Enlightenment (Bloomington, N: Indiana University Press, 2018).

61. Rachel Dolezal and Storms Reback, In Full Colour: Finding My Place in a Black and White World (Dallas: BenBella Books, 2017).

the commonalities and differences between the many, many German converts pushing into Jewish Studies and Rabbinical Studies, and what Native American scholars refer to as *ethnic fraud*, namely, the curious phenomenon of white people pushing into Native American Studies based on spurious claims to distant Native American ancestry?[62]

To evade the trap of exceptionalism, the entanglement of guilt and redemption in the German-Israeli and the Protestant-Jewish encounter needs to be studied as part of a broader history of emotions of the post-colonial and increasingly post-Christian West. Such a comparative and theory-guided approach might be usefully informed by the dynamics of vicarious ethnicity as a form of atonement, or, in the words of the psychoanalyst Irwin Rosen, "atonement as at-one-ment." For Rosen, atonement is an "identification with the fantasized victim of one's sadism," and "this identification constitutes the atonement (or at-one-ment) experience in which, magically, the aggressor seeks forgiveness, by becoming *one-in-suffering* with his victim."[63] Rosen's psychoanalytic model captures two distinct processes of atonement as at-one-ment, depending on the type of identification with the victim: concordant and complementary. In the *concordant* model of identification with the victim, the "guilty and self-accusatory concordant atoner" seeks to repair "that aspect of himself that has been identified with the victim,"[64] frequently through acts of reparation. Unlike these "repairers,"[65] their counterparts (who follow the complementary type of atonement) struggle with the "imaginatively enhanced, projectively ascribed retaliation of the vengeful victim who is now endowed with the same malevolence as that which impelled the abuser's original attack"[66] – as *"embracers of suffering."*[67]

If we apply this typology to the German politics of guilt, the Christian Philozionism of Aktion Sühnezeichen might be considered a concordant type of atonement, based on the idea of atonement as reparation. In contrast, the post-Christian Philozionism of the so-called "Anti-Germans" (*Antideutsche*) appears to be a complementary type, namely, atonement as suffering and vengeance. In other words, concordant atoners are drawn to acts of repentance, including the option of ideological, religious, and even ethnic conversion, as its most radical

---

62. Elizabeth Cook-Lynn, "Taku Inichiapi? What's in a Name?," in A Separate Country: Postcoloniality and American Indian Nations (Lubbock: Texas Tech University Press, 2012), 123–32.

63. Irwin C. Rosen, "The Atonement-Forgivenness Dyad: Identification with the Aggressed," Psychoanalytic Inquiry 29 (2009): 411–25, here at 414.

64. Ibid., 412.

65. Ibid., 420.

66. Ibid., 412.

67. Rosen, "The Atonement-Forgivenness Dyad," 420.

form. Complementary atoners, for their part, seek a projection screen for their fantasies of self-harm, or, as the Anti-Germans have put it in reference to the bombing of Dresden: "Bomber Harris – do it again."[68]

Of course, the two types of atonement are closely intertwined. The entanglement of Christian and post-Christian Philozionism in particular stands out in the writings of the late Eike Geisel, another former ASF volunteer in Israel. After publishing Nathan Weinstock's *Le sionisme contre Israël* in German,[69] Geisel later became an important inspiration for Philozionists in the German Left – and an acerbic critic of the self-serving German culture of faux atonement, including conversions to Judaism.[70] As the case of Eike Geisel shows, the ideological production of the Anti-Germans and their intellectual forebears can hardly be reduced to provocative statements, puzzling acts of self-flagellation, and the characteristic personality disorders of "compulsive confessors"[71] and "atonement addicts."[72] For scholars of Jewish-Protestant relations however, the shift from *Sühnezeichen* (sign of atonement) to *Antideutsche* (Anti-Germans) might indicate an intriguing theological movement: like other varieties of white guilt, the Anti-German ideology of a "revenge against the self"[73] resonates with the basic template of post-Christianity – all of the guilt, with none of the forgiveness.

Conclusion

As the case of the Temple Society (*Tempelgesellschaft*) demonstrates, the German Protestant presence in the Land of Israel predates both the State of Israel and the institution-building of the *New Yishuv*.[74] In the long history of German Protestant engagement with Jewish nationalism, the activities of *Aktion Sühnezeichen Friedensdienst* in Israel re-

68. For an insightful case study of left-wing Israeli bewilderment at the phenomenon of the Anti-Germans, see Amira Hass, "Korban Mi-She-Korban Acharon (He Who Is the Last Victim Is the True Victim)," Ha'aeretz, 2004, http://www.haaretz.co.il/1.957024.

69. Nathan Weinstock, Das Ende Israels? Nahostkonflikt und Geschichte des Zionismus, eds. Eike Geisel and Mario Offenberg (Berlin: Verlag Klaus Wagenbach, 1975).

70. Eike Geisel, "Deutsche Seelenwanderungen: Rückblick auf eine zehnjährige deutsch-jüdische Verwechslungskomödie," in idem, Die Banalität des Guten: Deutsche Seelenwanderungen (Berlin: Edition Tiamat, 1992), 9–34.

71. Rosen, "The Atonement-Forgivenness Dyad," 421.

72. Ibid., 420.

73. Ibid., 423.

74. For an intriguing case study of counterfactual history which explores what a German Protestant state project in the Land of Israel might have looked like, see Derek Jonathan Penslar, "What If a Christian State Had Been Established in Modern Palestine?," in What Ifs of Jewish History: From Abraham to Zionism, ed. Gabriel D. Rosenfeld (Cambridge and New York: Cambridge University Press, 2016): 142–65.

flect a compelling combination of paradoxes: a theology of Israel that is decidedly left-wing, an ethics of atonement which coexists with an entrenched culture of sarcasm, and a complex legacy of Philozionism that stretches all the way from Christian Zionism to the 'critical solidarity' of a strict equidistance, while sometimes foreshadowing the naïve Anti-German enthusiasm for all things Israeli.

For the study of contemporary Jewish-Protestant relations, the history of ASF is a vivid reminder that the Zionist project not only represents a rupture for Jewish history, but also for interfaith relations. Hence, both the most intense forms of contemporary Protestant sympathy and antipathy for the Jewish experience are no longer shaped by Diasporic statelessness, but by Zionist state formation in the Land of Israel. Especially in the German case, such a study of Protestant Philozionism and Antizionism should not be limited to the fields of theology and church history, but instead contribute to a broader history of emotions of the post-colonial and post-Christian West, with a special focus on the emotional politics of white guilt.

List of Contributors

Yaakov Ariel is Professor of Jewish History in the Department of Religious Studies at the University of North Carolina, Chapel Hill. He is also Director of the Minor of Christianity and Culture and Co-director of the Center for Jewish Studies. His areas of scholarly interest include Judaism and Evangelical Christianity in America, and the relationship between these two religious communities. Among his publications are: *On Behalf of Israel*: *American Fundamentalist Attitudes Towards the Jewish People and Zionism* (1991); *Evangelizing the Chosen People*: *Missions to the Jews in America 1880–2000* (2000); and *An Unusual Relationship*: *Evangelical Christians and Jews* (2013).

Irene Aue-Ben David is Director of the Leo Baeck Institute Jerusalem. Her research interests include modern German-Jewish historiography, Gender History, and the History of German-Israeli relations. Among her publications are: *Deutsch-jüdische Geschichtsschreibung im 20. Jahrhundert. Zu Werk und Rezeption von Selma Stern*. Göttingen: Vandenhoeck & Ruprecht, 2017 (Schriftenreihe des Simon Dubnow Instituts, Leipzig. Band 28); C*onstantin Brunner im Kontext*. Ed. with Gerhard Lauer und Jürgen Stenzel. Berlin: De Gruyter/Magnes 2014; Constantin Brunner (1862–1937). *Ausgewählte Briefe*. Annotated and edited with Jürgen Stenzel. Göttingen: Wallstein Verlag, 2012; Special Section: *Deutsch-israelische Annäherungen in Geisteswissenschaften und Kulturpolitik*, Edited by: Irene Aue-Ben-David, Michael Brenner und Kärin Nickelsen, in: Naharaim. Journal of German-Jewish Literature and Cultural History 11 (2017); with Yonatan Shiloh-Dayan, "Observant Ventures: Early German-Israeli Conferences on German History", in *Jahrbuch des Simon Dubnow Instituts* 15 (2016), 315–339.

Johannes Becke is Assistant Professor for Israel and Middle East Studies at the Heidelberg Center for Jewish Studies (Hochschule für Jüdische Studien Heidelberg), where he specializes in the Comparative Politics of Israel and the Middle East. His recent publications have appeared in the *Journal of Israeli History, Israel Studies, Inter-*

ventions, *Jewish Studies Quarterly*, and *Political Geography*. He is currently working on a monograph on territorial expansionism in the Middle East, and he co-edited *Studien: Geschichte, Methoden, Paradigmen* (Wallstein, 2019).

DEAN PHILLIP BELL is President/CEO and Professor of Jewish History at Spertus Institute for Jewish Learning and Leadership in Chicago. A former member of the Board of Directors of the Association for Jewish Studies, he is the author of *Sacred Communities*: J*ewish and Christian Identities in Fifteenth-Century Germany* (2001), *Jewish Identity in Early Modern Germany: Memory, Power and Community* (2007), and *Jews in the Early Modern World* (2008). He edited The Bloomsbury Companion to Jewish Studies (2013), *The Routledge Handbook of Jewish History and Historiography* (2018), and *Plague in the Early Modern World: A Documentary History* (2019); and (with Stephen G. Burnett) co-edited *Jews, Judaism and the Reformation in Sixteenth-Century Germany* (2006). His current research focuses on cultural responses to natural disaster in early modern Germany.

AYA ELYADA is Senior Lecturer at the Department of History, the Hebrew University of Jerusalem. Her research interests include German and German-Jewish history, Christian-Jewish relations, and the social and cultural history of language and translation. Among her publications are: "Yiddish – Language of Conversion? Linguistic Adaptation and Its Limits in Early Modern *Judenmission*," *Leo Baeck Institute Year Book* 53 (2008), 3–29, "Protestant Scholars and Yiddish Studies in Early Modern Europe," *Past and Present* 203 (2009), 69–98, "Early Modern Yiddish and the Jewish Volkskunde, 1880–1938," *Jewish Quarterly Review* 107 (2017), 182–208, "Bridges to a Bygone Jewish Past? Abraham Tendlau and the Rewriting of Yiddish Folktales in Nineteenth-Century Germany," *Journal of Modern Jewish Studies* 16 (2017), 1–18. Her book, *A Goy Who Speaks Yiddish: Christians and the Jewish Language in Early Modern Germany*, appeared in 2012 with Stanford University Press.

LARS FISCHER is an Honorary Research Associate in the Department of Hebrew & Jewish Studies at UCL (University College London), teaches at the FernUniversität in Hagen, and runs The History Practice in Berlin. His scholarship centers on the history and theory of antisemitism and Jewish/non-Jewish relations, Critical Theory, and the use of music as an historical source. His publications include a monograph titled *The Socialist Response to Antisemitism in Imperial Germany* (2007), "A difference in the texture of prejudice". *Historisch-konzep-*

tionelle Überlegungen zum Verhältnis von Antisemitismus, Rassismus und Gemeinschaft (2016), and some thirty papers on a range of relevant topics. He edits the review section of *Jewish Historical Studies*, the website of the *Critical Theories of Antisemitism Network*, and *H-Music*: *H-Commons Network Music in History*.

JOHANNES GLEIXNER is a research assistant at Collegium Carolinum – Research Institute for the History of the Czech Lands and Slovakia. Since 2018, he has represented this institution's newly established branch office in Prague, Czech Republic. His areas of interest include the history of secularism and anti-religion in Eastern and East Central Europe, as well as the history of ideas. His latest book is titled '*Menschheitsreligionen*' *zwischen sakraler Nation und ziviler Religion*: *Die religiöse Bedingtheit neuer Gesellschaften bei T.G. Masaryk und A.V. Lunačarskij* (2017). He also edited the volume *Konkurrierende Ordnungen*: *Verschränkungen von Religion, Staat und Nation in Ostmitteleuropa vom 16. bis zum 20. Jahrhundert* (with D. Tricoire et. al., 2015). His most recent articles address socialist freethought in East Central Europe and Economic reform during the Prague Spring.

OFRI ILANY is a post-doctoral fellow at the Polonsky Academy for Advanced Study at the Van Leer Jerusalem Institute and a lecturer at Tel Aviv University. His book, *In Search of the Hebrew People*: *Bible and Nation in the German Enlightenment*, was published in 2018 by Indiana University Press. Ilany's research interests include the history of Orientalism, the history of Bible research, and the history of sexuality. His column, "Under the Sun," is published in the Haaretz Weekly Supplement.

KYLE JANTZEN is Professor of History and Chair of the Department of Humanities at Ambrose University in Calgary, Canada. His areas of scholarly interest include the Protestant churches in National Socialist Germany, North American Christian responses to Nazism and Jewish persecution, and postwar German immigrants in Western Canada. Among his publications are various chapters and articles on these topics and his book, *Faith and Fatherland*: *Parish Politics in Hitler's Germany* (2008).

MARKÉTA KABŮRKOVÁ is curator in the Archive of the National Museum in Prague. She studied Jewish Studies and Theology at the Charles University in Prague, Ben-Gurion University of Negev in Beersheva, was a FIIRD post-doc fellow at the University of Geneva and at the Kurt and Ursula Schubert Centre for Jewish Studies at Palacký University in Olomouc. Her research focuses on Jewish-Christian religious polemic in the medieval and early modern periods and its function within Jewish-Christian relations, identities, and (self)perceptions. Among her recent publications are: "Tela Ignea Satanae: Christian Scholars and the Editing of Hebrew Polemical Literature" in *Revealing the Secrets of the Jews: Johannes Pfefferkorn and Christian Writings about Jewish Life and Literature in Early Modern Europe* (eds. Jonathan Adams and Cordelia Heß, Berlin/Boston: De Gruyter 2017), and "Reflection of *Other* Sources in the Works of Berechiah ben Natronai ha-Naqdan and Jacob ben Reuben in Quest for God's Unity" in *Polemics, Biology, and Gender: New Perspectives on Medieval Jewish Philosophy* (eds. Tamás Visi et al., Olomouc: Palacky University Olomouc 2018). Currently, she is working on a project concerning religious encounters between Jews and Christian anti-Trinitarians in the Polish-Lithuanian Commonwealth for Käte Hamburger Kolleg in Bochum.

URSULA RUDNICK is an ordained Lutheran minister who works on the topic of Jewish-Christian relations and teaches at Leibniz University Hanover. Her scholarly interests center on contemporary Jewish-Christian relations in Germany. Her publications include Kon-Texte – Kirche und Judentum. Impulse zur Verfassungsänderung der Ev.-luth. Landeskirche Hannovers, (2015); "Auf dem langen Weg zum Haus des Nachbarn." *Positionen der evangelischen Kirchen im christlich-jüdischen Gespräch und ihre Verortung in der Theologie.* (2006) and "Aber wie kommt es in jedes Haus und jedes Dorf?" Analyse ausgewählter religionspädagogischer Materialien zum Thema "Judentum" und "christlich-jüdisches Gespräch" (2005).

DIRK SCHUSTER, PhD, is research assistant in the Study of Religion/ Christianity at the Institute for Jewish Studies and Religious Studies at the University in Potsdam. His fields of research include the interdependences between religion and politics, religion in Nazi Germany, the history of the Evangelical Regional Church A.B. in Romania, and atheism. His latest book is *Die Lehre vom "arischen" Christentum. Das wissenschaftliche Selbstverständnis im Eisenacher "Entjudungsinstitut"* (2017), and he edited (with Ulrich A. Wien) *Siebenbürgen im Nationalsozialismus* (2016).

MOSHE SLUHOVSKY is Paulette and Claude Kelman Professor in the Study of French Jewry at the Hebrew University of Jerusalem and the head of the Lafer Center for the Study of Women and Gender and of the Institute of History. His latest books are: *"Believe not Every Spir-*

it": *Demonic Possession, Mysticism,* and *Discernment in Early Modern Catholicism* (2007) and *Becoming a New Self: Practices of Belief in Early Modern Catholicism* (2017). He is the editor of *Into the Dark Night and Back: A Collection of Writings by Jean-Joseph Surin* (2019), and (with Miri Eliav-Feldon) of a special issue of *Zmanim* commemorating the 500th anniversary of the Protestant Reformation.

ALEXANDER VAN DER HAVEN is a Research Fellow at the I-CORE (Israeli Centres for Research Excellence) Centre for the Study of Conversion and Inter-Religious Encounters, Ben-Gurion University of the Negev. Among his recent publications are: שרה האשכנזיה מלכת השבתאים (*From Lowly Metaphor to Divine Flesh: Sarah the Askhenazi, Sabbatai' Messianic Queen and the Sabbatian Movement*, 2018), articles about early modern Jewish-Christian relations in the Dutch Republic, articles about various themes related to religion and modernity, and the edited volume (with Sebastian Schüler and Lutz Greisiger) *Religion und Wahnsinn um 1900: Zwischen Pathologisierung und Selbstermächtigung. Religion and Madness Around 1900: Between Pathology and Self-Empowerment* (2017).

CHRISTIAN WIESE holds the Martin Buber Chair in Jewish Thought and Philosophy at the Goethe University in Frankfurt. His publications include *Challenging Colonial Discourse: Jewish Studies and Protestant Theology in Wilhelmine Germany* (2005), and *The Life and Thought of Hans Jonas: Jewish Dimensions* (2007). He has edited numerous volumes, including *Janusfiguren: "Jüdische Heimstätte", Exil und Nation im deutschen Zionismus* (with Andrea Schatz, 2006); *Redefining Judaism in an Age of Emancipation: Comparative Perspectives on Samuel Holdheim* (1806–1860) (2007); *Modern Judaism and Historical Consciousness: Identities – Encounters – Perspectives* (with Andreas Gotzmann, 2007); *Judaism and the Phenomenon of Life: The Legacy of Hans Jonas: Historical and Philosophical Studies* (with Hava Tirosh-Samuelson, 2008); *Years of Persecution, Years of Extermination: Saul Friedländer and the Future of Holocaust Studies* (with Paul Betts, 2010); *German-Jewish Thought Between Religion and Politics: Festschrift in Honor of Paul Mendes-Flohr on the Occasion of his Seventieth Birthday* (with Martina Urban, 2012); *Jüdische Existenz in der Moderne: Abraham Geiger und die Wissenschaft des Judentums* (with Walter Homolka and Thomas Brechenmacher, 2013); *Reappraisals and New Studies of the Modern Jewish Experience: Essays in Honor of Robert M. Seltzer* (with Brian Smollett, 2014).

www.ingramcontent.com/pod-product-compliance
Lightning Source LLC
Chambersburg PA
CBHW042113100526
44587CB00025B/4038